PENAL CENSURE
ENGAGEMENTS WITHIN AND BEYOND DESERT THEORY

This exploration of penal censure is inspired by the 40th anniversary of the publication of Andreas von Hirsch's Doing Justice, which opened up a fresh set of issues in theorisation about punishment that eventually led von Hirsch to ground his proposed model of desert-based sentencing on the notion of penal censure. Von Hirsch's work thus provides an obvious starting-point for an exploration of the importance of censure for the justification of punishment, both within his theory of just deserts and from the perspectives of other theoretical approaches. It also provides an opportunity for engaging with censure more broadly from philosophical, sociological–anthropological and individual–psychological perspectives. The essays in this collection map the conceptual territory of censure from these different perspectives, address issues for desert theory that arise from fuller understandings of censure, and consider afresh the role of censure within the jurisprudence of punishment. They show that analyses of censure from different vantage points can significantly enrich punishment theory, not least by providing a conceptual basis for perceiving common ground between and thus connecting different strands of penal theory.

Studies in Penal Theory and Penal Ethics: Volume 7

Studies in Penal Theory and Penal Ethics

A Series Published for
the Centre for Penal Theory and Penal Ethics
Institute of Criminology, University of Cambridge

FOUNDING EDITOR:
ANDREW VON HIRSCH

GENERAL EDITORS:
ANTHONY E BOTTOMS, ANTJE DU BOIS-PEDAIN

Ethical and Social Perspectives on Situational Crime Prevention
edited by Andrew von Hirsch, David Garland and Alison Wakefield

**Restorative Justice and Criminal Justice: Competing or
Reconcilable Paradigms?**
edited by Andrew von Hirsch, Julian Roberts, Anthony E Bottoms,
Kent Roach and Mara Schiff

Incivilities: Regulating Offensive Behaviour
edited by A P Simester and Andrew von Hirsch

Previous Convictions at Sentencing: Theoretical and Applied Perspectives
edited by Julian V Roberts and Andrew von Hirsch

Setting the Watch: Privacy and the Ethics of CCTV Surveillance
Beatrice von Silva-Tarouca Larsen

Criminal Law and the Authority of the State
edited by Antje du Bois-Pedain, Magnus Ulväng and Petter Asp

Penal Censure: Engagements Within and Beyond Desert Theory
edited by Antje du Bois-Pedain and Anthony E Bottoms

Penal Censure

Engagements Within and Beyond Desert Theory

Edited by
Antje du Bois-Pedain
and
Anthony E Bottoms

·HART·
OXFORD · LONDON · NEW YORK · NEW DELHI · SYDNEY

HART PUBLISHING

Bloomsbury Publishing Plc

Kemp House, Chawley Park, Cumnor Hill, Oxford, OX2 9PH, UK

HART PUBLISHING, the Hart/Stag logo, BLOOMSBURY and the Diana logo are
trademarks of Bloomsbury Publishing Plc

First published in Great Britain 2019

A catalogue record for this book is available from the British Library.

Library of Congress Cataloging-in-Publication data

Names: du Bois-Pedain, Antje, editor. | Bottoms, Anthony E., 1939- editor.

Title: Penal censure : engagements within and beyond desert theory /
edited by Antje du Bois-Pedain, Anthony E Bottoms.

Description: Oxford, UK ; Portland, Oregon : Hart Publishing, 2019. | Series: Studies in penal
theory and penal ethics ; volume 7 | Includes bibliographical references and index.

Identifiers: LCCN 2018048702 (print) | LCCN 2018049201 (ebook) |
ISBN 9781509919796 (Epub) | ISBN 9781509919789 (hardback)

Subjects: LCSH: Punishment—Philosophy. | Sentences (Criminal procedure) |
BISAC: LAW / Comparative.

Classification: LCC K5103 (ebook) | LCC K5103 .P463 2019 (print) |
DDC 345/.0773—dc23

LC record available at https://lccn.loc.gov/2018048702

ISBN: HB: 978-1-50991-978-9
        ePDF: 978-1-50990-428-0
        ePub: 978-1-50991-979-6

Typeset by Compuscript Ltd, Shannon
Printed and bound in Great Britain by TJ International Ltd, Padstow, Cornwall

To find out more about our authors and books visit www.hartpublishing.co.uk.
Here you will find extracts, author information, details of forthcoming events
and the option to sign up for our newsletters.

Table of Contents

PART III
CENSURE, DESERT AND THE JURISPRUDENCE OF PUNISHMENT

List of Contributors

Andrew Ashworth, Vinerian Professor of English Law Emeritus, University of Oxford; Emeritus Fellow of All Souls College, Oxford.

Christopher Bennett, Reader in Philosophy, University of Sheffield.

Anthony E Bottoms, Wolfson Professor of Criminology Emeritus, University of Cambridge; Life Fellow of Fitzwilliam College, Cambridge.

Rob Canton, Professor in Community and Criminal Justice, De Montfort University.

Alessandro Corda, Lecturer in Law, Queen's University, Belfast.

Antje du Bois-Pedain, Reader in Criminal Law and Philosophy, University of Cambridge; Fellow of Magdalene College, Cambridge.

Netanel Dagan, Adjunct Lecturer, Institute of Criminology, The Hebrew University of Jerusalem.

Andreas von Hirsch, Emeritus Honorary Professor of Penal Theory and Penal Law, University of Cambridge and Honorary Professor of Penal Theory, Goethe University Frankfurt.

Tatjana Hörnle, Professor of Criminal Law, Comparative Law and Legal Philosophy, Humboldt University, Berlin.

Jonathan Jacobs, Professor of Philosophy, John Jay College of Criminal Justice and Director, Institute for Criminal Justice Ethics, City University of New York.

John Kleinig, Professor of Philosophy Emeritus, John Jay College of Criminal Justice, City University of New York.

Liat Levanon, Lecturer in Law, King's College London.

Matt Matravers, Professor of Law and Philosophy, University of York.

Julian V Roberts, Professor of Criminology, University of Oxford; Supernumerary Fellow of Worchester College, Oxford.

Michael Tonry, Professor of Law and Public Policy, University of Minnesota.

Introduction

ANTJE DU BOIS-PEDAIN AND ANTHONY E BOTTOMS

I$_{N}$ INTRODUCING A book on penal censure, it is valuable to remind ourselves that all societies censure some acts. Indeed, Colin Sumner has argued that, sociologically, 'social censures have a profound existence: at the heart of intense emotional patterns, in the centre of politically and economically signifi-cant moral-ideological formations ... they are vital forces in the constitution of societies'.[1] If this is correct, social censures are clearly open both to sociological analysis (for example: 'How did this censure arise? 'What role does it currently play in our society?') and to critical normative analysis and evaluation (for example: 'Is it justified to maintain this censure?'; 'Should we not be formally censuring [a particular activity]?').[2] The principal concern of this volume lies in the field of critical normative analysis and evaluation, applied to the special field of criminal punishment. In developed societies, the criminal law is always a major vehicle (although of course not the only vehicle) through which social censure is conveyed; and normatively speaking, criminal censures need to be understood as a special kind of social censure, in respect of which analysts must be especially sensitive to the general terms of the relationship between citizens and the state.

Given the above, it is not surprising that the concept of censure now plays a major role in theorisation about criminal punishment. What is much more surprising is that this was not at all the case 40 or 50 years ago, when utilitarian justifications of punishment were dominant both in the academy[3] and, at least in some influential jurisdictions, in practice also.[4] An important basic difference

---

[1] C Sumner, 'Rethinking Deviance: Towards a Sociology of Censure' in C Sumner (ed), *Censure, Politics and Criminal Justice* (Milton Keynes, Open University Press, 1990), 15 at 28–29. For more on Sumner on censure, see A Amatrudo (ed), *Social Censure and Critical Criminology: After Sumner* (London, Palgrave Macmillan, 2017).

[2] It follows, of course, that views about what should be censured can change over time. For exam-ple, in England and Wales, the criminal censure of drink-driving is now universally accepted, and homosexual couples may marry. But just over half a century ago (before the Road Safety Act 1967 and the Sexual Offences Act 1967), there was no law against drink-driving unless one was incapably drunk, and a fully consensual homosexual act between adult males was a criminal offence.

[3] See for example T Honderich, *Punishment: the Supposed Justifications*, revd edn (Harmondsworth, Penguin Books, 1976).

[4] Especially in the United States. See the short survey of the sentencing regimes of different states in the 1950s in PW Tappan, 'Sentencing under the Model Penal Code' (1958) 23 *Law and Contempo-rary Problems* 528. Note especially Tappan's summary of the objectives underpinning the sentencing provisions of the American Law Institute's Model Penal Code at that time: these 'provisions ... are

between censure-based and utilitarian approaches to punishment is, of course, that censure theories justify punishment primarily by looking back to a wrongful act in order to censure it, whereas for utilitarian theorists punishment is justified by looking forward to its (on balance) perceived good consequences.[5] Perhaps surprisingly to contemporary ears, in the penology of the 1960s and 1970s the main utilitarian focus was not on deterrence but on rehabilitation; and in consequence, the penal policies of that era are often described as espousing 'the rehabilitative ideal'.[6] One very practical result of the adoption of such policies was the widespread enactment (particularly in the United States) of so-called 'indeterminate' prison sentences, in which the court pronounced simply a minimum and maximum term (for example, 'five to ten years'). Within that set range, a parole board (or similar body) would then decide when the prisoner would be released, based on his/her perceived response to the treatment or training offered. In such a system, therefore, the actual time served could depend more upon the prisoner's response to the sentence than on the seriousness of the crime committed.

The 'rehabilitative ideal' was forcefully challenged in the United States in the 1970s, on two separate grounds. First, influential overviews of empirical research findings strongly challenged the success of rehabilitative treatments, leading to a long-running academic debate which is still with us (although it is now much more sophisticated than it was in the 1970s).[7] But secondly, and just as importantly, some scholars and policy analysts developed a theoretical critique which, in a nutshell, claimed that the rehabilitative ideal, by playing down the importance of the offence(s) of conviction, and giving substantial discretionary power to parole boards, led to significant *injustices*. Among other complaints, it was pointed out that this system could and did allow situations whereby a person (P), who had been convicted of a relatively minor offence but who then reacted negatively to the prison regime, could serve significantly more time than another inmate (Q) who had committed a more serious offence but was subsequently a model prisoner. There was also a clear risk that the eventual duration of the punishment of a recalcitrant offender would cease to bear any reasonable relation to the seriousness of his offence.

---

predicated on the assumption that the law should endeavor to protect society as fully as may reasonably be possible, both by measures of general and individual prevention and by the rehabilitation of offenders' (at 528).

[5] We are aware that this is only a broad-brush statement. As will be seen later, some censure theorists have argued that such theories necessarily have a forward-looking dimension (although this is not seen as instrumental, unlike the utilitarian view). Moreover, in the literature there are many 'mixed' theories, with both backward-looking and forward-looking dimensions.

[6] FA Allen, *The Decline of the Rehabilitative Ideal* (New Haven, Yale University Press, 1981).

[7] The major 1970s text was D Lipton, R Martinson and J Wilks, *Effectiveness of Correctional Treatment: A Survey of Treatment Evaluation Studies* (Springfield MA, Praeger, 1975), which was preceded by the now notorious short article by R Martinson, 'What Works?: Questions and Answers about Prison Reform' (1974) 35 *Public Interest* 22. For a balanced overview of more recent studies, see F Lösel, 'Offender Treatment and Rehabilitation: What Works?' in M Maguire, R Morgan and R Reiner (eds), *The Oxford Handbook of Criminology*, 5th edn (Oxford, Oxford University Press, 2012) 986.

The reports of two non-official committees in the US were particularly influential in making this second (justice-based) challenge. First, in 1971, came a report from the American Friends Service Committee (AFSC),[8] which robustly declared that the 'individualized treatment model' (or rehabilitative ideal) was 'theoretically faulty, systematically discriminatory in application, and inconsistent with some of our most basic concepts of justice'.[9] In the same year, the Field Foundation set up an ad hoc Committee for the Study of Incarceration, chaired by a former US Senator and with a prestigious membership including academic luminaries such as the lawyer Alan Dershowitz, the historian of asylums David Rothman, the sociologist Erving Goffman and criminologists Stanton Wheeler and Leslie Wilkins. After four years' work, including 20 full committee sessions, the committee approved its final report (*Doing Justice*), which had two unusual characteristics. First, it was explicitly stated that the report had been written by the Committee's senior staff member (Executive Director Andrew von Hirsch)[10]; and secondly, alongside the main report the committee published several comments by members of the Committee which, while not disavowing the report, were certainly less than enthusiastic about it. (They indicated, broadly speaking, that the conclusions of the report could be supported only because they seemed to constitute the least worst option).[11]

Despite these lukewarm initial endorsements, *Doing Justice* has had a substantially longer shelf life than the AFSC report, and indeed it is widely perceived to have opened up a fresh set of issues in academic theorisation about punishment, based on the concept of 'penal desert'.[12] There is little doubt that at least some of this subsequent attention is attributable to the fact that the Committee for the Study of Incarceration had chosen an exceptionally talented Executive Director, who went on to work up the embryonic ideas in *Doing Justice* into a much more

[8] American Friends Service Committee, *Struggle for Justice: A Report on Crime and Punishment in America* (New York, Hill and Wang, 1971). The American Society of Friends (Quakers) had a standing Service Committee; they appointed a Working Party to prepare the report, which the AFSC then endorsed. The Working Party included several members who had served prison terms, and two criminologists (David Greenberg and John Irwin) whose later writings on penal issues were to be influential.

[9] Ibid at 12. All this was so, the text added, notwithstanding that this approach was one 'towards which reformers have been urging us for at least a century'. Other comments were equally hard-hitting: for example, '[accepted correctional practice] is dominated by indoctrination in white Anglo-Saxon middle-class values' (at 43); and (referring to sentencing and release decisions), 'criminal justice is the [last] surviving bastion of absolute legal discretion' (at 46).

[10] A von Hirsch, *Doing Justice: The Choice of Punishments* (Report of the Committee for the Study of Incarceration) (New York, Hill and Wang, 1976; reprint edn, Boston, Northeastern University Press, 1986). The author was then known as 'Andrew von Hirsch', but is now 'Andreas von Hirsch'.

[11] Ibid. See for example the Introduction by W Gaylin and D J Rothman ('our solution is one of despair, not hope': at xxxix) and the comment by Leslie Wilkins ('I cannot do other than add my signature to the report, but I do so without enthusiasm': at 177).

[12] It is important to note that *Doing Justice* was not the first 1970s text to discuss desert theory – see in particular J Kleinig, *Punishment and Desert* (The Hague, Martinus Nijhoff, 1973). But for various reasons *Doing Justice* attracted more subsequent attention.

sophisticated set of texts on penal theory.[13] As part of this process, Andrew von Hirsch developed the concept of censure (which is scarcely mentioned in *Doing Justice*)[14] as a key conceptual element within his overall theory of punishment[15] – both as regards the justification for state punishment systems, and as regards decisions about how, and how much, individual offenders should be punished.

Von Hirsch therefore played a key pioneering role in the development of modern censure theory, but – as he would be the first to point out – he is by no means the only contemporary penal philosopher who places censure centre-stage in their theorisation. Others who have done so with distinction include John Kleinig,[16] Antony Duff,[17] John Tasioulas[18] and Christopher Bennett,[19] as well as (more recently) younger scholars such as Hannah Maslen.[20] However, the fact that all these writers endorse and indeed emphasise communicative censure as a key feature of an adequate punishment theory does not mean that they agree on all features of such a theory; readers of their work will quickly discover many significant and thought-provoking differences of emphasis between them.

This brings us to the present volume, which has both a celebratory and an analytical dimension. The celebratory dimension is that, in September 2016, all the contributors to this volume attended a workshop that was organised to mark the fortieth anniversary of the publication of *Doing Justice*. It was the privilege of the current editors to organise that workshop on behalf of the Centre for Penal Theory and Penal Ethics at Cambridge, which Andreas von Hirsch had founded in 2000.[21] But the workshop was certainly not intended to be merely ceremonial. Although the concept of censure has now for some time been a

---

[13] See in particular A von Hirsch, *Past or Future Crimes: Deservedness and Dangerousness in the Sentencing of Criminals* (Manchester, Manchester University Press, 1986); A von Hirsch, *Censure and Sanctions* (Oxford, Oxford University Press, 1993) and A von Hirsch and A Ashworth, *Proportionate Sentencing: Exploring the Principles* (Oxford, Oxford University Press, 2005). For a recent summary restatement of the approach, see A von Hirsch, *Deserved Criminal Sentences: An Overview* (Oxford, Hart/Bloomsbury, 2017).

[14] John Kleinig (in n 2 of his chapter in this volume) points out that the word 'censure' appears only twice in *Doing Justice*.

[15] See in particular *Censure and Sanctions*, above n 13.

[16] Kleinig, above n 12; J Kleinig, 'Punishment and Moral Seriousness' (1993) 25 *Israel Law Review* 401; J Kleinig, *Ethics in Criminal Justice: An Introduction* (Cambridge, Cambridge University Press, 2008) chs 11 and 12.

[17] RA Duff, *Punishment, Communication and Community* (Oxford, Oxford University Press, 2001).

[18] J Tasioulas, 'Punishment and Repentance' (2006) 81 *Philosophy* 279.

[19] C Bennett, *The Apology Ritual: A Philosophical Theory of Punishment* (Cambridge, Cambridge University Press, 2008).

[20] H Maslen, *Remorse, Penal Theory and Sentencing* (Oxford, Hart, 2015).

[21] The Centre for Penal Theory and Penal Ethics is one of several topic-based research centres within the Institute of Criminology, University of Cambridge. It was founded in 2000 at the suggestion of Andreas von Hirsch, and with the enthusiastic support of the then Director of the Institute of Criminology, Michael Tonry. Andreas von Hirsch was the first Director of the Centre, and remained so (latterly as Co-Director) until 2016, when the two present authors took over the direction of the Centre. During his time as Director, Andreas also founded the book series 'Studies in Penal Theory and Penal Ethics', of which this volume is a part.

central concept in the theorisation of punishment, there remain many issues that require serious analysis. Among these topics are:

(a)   The precise meaning of 'censure';
(b)   How censure can be justified as a core concept within punishment theory, and whether that justification differs when one is considering the separate questions of: (i) the justification of a punishment system; and (ii) what punishments individual offenders should receive;
(c)   The relationship of censure to other important concepts within punishment theory, such as 'hard treatment', deterrence, remorse and rehabilitation;
(d)   Whether the censure for a given wrongful act can be justifiably different at different points in time;
(e)   The role of censure within penal systems understood sociologically; and in particular whether – as some have claimed – the explicit adoption of the concept of 'censure' within a penal system tends to lead to harsher sentencing;
(f)   What scope there might legitimately be, alongside a primarily censure-based penal system, for exceptional sentences intended to incapacitate offenders regarded as dangerous.

It is the hope of the editors that the chapters of this volume will, collectively, take forward the debates on some of these topics.

I. THE INDIVIDUAL CONTRIBUTIONS

We have arranged the 14 contributions into three main parts. Part one, Censure: Mapping the Conceptual Territory, deals with some core issues relating to the meaning and justification of censure within a state penal system. Part two, Censure and Just Deserts Revisited: Issues for Desert Theory, offers some distinctively fresh insights relating to a number of topics that have, in one way or another, already featured in the literature on desert theory. Part three, Censure, Desert and the Jurisprudence of Punishment, covers some important wider issues, including for example the role of victims' rights in punishment theory, and whether 'historic' offences (those punished many years after the crime itself) should receive the same punishment as a recently-committed crime.

A. Censure: Mapping the Conceptual Territory

The opening chapter, by John Kleinig, explores what he describes as the conceptual 'architecture of censure'. Kleinig identifies three dimensions to censure: a performative one, in which censure brings about a change in social status; an expressive one, in which censure rebukes or expresses condemnation; and a communicative one, in which what is conveyed to the offender is the seriousness of what he has done. He also argues that censure and sanction do not represent separate elements in a practice, but stand simply as distinguishable foci in a single practice that has a condemnatory as well as a sanctioning (or 'hard treatment') function. Kleinig's analysis further entails that censure – as a performative act – requires a certain social standing for the person conveying the censure, of a kind that only arises in institutional settings. Censure is therefore to be distinguished from, for example, expressions of blame among friends.

The next two chapters in the preliminary conceptual section are more concerned with psychological and sociological issues. Chapter two, by Jonathan Jacobs – a moral philosopher who is especially interested in issues of moral psychology – attempts to explicate a morally sound role for resentment, and for retributivist considerations in the understanding of censure and criminal sanction, building especially on the work of Adam Smith. Among other things, Jacobs highlights the significance of both the morally educative potential of civil society, and the importance of resentment in the moral economy of human interaction. One role of moral education is then to learn how to calibrate resentment appropriately. Jacobs' argument thus links the importance of resentment and its proper calibration to practices of censure, including state-imposed punishment. It holds that censure and sanction can be understood as appropriate responses to criminal conduct, provided that the responses are to be ordered and measured by a concern with justice within civil society.

In chapter three, Liat Levanon engages with censure from a different perspective, based on developmental psychology. In an individual-developmental context, censure (in its positive form) functions as a mechanism through which wrongdoing can be 'contained', that is to say, turned into an isolated instance of past behaviour that does not define or rule the wrongdoer. This containment is achieved through an interaction between the wrongdoer and the censuring authority. For this process to succeed, the censuring authority must act with critical self-reflection. Acknowledging the manifold differences between the educational-developmental settings for child development and the public-institutional settings of state punishment, Levanon points to ways in which an understanding of censure grounded in developmental theory can nevertheless inform penal practice, particularly through the use at the sentencing stage of some of the tools and techniques offered by restorative justice approaches.

Chapter four, by Christopher Bennett, like that of John Kleinig, undertakes a formal conceptual analysis, in Bennett's case focused on the question of how one can mount a justifiable argument for a censure theory of punishment. He argues that a successful penal censure theory will need to explain, first, why it is prima facie wrong not to censure wrongdoing; secondly, since it is not always wrong not to censure wrongdoing, what distinguishes cases where it is wrong from those where it is not wrong; and thirdly, how all this relates to punishment in real criminal justice systems. Bennett describes this approach as an attempt to outline a 'positive role for censure' within criminal justice, and he suggests that von Hirsch's writings, fruitful as they are, need to be supplemented by the provision of a fuller 'positive' account, for which the notion of 'disassociating' the political community from the wrong committed by the offender, is crucial.

B. Censure and Just Deserts Revisited: Issues for Desert Theory

Part two opens, in chapter five, with a short but important chapter by Andreas von Hirsch, in which he amends his previously published account of the General Justifying Aim of a penal system.[22] That previous account offered two separate, although linked, justifications for punishment, namely censure and crime prevention. However, the so-called 'hard treatment' element of punishment (loss of liberty through imprisonment; loss of resources through being fined, etc) was seen as contributing to the General Justifying Aim by furnishing a deterrent against injurious conduct, rather than through the dimension of censure. The revised account suggests that hard treatment also, and indeed principally, contributes to the General Justifying Aim through its *amplifying* and *grading* functions, which are dimensions of censure. Given the wide influence of von Hirsch's theory, this significant revision will no doubt generate considerable discussion among penal theorists.

Andrew Ashworth has worked closely with Andreas von Hirsch on issues relating to censure theory, notably in their joint book *Proportionate Sentencing*, published in 2005.[23] In chapter six, he focuses on one particular aspect of theories based on deserved censure – their relationship with principles of penal restraint. Do such theories *require* penal restraint; or is it simply that desert theories are usually held by liberals who also subscribe to principles of penal restraint? If the latter is true, could desert theories also be supported by those who believe that more severe sentencing is called for? In pursuit of answers to these questions, the chapter examines four 'restraining' arguments that have been put forward in Andreas von Hirsch's writings – the so-called 'drowning out' argument; progressive loss of mitigation for repeat offenders; the principle of parsimony; and decrementalism. The question is then raised whether these principles provide von Hirsch with adequate defences against those who favour enhanced severity in sentencing.

An important controversy within communicative censure theory has concerned the possible role of repentance within a justified penal system. Two major penal philosophers, Antony Duff and John Tasioulas, have – in different ways – defended a significant role for repentance, but Andreas von Hirsch has dissented from this view, particularly because of his doubts about 'the state's

---

[22] For a summary of von Hirsch's previous position, see *Deserved Criminal Sentences*, above n 13, ch 3. On the concept of the General Justifying Aim of a penal system, see HLA Hart, 'Prolegomenon to the Principles of Punishment' (1960) 60 *Proceedings of the Aristotelian Society (New Series)* 1, reprinted in HLA Hart, *Punishment and Responsibility*, 2nd edn edited by J Gardner (Oxford, Oxford University Press, 2008).

[23] Von Hirsch and Ashworth, above n 13.

proper standing to delve so deeply into moral attitudes'.[24] In chapter seven, Anthony Bottoms revisits this controversy. He argues that the issue cannot be resolved without a full discussion of what is meant by 'repentance', about which Duff and Tasioulas differ. Bottoms then explores a third meaning of the term, derived from within the Christian tradition, namely that of 'repentance as turning around'. He argues that this concept of repentance can be fully defended within a liberal penal system. Moreover, although this definition is different from that utilised by Duff, it is fully congruent with Duff's important argument that censure, properly understood, has a non-instrumental forward-looking dimension, as well as its more obvious backward-looking dimension.

Unlike the preceding three chapters, chapter eight by Julian Roberts and Netanel Dagan does not revisit an existing issue within the literature of desert and censure theory; instead, it focuses on what the authors consider to be an important evolution over time in retributive theorising, reflected – as they see it – in the terminological shift from 'desert' to 'penal censure' (see above). They argue that this shift has consequences for legal punishment that have not yet been sufficiently explored, and these consequences are captured in the sub-title of their chapter – 'from static desert to responsive penal censure'. They argue that early desert theory (articulated for example in *Doing Justice*) was relatively 'static', seeing the offender's desert (based on harm and culpability) as in effect 'sealed' from the moment of the offence. By contrast, more recent censure theory presents a more dynamic aspect, seeing penal censure as something that permits a positive reaction from the offender, and subsequent response from the state. Welcoming this shift, the authors go on to suggest some possible practical implications of it, including a 'second-look' sentence review to examine altered culpability in light of post-sentence events. Such reviews are seen as particularly apposite for those serving lengthy terms of custody.

Chapter nine, the final chapter in part two, by Alessandro Corda, addresses the issue of whether, and if so to what extent, increases in sentences beyond the censure-based deserved amount can be justified for offenders engaging in pre-inchoate terrorist activities. There has been previous controversy within desert theory about whether and when predictions of future dangerousness might justify the use of disproportionately severe punishments for offenders with a history of serious violence.[25] Here, however, the focus is different, because the offences in question (which have been recently created in many Western jurisdictions) often involve minor harm, yet they are defined as preparatory to terrorist acts, and thus considered dangerous. Corda argues that, in such situations, the potential impact of the ultimate harm cannot alone justify the imposition of extremely severe sentences. Judges should instead carefully assess whether in

---

[24] Von Hirsch, *Deserved Criminal Sentences*, above n 13 at 43.
[25] See AE Bottoms and R Brownsword, 'Dangerousness and Rights' in JW Hinton (ed), *Dangerousness: Problems of Assessment and Prediction* (London, George Allen and Unwin, 1983) 9; von Hirsch and Ashworth, *Proportionate Sentencing*, above n 13, ch 4.

practical terms the preparatory acts increase the likelihood of terrorist acts, and pay greater attention to the defendant's strength of intention.

C. Censure, Desert and the Jurisprudence of Punishment

The chapters in part three place desert theory within wider jurisprudential-penological concerns and debates on censure. Chapter ten, by Matt Matravers, is perhaps for censure theorists the most challenging in the volume. Entitled 'Rootless Desert and Unanchored Censure', it opens with a quotation from an early book review of *Doing Justice*, which wondered whether that Report's 'blatant and unembarrassed defense of desert by those concerned about the present severity of punishment may become perverted by those who think present punishment too lenient'.[26] For Matravers, this comment was all too prescient, not because the arguments of *Doing Justice* (or desert theory more generally) caused or were directly responsible for subsequent significant rises in punishment in many Western countries, but rather because desert theory leaves the question of cardinal desert to be settled ultimately by social convention.[27] This in turn, he argues, renders desert theory 'rootless' and thus unable to contain rising punishment levels in a post-anthropomorphic, post-theocentric, post-Nietzschean world.

Censure theorists typically emphasise that state punishment is different from punishment in other social contexts, and they also focus on punishment as a state-offender interaction. In chapter eleven, Tatjana Hörnle agrees with the first of these points, but she argues that the second is too restrictive, and that it is necessary to develop a more prominent role for victims within theories of state punishment. Rejecting the project of a one-size-fits-all punishment theory for victimising and non-victimising crimes, Hörnle contends that the victims of crimes against individuals (that is, crimes that have violated individuals' rights to non-intervention, such as the right to life, physical integrity, sexual autonomy and property) have a prima facie right to obtain a statement about the wrong done to them, in the form of a criminal court's condemnatory message. However, this prima facie right must be weighed against other appropriate legal considerations, so it does not follow from the analysis that states must necessarily grant victims a stronger position than at present in criminal proceedings

---

[26] MR Gardner, 'The Renaissance of Retribution – An Examination of *Doing Justice*' (1976) 3 *Wisconsin Law Review* 781 at 791.

[27] Von Hirsch's desert theory distinguishes between 'ordinal desert' (creating an ordinal list of offences, in descending order of seriousness) and 'cardinal desert' (which concerns settling questions about the anchoring points of the punishment scale, and questions concerning 'how much punishment should actually be given to an offence of a specified seriousness?'). It is conceded that there is no objective way of calibrating cardinal desert, hence 'when judged in absolute rather than comparative terms ... the censure expressed through penal deprivation is in part a convention': von Hirsch, *Deserved Criminal Sentences*, above n 13 at 60.

(including sentencing proceedings). This chapter is therefore a balanced call for victims' rights to be taken more seriously by censure theorists.

In chapter twelve, Antje du Bois-Pedain addresses the question how – if at all – the mere passage of time influences how much punishment an offender deserves. She focuses, in particular, on how the two main determinants of desert – wrongful harm and culpability – are affected over time. She argues that subsequent events can affect both of these components in either direction. A wrongful harm is not on a unidirectional slide towards 'historicisation' but can experience 'diachronic spikes' in its significance. The agent's culpability is importantly influenced by how he/she incorporates the crime into his/her personal history. Most importantly, the fact that penal desert claims are made in respect of spatially and temporally extended beings that qualify as agents means that it matters for the question of desert when – and with how much delay – punishment for crime is imposed in the life course of an offender.

We have seen above that a key aspect of *Doing Justice* was its contestation of central features of 'the rehabilitative ideal'. An important question therefore arises as to whether censure theory can be formulated in a way that positively affirms a role for rehabilitation in punishment theory. This question is answered positively by Rob Canton, who argues in chapter thirteen that censure theory must not rest content with attention to the pronouncement of sentence, its weight or even its form. Rather, Hannah Maslen's concept of responsive censure[28] should be built upon to explore a continuing process of dialogue between the state and the offender that moves through remorse and apology to reconciliation. Canton argues that the traditional disputes between proponents of rehabilitation and of 'doing justice' need to be reframed to take account of developments in rehabilitation theory. Rehabilitation is more than the 'corrections' that attracted the criticism of an earlier generation and, in the more rounded conception advanced by Fergus McNeill,[29] it is not only compatible with censure theory but required by it. Moreover, the state and civil society have active duties towards the offender if reconciliation is to be achieved and justice done.

The volume concludes in chapter fourteen with a significant overview of punishment theory, including censure theory, by Michael Tonry. Tonry argues that the retributive conception of punishment as a process for censuring blameworthy conduct is an important component of a complete theory of punitive justice, but by itself is not enough; and neither are 'mixed' theories that incorporate traditional retributive ideas as constraints on the pursuit of consequentialist crime prevention goals. If punishment were unidimensional, involving only first offenders convicted of a single offence, and based solely on censuring blameworthy behaviour, theorising would be easier. Such theorising would, however,

---

[28] Maslen, above n 20.
[29] F McNeill, 'Four forms of "offender" rehabilitation' (2012) 17 *Legal and Criminological Psychology* 18.

ignore the reality that (as Isaiah Berlin observed) difficult problems almost always implicate competing normative principles.[30] We need to recognise that punishment implicates not only blameworthiness, crime prevention, and norm reinforcement, but also fairness, equality and human dignity. In his final section, Tonry therefore suggests a normative framework for just punishment that incorporates retributive ideas within a wider set of values. Ordinal proportionality based on offence seriousness is a fundamental component; it provides tools for inter-offence comparisons, and sets intelligible limits on just punishments. So, however, independently, do fairness, equality, and human dignity.

II. ACKNOWLEDGEMENTS

We are most grateful to all who attended the workshop on Censure Theory in September 2016, and especially to those who have subsequently contributed chapters to this volume. We are especially grateful to Julian Roberts of Oxford University, who originally suggested to us the idea of a scholarly event to mark the fortieth anniversary of the publication of *Doing Justice*. Warm thanks, also, to Tom Hawker and to Joanne Garner for administrative help in mounting the workshop. For his generous and skilled help in preparing the manuscript for the publishers, we are greatly indebted to Francois du Bois.

---

[30] On Berlin's value pluralism, see the editorial introduction by H Hardy in I Berlin, *Liberty* (Oxford University Press, 2002) at ix–x.

Part I

Censure: Mapping the Conceptual Territory

1

The Architecture of Censure

JOHN KLEINIG

ANDREAS VON HIRSCH has done much to give censure a central role in the theory of legal or state punishment. He does not exactly identify censure with punishment, though he views it as integral to it. His conjunction, 'Censure and Sanctions' – the title of his influential 1993 monograph[1] – puts in a nutshell the two elements that, for him, together constitute state punishment.

The structural or architectural elements of the sanctioning or 'hard treatment' dimension of punishment have been endlessly (even if contentiously) discussed. Those of censure have garnered somewhat less attention.[2] If censure is intended to illuminate *punishment theory* in some way, is the light it brings clear enough? Is it of the right kind?[3] Does it introduce problematic issues of its own? My purpose in this chapter is to reflect on some of these questions, and to suggest that focusing on censure can distort the discussion in certain respects.[4]

---

[1] A von Hirsch, *Censure and Sanctions* (Oxford, Oxford University Press, 1993).

[2] There are of course some exceptions. Andrew von Hirsch has a fair amount to say in *Censure and Sanctions* (ibid, ch 2). Uma Narayan also focuses specifically on censure in 'Appropriate Responses and Preventive Benefits: Justifying Censure and Hard Treatment in Legal Punishment' (1993) 13 *Oxford Journal of Legal Studies* 166; and Thaddeus Metz offers a 'censure theory' in 'Censure Theory and Intuitions about Punishment' (2000) 19 *Law and Philosophy* 491 and several other articles. Joel Feinberg comes close – though perhaps not close enough – to discussing censure in 'The Expressive Function of Punishment' (1965) 49 *The Monist* 397.

[3] There is some irony here, as we reflect on the 40th anniversary of Andrew von Hirsch's *Doing Justice: The Choice of Punishments* (Report of the Committee for the Study of Incarceration) (New York, Hill and Wang, 1976). To the best of my knowledge, 'censure' barely registers in *Doing Justice* (at 49 and 85), and the second reference – in the chapter on 'Prior Criminal Record', where von Hirsch refers to the recidivist as having 'persisted in the behavior after having been forcefully censured for it through his prior punishment' – comes eerily close to the slightly radical account I am formulating in this essay.

[4] Our vocabulary of criticism and rebuke is quite rich. Apart from censure, its noun forms include: accusation, admonishment, animadversion, blame, castigation, condemnation, criticism, disapproval, denunciation, excoriation, judgment, obloquy, punishment, rebuke, reprimand, reproach, reproof, and stigmatisation. Its verbal option includes additional possibilities such as: berate, chastise, chide, dress down, take to task, tell off, and upbraid. My focus here, though, is primarily on 'censure' as a distinctive form of criticism and rebuke.

I argue that there are three dimensions to censure – a *performative* one, in which censure brings about a change in social status; an *expressive* one, in which censure rebukes or expresses condemnation; and a *communicative* one, in which what is conveyed to the offender is the seriousness of what was done. In other words, I'm going to give a stronger account of censure than is usual.[5]

Further, I suggest that although *censure* may have a central place in a moral theory of *state or institutionalised* punishment, it is not as well suited to the moral justification of punishment per se. It does not fit well with the moral framework envisaged by early liberal theorists, such as Locke, who saw the moral right to punish as *natural*, pre-existing the conventions of civil society.[6] Within that scenario, the moral criticism and rebuke – resentment/indignation and condemnation – that punishment expresses does not carry with it some of the conventional trappings that we generally associate with censure.

The importance of this is that censure is integral only to an account of institutionalised punishment, including that by the state. As we cede to civil authorities (inter alia) the task of securing our fundamental rights, so we also cede to those authorities a primitive or natural or moral right to punish certain of the wrongs that are inflicted on us or others.

So far as punishment theory is concerned, the primary focus should be on moral rebuke and communicative proportionality. In the case of *legal* or *conventionalised* punishment, censure – an institutionally constructed vehicle for condemnation – is also involved. In addition, I suggest that the institutionalisation of punishment helps to determine standing – the authority to be an agent of punishment, and thus potentially provides the state with a reason for its involvement in a form of social response that has its deepest (though not only) rationale in considerations of justice or moral desert.

Does this involve some major shift from what von Hirsch and I have argued and occasionally sparred over? Not really. Reading over what he and I have written in the past 40 years, I often have a sense of *déjà vu*. That said, I think of the present essay as offering a few clarificatory steps in what is mostly a jointly shared position.[7]

---

[5] The dictionary allows that 'censure' can sometimes refer simply to harsh criticism. I think my account better reflects its Latin origins (*censura*) and history. Note also that my use of 'expressive' and 'communicative' is contextually limited to articulating elements in the act of censuring/punishing. Both terms are widely and variously used in punishment theory, sometimes to characterise theories of justification. That is not the case here.

[6] J Locke, 'The Second Treatise of Government' [1690] in *John Locke: Two Treatises of Government* edited by P Laslett (Cambridge, Cambridge University Press, 1988).

[7] I consider von Hirsch's primary statements on punishment theory to be: *Doing Justice*, above n 3; *Past or Future Crimes* (New Brunswick, Rutgers University Press, 1985); *Censure and Sanctions*, above n 1; and (with Andrew Ashworth) *Proportionate Sentencing: Exploring the Principles* (Oxford, Oxford University Press, 2005). My own are: *Punishment and Desert* (The Hague, Martinus Nijhoff, 1973); 'Punishment and Moral Seriousness' (1993) 25 *Israel Law Review* 401; *Ethics in Criminal Justice: An Introduction* (Cambridge, Cambridge University Press, 2008) chs 11 and 12; and 'What Does Wrongdoing Deserve?' in M Tonry (ed), *Retribution Has a Past: Has it a Future?* (Oxford, Oxford University Press, 2011) ch 3.

I. STRUCTURAL ELEMENTS IN CENSURE

I begin with an exploration of what I take to be the implicit form adopted by acts of censure:

A censures B for Ø-ing, expressing and communicating it by Π-ing B

I/we censure you for Ø-ing, and express and communicate it by Π-ing you.

First of all, though, and perhaps as an explanation for offering a first-person form of the schema, I wish to make the point that, lest the first version be construed as a simple proposition that is true or false (what JL Austin termed a 'constative') or even as the communication of such a proposition, censure is better seen as a complex version of what he characterised as a 'performative'.[8] That is, a suitably placed person who pronounces 'I censure you for Φ-ing' or 'I convict you for Ø-ing' *acts* to censure the other (by, inter alia, Π-ing B). The verbal act of censuring – which marks someone out as a transgressor – includes but is not exhausted by the particular form of words that convey censure. In other words, Π-ing B without words of censure does not amount to censure, and uttering 'I hereby censure you', or another phrase understood to express censure, without conveying this through Π-ing, falls short of censure.[9] There is more to censuring someone than looking disapprovingly at, reprimanding, or even imposing a hardship on that person.

A critical phrase is, of course, 'suitably placed'. There are conditions that must be satisfied if a censuring act is to be 'felicitous' (another Austinian term of art) or successful (rather than true or false).[10] These felicity conditions (*fc*) include, somewhat schematically:

- *fc-1a* There must exist an accepted conventional procedure having a certain conventional effect, a procedure that *includes* the uttering of certain words by certain persons in certain circumstances and, further,

- *fc-1b* the particular persons and circumstances in a given case must be appropriate for the invocation of the particular procedure invoked.

- *fc-2a* The procedure must be executed by all participants both correctly and

---

[8] JL Austin, *How to Do Things With Words* (Oxford, Oxford University Press, 1976) 14f. Later in the series of lectures (which were published posthumously), Austin was to abandon the simple performative/constative dichotomy; instead, he distinguished five general though overlapping classes of performative utterances, which he classified according to what he spoke of as their illocutionary force (at 151ff). They are: (i) Verdictives (used to judge something: estimate, reckoning, appraisal); (ii) Exercitives (used to exercise powers, rights or influence: appointing, voting, ordering); (iii) Commissives (used to commit oneself to doing something: promising); (iv) Behabitives (used to express attitudes or social behaviour towards someone: congratulating, challenging); and (v) Expositives (make plain how one is using words: 'I illustrate').

[9] Von Hirsch takes issue with this in *Censure and Sanctions* (above n 1 at 12), though in terms that I reassert here.

[10] Austin, above n 8 at 14f.

- *fc-2b* completely.
- *fc-3a* Where, as often, the procedure is designed for use by persons having certain thoughts or feelings, or for the inauguration of certain consequential conduct on the part of any participant, then a person participating in and so invoking the procedure must in fact have those thoughts or feelings, and the participants must intend so to conduct themselves, and further
- *fc-3b* must actually so conduct themselves subsequently.

I think that Austin overformalised these conditions – they function more as paradigmatic than as necessary and sufficient conditions. For example, I can imagine a situation in which a judgement of censure does not get to its object, B (because B died prior to its communication) – but I doubt whether that would cause me to claim that B was not, after all, censured. I don't think that treating them as paradigmatic conditions makes Austin's conditions less useful, as they capture something of importance for the overall structure of censure.

As Austin put it, performatives are infelicitous if they misfire or constitute abuses of the convention. *Misfires*, which invalidate the act, occur when there is a failure with respect to conditions *fc-1* or *fc-2*. In such cases, what is said or done does not achieve its intended purpose.[11] There is no censure. *Abuses* occur when the conditions associated with *fc-3* are violated, and the act is deemed 'unhappy' though not void.[12] The censure is inappropriate.

Let me, then, turn in order to A (the censuring party), B (the censured party), Ø (the censured behaviour), and Π (the act of censure).

A. The Censuring Party *(A)*

Who or what may censure?

We need not spend too much time debating the idea that censure is centrally a human activity. Machines and mere biota do not censure. Even animals do not censure: that most domesticated of animals, the dog, is often loved precisely because it appears to be free from the judgemental and censuring behaviour that often makes the company of our fellow humans so onerous.[13]

But may anybody censure?

First, to develop the point just raised, censure requires the development or possession of certain internal capacities. Infants cannot censure; nor can those in certain states of decline or unconsciousness. It also requires various active capacities for normative judgement. Censure is ordinarily an expression of responsible (in contrast to non-responsible rather than irresponsible)

---

[11] Ibid at 16.
[12] Ibid at 15, 41, 43.
[13] True, dogs may retaliate, though without censure. (Some of course may claim that I underestimate dogs, though there is also a linguistic deficit.)

agency. That agency will involve the development of self-consciousness and certain cognitive, emotive, and conative capacities – making it unlikely that a mere machine, however capably programmed, could censure (as distinguished from conveying the censure of others).[14] In addition, censure almost certainly requires, on the part of the censurer, a certain self-conception or self-consciousness of what is being done when censuring takes place. In censuring, one knows (or should know) what one is about. There is an intentionality about censure, captured in Austin's idea of an illocutionary act. But that is not all.

Second, perhaps the most general and undifferentiating point, censuring seems to presume someone with appropriate standing. May a child censure a parent, a citizen censure the government, a church member the priesthood? At first, and maybe second, blush it is questionable whether they can. At least it sounds somewhat stilted to suggest that they can. Or, if they can, we need to tell a story to make plausible sense of it.[15] Certainly they can complain about or criticise their respective objects, express disapproval of them, and even (in some sense) blame them. But censure seems to require something more: positional standing.[16]

Before I say more about the character of that positional standing, however, I note that the agent with standing need not be a particular individual but could be some institution, collectivity, or group – such as a committee, church, or court.[17] Some years ago, within the US Congress, a committee was formed to determine whether President Bill Clinton should be censured for lying to Congress about his relationship with Monica Lewinsky. Even though the censure motion that was recommended did not – in the end – garner the required Congressional votes, it illustrated how certain formalised censures could be imposed by a collective body.[18]

Of course, highly formalised censure of the kind involved in the Clinton case is more tightly structured than is commonly the situation when *A* censures *B*,

---

[14] I leave to one side ongoing debates about the possibilities of artificial intelligence.

[15] Not everyone may share my ear for this – some may be willing to speak of a child censuring a father for falling short of a promise – but I would be inclined to argue (a) that other characterisations (rebuke; reprove) are equally available, and (b) that to the extent that we wish to use the language of censure, it is because the promise made to the child gives it a certain standing.

[16] I have a problem with views of censure that see it simply as condemnation or rebuke. Narayan says that she understands '"censure" to be the expression of condemnation or blame directed at a responsible wrongdoer for the reason that she has committed a wrongful act' (above n 2 at 167). However, as her account of what censure is evolves, it becomes clear that she sees it as including a further element – 'authority to censure' (168) – which would bring it closer to the account I provide here. Metz, who does accept that there is a distinction between censuring and condemning (above n 2 at 494 n 3), also fails, in my view, to accommodate what I call the 'positional standing' that censuring involves.

[17] I don't think that for present purposes we need to resolve questions about the 'ontological' status of such collectivities – whether, for example, they should be seen as persons.

[18] For some documentation, see J Maskell, *Expulsion, Censure, Reprimand, and Fine: Legislative Discipline in the House of Representatives* (Washington, DC, Congressional Research Service, 2016) available at www.fas.org/sgp/crs/misc/RL31382.pdf.

but the censure that punishment theorists have in mind differs in degree rather than kind. And that, I suggest, is probably because most punishment theorists tend to think about punishment within a legal/criminal offence paradigm. It is the court that censures (on behalf of the community? state? sovereign?) when it passes judgment and imposes a penalty.[19]

Returning to the issue of standing, censure includes for the most part a formalised or institutionalised judgment, requiring that the person who censures has the standing or authority to pass such a judgment (and whatever else expresses it), communicating it to the wrongdoer. Whether that authority is to be thought of simply as some kind of moral authority or is more appropriately seen in terms of certain conventions that ascribe inter alia the authority to censure is an issue to which I return near the end of this essay. Nevertheless, I want to suggest that to the extent that we link punishment with censure, the paradigm for censure will be an appropriately situated person or collective. This is why the dominant account of punishment in the literature sees it as an *authoritative* act.[20]

Casting this in terms of Austin's conditions for a felicitous performative, *fc-1a* and *fc-1b* capture what is required for standing. There must be conventions about who may perform the particular act and how the particular act is performed. That may be one reason for reluctance to call the acts of a lynch mob punishment, even if the language of vengeance may sometimes be apposite. As conventions, there may be little that is of deep or natural entitlement. In many cases, censure will be an option within an organisation that wishes to pass judgment upon and no doubt deter its members from conduct (Ø-ing) that is deemed to bring the organisation or collectivity into disrepute. There will be some understanding about what it is that brings such a body into disrepute, some procedure that it accepts for determining whether *B*'s acts have brought it into disrepute, and a process for declaring that *B* is or is not to be censured.

Standing to censure is likely to be relatively particularised and specific in the sense that social context will determine those who are accorded such standing and those with it will not *ipso facto* have the standing to perform other acts that require standing unless there are conventions giving them a wider remit. That is, if I have standing to censure *B*, someone else otherwise similarly situated may not have that standing, and if (say, in an employment context) I have standing to censure *B* I may not have standing to fire *B*. (Some parents might wish they had power to fire their children!) Parents may conventionally be seen as having standing to censure their child. That standing, however, may not always be thought to

---

[19] I acknowledge, though, that RE Myers has argued otherwise: 'Requiring a Jury Vote of Censure to Convict' (2009) 88 *North Carolina Law Review* 137. Without taking too much issue with his point, I would see him as wanting to emphasise – and bring to the fore – the expressive function of punishment stressed by Feinberg, above n 2.

[20] See for example AGN Flew, 'The Justification of Punishment' (1954) 29 *Philosophy* 294. The view is an old one, however: see T Hobbes, *Leviathan* [1651] edited by JCA Gaskin (Oxford, Oxford University Press, 1996) ch 28.

transfer to another's child: 'If you have a problem with my child – come and see me!' And the kinds of censure available to a particular censuring authority may be quite limited. A school may censure a student by suspending her, but not by imprisoning her.

One final note. To the extent that censure is a performative, an act that has 'social' consequences of some kind, it is not removed or withdrawn by a change of heart (or the will of the person censured), but only as a result of some determination by the censurer or authority that oversees the act of censure. A Congressional censure can be removed only by Congressional action; an ecclesiastical censure can be removed only by absolution – unless, that is, a condition for its automatic removal is built into the original act of censure (say, being placed under censure for five years).

B. The Censured Party *(B)*

The object of censure is also typically a responsible agent, whether an individual or collective body. Unless one considers it capable of deliberate or at least culpable wrongdoing, it is inappropriate to censure an animal, even though one may rebuke, criticise or discipline it. Or, perhaps to put the point more neutrally, unless one views one's pet as a person or responsible, censure will not be viewed as appropriate. Insofar as censure involves the accusation of culpable wrongdoing – which, I believe, it normally does – then the object of censure must be deemed capable of understanding and appreciating the act of censure in a certain way. (Whether or not it does understand and appreciate it in that way is another matter.)

The case of children is more complex. Although parents have positional standing, we may sometimes resist the language of censure because of the developmental nature of child-raising.[21] We chastise and discipline children as readily as we censure and punish them.

May one censure the dead? I guess that insofar as the act of censure may involve certain formal processes, those formal processes could be followed in the event that their object is no longer alive. The censure would apply to what was done by the person while alive and would be seen as affecting the person's legacy. Take President Andrew Jackson, in respect of whom a 1837 Congressional vote expunged the 1834 censure that Congress had imposed on him for his refusal to hand over certain documents. Plausibly, this vote would have been considered (by some) as important to his legacy, even if the President had died prior to the censure being expunged.[22] Nevertheless, the idea of censuring someone who has

---

[21] But compare Liat Levanon's chapter in this volume, which draws on developmental theory to develop an account of positive censure.

[22] See, briefly, 'Congress Censures Jackson', *This Day in History*, March 28, 1834, available at www.history.com/this-day-in-history/congress-censures-jackson. What is true of the effect of expungement on a legacy may also be true of a posthumous censure on a legacy.

died loses something in its implementation, as it is generally intended to impact the person who is censured. In political censures, as well as others, it is usually important that the censured person is present when the act of censure is formally announced.[23]

Because censure is an act in which, inter alia, someone is rebuked for culpable wrongdoing, it often – even if not necessarily – constitutes a form of public shaming. One's public status is altered. Although some sense can be given to the idea of a private censure, in which the censured person is not named, or the censure is conveyed privately to someone by means of a letter of censure, the expectation when someone is censured is not only that the person is confronted with the claim that s/he had acted wrongly, but is openly condemned for such wrongdoing. This would be true of most formal censures, but may often be true of other conventionalised censures, as when a parent censures a child or a church censures one of its members, or a court censures a defendant. The person who is censured is subject to a socially sanctioned or approved or conventionalised judgment.[24]

C. The Censured Behaviour (*Ø*)

Agents are not censured *in vacuo* but censured for some act or activity for which it is presumed they can appropriately be held responsible.

Does the activity in question have to be morally condemnable? There is some temptation to think that it must. That temptation is fed by the confinement of censure to those who can be regarded as responsible or moral agents. And I think there is an argument for considering that censure generally includes a suggestion of moral obloquy. Censure involves strong criticism of another, and is intended to expose the one criticised to judgment and serious condemnation. Even when censures are expunged, those censured may feel the ongoing burden of having been held in some sort of moral contempt.

Nevertheless, it may be too strong to argue that all censure involves moral obloquy, even though it often comes close to it. Historically, people have been censured for their political judgements, theological beliefs and religious practices as well as their moral or role-related conduct. Such censure 'comes close' to moral obloquy because the beliefs and practices in question tend to be closely

---

[23] Here I take issue with Metz (above n 2 at 495–96), who disputes the idea that censure requires communication. I think that Metz sometimes conflates the more basic and less institutionalised notion of condemnation with censure. Censure may also serve other purposes, such as assuring victims that their dignitarian status and the harm done to them is taken seriously. But I am less convinced that this is as central as expressing and communicating to the wrongdoer the wrongness and seriousness of his/her wrongdoing.

[24] Where censure is privately conveyed, it will usually (though not always) be in the context of a private institution. Others within the institution may be witnesses to it, though not outsiders.

intertwined with moral expectations. The spiritual failing is not simply a ritual failing but one that also reflects a character failure.[25]

Interestingly, though perhaps not surprisingly, given my understanding of censure, ecclesiastical censures were not mere judgments of serious deviation but were also punishments. They were, at the same time, sanctions as well as censures. Focusing on the censuring judgment served to emphasise one dimension of a complex whole. This is not surprising because 'censure' derives from the Latin *censura*, which designated an office that was initially intended to keep a register of citizens (hence, census) and subsequently bifurcated, on the one hand, in the direction of censorship (official control over the flow of information) and, on the other, of expressed condemnation, including discipline, of those who violated manners and mores. The latter function (as well as the former) was taken over by the Roman church, which usually excluded those who were censured from access to some of the church's privileges until they had reformed their ways.[26] Such censures were directed primarily to correction or reformation, and were 'vindictive' only when restoration failed.

D. The Act of Censure (*Π*)

One of the complexities of censure is that the act of censuring (*Π*-ing) ordinarily carries with it certain material consequences.[27] This is one important respect in which my account of censure differs from one that has been common in punishment theory, where censure is viewed as one thing, and sanctions/hard treatment/punishment are viewed as another. Generally, though, the expression of censure involves more than a formalised rebuke that stigmatises. For example, if a member of the US Congress is censured, he or she may no longer be permitted to serve on certain Congressional committees. Censure may include disqualification, and, in some documents, censure is characterised as a form of punishment that may be distinguished from other forms of punishment such as impeachment, fines, or rebukes.

Thus, part of what I am suggesting is that censure and sanction do not represent separate elements in a practice but stand simply as distinguishable foci in a single practice that has a condemnatory as well as a sanctioning or hard treatment function. The point then is not to isolate a form of behaviour that is censure and then add to it certain sanctions that, though they may be

[25] Other cases, however, are less likely to be seen as involving moral judgement. A person could be censured for failing to perform an administrative duty and penalised thereby. We need to keep a distinction between penalties and punishments, and in certain cases an institutionalised notion such as censure can be employed either way. This is difficult to do with the more primitive notions of condemnation and rebuke.

[26] For a useful discussion of such censures, see Leo Gans, 'Ecclesiastical Censures', *The Catholic Encyclopedia* (New York, Robert Appleton Co, 1908), available at www.newadvent.org/cathen/03527a.htm.

[27] Cf the quotation from von Hirsch given in n 3 above.

appropriate to it, are nevertheless not part of it. The material consequences of censure, those elements that make censure what it is, are integral to it because the expressive and communicative dimensions of censure cannot be detached from some notion of proportionality. In focusing on censure we are often emphasising the condemnation involved; in focusing on punishment we are often emphasising the hard treatment that comes with condemnation.

Not that the punitive dimension of censure is always proportionate to the wrong indicated by B's Φ-ing. But *ceteris paribus*, the authority that fails to censure proportionately will – absent considerations mentioned below – often be criticised for giving (at most) a mere 'slap on the wrist'. There is something seriously defective in such censure. Such censure is deserving of criticism for its failure to communicate seriousness with accuracy. What we term (state) punishment, then, is not so much the welding of a separate censure with sanctions; rather, it is a performative in which a certain process takes place comprising an authoritative condemnatory judgment that is partially expressed and communicated through certain sanctions, sanctions that *ceteris paribus* convey proportionate seriousness.

The failure of a censuring act to communicate the seriousness of what was done (a failure of proportionality) is not a simple conceptual deficiency – a failure in felicity – but a potential deficiency in the legitimacy of the censure. And yet, as a legitimacy consideration, it does not operate in isolation and, as I will indicate, is not necessarily determinative.

What is sometimes viewed as an evolution in von Hirsch's theory of punishment – from 'just deserts' to 'censure and sanctions' is therefore not to be construed as leaving behind one type of consideration (just deserts) for another (censure and sanctions) but as refocusing a complex institutionalised response to public wrongdoing from one of its aspects to another. The proportionality implicit in the communicative dimension of censure reflects the cardinal and ordinal deserts of just desert theory.[28]

A large cluster of questions arises at this point, but I want to make clear that although proportionality in censure is a morally important consideration, it is not determinative with respect to what ought, in the end, to be done. A person's moral or pre-institutional deserts may be out of proportion to what we may ultimately be justified in imposing on them (as in crimes against humanity). They may need to be moderated by what John Deigh refers to as a principle of humanity.[29] Communicative expressions of censure may also need to take

---

[28] Although this is not the place to offer a defence of proportionate deserts, I do not wish to underestimate the problems associated with their determination. Those problems are well articulated by Matt Matravers in his chapter in this volume. My own efforts to address the difficulties can be found in *Punishment and Desert*, above n 7, section VIIa. See also A Ristroph, 'Proportionality as a Principle of Limited Government' (2005) 55 *Duke Law Journal* 263.

[29] J Deigh, 'Punishment and Proportionality: Part 2' (2016) 35 *Criminal Justice Ethics* 21; cf A Fichtelberg, 'Crimes Beyond Justice: Retributivism and War Crimes' (2005) 24 *Criminal Justice Ethics* 31.

into account such things as remorse, repentance, the effect of penalties, victim forgiveness/reconciliation, and so on.[30] Desert is only one factor that impacts the final outcome, even though it may provide a critical moral backdrop.

The important point to recognise, however, is that the background against which these often moderating factors impact on the actual practice of censure is one in which proportionality is presumed.

II. PRE-CENSURE PUNISHMENT THEORY

Although traditional penal theory in the Lockean tradition hearkens back to a state-of-nature in which, as a matter of pre-institutional desert, wrongdoing of certain kinds warranted a proportionate response, including punishment,[31] it is the conviction of the tradition's proponents that the state of nature is an inadequate vehicle for such responses. Civil society, although subject to failures of its own, offers an overall better way of responding to human conflict and wrongdoing. It institutes broadly acceptable procedures for handling human ignorance, obtuseness, vengefulness, and failure, and its institutionalised procedures – laws, police, courts, and sentences – function overall as a morally acceptable though revisable attempt to capture what would remain insecure in a state of nature.

Punishment in liberal democratic civil societies – state punishment, for the most part – represents a formalised and consensual compromise that preserves and maximises our deepest moral concerns – rights, dignity and the conditions for human flourishing. Although it reflects cultural conventions, it must remain responsive to such moral concerns. Worries about cruel and unusual punishment, for example, are not to be resolved solely in terms of legal precedent, but must go deeper into the conditions that make human life the distinctive phenomenon it is and individual humans worthy of dignitarian regard.[32]

Given these contentions, my argumentative path takes the following direction. If I am right that censure is a performative act requiring standing, then censure does not seem to provide an appropriate starting point for a discussion of the morality of punishment per se. The primary reason for this is that

---

[30] Other chapters in this volume, for example those by Andrew Ashworth and Michael Tonry, also emphasise the moral importance of penal restraint and other considerations. Although I would not adopt their talk of a static desert and flexible censure, Julian Roberts and Netanel Dagan (this volume) reasonably point to other factors that may bear on the ultimate severity of the sanction. One failing of my earlier work as well as of *Doing Justice* was the tendency to believe that all things considered, people ought to get what they deserve, whereas it would be more correct to say that, *ceteris paribus*, people ought to get what they deserve. *Ceteris paribus* may often not be the case, and though it would be unjust to give people more than they deserve, there are other considerations, both before sentencing and subsequently, that may justify a mitigation to giving people as much as they deserve.

[31] Locke, above n 6.

[32] For an articulation, see J Kleinig and NG Evans, 'Human Flourishing, Human Dignity, and Human Rights' (2013) 32 *Law and Philosophy* 539.

punishment – or at least the moral right to punish (or retaliate?) pre-exists the institutional trappings of censure. If I can cast this in the traditional language of social contract theory, punishment has its foundations in a state of nature – that is, as a naturally appropriate response to certain kinds of acts. This has two aspects – first, the debate we now commonly associate with PF Strawson, concerning natural attitudes to the acts of others, including resentment/ indignation in the face of certain kinds of wrongdoing and condemnation/ rebuke based on that resentment;[33] and second, the idea that the punishment of wrongdoers is defeasibly appropriate or fitting to or justly deserved by wrong-doing even if there are no positional authorities of the kind that we associate with state or legal punishment. At bottom, and *ceteris paribus*, those wrongly done by are morally positioned to punish.[34]

My suggestion, then, is that the fundamental moral question is not: why, beyond censure, are sanctions justified? But: why, beyond condemnation, is hard treatment justified? This is because punishment's justification must lie in the deeper moral concerns that arise in the so-called state of nature – a social arrangement that does not possess the institutional conditions for censure, but does have room for condemnation and what it deservedly warrants by way of a just response. When we contemplate civil society, with its institutional conditions for censure, the central question becomes: what gives this or that person or agency the authority to censure?[35] I don't deny that there may be a similar (though not strictly analogous) question about condemnation and the punishment that communicates the seriousness of what was done: Insofar as punishment is justified, what gives this or that person the *moral* authority to punish? Is it restricted to those who have been wronged? May anyone who is aware of wrongdoing be its agent? Are there disqualifying considerations?

I offer a few reflections on these questions. Some of these thoughts have been developed (and criticised!) extensively in the literature. So what I suggest here are merely some indications of the direction taken by my thinking rather than an extended argument.

One strategy might be to argue that the social contract theorists' view that there is a natural or basic moral right of retaliation or punishment is misguided, and that at most there is a natural right of self-defence or condemnation (under-stood as denunciation). HLA Hart comes close to this at one point when he says that the appropriate response to wrongdoing is condemnation, not punishment,

---

[33] See PF Strawson, 'Freedom and Resentment' (1962) 48 *Proceedings of the British Academy* 1.

[34] This doesn't rule out the possibility of consequentialist considerations having some role, though Locke and those of his ilk give such considerations a place within a generally retributivist frame-work. There is also a further debate here, pursued at some length by John Simmons, about whether only those wronged by others may punish them or whether, absent the trappings of civil society, others may be morally justified in punishing wrongdoers. (Cf the debate about self-defence and defence of others.) See AJ Simmons, 'Locke and the Right to Punish' (1991) 20 *Philosophy and Public Affairs* 311.

[35] There are, of course, several subsidiary questions in each case.

and that condemnation may be conveyed by words. Hard treatment requires some further justification.[36] I certainly agree that condemnation is an appropriate response to wrongdoing as such, but so far as hard treatment is concerned the seriousness of condemnation needs to be manifested in a range of responses from mere rebukes to various kinds/degrees of hard treatment.[37] Condemnation of (serious) wrongdoing without sanctions is evacuated of its seriousness, and some measure of proportionality is built into condemnation. Narayan criticises an earlier attempt of mine to suggest that hard treatment is required by *our human resistance*, when we have acted wrongly, to taking condemnation seriously without – *ceteris paribus* – its hard treatment expression.[38] I think she was right to find fault with that – at least as a complete account – even if we are in need of more forceful expressions of condemnation.[39] It is the seriousness of the wrongdoing, not the mere intransigence of the wrongdoer that warrants the hard treatment as the censure's expressive and communicative content.[40]

When it comes to the form taken by expressions of censure, my suggestion is that we need to look at the social role of the censuring person or agency, and therefore at the way in which censure/hard treatment fits into the rationale for that social role.[41] Different authorities will have different roles and particular

[36] HLA Hart, *Law, Liberty, and Morality* (Stanford, Stanford University Press, 1963) 65–66.

[37] It's unclear to me why hard treatment should require some additional justification beyond condemnation and rebuke, particularly if the wrongdoing is serious. I grant that there may sometimes be reasons for withholding hard treatment, but that is another matter. Do those who find a gap between condemnation and punishment see a similar gap between praise and gratitude and reward, especially when the good done is significant? Are words enough? Von Hirsch also addresses this question in his chapter for this volume.

[38] See Narayan, n 2 above at 178 in respect of my 'Punishment and Moral Seriousness' n 7 above. The point can be made, not only with respect to our own wrongdoing, but also in regard to how we see responses to others' wrongdoing. Insofar as we see others as we see ourselves, hard treatment will be apposite.

[39] There is some symbolic and material value (especially given the problem of recidivism) in choosing punishments that could elicit penitential or apologetic responses (see for example RA Duff, *Punishment, Communication and Community* (Oxford, Oxford University Press, 2001); C Bennett, *The Apology Ritual: A Philosophical Theory of Punishment* (Cambridge, Cambridge University Press, 2008)). There is also an important disvalue in imposing punishments that demoralise (see Jonathan Jacobs and Rob Canton in this volume). Nevertheless, I do not think that the former should determine the amount of punishment to be imposed. The initial and primary emphasis should remain on the seriousness of the wrong done. In her chapter for this volume, Tatjana Hörnle touches on the fraught question concerning the relevance of the victim's perspective to determinations of such seriousness. And Alessandro Corda asks whether, in the light of terrorist challenges, desert-based theories of punishment can accommodate pre-inchoate crimes (via determinations of dangerousness). I accept the challenge posed by such developments, but would argue that we should not lose hold of the moral constraints constituted by desert theory. Sometimes a theory of quarantine may be more appropriate.

[40] Andreas von Hirsch, in his chapter in this volume, develops a similar institutional ground for the necessity of hard treatment that is based on the scaling function of hard treatment. This way of forging a closer connection between censure and hard treatment is compatible with what I say here. Von Hirsch's talk of the scaling function of hard treatment comes close to what I see as the proportionality involved in the expressive dimension of censure.

[41] Ecclesiastical censure may have a different set of ends from criminal censure. In my early writing on punishment, this is where I saw a place for consequentialist considerations in the justification of institutional punishment. See my *Punishment and Desert* above n 7, section VIId.

forms of censure/hard treatment need to be shown to advance that role in various ways.[42] This, for me, is where consequentialist considerations come in – not in the justification of censure/punishment, but in providing a particular person or agency with the authority to determine and impose that censure. This is why we recognise the state's authority to punish certain wrongs but not others, and why we have the limits we do on parental punishment (recognising of course that the various limits we place on authorities are contestable).[43] It is also why some expressions of censure, even if sensitive to considerations of proportionality, may be more appropriate than others: they further or fail to further the purposes of the institution.

This response leaves some room for claiming that a censuring/punishing authority lacks the *moral* authority to punish, that is, to give a wrongdoer what he or she negatively deserves. There is a presumption that the punishment of wrongdoing has moral as well as role-based underpinnings. We saw this in some of the older literature on punishment, in which it was argued that only God had the authority to punish moral wrongdoing.[44] If the contractual role that the state is given is abused in some way – for example, if the state maintains a social order in which immoral laws are promulgated or in which the violation of laws is made necessary – then, despite the role-based reasons it may have for punishing crime, it may lose its moral authority to punish/censure or have that authority greatly circumscribed. What is transferred from the state of nature to civil (and other) authorities is a moral authority to punish, and even if it is appropriately constrained by institutional roles, it may still be subject to forms of abuse.[45] In recent literature I think this has also been one – though perhaps not the only – consideration informing the argument against private prisons – at moving what may be appropriate to the state as an agent of the community to a private organisation. Although profiting from the wrongdoing of others may be unseemly, even a non-profit punishing authority could be viewed as failing to acknowledge the dignitarian claims of wrongdoers.[46]

I think a failure of moral authority can also occur in the informal context of a state of nature.[47] The agent who retaliates may be morally compromised

[42] I think this a major reason why legal punishment is to be limited to public wrongs, not private ones (if I can exploit that problematic distinction for present purposes).

[43] I am thus slightly uneasy about Liat Levanon's argument (in this volume), which draws on child developmental theory to illuminate a possible aspect of legal punishment.

[44] Eg, JD Mabbott, 'Punishment' (1939) 48 *Mind* 155.

[45] We might think of North Korea in this context. Cf also J Murphy, 'Marxism and Retribution' (1973) 2 *Philosophy and Public Affairs* 217.

[46] Alon Harel has written several articles criticising the privatisation of government functions. See, most recently, A Harel, 'Why Privatisation Matters' in A du Bois-Pedain, M Ulväng and P Asp (eds), *Criminal Law and the Authority of the State* (Oxford, Hart/Bloomsbury, 2017) 229. Admittedly, Harel's views have drawn some strong reactions: see, eg A Volokh, 'Privatisation and the Elusive Employee-Contractor Distinction' (2012) 46 *UC Davis Law Review* 133.

[47] Although I'm inclined to think of a state of nature as a theoretical construct, Simmons has a more generous account, allowing that it also covers 'the state into which each of us is born today, and

in ways that makes him/her an unseemly agent of punishment. If, for example, the person who punishes will profit from the punishment and that corrupts his motivation, he is almost certainly an inappropriate agent of punishment.

If we focus on the hypothetical state-of-nature case, it would seem reasonable that the moral authority to punish would ordinarily reside with the person wronged. Writers such as Locke appear to grant that those who are victimised in a state of nature have a privileged authority to punish those who wrong them. But he casts the net wider than this.[48] After all, the wronged person may not be in a position to administer punishment. May others who are familiar with the wrongdoing? I see no decisive reason against it. After all, that is standard practice in civil society. Nevertheless, the propensity for mistake – one of the factors that underlies the complex procedures we have in civil society – is troubling. And there may be additional problems concerning motivation. More deeply, though, Locke sees the wrong done to one as being – as we acknowledge in criminal cases – a wrong done to all.[49] Dealing with this can of worms, however, is better left to another time and place.

III. CONCLUSION

The thrust of my argument, admittedly brief in places, has been that, as a matter of justice, we condemn and rebuke wrongdoing but, in addition, convey the seriousness of that condemnation and rebuke by acts that express and communicate it, viz (penalties and) punishment, defeasibly measured by considerations of desert. When institutionalised, such condemnation and rebuke take the form of censure. Insofar as the institutions through which we censure are functionally justified, the authority to censure will most likely be normatively constrained by the social purposes that we believe such institutions legitimately have, and these will in turn constrain the forms that such censure takes.

in which we remain until we consent to join some commonwealth. It is the state to which we return when our political society dissolves (as in times of civil war), and perhaps also when our political leaders overstep the bounds of their rightful authority (i.e., cases of tyranny). It is the state in which all political rulers stand with respect to one another, and in which all citizens of one state stand with respect to citizens of another state' (Simmonds, n 34 above at 319). His arguments for this reference his 'Locke's State of Nature' (1989) 17 *Political Theory* 449.

[48] Locke, above n 6.

[49] Simmons teases out these elements in Locke's account in 'Locke and the Right to Punish' n 34 above.

2

Censure, Sanction and the Moral Psychology of Resentment and Punitiveness

JONATHAN JACOBS

T HIS CHAPTER EXPLICATES a morally sound role for resentment and for retributivist considerations in the understanding of censure and criminal sanction.

Addressing issues of moral psychology, normative issues and relations between these two types of issue, it elaborates a view of censure and sanction that owes much to Andreas von Hirsch's treatments of these topics but also pursues some avenues of approach not explicitly developed in his work. In particular, it draws on considerations of moral psychology that build upon the work of Adam Smith.

The first section highlights the significance of the morally educative potential of civil society in liberal democracies. Section II focuses on the importance of resentment in the moral economy of human interaction, and connects moral education to learning how to calibrate resentment appropriately. Section III links the importance of resentment and its proper calibration to practices of censure, including state-imposed punishment. It argues that censure and sanction can be understood as appropriate responses to criminal conduct, provided that the responses are to be ordered and measured by a concern with justice in a sphere of agents capable of acting for reasons. Censure thus has a *point*, a significance that is not appropriately explicated in exclusively consequentialist terms. This theme is further developed in section IV, which addresses the desert-censure-proportionality-parsimony nexus, and in section V, which brings to light reasons to reject a strictly consequentialist conception of the aims and justification of criminal sanctions. Taking consequences seriously is, of course, part of any plausible moral view. However, an exclusively consequentialist conception of censure and sanction is problematic in ways that render it untenable. The chapter argues that the ills of current policies ostensibly based on retributivist notions need to be addressed within a framework of thought that recognises the propriety and importance of the moral sentiments that underpin penal practice.

The discussion is shaped by concerns motivated by contemporary criminal justice practices in the US and UK, although the main points also apply more generally. All of these points chiefly concern criminal justice in a broadly liberal democratic polity.

I. CIVIL SOCIETY'S MORALLY EDUCATIVE ROLE AND THE RELEVANCE OF LIBERAL POLITICAL ORDER

The fact that we are discussing criminal justice in liberal democracies is important to the issues. Some brief remarks concerning that type of political order are necessary as background to the claims at the centre of the discussion. The liberal dimension of liberal democracy concerns the protection of extensive rights and liberties of individuals and the fact that the state does not enforce or impose some specific way people are to lead their lives. Individuals have a significant measure of moral independence.[1] The democratic dimension concerns the existence of meaningful forms of participation in the political process, including (for example) election of legislative representatives and those in executive offices, as well as the opportunity to compete for election. Those who govern are accountable to the governed, even if, as in Great Britain, the specific political form is a constitutional monarchy rather than a republic.

Among the most important features of a liberal democratic political order is that it creates and preserves conditions for a diverse, dynamic civil society, comprising the many contexts in which individuals (and groups) engage in a broad range of activities voluntarily.[2] In a polity in which individuals have extensive rights and liberties, civil society will extend to numerous spheres, such as education, economic activity and occupations, religious life, leisure and cultural activities, sports, the media and various others. While there may be a good deal of government regulation and administrative apparatuses of many kinds, civil society exists where people engage in activities and associations voluntarily and when the forms of those activities and associations are largely self-chosen and of their own design. There is a great deal of that kind of activity in many liberal democracies.

Participation in the various spheres of civil society can play an important role in moral education. This is so because in many of those spheres, people

---

[1] By moral independence I mean that individuals are not required or forced by the state to have a specific, comprehensive view of how to live, what is worthwhile, and what matters most. Of course, it is important that individuals should endorse certain shared values, but those can allow for extensive diversity in people's conceptions of how to lead their lives. The state does not impose confessional requirements.

[2] The notion of civil society I employ is influenced by Edward Shils. See his *The Virtue of Civility* edited by S Grosby (Indianapolis, Liberty Fund, 1997).

engage in criticism, encouragement, rebuke and guidance of various types and in settings that are not narrowly confined only to those who strongly share one's values. They are thus contexts in which people's 'skills of civility' can be developed, skills such as respectful disagreement, cooperation and compromise, and the recognition and toleration of perspectives different from one's own. By contrast, in strongly illiberal societies, ones in which ideological conformity is demanded or religious confession is of the first importance, moral learning is a very different process. In a liberal polity's civil society numerous forms of criticism and censure would be compatible with trust. Different groups will regard each other as equal participants in the social world and interaction and mutual education can occur in meaningful ways.

In discussing how civil society depends on attitudes and dispositions that differ from those of repressive political order or a social world fraught with ideological brittleness, Edward Shils wrote of the need for

> an outlook which attempts to do justice to all the interests which involves also holding them in check – and thus maintaining the traditional pattern of plurality within a common society which is of intrinsic value … This quiescence [of ideological politics] can be sustained only if an effective alternative is available. Civil politics are this alternative.[3]

Civility understood in this way is crucial to a political culture in which there are respectful relations between people in their regard for each other as participants in a common, if not homogeneous social world. There can be sharp political differences between various groups without those differences threatening the basic elements of the political order. Civil society can present a huge variety of morally relevant contexts and challenges. In different contexts one encounters different rules, norms, and expectations, and one might have a range of different responsibilities and modes of interacting with others. Sensibility is developed, patterns of motivation are formed, and aspects of one's acquired character are shaped by experience in the various contexts of civil society.

In a pluralistic society groups will have different traditions with some different customs and outlooks, and the social world will accommodate diversity. There may be various sources of friction, and issues that aggravate moral disagreement (consider same-sex marriage, abortion, drug use, euthanasia, capital punishment, for example), but there will also be interaction and a measure of mutual influence. Also, there may be assimilation to some extent as a shared political culture develops when groups are tolerant and willing to regard each other fully as members of the same political community. Yet, groups will have freedom to maintain many of their distinctive perspectives and traditions. Broadly based endorsement of principles of liberal democracy need not erase or diminish the genuineness of differences between groups.

---

[3] Ibid at 49.

However, in a troubling way the civility of society seems to be diminishing in important respects. One indication of this is the proliferation of criminalisation. In the US, recent decades have seen a dramatic growth in types of conduct that are criminalised and an increase in the severity of many sentences. Such developments can weaken the moral point of censure and sanction even if the cost to those punished increases. When there is increasing reliance on criminalisation, law enforcement and criminal sanction, the capacity of civil society and the capacity of criminal justice to communicate moral messages effectively are diminished and the morally educative role of civil society is reduced.[4]

Given the ways those trends are threats to civility it may seem odd to argue for an important role for resentment and censure in criminal justice. Yet, there is such a role, and much that is morally objectionable about contemporary criminal justice is that it reflects corrupt and disordered forms of resentment and censure. We need therefore to explicate the outlines of their morally proper forms.

II. A MORALLY PROPER ROLE FOR RESENTMENT

Many critics of contemporary criminal justice argue that the basis of many of its problems is the liberal political order and the ways that highly punitive resentment are institutionally realised. However, I will argue that there is a role for resentment and for retributivist considerations in criminal justice in a broadly liberal polity, and that they are centrally important to *morally defensible* censure and sanction. There surely are ways that resentment and retributive sentiments can go morally off the rails and do considerable damage. But that is not because they are inherently morally problematic. Resentment can be a morally appropriate sentiment and it can have a morally apt role as a basis for censure.

Adam Smith's *The Theory of Moral Sentiments* provides us with a helpful perspective on this issue. Smith argued that gratitude and resentment are *fundamental* moral sentiments.[5] He pointed to the fact that human beings are capable of acting for reasons, of having purposes and concerns, and of being motivated by a multitude of feelings and perspectives. Moreover, they can consider those feelings and attitudes, and reflect on their purposes and concerns. They can decide to act, or refrain from acting, on the basis of such reflection. Human beings can negotiate the world and interactions with each other on the basis of

---

[4] See, for example DS Nagin, 'Criminal Deterrence Research at the Outset of the 21st Century' in M Tonry (ed), *Crime and Justice: A Review of Research* volume 23 (Chicago, University of Chicago Press, 1998) 1. Also see DS Nagin, FT Cullen and C Jonson, 'Imprisonment and Reoffending' in M Tonry (ed), *Crime and Justice: A Review of Research* volume 38 (Chicago, University of Chicago Press, 2009) 1; A von Hirsch, AE Bottoms, E Burney and P-O Wikström, *Criminal Deterrence and Sentence Severity* (Oxford, Hart Publishing, 1999).

[5] A Smith, *The Theory of Moral Sentiments* [1759] edited by DD Raphael and AL MacFie (Indianapolis, Liberty Fund, 1982) esp. 67–78 (Part II, Section I).

what they think good and worthwhile, and on the basis of motives they regard as appropriate and commendable. Each mature individual is a locus of account-ability, and being responsible is a crucial feature of the sphere of human action. On this basis, Smith argues that:

> Gratitude and resentment, therefore, are the sentiments which most immediately and directly prompt us to reward and to punish. To us, therefore, he must appear to deserve reward, who appears to be the proper and approved object of gratitude; and he to deserve punishment, who appears to be that of resentment ... To punish, too, is to recompense, to remunerate, though in a different manner; it is to return evil for evil that has been done.[6]

The notion of 'evil' here is just that punishment is something unpleasant, unde-sired. It is certainly not the notion of 'two wrongs making a right' or mere vengeance.

One can thus summarise Smith's argument as follows: Human beings can exercise their abilities as voluntary, accountable agents in ways that merit appre-ciation and praise – meriting *gratitude*; and in ways that merit censure and blame – meriting *resentment*. Gratitude and resentment are fundamentally important as responses to unavoidably normative aspects of human action. Each is a basic normative valence of desert, and desert is an integral aspect of morality. In the complete absence of considerations of desert a putative moral order would be barely recognisable, and – at the least – incomplete in a significant respect.

Even supposing Smith may have overstated the significance of gratitude, what he says about the significance of resentment (which in his discussion also includes what we would call 'indignation') is highly plausible. Moreover, Smith saw that resentment can be disproportionate and become embittered, that it can become maliciously punitive. There is nothing automatic about resentment having its proper object, being felt to the proper degree, and being expressed appropriately. Aristotle had argued that passions need to be moulded by habit, guidance, censure, encouragement, and effort into a well-ordered second nature.[7] Smith, too, saw that having apt and fit sentiments is not automatic. There may be various sentiments that by nature we are prone to, but one needs to *learn* to have them in the proper circumstances, in proper measure, and directed at proper objects. Such learning is a crucial element of moral education.

He wrote:

> Nothing is more graceful than the behaviour of the man who appears to resent the greatest injuries, more from a sense that they deserve, and are the proper objects of resentment, than from feeling himself the furies of that disagreeable passion; who, like a judge, considers only the general rule, which determines what vengeance is due for each particular offence; who, in executing that rule, feels less for what himself

[6] Ibid at 69.
[7] Aristotle *Nicomachean Ethics* translated by T Irwin (Indianapolis IN, Hackett Publishing Company, 1999) Bk I, ch 13 and Bk II, chs 1, 2.

has suffered, than for what the offender is about to suffer; who, though in wrath, remembers mercy, and is disposed to interpret the rule in the most gentle and favourable manner, and to allow all the alleviations which the most candid humanity could, consistently with good sense, admit of.[8]

There is a kind of dignity in resenting properly, in judging what a wrongdoer deserves on the basis of what the person has done and how that person was motivated and not just on the basis of how one has been affected by the wrongful conduct. It is not so surprising that many people resent too much or too long, but it is damaging. However, there is a morally significant role for resentment. As Smith explained, it

> is the safeguard of justice and the security of innocence. It prompts us to beat off the mischief which is attempted to be done to us, and to retaliate that which is already done; that the offender may be made to repent of his injustice, and that others, through fear of the like punishment, may be terrified from being guilty of the like offence. It must be reserved therefore for these purposes, nor can the spectator ever go along with it when it is exerted for any other.[9]

Smith saw that sentiments have an integral role in shaping moral judgement and response; they are not just distractions from or impediments to sound judgement. Resentment and punitiveness can communicate appropriate judgement and affective stances toward persons' conduct, reflecting shared conceptions of what it is reasonable to expect of people. In that regard, they can be forms of guidance as well as expressing valuations. And, as such, there are contexts in which they can have a morally educative role as well as being appropriate.

There is something contrived and implausible about claiming that we should 'transcend anger,' 'overcome resentment' or 'grow out of such negative sentiments and attitudes' as though they are uncivilised, morally brutish, and always morally dubious. We should not evaluate the moral role and significance of a sentiment or attitude or motive just on the basis of whether forms of it *can* be associated with harmful conduct, disreputable passions or failures of self-control. In addition, we should not forget that there are such things as misplaced compassion, uncalled for apology, misguided forgiveness, and so forth. Whether a sentiment or attitude is agreeable or disagreeable, whether it tends to motivate benefiting others or not, there is the question of whether it is merited or unmerited, appropriate or inappropriate. That involves more than causal considerations.

This is the case even with regard to anger. John Casey writes:

> To be angry with someone is to be disposed to rebuke him, to remonstrate with him, demand that he apologize, have him punished. One could not satisfy one's anger simply by causing another person to be harmed. One cares about his attitudes as well as his acts. If one's anger cannot be appeased by apology or restitution, and if it

[8] Smith, above n 5 at 172.
[9] Ibid at 79.

concentrates not upon someone's attitudes and emotions, but purely on what he has done, or even on what he is, then it has ceased to be anger and has become hatred.[10]

Casey adds that,

> it is part of the nature of anger that one make certain demands, that one seek a certain response. The angry man claims that his feelings and attitudes be taken seriously. He makes certain claims, and considers himself justified. Anger and apology are concerned with claims, justification, recompense.[11]

He goes on to observe that 'Anger entails reacting to someone personally, setting a value on his attitudes and intentions. It implies treating him as an agent capable of accepting or rejecting reasons for action. And that means treating him as free.'[12] This illuminates our discussion of Smith's views. The resentment Smith refers to is a form of anger that is motivated by an agent acting unjustly. Smith argues that it is anger motivated by the agent's ill-desert, and we can resent wrongs done to others. The anger is not confined to injustice done to oneself. While there is such a thing as blind rage or being overcome with anger to the point of irrationality, anger is a sentiment that only a rational creature can experience. This is because of the ways in which normative considerations figure in anger.

As Casey points out, to be angry on behalf of another person involves sympathetic appreciation of the wronged person's injury and sympathetic appreciation of the motives and aims of the person who has committed the wrong. Anger motivated by the injustice of another or by seeing someone needlessly but purposely harmed involves a conception of the object of anger as an agent and not just an unwelcome thing. Moreover, when someone (with reason) is angry with us, we experience that anger

> as a claim that we treat the other as a person, take his attitudes seriously, enter into a world of reciprocal relations where rebuke, apology, forgiveness, are intelligible. And that must be the world of beings who can make claims, can incur and acknowledge obligations, can be wronged, can be the objects of and can reciprocate love, respect, hatred and contempt.[13]

Casey goes on to note that if all I feel is 'dumb, subterranean resentment' that is not proper anger and 'I may be failing to regard myself as on terms of equality with the person at whom my feeling is directed'.[14] There certainly is such resentment, and that is one of the toxic varieties. There is also healthy, proper resentment and it is connected with beliefs about oneself and others and with a judgement of the fitness of certain affective states and acts motivated by those

[10] J Casey, *Pagan Virtue* (Oxford, Clarendon Press, 1991) 12.
[11] Ibid at 13.
[12] Ibid at 15.
[13] Ibid at 21.
[14] Ibid.

beliefs and that affect. Certainly the resentment Smith focused on is not 'dumb, subterraneous' anger. It has to do with proper acknowledgment of the status of the parties involved – wrongdoer, victim and the person feeling resentment – and it concerns a complex notion of what is due to each, that notion achievable through a training of the capacity for sympathy and imagination and regulation of one's sensibility.

The notion that there is a morally appropriate role for resentment has received recent expression; it is not a view confined to the eighteenth century. PF Strawson's 'Freedom and Resentment' has been an enormously influential explication of the non-optional character of a wide range of moral sentiments and attitudes.[15] Strawson argued that an attempt to regard all of human conduct as causally explained in such a way that an 'objective' attitude toward it would be appropriate would involve a 'conceptual shock' of a kind that could only be overcome by 'attending to that complicated web of attitudes and feelings which form an essential part of the moral life as we know it, and which are quite opposed to objectivity of attitude'.[16] The objective attitude would involve seeing persons and actions merely as things and events rather than morally meaningful doings of agents with perspectives, concerns and responses. In some respects, Strawson's analysis resonates with the thought of the early modern British Moralists and with Smith's thought in particular. It also reso-nates with something like Kant's doctrine of the two standpoints. Strawson did not invoke Kant's distinction between *phenomena* and *noumena*[17] or even the distinction between laws of nature and a law of reason. He did, however, emphasise the distinction between the 'participant reactive attitude' and the 'objective attitude', and while he did not endorse a metaphysical underwriting of it, he did regard the participant reactive attitudes as 'essential elements in the concepts of *moral* condemnation and *moral* responsibility'.[18] The chief point is that resentment (and what we would call 'indignation') is among basic moral sentiments integral to a conception of human beings and human action that is non-discretionary. In other words, it is not a theory that we could choose to discard in favour of another.

Matt Matravers points out the affinity between Strawson's view and the argument of HLA Hart that our intentions, choices, reactions, and feelings – of course, including resentment – and the distinction between voluntary and

---

[15] PF Strawson, 'Freedom and Resentment' (1962) 48 *Proceedings of the British Academy* 1, reprinted in Russ Shafer-Landau (ed), *Ethical Theory: An Anthology* (Chichester, Wiley-Blackwell, 2013) 340.

[16] Ibid at 350.

[17] See I Kant, *Foundations of the Metaphysics of Morals* [1787] in *The Cambridge Edition of the Works of Immanuel Kant: Practical Philosophy* translated by M Gregor with introduction by A Wood (Cambridge: Cambridge University Press, 1996) section III.

[18] Strawson, above n 15 at 349. In that regard Strawson's view also shows the influence of the later Wittgenstein (L Wittgenstein, *Philosophical Investigations*, 4th edn edited by PMS Hacker and J Schulte (Chichester, Wiley-Blackwell, 2009)) Strawson's view is that of a post-Wittgensteinian, Kantian-influenced British Moralist.

involuntary conduct 'is how human nature in human society actually is'.[19] Though we recognise cases in which someone's behaviour really is just bodily motion or is caused in a manner that exempts it from moral judgement or legal responsibility, our regarding each other and ourselves as responsible individuals is not a conceptual or theoretical *choice*. Moreover, judgements reflecting that kind of regard 'pervade the whole of our social life'.[20]

Views such as those of Smith, Kant and Strawson are diverse articulations of the insight that it is a fundamental feature of the context of human action that certain basic types of responses are merited. That is part of the explication of the intelligibility of various reactions and judgements and of their normative grounds. Smith articulates his moral theory on the basis of facts about sensibility, imagination, and the possibility of adopting an impartial view of them. Kant articulates his moral theory in terms of what he takes to be an a priori principle of practical reason. Strawson's discussion shows the influence of the later Wittgenstein and his insights concerning how our conceptual schemes relate to the practices and judgements integral to leading human lives. Still, they share the fundamental claim that certain types of responses are partially constitutive of moral life. That does not mean that actions motivated by them are automatically morally validated. But *it does mean that there is a substantial basis for regarding considered, critically reflective actions that enact those responses as having a grounding that is more than merely expressive.* Of course, acts motivated by resentment and censure do have an expressive function and the language of such acts has expressive meaning, but in no case is their significance exclusively expressive. We can see the plausibility and aptness of Feinberg's analysis in 'The Expressive Function of Punishment' without concluding that we are, in that context, restricted to expressive significance.[21]

Resentment is not a 'tax' we pay for being affective creatures, vulnerable to being morally misguided by passions. Whether or not we agree with Smith's metaethics the notion that *merited censure is integral to our understanding and appreciation of human action* seems right. It is integral to the normative valence of human action.

Blame, derision, contempt and other negative sentiments, attitudes and judgements are disagreeable inasmuch as they are painful to feel. Also, they can easily play a role in motivating morally dubious conduct. Nonetheless, voluntary, accountable agents are susceptible to being objects of such attitudes on the basis of what they are like and what they do. The sentiments and attitudes mentioned are not examples of moral immaturity or of a sensibility that is insufficiently oriented to justice or the good. Most, if not all, are among the responses

---

[19] M Matravers, *Responsibility and Justice* (Cambridge, Polity Press, 2007) 128. The quote from Hart is from: HLA Hart, *Punishment and Responsibility* (Oxford, Oxford University Press, 1995) 183.

[20] Hart ibid at 183.

[21] J Feinberg, 'The Expressive Function of Punishment' (1965) 49 *Monist* 397.

and forms of regard appropriate on the basis of persons' features and conduct, the features and conduct of rational agents capable of reasoned conceptions of what to do and how to respond.

III. A MORALLY PROPER ROLE FOR CENSURE AND RETRIBUTIVIST CONSIDERATIONS

Critics of retributivism often argue that it is either just a disguised form of vengeance or that it relies heavily on metaphors and images (such as 'balancing the scales of justice' or 'nullifying an erroneous claim of superiority') that cannot be explicated persuasively. Moreover, some have suggested that it is not possible to explicate just desert in non-consequentialist terms; notions of what is fitting and what is appropriate need to be spelled out in consequentialist terms.

HLA Hart thus observed of several retributivist theories, that they 'all either avoid the question of justification altogether or are in spite of their protestations disguised forms of Utilitarianism'.[22] Retributivism also often meets with the charge of gratuitously bringing more suffering and injury into a world already abundantly supplied.[23] In his critique of retributivism, Anthony Kenny wrote: 'Popular wisdom, which has many adages which seem to favour the retributive theory, has one which is conclusive against it: two wrongs don't make a right. We must not render evil for evil.'[24] Kenny went on:

> Oddly enough, the root of the error contained in the retributive theory of punishment is the same as the root of the error contained in the purely remedial theory. Both theories attempt to give an account of crime and punishment as two episodes in a criminal's life, considered in isolation both from the authority imposing the punishment and the society in which the criminal lives. The retributive theory, starting from the premiss that it is just to punish, reaches the conclusion that it is just to render evil for evil. The remedial theory, starting from the premiss that it is unjust to render evil for evil, reaches the conclusion that it is unjust to punish.[25]

TM Scanlon said (of retributivism), 'I regard as morally repugnant [the idea] that it is good that people who have done wrong should suffer'.[26] There are numerous other examples of retributivism being portrayed as thinly disguised vengeance or resting on little more than a (morally questionable) intuition that justice involves payback of the sort that can be realised by imposing suffering. Yet, as Jeffrie Murphy has remarked,

> The concept of suffering I regard as central in retributivism, however, is to be found in the original and primary meaning of the word: 'to endure something that is not

---

[22] Hart, above n 19 at 9.

[23] Ibid.

[24] A Kenny, *Freewill and Responsibility* (New York, Routledge and Kegan Paul, 1978) 73.

[25] Ibid at 73–74.

[26] TM Scanlon, 'Giving Desert Its Due' (2013) 16 *Philosophical Explorations* 101.

within the control of one's own will.' (Think here of 'To suffer woes which hope thinks infinite' from Shelley's Prometheus or the common phrase 'He does not suffer fools gladly.')[27]

I shall suggest that retributivist considerations and notions of proportional censure and sanction are defensible in significant respects, and that many of the critiques of retributivism object to versions of it that involve features that are not essential to it.

There are indeed versions of retributivism that employ the idiom of 'balancing the scale of justice', or 'annulling a wrong assertion of value by the offender', or imposing a burden on an agent who violates rules of fair play, and there are difficulties attending such conceptions. We might find the metaphors and images less than compelling, but even those conceptions of retributivism are clear in not assigning a role to returning evil for evil or taking there to be good in the offender's experiencing pain and misery. Moreover, the retributivist's insistence on proportionality is sometimes ignored or the 'eye for an eye' notion is portrayed as sanctioning mutilation rather than demanding proper proportionality. (In fact, the tradition of Jewish law makes it clear that 'eye for eye' punishment was not meant literally. It indicated proportionality that is never to be exceeded, and in the vast majority of types of cases, even that was translated into monetary compensation.[28] In a great many cases regarding that notion people fail to consult the actual legal tradition.)

One of the implications of the discussion of resentment is that censure and sanction can be understood as appropriate responses to criminal conduct if the responses are to be ordered and measured by a concern with justice in a sphere of agents capable of acting for reasons. That is the sort of response encouraged by a genuinely civil society. Censure can express not only anger or disapproval; it can reflect regard for the dignity and status of the person harmed by wrong conduct and it is a response to the accountable agency of the wrongdoer. (We don't resent lightning strikes, stock market declines or influenza. We might resent someone giving us what that person knew to be unsound investment advice.) Censure has a *point*, a significance that is not appropriately explicated in exclusively consequentialist terms. It is a mistake to interpret censure as exclusively or most fundamentally a *means* to something. Similarly, gratitude might prove to be a means of strengthening relations between two persons but it has a point, a significance that is not fully captured by thinking of it as a means to such strengthening.

---

[27] J Murphy, 'Last Words on Retribution' in J Jacobs and J Jackson (eds), *Routledge Handbook of Criminal Justice Ethics* (Abingdon, Routledge, 2017) 28 at 33.

[28] Sources as ancient as the *Talmud* (see Baba Kamma 83b–84a in *Talmud*) as well as numerous medieval sources (eg Maimonides's *Mishneh Torah*) interpret 'eye for an eye' in terms of monetary compensation. Such an approach is found in a great deal of Jewish legal thought and Biblical interpretation.

Censure communicates condemnation of conduct, but it is not limited to a thin, emotive meaning or mindless anger. Censure is a practical aspect of a judgement that the agent's conduct is unacceptable, wrong, perhaps meriting punishment. Thus, if a society has a shared sense of acceptance of the rule of law and largely endorses the laws under which people live, censure can express commitment to the relevant values of the society. Censure and retributivist considerations can reflect regard for both victim and offender as full participants in the community as subjects of rights and as responsible agents to whom various expectations reasonably apply. The fact that censure communicates the community's disapproval of conduct and regard for it as blameworthy does not mean that censure and punishment are no more than institutionally regulated vengeance. That is a selective, pejorative interpretation.

To be sure, ascertaining just what is proportional as punishment is a difficult challenge – for any conception of punishment. But proportionality reflects commitment to a moral concern that is not an essential feature of a consequentialist view, one maintaining that we should regard criminal conduct as an occasion for promoting some sort of social good without regard to retributivist considerations. To strip out retributive considerations (except, perhaps, for the fact of criminal conduct being a justifying ground of sanction) shrinks the moral relevance of both the victim and the offender in a way that makes regard for each as an agent much less important. How are we to understand a system of law for rational agents if that system does not include (among other notions, of course) the notion of culpable wrongdoers and of wrongdoing as meriting censure?

That is not to say that punishment should *not* be concerned with possibly doing some kind of good. However, if we mean to (i) maintain the fundamental political value of individuals' rights, liberties, and dignity, and (ii) regard and treat persons as being worthy of respect as accountable agents, capable of acting for reasons and having valuative commitments, then there is a significant role for retributive censure in criminal sanction. Overstating the point somewhat, we might say that it is the difference between focusing on 'What are we to bring about?' versus focusing on 'What guiding values are we to be responsive to?' It is through retributive censure that the values of desert and proportionality can be actualised or enacted. That does not mean that what is brought about is not significant, but it does mean that thinking only in terms of what can be brought about would constitute a quite radical challenge to how we regard each other as agents.

When there is a significant breakdown in the community of sentiment and when there are doubts regarding the legitimacy of law, law enforcement and sanction, then censure is not able to communicate in a clear manner and it is more likely to be – or at least be perceived as – an expression of anger and mere punitiveness. That is one of the most troubling issues concerning criminal sanction in the US at present. When censure does not communicate in a widely intelligible and unconfused way it is less likely to have any morally educative significance.

The liberal political order is not, as such, the cause of the serious moral defects of contemporary criminal justice. In fact, those defects reflect significant respects in which contemporary criminal justice fails to be in accord with some of the basic principles and values of that order.

IV. DESERT, PROPORTIONALITY, AND PARSIMONY

It is notable that in a great deal of political theorising during recent decades the notion of desert has played a very modest role apart from having a place in criminal justice. Many of the most influential political theorists (Rawls is a good example[29]) assign little or no role to desert in the sphere of politically just institutions and arrangements and in distributive justice. I am not going to argue for a reinstatement of desert in the conception of political justice, or even pursue the issue of why desert has been much less prominent than during earlier periods in political thought, except to note that desert is thought to threaten some of the forms of egalitarianism and the positive rights many theorists endorse. The main point here is that desert certainly has a central role in criminal justice, including criminal sanction, and it is a key element of a non-consequentialist conception of criminal sanction.

To see the appropriateness of desert in the context of criminal justice we can ask, 'Are there any features of actions (and the persons who perform them) that constitute reasons for responding on the basis of what the agent merits rather than in terms of what desirable states of affairs could be brought about in the situation that has been created?' and 'Can we identify those features without making reference to the harm and culpability of the conduct in violation of law?' We have already challenged the notion that there are no rationally merited responses of a sort that motivate censure and sanction. It is not true that all anger, all retributive sensibility is vengeful, a failure of self-control or rationality. It is simply a mistake to insist that retributivist considerations are inevitably poorly disguised rationalisations of anger and vengeance. Granted, it is a difficult matter to ascertain what punishments are proportional to which offences. But it is worth striving to construct a morally defensible view of that matter because of the strong case there is for sanction being *deserved*.

As discussed above, we regard ourselves as agents in that sense, and the conceptual revision required to abandon this way of regarding ourselves and others would be radical in ways it is actually difficult to imagine. Not only are certain sentiments and attitudes deeply rooted in how we conceptualise ourselves as human beings, but so too are the rationales for certain practices, such as reward and punishment. This is not to say that they have a non-rational biological basis. Rather, the point is that they are not altogether rationally discretionary,

---

[29] J Rawls, *A Theory of Justice* (Cambridge, MA, Harvard University Press, 1971).

a matter of preference or choice. Only when we fail to properly acknowledge persons as agents who act for reasons, and also what it is reasonable to expect of participants in a community informed by moral and legal considerations, does there seem to be no significant connection between accountability and censure as part of a fabric of concepts through which action, decision, and conduct are intelligible.

Strictly consequentialist conceptions of criminal sanction make that mistake. The consequentialist notion that any state of affairs of whatever type, or any act, no matter how it was brought about, should be regarded as an occasion for maximising some good is an item of theoretical enthusiasm that is not only morally dubious on multiple grounds but also a practical impossibility. Human beings – and not just some of their habits and beliefs – would have to be quite different for such an approach to action and evaluation to be imagined as feasible. It is one thing to offer the view as a theoretical construct, it is quite another thing to really, genuinely regard actions as morally significant only in terms of being occasions for trying to bring about states of affairs with some specific feature.

Censure and sanction have a moral *point* in the sense that they express commitment to the values reflected in the law and they reflect the community's judgement of what can be legitimately required of those who engage in criminal conduct. Speaking of what he calls the 'commensurate-deserts principle' von Hirsch says:

> For the principle, we have argued, is a requirement of justice, whereas deterrence, incapacitation, and rehabilitation are essentially strategies for controlling crime. The priority of the principle follows from the assumption we stated at the outset: the requirements of justice ought to constrain the pursuit of crime prevention.[30]

This is why the desert-censure-proportionality-parsimony nexus is normatively and practically well suited to criminal justice in a liberal polity (interpreted broadly to encompass diverse versions of liberal democracy). That nexus reflects the notion of persons as responsible agents, capable of grasping the rationality of proportional sanction, which is meant to inflict the minimum of state-inflicted sanction to be endured on account of criminal conduct.[31] The reasons to avoid needless suffering are not only consequentialist reasons. As noted above, it is very difficult to ascertain what are proportional punishments, but that is a problem for practical rationality in general and we are not limited to only arbitrary ways of addressing it.

Current policy and practice fail badly to meet the conditions of the desert-censure-proportionality-parsimony nexus. Indeed, it is the morally objectionable features of contemporary criminal justice that motivate the case for the view

---

[30] A von Hirsch, *Doing Justice* (Boston, Northeastern University Press, 1986) 75.
[31] See also Andrew Ashworth's and Andreas von Hirsch's chapters in this volume.

defended. However, as already noted, the retributivism of current sanction, and the liberal values and principles supporting it are not, *as such*, among the chief reasons for it being morally rotten. The excesses of punitiveness are a social and political issue, not an implication of retributivism. Over-criminalisation is not an inevitable consequence of liberal values, and neither are discrimination against minorities and the poor. Those are all ways of failing to uphold values and principles of the liberal polity, and remedy for the failure can be formulated on the basis of those values and principles.

Legitimate legal sanction (except perhaps for a narrow range of strict liability) should communicate blame, disapproval and the judgement that such conduct is unacceptable because wrong. It is not just an unwelcome, inexplicable imposition on the person sanctioned. Imposing punishment while denying that it has a basic normative point or significance would be a morally problematic project. Or, suppose it had an exclusively consequentialist rationale; then it could be – as far as the persons sanctioned are concerned – an unwelcome, inexplicable imposition unconnected with desert and proportionality. Censure is a morally intelligible, merited response to ill-desert, and sanction is an enactment of censure. Agency, desert and the requirements of criminal justice are explanatorily and normatively interrelated.

This does not imply or presuppose that there is stable consensus on the values reflected in criminal law. There may well be numerous disputed issues, and in a pluralistic, diverse society it would be surprising if there were not. Acknowledging the legitimacy of the liberal rule of law involves recognising that one may disagree with some matters of law without also thinking that such disagreement is an adequate basis for flouting the law or for regarding obedience to law as a discretionary matter (assuming that the cases in question are genuinely disputable rather than egregious examples of bad law). As Antony Duff has argued:

> In such instances, what the law says to those who dissent from the stand it takes is not simply and unqualifiedly that the conduct in question is wrong, but rather that this is now the community's authoritative view. Even if they dissent from its content, they have an obligation as members of the community to accept its authority – to obey the law, even if they are not persuaded by its content, unless and until they can secure a change in it through the normal political process.[32]

Part of a civil disposition is the willingness to accept, and regard as legitimate, some laws one does not personally endorse, and to acknowledge as acceptable some types of conduct one finds objectionable. In a society that has achieved a high level of civility there are disagreements without the degree of hostility that threatens the integrity of the political process. When civility is scarcer than we would like, one way to threaten the integrity of the political process is to

---

[32] RA Duff, *Punishment, Community, and Communication* (Oxford, Oxford University Press, 2001) 59.

institute censure and sanction even if there are not good grounds on the basis of culpable harm. That sort of threat – using legislation as a political weapon – is more common when politics has become ideological and illiberal.

While there are not rationally evident, uncontroversial measures for desert, censure, proportionality and parsimony, that does not mean that instantiations of them can only be the result of brute political force or the least dignified forms of democratic populism. Of course, both of those have done much to corrupt criminal justice in the US and to some extent in the UK as well. Nevertheless, there remain important connections between the normative nexus highlighted and the civility of society under a liberal democratic rule of law. A great deal of needless harm is being done by various features of current carceral practice and criminal justice policies and practices generally. It should be possible to address much of that harm. Taking parsimony seriously, doing as little needless harm as is consistent with proportional sanction, would make a significant, welcome difference.

In addition, rolling back some of the tide of over-criminalisation, making improvements to the worst of prison conditions, providing more training for, and oversight of members of the Prison Service ('Corrections' in the US); these are among the changes that would alleviate some of the most pronounced flaws of contemporary criminal justice in ways that do not require a great deal of intellectual imagination or forays into uncharted territory. It is part of the conception of a liberal political order that, while the state should not require persons to acquire virtues, neither should its practices and policies harm or worsen people in known and regular ways. To a large extent, that seems to have been forgotten or overlooked.

We almost certainly have a better understanding of how current conditions are *impediments to encouraging desistance* than we have of what specific, positive steps would effectively encourage desistance or on what scale they would do so. However, there is an important relation between the issues. A cogent basis exists for *doing much less harm* and reforming some of the most egregiously awful features of incarceration even if we are not sure what sorts of additional, positive programmes should or could be implemented. Even without agreement on possible new initiatives, there is abundant justification for the removal of the damaging, morally unjustifiable aspects of incarceration. The recidivism we are 'purchasing' with the current practices and resources is certainly not worth what we are paying for it.

V. DOING NO HARM VS MAXIMISING THE GOOD

It would be a mistake to conclude from the facts about contemporary criminal justice that it should be recast on a systemic level to be governed by consequentialist considerations and that those should provide the basis for decisions regarding policy. That would involve a loss of normative focus fraught with risk to the standing of persons as members of a political community and as responsible agents.

To avoid misunderstanding, we should distinguish between 'consequentialism' as naming a distinctive, specific approach to moral theorising (ie, focusing on certain features of states of affairs as the locus of moral value) and taking consequences seriously, recognising that consequences as well as other factors can have a place in making moral judgements. By commitment to the former we are committed to maintaining that, in our response to criminal conduct, we should focus on the overall project of promoting the good, in whatever way that is specified. The rational agency of the offender, and the rights and interests of the victim – that is to say, the most basic respects in which the conduct in question might seem to have moral significance – have no independent moral weight. If they have any weight it is on the basis of the extent to which they contribute to bringing about states of affairs with the specific feature that is identified as the ground of value. Any moral value is to be specifiable in terms of features of states of affairs.

Consequentialists often point to Kant as the most egregious example of a retributivist desert theorist, but at the same time they fail to account for the Kantian insight that we unavoidably think of ourselves (and have reason to think of others) as practically reasoning agents, in contrast to being *things*. The distinctions between agents, states of affairs, events, and things are critically important to the intelligibility of the world and human action, and in ways that underwrite desert. If we think of morality in strictly consequentialist terms we will have to overlook some of the most basic normative valences of actions and motives. We will have to suppress or redirect some of the most apt-seeming responses and passions. In doing so we can easily lose our grip on the importance of agency, accountability and persons as having a morally significant status.

A consequentialist may try to block the implication that, on consequentialist terms, 'anything goes', by insisting that rights and human dignity and limits on how persons can be regarded and treated can be part of a consequentialist view. But if what ultimately matters most is that certain kinds of states of affairs obtain, how would values such as dignity be anchored? Moreover, if we think of moral reasoning as primarily concerned with bringing about certain types of states of affairs that approach will assimilate all moral judgement to one kind of consideration. There remains a fundamental difference between the concern, 'what values are being respected and enacted?' and 'is this the way to bring about the most of X?'

In addition, the practical matter of how, in fact, such judgements are to be made is fraught with difficulty. In many contexts, we can probably make reliable judgements on the basis of a good deal of accumulated wisdom concerning human experience. (Mill made just this point in his *Utilitarianism*.[33])

---

[33] JS Mill, *Utilitarianism* [1863] edited by G Sher (Indianapolis, Hackett Publishing Co, 2001) ch 2.

However, with regard to important, large-scale matters of criminal justice policy, our epistemic position is less strong, especially with respect to comparative judgements and anticipating the consequences of new approaches (or even familiar approaches but in changing circumstances). In the abstract, the notion that we should make empirical judgements of states of affairs sounds manageable and feasible. In practice, the complexities and uncertainties could be overwhelming. We need to realise that in order to make consequentialist judgements we either have to radically oversimplify moral reality or be willing to rely on judgements that are informal and commonsensical but lack genuine, empirically elaborated grounds.

Are we able to ascertain the deterrent impact of a specific sanction? Are we able to ascertain the extent to which people obey the law in order to avoid the unpleasant consequences of not doing so? There may be a considerable gap between what we aim to achieve and what actually results, and we may not have a very accurate grasp of the latter. In fact, regarding the deterrent effect of many sanctions that seems to be the case. I do not mean that desert, censure and sanction should be understood without reference to consequences. *Of course* the results of actions matter, but one can acknowledge that results and consequences matter morally without being a consequentialist, taking the states of affairs brought about as the exclusive locus of moral value.

Retributivist justification, focusing on desert and censure, is not to be interpreted as a bet that our luck will be good if we punish, that there will be desirable consequences. Luck, in the sense of circumstances and outcomes that are not under our control or directly responsive to our intentions and purposes, makes for looseness between any consequentialist justification and the actual states of affairs brought about by the practice. The connection between the practice of punishment and the aims of punishment is less like the connection between mandatory immunisation and reduction in the incidence of disease, and more analogous to the relation between sex education for adolescents, and their adolescent and adult sexual behaviour, or between inflation and unemployment.[34]

An important upshot is that we do not know to what extent punishment accomplishes the various ends that have been set for it (which are often multiple and not particularly complementary, and often also lack the relevant sorts of institutional infrastructure and support). In that regard, claims about what punishment is aimed at, *when offered as part of a justification of punishment*, are, as mentioned above, vulnerable on epistemic grounds, independently of any moral reservations we might have about consequentialist justifications. And that is a serious matter for a consequentialist justification. We would be on firmer ground focusing on what is the moral point of censure and sanction rather than focusing on what are we likely to bring about (or hope to bring about) through

---

[34] This is a point I first presented in J Jacobs, 'Luck and Retribution' (1999) 74 *Philosophy* 535.

censure and sanction. Under what description are we to judge the consequences of an action? Is it necessary to take into account multiple descriptions, given that there can be several different kinds of consequences or consequences at multiple levels and over different time periods? Deterrence is one possible consequence, but in addition to deterrence there are plenty of other consequences. How much weight should each type have? What if the consequences regarding desistance are quite different from those regarding deterrence? Which should have more weight?

Imagine a social world in which no one felt resentment or indignation. That would be a world in which no one felt resentment on anyone else's behalf as well as not resenting wrongful injuries done to oneself. That may seem like a world liberated from a variety of morally unconstructive, potentially harmful feelings, motives and behaviours. Perhaps, instead of concern with what is merited, the response to crime would be primarily in terms of what opportunity for socially beneficial action is presented. Consequentialist theorists might delight at the prospect of a resentment-free world. It might be free of revenge, and the consequentialist might argue that it is thereby also free of several varieties of needless harming, the types that are matters of payback, extracting a debt allegedly owed to society, balancing the scales of justice, and so forth. But we should take care with the 'thereby' part of the claim. If it is meant to indicate that nothing constructive, nothing with moral propriety would be sacrificed by the utter absence of resentment, then we have reason to have our doubts.

As noted above, participation in civil society can be morally educative. Through such participation a person learns the norms and standards of different kinds of conduct and interaction in different contexts, and one also learns ways of engaging with others in the diverse ways distinctive of different spheres of activity. The individual's capacity for practical reasoning can be realised, different kinds of judgement and evaluation can be learned, and one gains experience responding to the agency of other persons. One's capacities for rational activity are not actualised and rendered effective in operation and informed by use, except through their employment in the various contexts of civil society. Mature, rational self-determination is not a stage at which one 'naturally' arrives just by reaching a certain age. The realised capacity for it must be acquired through one's experiences in acting, interacting and responding as an agent. Experience is vitally important to learning how to interact with other persons in diverse relationships, with diverse responsibilities, with a view to diverse ends.

An additional reason for doubts concerning consequentialist approaches is that, however well-intentioned a consequentialist programme of overall reform might be, it extends the scope of the state's coercive power by putting more projects under its authority, and it leaves open, in an indeterminate (presumably consequences-validated) way, the questions of 'how long', 'how much', and directed 'at whom'. The vital role – and it is a limiting role as well as a communicative one – of proportional censure and sanction could become obscured by various competing strategies for doing the most good. Do we (or would we) have a satisfactorily supportable basis for undertaking large-scale initiatives aimed at producing certain consequences or is it much more likely that we will not be in the appropriate epistemic position and actually will not have a very good idea of what will be brought about? If multiple approaches to offending seems to offer the best results overall, decisions will need to be made about which groups of offenders are treated in which ways, and that could raise serious complications regarding fairness and consistency. Consequentialist approaches sound promising, but are much more complicated and more fraught with significant epistemological and moral problems than they seem.

Certainly, an important part of the answer to the question, 'Why is there criminal law and criminal sanction?' is that they have the purpose of deterring harmful, culpable conduct. Taking consequences seriously is part of the overall rationale for criminal law and criminal sanction. That is not a reason for being a consequentialist. What is in favour of the nexus of desert-censure-proportionality-parsimony as the core conceptual architecture of criminal sanction is that it reflects values concerning the agency, dignity, and accountability of persons, and it reflects commitment to values not limited to specific features of states of affairs. Consequentialists often argue that values such as liberty or autonomy or the significance of rights can be accounted for in consequentialist terms. Even if this is more than a verbal manoeuvre, it is doubtful that the significance of those 'other' values actually is fully captured and expressed in consequentialist terms. Those are clearly not the terms in which they were introduced into moral and political thought, and it is not all clear why they should be reconstructed in consequentialist terms. Moreover, a political/legal order that is not committed to non-consequentialist values in a fundamental manner will lack a principled basis for opposing all manner of extensions of the state's coercive power via claims to be pursuing policies that promote desirable ends.

VI. CONCLUSION

I have argued that there is a morally appropriate role for resentment, that there is a role for retributivist considerations in criminal sanction, and that consequentialism is fraught with epistemic difficulties and risks undermining values we would do well to preserve. In an important respect, the larger context of these disputed issues is the question of whether the values and principles of the liberal polity are to blame for many of the most objectionable features of criminal justice. The notion of individuals as accountable, voluntary agents acting for reasons is generally a key element of the liberal conception of politics. Much current debate concerning criminal justice focuses on whether that notion is a plausible, realistic element of a desirable conception of politics, or part of an objectionable ideology that has given rise to a host of moral failures. Several of the worst features of contemporary criminal justice are antithetical to principles and values of liberal democracy, rather than exhibiting inherent features of that form of political/legal order. It is a serious error to regard corrupt forms of resentment, punitiveness, desert and retributive sanction as what each of those inevitably becomes. Realising and sustaining the proper forms depends on commitment and effort, as is the case with a great many values.

A realistic moral psychology, plausible normative considerations, genuinely defensible moral aspirations, and institutions and policies that are conducive to the civility of society are required to remedy the many troubling aspects of contemporary criminal justice. Some of the most important elements of such views are found in works of Andreas von Hirsch, or are elaborations of views consistent with much of his thought. This is a moment when much can be gained by looking back at his thought on desert, censure, and sanction while also looking ahead toward strategies of value-and-principle-anchored remedy for the numerous, serious challenges we face.

3

Reflective Censure: Punishment and Human Development

LIAT LEVANON

M Y SON IS in year 5. Being one of the youngest in class, he has not yet reached the age of criminal responsibility, but many of his friends have. His teacher thinks his cohort is one of the best the school – which is known as a good school – has had. Yesterday they had the police come over. All the year 5 boys were gathered in the hall for a talk with PC Chris. At that point, my son and some of his friends were sent back to class, so he is not sure about the details. Apparently some of the boys arranged a fight club in connection with their football matches. PC Chris was telling them off for keeping him busy while he should have been helping an old lady whose house had been burgled.

I am not sure about the wisdom of calling the police in that instance, but I find it very telling. In theoretical terms, this incident demonstrates interaction between two systems that respond to wrongdoing through sanctions: the school system and the criminal justice system. In this interaction, the two systems feed into each other: the school becomes a sphere of the law, and the law enforcement officer becomes an arm of the school operating in ways that remind of school discipline rather than criminal investigation. This actual momentary merger of the systems indicates that school discipline and legal punishment may have much in common.

That school discipline and legal punishment are two types of censure seems obvious enough. The more pressing question is to what extent the theory that underlies school discipline reflects general truths about censure, from which penology can learn. To what extent, in other words, might the body of knowledge feeding school discipline contribute to our understanding of legal punishment? Assuming that the body of knowledge that informs school discipline can be shown to be relevant for the understanding of criminal punishment, we then need to ask what exactly this body of knowledge consists of. The theory of school discipline may be drawing, for example, on behavioural approaches of control based on provision of 'sticks and carrots', perhaps to an even greater extent than it draws on developmental theory. Which of these theories has the potential to contribute to an account of criminal punishment? Once the relevant body of knowledge has been identified, it should still be clarified what exactly it can contribute to penology, and what might be the implications of the analysis for the criminal justice system.

This chapter tries to answer these questions. It advances the argument that the body of knowledge that informs school discipline has much to contribute to our understanding of legal punishment; that the most relevant part of this body of knowledge is developmental theory; and that exploration of developmental theory can provide a sound naturalistic foundation for a requirement of critical self-reflection by the punishing authority.

The chapter begins with an exploration of the general concept of censure and its interpretation in penology. It then turns to the theory of school discipline, and particularly to developmental theory that informs it, as a potential source of a sounder interpretation of censure. We shall see that developmental theory is already being relied on in the context of school discipline. In addition, Axel Honneth has provided a useful theoretical link between developmental theory and criminal law. Developing Honneth's point, the chapter explores Donald Winnicott's and Wilfred Bion's developmental theories to provide us with a richer understanding of positive censure. Their work also provides a naturalistic foundation for a requirement of self-reflection by the censuring authority throughout the censuring interaction. Last, the chapter returns to penology and examines possible implications of the self-reflection condition for the criminal justice system. It argues that this condition can provide a theoretical foundation for the use at the sentencing stage of some of the tools and techniques employed by restorative justice approaches.

I. CENSURE IN PENOLOGY: POSITIVE AND NEGATIVE

Censure is a key concept in penology. It is central to von Hirsch's retributivist account of punishment that has been developed in his *Doing Justice*[1] and in *Censure and Sanctions*,[2] and it is also a key concept in the closely related communicative strand, especially as developed in Antony Duff's theory of punishment.[3] Nevertheless, penology has only little to say about the general concept of censure. For von Hirsch, conveying censure or blame is condemnatory.[4] Referring to PF Strawson's account, he mentions that 'Censure consists of the

---

[1] A von Hirsch, *Doing Justice: The Choice of Punishments* (Report of the Committee for the Study of Incarceration) (New York, Hill and Wang, 1976).

[2] A von Hirsch, *Censure and Sanctions* (Oxford, Oxford University Press, 1993).

[3] RA Duff, *Punishment, Communication, and Community* (Oxford, Oxford University Press, 2001).

[4] Von Hirsch, above n 2 at 9.

expression of … judgement, plus its accompanying sentiment of disapproval'.[5] For Duff too, censure is condemnation; he further cites Feinberg to explain that punishment 'is a conventional device for the expression of attitudes of resentment and indignation, and of judgements of disapproval and reprobation, on the part either of the punishing authority … or of those in whose name the punishment is inflicted'.[6] Thus, censure is generally referred to as an expressive or communicative practice that conveys moral reprobation and accompanying moral sentiments.

Adverse moral sentiments can take different forms. In some instances, they might take a destructive form, and then punitive censure can be described as negative. In negative punitive censure, outrage is translated into toxic hostility, and this toxic hostility remains part of the relationship between the wrongdoer and the punishing authority throughout the process of censure. This process has been captured by Jonathan Jacobs in his discussion of Adam Smith's *The Theory of Moral Sentiments* in this volume. Jacobs notes: 'Smith saw that resentment can be disproportionate and become embittered, that it can become maliciously punitive. There is nothing automatic about resentment having its proper object, being felt to the proper degree, and being expressed appropriately.'[7] Negative punitive censure is such a case of 'malicious punitiveness'. Its outcome is merely repressive: the dynamics between the offender and the public remains one of conflict.

But censure can also be positive. When this is the case, the hard sentiment directed at the wrongdoer takes an appropriate and productive form. The anger and outrage provoked by wrongdoing are translated into a constructive demand that the offender be held accountable. Such a type of anger 'entails reacting to someone personally, setting a value on his attitudes and intentions. It implies treating him as an agent capable of accepting or rejecting reasons for action. And that means treating him as free'.[8] Furthermore, holding the offender accountable restores the disrupted social order thus allowing all the parties involved to move on. Positive censure therefore works to mend that which has been torn or broken by the wrongdoing. It engages the wrongdoer in a constructive process, communicates with potential wrongdoers, restores social values, and re-establishes mutual recognition between the wrongdoer and the authority. Examination of the penological literature reveals the gradual development of a conception of punishment as a form of positive censure.

---

[5] Ibid, referring to PF Strawson, 'Freedom and Resentment' (1962) 48 *Proceedings of the British Academy* 1.

[6] Duff, above n 3, citing J Feinberg, 'The Expressive Function of Punishment' in J Feinberg, *Doing and Deserving* (Princeton NJ, Princeton University Press, 1970) 95 at 98.

[7] J Jacobs, 'Censure, Sanction and the Moral Psychology of Resentment and Punitiveness' in this volume, referring to A Smith, *The Theory of Moral Sentiments*, edited by DD Raphael and AL MacFie (Indianapolis, Liberty Fund, 1982), esp Part II, Sec I, 67–78.

[8] J Casey, *Pagan Virtue* (Oxford, Clarendon Press, 1991) 15, cited by Jacobs, ibid.

II. POSITIVE CENSURE IN PENOLOGY

Existing penological accounts elaborate several characteristics of punishment that fit squarely within a conception of positive punitive censure. Examination of von Hirsch's theory of punishment as censure,[9] Duff's communicative account,[10] and Hannah Maslen's dialogic theory of punishment[11] indicates the gradual emergence of a requirement of interaction with the offender in the process of censure. Antje du Bois-Pedain has traced to Hegel's work[12] a requirement that the punishing authority critically self-reflect on its fallibility as part of this interaction. These two requirements characterise respectful and constructive censure.

In von Hirsch's account of punishment as censure, censure is interactional yet still mostly unilateral: while it addresses the defendant, the victim, and third parties,[13] it does not aim to produce a response by these addressees:

> [Censure] deals with the person *externally*. The disapproval conveyed by the sanction gives the actor the opportunity to reconsider his actions and to feel shame or regret. However, it is left to him to respond. Censure... need not specifically be fashioned to elicit certain sentiments in him – whether those be shame, repentance or whatever.[14]

Thus, for von Hirsch, censure consists of one moment in which the punitive authority takes an expressive stance. That censure consists of only one moment is crucial for von Hirsch, as he conceives the continuation of the interaction between the censuring authority and the criminal as overly intrusive and coercive. This is the case, for him, even if the criminal indicates that she wishes to continue the interaction, for example by way of expressing remorse and thereby, presumably, expecting the censuring authority to respond to this remorse in an affirmative way.

Duff has moved from a unilateral understanding of censure to a more bilateral one. In his *Punishment, Communication, and Community*, he contrasts expression of censure with communication of censure, explaining that in the first only the punishing authority is an active player, whereas the second aims to engage the offender.[15] Duff foregrounds communication, as he thinks that the idea of a liberal community entails seeking citizens' understanding and acceptance of the community's demands, and doing so in ways that treat them as moral agents and as members of a moral community.[16] Thus, in Duff's account

---

[9] Von Hirsch, above nn 1 and 2.

[10] Duff, above n 3.

[11] H Maslen, *Remorse, Penal Theory, and Sentencing* (Oxford, Hart, 2015).

[12] A du Bois-Pedain, 'Hegel and the Justification of Real-world Penal Sanctions' (2016) 29 *Canadian Journal of Law and Jurisprudence* 37.

[13] Von Hirsch, above n 2 at 10.

[14] Von Hirsch, above n 2 at 72.

[15] Duff, above n 3 at 79–80.

[16] Ibid at 80–81.

censure consists of two logical moments: one in which the punishing authority delivers a message, and another in which the offender becomes engaged as the receiver of this message.

Hannah Maslen has taken a further step by developing the idea of bilateralism. Her work emphasises the essential dialogic nature of communication and the derivative need for the punishing authority to 'go back to itself' in the process of communication and thus respond to the offender's remorse. When explaining the case for dialogic and responsive censure, Maslen writes:

> [T]he term 'dialogue' … is *responsive* – what is communicated by participant A is influenced by the prior communication of participant B, with a view to his subsequent response … it necessarily involves *attention to one's interlocutor* – one is not involved in dialogue if one ignores the other participant's input.[17]

Thus, for Maslen, censure consists of three logical moments: one in which the punishing authority develops a preliminary response to wrongdoing; another in which the offender communicates his or her own response to the wrongdoing and/or to the punishing authority's preliminary response; and a third where the punishing authority goes back to itself and develops a response to the offender's communication. Julian Roberts and Nethanel Dagan have further argued that these three moments need not all occur at the sentencing stage; rather, later remorse should also bring about a response by the censuring authority.[18] While the time limits of the interaction and the appropriate way to respond to remorse are the object of debate,[19] the requirement that the punishing authority go back to itself and reflect in the process of censure is not difficult to accept.

Nevertheless, neither Maslen nor Dagan and Roberts explicitly discuss the full implications and scope of the requirement that the punishing authority go back to itself in the process of communication. Specifically, Maslen and Dagan and Roberts emphasise the required change of attitude towards the offender, but they do not discuss the required change of attitude by the punishing authority *towards itself* in its interaction with the offender. Without yet aiming to fully describe this required change or to provide it with theoretical foundations, it can be briefly explained as follows: the interactive process of going back and forth from self to other aims to establish a channel through which messages can be effectively delivered to the offender rather than emptily pronounced. For this purpose, the process has to involve internal movement in the punishing authority – movement from pure resentment to the development of a measure of sympathy towards the offender (without foregoing resentment). This sympathy is the channel through which the message of resentment can be delivered. It is also the substrate for the punishing authority's eventual willingness and ability to reintegrate the wrongdoer in society. As David Hume explained in

---

[17] Maslen, above n 11 at 99–100 (emphasis in original).
[18] Roberts and Dagan, in this volume.
[19] See eg Duff's discussion of 'The Already Repentant Offender', above n 3 at 118–21.

his analysis of human sentiments, sympathy is developed upon encounter with traits and affects one can trace in oneself.[20] Accordingly, the interaction between the punishing authority and the offender must involve introspection and recognition by the punishing authority of its own fallibility – fallibility that it shares with the offender and that provides an effective foundation for meaningful reintegrative interaction.

The condition of critical self-reflection has not yet been fully developed in penological literature. Tracing its initial development requires, first, going back to von Hirsch and Duff. One of von Hirsch's preliminary assumptions in devising his theory of punishment is that 'A sanctioning system should not be seen as one which "we" devise to prevent "them" from offending. Rather, it should be one which free citizens could devise to regulate their *own* conduct.'[21] Duff further develops this point in his discussion of von Hirsch and Narayan's[22] account:

> One merit of this account is that it avoids the exclusionary conception of offenders as a 'them' against whom 'we' must protect ourselves. Punishment, as a system of prudentially supplemented censure, is something that we can plausibly threaten against and impose on *ourselves*, as moral agents who recognize our own moral weaknesses, to help us to act as we know we should. It addresses potential offenders not as outsiders, whose membership of the normative community is thus cast in doubt, but as fellow members of that community.[23]

While Duff ends up rejecting von Hirsch and Narayan's analysis, his comments do seem to imply that he embraces the inward-looking acknowledgement of our own fallibility as at least desired, even if not essential for justifying punishment.

Another implicit yet important reference to the requirement of critical self-reflection can be found in the literature on legitimacy of law enforcement agencies. Anthony Bottoms and Justice Tankebe have argued that to exercise authority legitimately, power-holders must engage in continuous dialogue with their audience.[24] This dialogue entails examining and re-examining their claims for authority in response to the audience's responses. Willingness on behalf of the power-holders to listen to their audience is part of this process of examination and re-examination.[25] The authors do not discuss explicitly the inward-looking perspective essential for true and receptive listening in an honest dialogue. Yet they do make an interesting reference to Axel Honneth's work on

---

[20] Hume developed his theory of moral feelings especially in *A Treatise of Human Nature* [1739–40] edited by DF and MJ Norton (Oxford, Oxford University Press, 2000). His thoughts have implicitly influenced the developmental theories discussed later in this paper.

[21] Von Hirsch, above n 2 at 5.

[22] A von Hirsch and U Narayan, 'Degradingness and Intrusiveness' in von Hirsch, above n 2, ch 9.

[23] Duff, above n 3 at 86–87.

[24] AE Bottoms and J Tankebe, 'Police Legitimacy and the Authority of the State' in A du Bois-Pedain, M Ulväng and P Asp (eds), *Criminal Law and the Authority of the State* (Oxford, Hart, 2017) 47, esp at 57–61 and 70–76.

[25] Ibid.

mutual recognition as providing the foundations for their argument. As we shall see below, Honneth's work establishes an effective link between political theory and developmental theories that embrace the inward-looking perspective.

There have also been some explicit references to this required attitude in the literature. In a couple of articles, Antje du Bois-Pedain has proposed an account of criminal punishment as an inclusionary and reintegrative practice that might in this essential respect be analogous to parental punishment and, possibly, to other forms of relational action.[26] To develop and support this account, Du Bois-Pedain has drawn on the theories of several philosophers who examined criminal punishment. The most important of these discussions for current purposes is Du Bois-Pedain's analysis of Hegel, in which she expressly identifies the need for critical self-reflection and acknowledgment of the punishing authority's own fallibility as a condition for the legitimate imposition of punishment. Considering Hegel's account of punishment as an instance of his general philosophy of action, Du Bois-Pedain writes:

> [T]he punishing agent, in punishing, discovers something unpleasant about itself: it discovers what Hegel calls its hard heart, its motivation in self-assertion through revenge. There is no punishment in which the punishing agent does not take a stance, does not involve itself through the act of punishing in an ongoing struggle for recognition … To punish means to engage with the offender, and that means that *it can and must always be asked what treating the offender in this or that way says about yourself.*[27]

In Hegel's philosophy of action, every significant action carries with it the risk of transgression. What follows transgression to restore relations is a sequence of owning up to the action ('confession') and a response releasing both parties from the moral injury of that transgression ('forgiveness'). Given the ubiquity of transgression, human action thus unfolds through interaction involving violation-confession-forgiveness and culminating in mutual recognition.[28] Crime and punishment are one instance of this process. In this context, self-reflection is one element of the general process of mutual recognition; without it, we are left with mere violent repression (or negative censure).

One implication of the Hegelian analysis is thus that self-reflection and acknowledgement of one's fallibility is not a merely internal process. Given that it is part of an interaction, it should be demonstrated externally in a way that makes it available to the other party. In the instance of crime and punishment, the punishing authority's acknowledgment of its own fallibility should be communicated, thus made accessible to the offender in his or her position as an

---

[26] A du Bois-Pedain, 'Punishment as an Inclusionary Practice: Sentencing in a Liberal Constitutional State' in Du Bois-Pedain, Ulväng and Asp (eds), above n 24, ch 9; Du Bois-Pedain, above n 12.

[27] Du Bois-Pedain, above n 12 at 65 (emphasis added).

[28] For an illuminating analysis see JM Bernstein, 'Confession and Forgiveness: Hegel's Poetics of Action' in R Eldridge (ed), *Beyond Representation: Philosophy and Poetic Imagination* (Cambridge, Cambridge University Press, 1996) 34, and the brief summary in Du Bois-Pedain, ibid at 64–65.

active party in the interaction. This allows the offender to find common grounds with the punishing authority, and thus also to relate to its communication of censure.

We are, however, left with a puzzle. Unlike the other requirements, the requirement of self-reflection and acknowledgment of fallibility has so far been founded only on Hegelian premises. To embrace this requirement we must embrace Hegel's notion of mutual recognition and the metaphysical assumptions that underlie it. This may be more than we are willing to do. The task of the next section is to provide a naturalistic foundation for the requirement of critical self-reflection by the punishing authority. For this purpose, it observes punishment as a practice that the legal system has in common with institutions such as the school system and the family. In these social and political contexts, naturalistic foundations for the requirement of critical self-reflection have already been offered.

III. FROM PENOLOGY TO NATURALISTIC DEVELOPMENTAL THEORY: THE SPHERE OF SCHOOLS

The requirement of critical self-reflection by the punishing authority is more readily visible in the context of school discipline, where the imposition of sanctions is informed not only or mainly by penology, but also by developmental theory. Developmental theory is founded on naturalistic premises; in its relevant parts, it reflects many of Hume's assumptions about sentiments. Thus, it has the potential to fill gaps in naturalistic penology. This section advances the argument that observation of school discipline – with its reference to developmental theory – can inform penology.

Punishment is a general category; it is commonly defined as an intentional imposition of deprivation or pain on a wrongdoer by an authority, in response to wrongdoing for which the wrongdoer has been determined to be in some way responsible.[29] So defined, punishment encompasses a range of subcategories, including legal punishment, parental punishment, disciplinary measures imposed by schools, and other disciplinary measures imposed on adults in various professional contexts. Each of these subcategories represents a different sphere in which punishment is imposed (the family, school, the legal sphere, etc). The nature and characteristics of each sphere affect the nature and characteristics

---

[29] The most famous and widely acceptable definition is the Flew–Benn–Hart definition, slightly different variants of which appear in A Flew, 'The Justification of Punishment' (1954) 29 *Philosophy* 291; SI Benn, 'An Approach to the Problem of Punishment' (1958) 33 *Philosophy* 331; and HLA Hart, 'Prolegomenon to the Principles of Punishment' (1959–60) 60 *Proceedings of the Aristotelian Society* 1. For discussions of this definition, see T McPherson, 'Punishment: Definition and Justification' (1967) 28 *Analysis* 21; DE Scheid, 'Note on Defining "Punishment"' (1980) 10 *Canadian Journal of Philosophy* 453, and the references there. See also J Kleinig, *Punishment and Desert* (The Hague, Martinus Nijhoff, 1973) ch 2.

of punishment in this sphere. And yet, observation of punishment in one sphere can enrich the analysis of punishment in another (closely related) sphere. There are two main reasons for this. First, analysis of one subcategory of punishment can contribute to the analysis of punishment in general, and hence also to the analysis of other subcategories. Second, analysis of one subcategory can highlight characteristics that it has in common with another subcategory, and hence contribute to the analysis of punishment in that subcategory. As mentioned above, Du Bois-Pedain has already demonstrated the potential of such an approach when drawing a cautious analogy between parental punishment and criminal punishment in her account of inclusionary criminal punishment.[30] Yet, as Du Bois-Pedain notes, there are significant differences between the familial sphere and the legal sphere, and this might raise the question whether the analogy is not too remote.

Analysis of punishment in the school system can help bridge the gap between the familial sphere and the legal sphere. It can therefore contribute to the analysis of these two subcategories of punishment, and significantly to the analysis of legal punishment. In typological terms, the sphere of schools is located between the sphere of the family and that of the criminal justice system. Schools share some of the aims of the family, such as education and development of the child's subjectivity; and some of the aims of the criminal justice system, such as censuring wrongdoing. The subject of the school system is the child, who still requires familial protection and direction, but at the same time can understand and take censure from more formal authorities such as the state. The authority exercised by teachers manifests some of the intimate characteristics of parents and some of the formal and institutional characteristics of the state. Both parents and the state feed the school system and guide its actions to some extent. This combination of characteristics produces the subcategory of school discipline and punishment, and it can serve to highlight the role and significance of similar characteristics in the familial and legal contexts.

One possible understanding takes these characteristics as forces pushing in different directions. Where commonalities with the criminal justice system take over, censure is constructed as an act of control that bears similarity to crime-control strategies deployed by the criminal justice system.[31] Schools may then slip down to criminalisation models;[32] or, in extreme cases, even divert pupils to the criminal justice system.[33] Where commonalities with the family take over,

---

[30] Du Bois-Pedain, above n 26 at 202–06.

[31] For an overview of such developments in education theory, see M Watson, 'Developmental Discipline and Moral Education' in LP Nucci and D Narvaez (eds), *Handbook of Moral and Character Education* (New York and London, Routledge, 2008) 175.

[32] See PJ Hirschfield, 'Preparing for Prison? The Criminalisation of School Discipline in the USA' (2008) 12 *Theoretical Criminology* 179; CY Kim, 'Policing School Discipline' (2012) 77 *Brooklyn Law Review* 861.

[33] KC Monahan et al, 'From the School Yard to the Squad Car: School Discipline, Truancy, and Arrest' (2014) 43 *Journal of Youth and Adolescence* 1110.

discipline takes a less formal stance. In such cases, the system relies heavily on developmental theory:[34] it considers the psychological effects of censure on children, shows awareness of the risks of negative repression, and exercises critical self-reflection.[35] It calls on teachers to acknowledge their fallibility as appropriate in their daily interactions with pupils: 'The good enough teacher genuinely tries and when he or she fails, apologizes, reflects, and goes on trying'.[36] Significantly, these characteristics exist in the daily work of professionals who are part of the system.[37]

This 'competing-forces' understanding seems, however, too simplistic. It fails to account for the fact that neither set of commonalities (with the criminal justice system and with the family) can ever fully 'take over'. The human condition is too rich for any one set of commonalities to dictate the nature of punishment in the school system exclusively and satisfactorily. Significantly, there always remains a developing child in every well-developed child (and indeed in every adult), and there always remains a person in every authority – formal as it may be. Accordingly, every censure has a measure of each of the abovementioned 'forces' in it. The concept of censure thus must be understood to include all the above-mentioned characteristics, even if at times they make themselves more or less apparent, or exist in different amounts.

An alternative understanding suggests itself. Rather than forces pushing in different directions, all the characteristics that have been identified in the context of school discipline are actually the building blocks of a unified concept of censure – elements that exist in every censure. These elements become more apparent when focusing not on the extremes (the family and the criminal justice system) but on the middle ground of the school system. Accordingly, punishment in the school system is informed by more than one theoretical approach. It is, in fact, an arena where developmental theory and penology meet. It is an arena where different aspects of punishment highlighted by each of these disciplines can be effectively traced, examined and integrated into richer and fuller concepts. On this understanding, observation of punishment in the school system highlights the relevance of developmental theory for a full theory of punishment. At the same time it also serves to highlight the modifications that are needed if developmental theory is to be used to enrich penology.

As already noted, one obvious advantage of using developmental theory to enrich penology is its naturalistic foundation. This advantage has already been identified and exploited by Axel Honneth, whose work therefore provides a good

---

[34] Watson, above n 31. On the psychological impact of punishment, see JS Kounin and PV Gump, 'The Comparative Influence of Punitive and Non-Punitive Teachers upon Children's Concepts of School Misconduct' (1961) 52 *Journal of Educational Psychology* 44.

[35] Watson, above n 31; M Cameron and SM Sheppard, 'School Discipline and Social Work Practice: Application of Research and Theory to Intervention' (2006) 28 *Children and Schools* 15.

[36] Watson, above n 31 at 196.

[37] See eg, Cameron and Sheppard, above n 35.

starting point for a theoretical examination of the relevance of developmental theory for penology.[38] Like Du Bois-Pedain's analysis, Honneth's critical theory is Hegelian; however, Honneth aims to provide naturalistic foundations for Hegel's notion of recognition. He does so with particular reference to Donald Winnicott's object-relation theory[39] and to Herbert Mead's social psychology.[40]

In *The Struggle for Recognition*, Honneth does not analyse punishment, but he does analyse crime, and this analysis provides an effective jumping board for the analysis of punishment. For Honneth, grave crime violates more than legal rights. Referring to grave interpersonal crimes such as rape and torture, he writes:

> Physical abuse represents a type of disrespect that does lasting damage to one's basic confidence (learned through love) that one can autonomously coordinate one's own body ... this affects all practical dealings with other subjects, even at a physical level ... The successful integration of physical and emotional qualities of behaviour is, as it were, subsequently broken up from the outside.[41]

Crime is therefore understood as an attack on (the victim's) self-integration that is learned through love. Self-integration learned through love is explained, in turn, with reference to Winnicott's object relation theory. Winnicott's theory describes 'the interactional process by which "mother" and child are able to detach themselves from a state of undifferentiated oneness in such a way that, in the end, they learn to accept and love each other as independent persons'.[42] That which crime breaks is therefore independence or self-containment within the scope of one's personal boundaries.

This analysis of crime can be taken further to explain the offender's experience in committing crime and the appropriate response to this experience. Indeed, similarly to Hegel's analysis of transgression and his notion of crime as an act of self-contradiction by which offenders deny the recognitional structure of human interaction on which their own recognition depends, Winnicott's own analysis of crime observed not only and not even mainly the disintegration of the victim, but also that of the offender. For Winnicott, in committing crime, the offender attempts to deny the existence of his or her own boundaries – the boundaries that confine him or her into their own body, property, etc. And it is

---

[38] A Honneth, *The Struggle for Recognition: The Moral Grammar of Social Conflicts* translated by J Anderson (Cambridge, Polity Press, 1995).

[39] See DW Winnicott, *The Child, the Family, and the Outside* World (London, Penguin Books, 1964); DW Winnicott, 'The mother-infant experience of mutuality' (1970) *Parenthood: Its Psychology and Psychopathology* 245; DW Winnicott, *The Maturational Process and the Facilitating Environment: Studies in the Theory of Emotional Development* edited by MMR Khan (London, Hogarth Press and Institute of Psycho-Analysis, 1965); DW Winnicott, 'The Theory of Parent-Infant Relationship' (1960) 41 *International Journal of Psychoanalysis* 585. For a brief summary, see M Jacobs, 'D.W. Winnicott' in W Dryden (ed), *Key Figures in Counselling and Therapy* (London, Sage, 1995) 34–37.

[40] GH Mead, *Mind, Self and Society* (Chicago, Chicago University Press, 1934).

[41] Honneth, above n 38 at 132–33.

[42] Ibid at 98.

the role of authority to reconstitute these boundaries in processes that share the basic structure (though not necessarily the content) of the constitution of boundaries through love.

IV. DEVELOPMENTAL THEORY: WRONGDOING AND CONTAINMENT

A. Winnicott on Crime and the Response to it

Winnicott's object-relation theory[43] is concerned with the baby and child's developing senses of integration and of being-in-time. These senses are, for Winnicott, not inborn; they are developed through good interaction with the child's mother. This interaction consists of moments of absolute merging and of gradual separation through which the child comes to know his bounded self. In line with these assumptions, Winnicott analyses crime as reflecting some deficiency in the interaction with the mother figure. Crime, for Winnicott, is an infantile attempt to merge – an attempt made where the original process of merging and separation has failed.

If crime reflects a failure in the development of a sense of bounded and independent self, then the response to crime should address this failure. This is precisely what Winnicott suggests should be done. When Winnicott analyses the case of a stealing child, he writes as follows: 'If parents understand what this phase of a more compulsive type of stealing means they will act sensibly. They will tolerate it, for one thing … Above all, parents who understand this situation will not come down like a ton of bricks on the child and demand confession.'[44] Winnicott thus proposes two possible responses to the act of stealing. The first response consists in containing the act and in this way also the child's personality that is reflected in the act. Containment, through interaction, makes the underlying sentiments bearable by acknowledging them and moving beyond them. When contained, the wrongdoing loses its 'life' within the wrongdoer. While the process of containment is unlike the process of positive censure, it is important to note that containment thus achieves one of the objectives of positive censure – it turns the wrongdoer away from wrongdoing. (The processes may also share other important features, such that Winnicott's model may enrich and inform the conception of positive censure. This point is addressed further below.) The second response Winnicott offers to the act of stealing is hard and punitive. For Winnicott, hard treatment keeps the theft or the wrongdoing 'alive', thus we should expect more wrongdoing which is then repressed once again in a vicious circle. Hence, punishment is a negative form of censure. Winnicott suggests that while being a bad response to wrongdoing, punishment is unavoidable in the

---

[43] See references at n 39 above.
[44] Winnicott, *The Child, The Family and the Outside World,* above n 39 at 164.

public sphere of the state due to the need to address the feelings of the victim and the community.[45]

Winnicott's developmental analysis best fits young children acting in the familial context, where punishment is indeed often inappropriate or counter-productive; it fits less well older children acting in more formal structures such as schools, where sanctions are commonly used and often seem appropriate. Nevertheless, Winnicott's analysis has implicitly nourished developmental approaches to school discipline that consider punishment an inappropriate response to wrongdoing. For instance, Marilyn Watson (who has coined the term 'the good enough teacher' by paraphrasing Winnicott's well-known notion of 'the good enough mother'), objects to punishment in the school system altogether. She explains:

> From a developmental perspective, punishment as an inducement to moral growth is at best ineffective and at worst counterproductive … For oppositional children, those who have little trust and a confrontational stance toward the world, it will do little good and is likely to reinforce their untrusting, defiant stance.[46]

However, Watson's idea that schools should refrain from imposing punishments has not been widely received, and this does not seem surprising. Arguably, her proposed generalisations are too sweeping. Winnicott's analysis requires adapta-tions if it is to fit non-familial social institutions such as schools or indeed the criminal justice system.

Refining and modifying Winnicott's ideas to fit well with the nature and characteristics of the school system or with those of the criminal justice system requires acknowledgment of the differences between the young child acting in the context of the family and the more mature child acting at school or in civil society. Unlike the mature child or the adult, the young child acting in the familial context is still in early stages of development of his/her self. The consciousness of such a child is not yet differentiated; she has no clear sense of boundaries between herself and others (especially her mother), between herself and the outside world, and between her self and her actions, emotions, and mental states.[47] This phenomenon has been identified and analysed in more than

---

[45] Ibid at 165.

[46] Watson, above n 31 at 191.

[47] The gradual differentiation of consciousness is central to Hegel's account of spirit in his *Phenomenology of Spirit* [1807] translated by AV Miller and edited by JN Findlay (Oxford, Oxford University Press, 1977). This differentiation and the related ability to further distance oneself from some acts, mental states, and emotional states have also been discussed extensively by later thinkers. For a concise philosophical exploration of this ability, see esp M Dan-Cohen, 'Responsibility and the Boundaries of the Self' (1992) 105 *Harvard Law Review* 959, and the sources there cited. Dan-Cohen discusses the capacity of the self to actively participate in its own constitution. He defines this capac-ity as 'the self's ability to *identify* with various elements and thereby integrate them into itself, or to distance itself from them by objectifying them and holding them at arm's length' (at 966). Follow-ing Harry Frankfurt, Jean-Paul Sartre, Maurice Merleau-Ponty, and Erving Goffman, he notes that these elements can be mental (for example wills), social (social roles), or physical (body, property).

one philosophical context,[48] and it is the cornerstone of Winnicott's analysis of the process of differentiation, separation, and gradual movement towards independence.

This lack of differentiation of the young child's consciousness has implications for the appropriate response to her crime. Since the ability to distance oneself from external or internal elements is not yet formed, the young child fully identifies with all her actions, emotions and mental states. Accordingly, the response to the young child's act (or, for that matter, the response to the child's thoughts or emotions) and the response to this child's self or personality are experienced as one and the same. Any censure of an act is received as censure of the child's undifferentiated self. But censure of the undifferentiated self is always negative and repressive, since it leaves no room for constructive acceptance of the self. For this reason, when it comes to young children, Winnicott recommends full and sweeping containment of crime and of child. Only such a response would not turn out to be oppressive; only such a response would provide the child's personality a sufficiently protective environment in which boundaries can be gradually and comfortably learnt and internalised, and in which consciousness can gradually mature and differentiate. Yet despite this sweeping recommendation, it seems that the heart of Winnicott's recommendation does not lie in the containment of the crime, but only in the protective containment of personality.

If this is indeed the case, then the appropriate response to wrongdoing by a mature child in school settings or to crime by an adult need not and should not be full containment of act and personality. At least after the child has matured enough, wrongdoing and the personality that produced it are no longer one and the same: the mature child and the grown-up have learnt that they can identify with their acts or distance themselves from them.[49] This realisation on the side of a wrongdoer also allows the authority to treat the act and the person separately – censuring one and containing the other. Thus, Winnicott's position can be refined to allow positive punitive censure that accepts and contains the personality that produced crime, but rejects the criminal act. The remaining question is how this can be achieved.

B. Bion on Containment

The conditions under which a response to crime contains the personality that produced the crime (while rejecting the criminal act) should now be laid down. Winnicott makes references to the concept of containment, but he does not bring this concept to its full development (his main concept is that of holding). The concept of containment has been fully developed by Alfred Bion. Bion

---

[48] See the works cited in the preceding footnote.
[49] See, generally, the works cited in n 39 above.

(whose specific concern is not with the baby's sense of being-in-time but with the development of the capacity to think through processing of impressions and raw emotions[50]) has suggested a developmental structure that bears similarities to that proposed by Winnicott.[51] We can start with a brief account of Bion's main developmental structure that will serve to introduce its potential. According to Bion, in early stages of development the baby and the mother create a container-contained structure. In this structure, the baby incorporates in her personality a range of raw emotions that the baby cannot process. These emotions are 'contained' by the mother when she experiences them and processes them by way of thinking them, thereby transforming them into bearable elements. The mother (as the emotion's 'container') then returns them to the baby (the 'contained') in their new processed and bearable form.[52] With time, the baby internalises the entire container-contained structure and becomes capable of independent processing that involves independent thinking.

Bion's account has potential implications for a range of contexts. Bion himself has drawn attention to the fact that his account of the sentiments of containment has close affinities with Hume's more general account of sympathy.[53] David M Black similarly points out that 'Bion's account of maternal reverie… clearly implies the existence of sympathy'.[54] Hume's account concerns what he calls 'human nature', and its application is not limited to developmental/familial or educational contexts; indeed, these contexts are not Hume's typical concerns.[55] Hume's account has already been relied on in section III above to provide an initial justification for the requirement of critical self-reflection by the punishing authority. The similarities between Hume's and Bion's observations gives us reason to expect that Bion's account may usefully be considered in contexts other than parental and therapeutic ones.

It is apparent that, for Bion, containment works primarily at the level of attitudes, emotions and sentiments rather than at the level of actions and rational considerations. Only once containment of sentiments is achieved can work commence at the level of actions and reasons, which involves independent thinking. Applied to responses to wrongdoing, Bion's model thus opens the door

---

[50] This is a significant difference between Bion's and Winnicott's theories. For elaboration see TH Ogden, 'On Holding and Containing, Being and Dreaming' (2004) 85 *International Journal of Psychoanalysis* 1349.

[51] WR Bion, *Learning from Experience* [1962] (London, Karnac Books, 1984); WR Bion, 'Attacks on Linking' (1959) 40 *International Journal of Psychoanalysis* 308.

[52] Bion, *Learning*, ibid at 90–94.

[53] See Bion's comments in *Learning*, ibid at 90–94. On the connections between Hume and Bion, see further L Braddock, 'Natural Evil, Extreme States of Mind, and the Disruption of Sympathy', talk given in December 2012 for the London Philosophy and Psychoanalysis Group, manuscript pp 7–8 available at www.philosophy-psychoanalysis.org.uk/wp-content/uploads/2013/01/LB-evil_talk.pdf.

[54] DM Black, 'Sympathy Reconfigured: Some Reflections on Sympathy, Empathy and the Discovery of Values' (2004) 85 *The International Journal of Psychoanalysis* 579.

[55] Hume, above n 20.

for responses that work at different levels – the level of sentiments, attitudes and emotions, and the level of actions and reasons. At the level of sentiments, such responses would acknowledge and process the wrongdoer's rage, greed, confusion, helplessness, etc. This would involve an attempt to understand the full personal context of the wrongdoer's act, including situational factors and personality factors that might have stimulated negative sentiments. Only familiarity with the full personal context enables someone to experience, identify, acknowledge and isolate negative sentiments through processes involving emotion and thought. Acknowledgement and isolation of these sentiments make them bearable for the wrongdoer. As the sentiments are made bearable for the wrongdoer, more advanced reflection at the level of actions and reasons becomes possible. At the level of actions and reasons, the appropriate response can now further echo what the wrongdoer is already capable of seeing by herself from her new reflective position – that her choice was harmful and wrong.

It is now left to consider whether Bion's model is applicable, in full or in part, outside the familial and therapeutic contexts, and particularly in the legal context. To examine the fuller potential of Bion's model as well as its limitations, the next section further elaborates on Bion's account of the ongoing interaction between container and contained. It identifies its logical moments and examines which of those can find full or partial expression in legal realities.

V. BACK TO PENOLOGY: PUNISHMENT, CRITICAL SELF-REFLECTION AND POLITICAL CONTAINMENT

If Bion's model is to be applied to the legal context, then the legal response to crime must have different levels that manifest not only rejection of crime and its reasons, but also acceptance and containment of the offender's person. Bion's account of containment includes several logical moments,[56] each of which can be fully or partly identified in existing or at least possible legal realities.

The first logical moment is Bion's moment of experiencing, where the container actually experiences the strong difficult emotions incorporated in the contained. In the context of responses to wrongdoing, this would happen as the authority takes the wrongdoing into itself and experiences its destructiveness and its separateness-denying quality. In the more particular context of crime and punishment, this takes place as the state (or rather the persons representing its authority, like the juries or the judge) experience the challenging and violent rage of crime. This would not take the form of identification with the criminal's attitudes towards protected legal interests, but of mirroring rage that hearing detailed accounts of crime may provoke in juries and judges. This rage may well now be directed at the offender.

---

[56] These moments are elaborated mainly in *Learning from Experience* and in 'Attacks on Linking' both above n 51.

Bion's second logical moment is that of independence, where the container resists full identification with the violent sentiment of the contained and manages to critically reflect on it. Such critical self-reflection involves isolating the violent sentiment from the container's fuller person, thus being able to acknowledge it without risking self-destruction. In the context of responses to wrongdoing, this would happen as the authority identifies and acknowledges destructive and separateness-denying qualities in its own rage over the wrongdoing. In the more particular context of crime and punishment, this takes place as the state (or rather the persons representing its authority) become aware of the possible arbitrariness and harmfulness of the punitive action they are inclined to impose out of rage over crime. As we shall see in the next section, awareness of the possibility of arbitrariness is often manifested in, and further facilitated by, demonstrations of human fallibility by the representatives of the authority. Awareness of the harmfulness of the punitive action is well documented in empirical research of sentencing. For example, in Judith Rumgay's research, a magistrate noted that 'The very vast majority of us feel that custody is the most negative thing of all from everybody's point of view'.[57] Other empirical studies have likewise found that judges perceive prison as 'a frightening experience for many and often just a way of making [offenders'] lives go worse'.[58]

Bion's third logical moment consists of the act of 'digesting' where the raw sentiment turns into a less terrifying substance that can be accepted.[59] In the context of responses to wrongdoing, this would happen as the authority takes regulative actions that turn its fallibility and destructiveness into something that can be lived with. In the more particular context of crime and punishment, this takes place as the state (or the persons representing it) take measures to address their fallibility by limiting their own punitive power. Some of these measures are set in legal rules that limit punitive power; others are spontaneously carried out by juries, judges, or magistrates who self-restrain in the courtroom. This self-restraint is described in Du Bois-Pedain's account of judges' experiences of sentencing when she points to judges' acute awareness that, 'if they imposed a custodial sentence, it would be *their* decision to make the defendant's life go worse in this particular way, for which they would have to carry a moral responsibility'.[60] It is also reflected in a magistrate in Rumgay's research noting that: 'I would do anything rather than send somebody to prison, if there's a hope of something else being more effective.'[61]

---

[57] J Rumgay, 'Custodial Decision Making in a Magistrates' Court – Court Culture and Immediate Situational Factors' (1995) 35 *British Journal of Criminology* 201 at 205.

[58] A du Bois Pedain, 'In Defence of Substantial Sentencing Discretion' (2017) 28 *Criminal Law Forum* 391 at 418 (referring to and summarising findings of empirical studies reviewed in the article).

[59] The second and the third moments partly overlap; I have made a distinction between them in order to emphasise the regulation of the processed emotion in the third moment.

[60] Du Bois-Pedain, above n 58 at 418.

[61] Rumgay, above n 57 at 205.

Bion's fourth logical moment involves internalisation by the contained of the entire container-contained structure in a way that gives him independent reflection and 'digestion' capabilities and frees both parties. In the context of responses to wrongdoing, this would happen as the authority addresses the wrongdoer with its processed and now-bearable rage; the wrongdoer internalises the ability to process rage and other negative sentiments in calm critical self-reflection; and both parties engage together in critical reflection on the wrongful act. In the more particular context of crime and punishment, this takes place in a comfortably-regulated process of sentencing that enables the state (or rather its representatives) and the offender to start reflecting on the offender's crime. The offender who has faced state-representatives for whom arbitrariness and harmfulness are manageable can now identify with the state and internalise its capacity for calm critical self-reflection. Under these conditions, the sentencing process merely echoes what the offender is already capable of seeing by herself – that she is a full fallible person whose fullness enables isolating difficult sentiments and critically reflecting on them without risking self-destruction; that she has indeed done wrong; and that her wrongful act requires condemnation. This process, too, is arguably reflected in existing legal rules and realities, such as sentencing guidelines that require observation of the full personal context of crime commission; and it also finds expression in judges' perceptions of sentencing. Take Du Bois-Pedain's conclusion from the empirical literature that '[sentencers] saw themselves very much as responding to the person of the offender' and 'wanted to understand the kind of person they were imposing their sentence on'.[62] It is worth noting that this creates a relationship with certain qualities between the offender and the sentencers: 'When sentencers see it as part of their task to respond to the person of the offender, sentencing acquires aspects of an everyday moral interaction between the offender and the sentencer. In particular, judges have been observed to "try to build up a rapport" with the offender.'[63] And in the context of this relationship, critical self-reflection is made possible.

Yet a difficulty remains. In the above discussion I have used 'the state' and 'state representatives' interchangeably, as if the state and its representatives were identical as far as Bion's model is concerned. However, this is not the case. The lack of identity between the state and the persons representing it can stand in the way of full application of Bion's model in the legal context. This lack of identity can stop the offender from perceiving the state's representatives (judge, juries, etc) as the ultimate authority that can contain her person. For the offender, even if a particular judge has some human characteristics that potentially allow containment, she lacks ultimate authority; and the ultimate authority (the state) might not be containing at all – it might still be rejecting her person as well as

---

[62] Du Bois-Pedain, above n 57 at 419.
[63] Ibid at 421.

her act. When full containment by the authority is lacking from her experience, the offender is not helped to critically self-reflect on her act.

This tension is unresolvable. It exemplifies the extent of the challenge for the criminal justice system – the challenge of concrete people representing an abstract authority. Moreover, this tension should not be resolved. We should think of the criminal justice process as offering 'political containment', and such 'political containment' is distinct from, and should not strive to be, full containment in Bion's sense. Rather, political containment is a replica of full containment that points to its possibility. The state is neither a parent nor a therapist – indeed it must not be – but it can and should demonstrate positive authoritative interaction that gives the offender as much as can be given without undermining its own (essential) abstract status. In this respect, political containment is the beginning of a journey for the offender rather than its end. It gives the offender a lead to follow up in the search for full containment.

The next section further discusses the challenge of political containment. It proposes a way to manage the tension between concrete representatives and abstract authority in a slightly more satisfactory manner. It focuses on the second logical moment, namely that of critical self-reflection by the punishing authority; and it proposes its full institutionalisation in a way that narrows the gap between the fallible representative and the institution it represents.

VI. FURTHER IMPLICATIONS FOR THE CRIMINAL JUSTICE SYSTEM: RETHINKING THE PLACE OF RESTORATIVE JUSTICE PRACTICES

Critical self-reflection is already incorporated in the criminal justice system, and it serves both to justify and to legitimise it. The clearest examples of critical self-reflection are principles, rules, structures and procedures that construct and limit the state's power to impose punishment. One such obvious principle concerns judicial independence and the duties that arise from it;[64] but self-reflection goes way beyond that. The very structure of the system and its constant efforts to deal with the risk of false convictions through almost every rule of evidence and of procedure manifest awareness of fallibility. Thus, it could be argued that the concept of reflective censure has limited normative implications beyond those that are already taken into account in virtually every modern legal system.

Yet this critical self-reflection at the structural level is often accompanied by a formal authoritative stance that conceals it in specific cases. During trial the formal authoritative stance overarches adjudication and makes fallibility almost invisible. The architecture of the courtroom, the appearance of participants (wearing gowns and wigs), the legal language, the ceremonial nature of the trial

---

[64] Principles on judicial independence are set in the Bangalore Principles of Judicial Conduct that were endorsed by the United Nations Human Rights Commission in April 2003. For England and Wales, see *Guide to Judicial Conduct* (Judiciary of England and Wales, March 2013).

and the announcement of the verdict – all these give the impression of absolute and perfect authority that operates in a different sphere than that of fallible humans.[65] This formal authoritative stance too has important justificatory and legitimising functions.

The tension between critical self-reflection and a formal authoritative stance of infallibility is not only unavoidable, it plays an important role in the case for positive punitive censure in the public-political context of criminal justice. It is through positive censure that this tension is managed in a way that culminates in as much containment as the political structure allows. As already noted, this would never be full containment in Bion's sense. Political containment is a limited form of containment that nevertheless points to the possibility of full containment.

Such political containment requires, first, the establishment of a container-contained structure and of some content that can potentially be contained, and second, an interaction that includes the moments of containment. This can be achieved if the tension between fallibility and infallibility is dynamic and managed differently in the two stages of the trial: the stage of determination of liability (the fact-finding stage) and the sentencing stage. Demonstrable authority should dominate the fact-finding stage and demonstrable fallibility should dominate the sentencing stage.

The fact-finding stage sets the grounds of political containment; it sets 'the rules of the containment game'. Throughout this stage, the container-contained structure is established and reinforced: the state is placed as a potential container and the offender is placed as potentially contained. In addition, the content of future interaction is determined: the fact-finding stage establishes the offender's wrongdoing as a public truth that is the basis for further containing interaction. For this substrate to be established and accepted by all, a moment dominated by clear authority is required. Personalities in need of containment would not regard anyone who primarily engages in critical self-reflection as a potential container; offenders cannot regard any state that is less than confidently authoritative as capable of reintegrating them in society. This does not mean that there cannot be a healthy measure of critical self-reflection embedded in the system. But this critical self-reflection cannot dominate the initial concrete interaction between the offender and the state.

Things are different in the sentencing stage. Here, structures are already well-established, and the task for the authority is finer and more delicate: the offender's wrongdoing still has to be censured, but this should be done in a way that contains his or her personality. As we have seen, containment works at the level of attitudes and sentiments rather than of acts or even rational reasons. Engagement with attitudes and sentiments requires a less authoritative

---

[65] See M Edelman, *From Art to Politics: How Artistic Creations Shape Political Conceptions* (Chicago and London, University of Chicago Press, 1995) 93–94.

stance. It requires interacting with the offender directly and with a measure of sympathy. As we have further seen, sympathy develops on a common ground – the common ground of acknowledged fallibility. Accordingly, the authority should make critical self-reflection and acknowledgement of the fallibility it shares with the offender more pronounced and dominant; and the process of critical self-reflection should be fully institutionalised.

The criminal justice system already goes at least one step in this direction: in sentencing, the focus is no longer only on the defendant's act, but also on his or her personal circumstances.[66] This allows the court to relate to the offender as a fallible human being, and such relation is likely to give rise to identification and sympathy in a way that allows containment. Furthermore, statements of the effect of the offence on the victim, the victim's family, or others can be introduced in the sentencing stage.[67] This allows the offender to relate to the human vulnerability of those in the name of whom, partly, the criminal justice system speaks. Once the offender identifies the other side's humanity, the process of containment progresses further. Thus, the change of focus in the sentencing stage from the wrongful act to the personalities it involved serves to promote the process of reflective censure.

Yet it is arguable that the visible and institutionalised exercise of critical self-reflection in the sentencing stage should be taken further. The sentencing stage should be constructed less like a natural continuation of the fact-finding stage and more like a distinct process that bears resemblance to alternative dispute resolution processes that adopt restorative justice as their underlying premise. Restorative justice provides tools and techniques that seem appropriate and helpful, yet it is doubtful whether its basic premises rest on sound theoretical foundations.[68] The requirement of critical self-reflection by the punishing authority can provide theoretical foundations for these tools and techniques, while at the same time pointing to necessary modifications in their use and in the understanding of their role.

To see this, let us briefly consider restorative justice. Restorative justice is commonly defined as a process by which all the parties with a stake in an offence come together to resolve collectively how to deal with its implications.[69] This would usually include the taking of responsibility by the offender, acknowledgement by the offender of the harm to the victim, apology, and some form

[66] See Sentencing Guidelines Council, *Overarching Principles: Seriousness (Guideline)* sections D(ii) and D(iii) (2004).
[67] *Criminal Practice Directions* 2015 Division VII (Sentencing), F and G.
[68] Some theorists of punishment therefore propose integrating insights from restorative justice into better-established justifications of punishment. See eg RA Duff, 'Restoration and Retribution' in A von Hirsch et al (eds), *Restorative Justice and Criminal Justice: Competing or Reconcilable Paradigms?* (Oxford, Hart, 2003) 43.
[69] J Braithwaite, 'Restorative Justice: Assessing Optimistic and Pessimistic Accounts' (1999) 25 *Crime and Justice* 1 at 5. Braithwaite's republican version of restorative justice has consequentialist undertones, but compare with M Wenzel et al, 'Retributive and Restorative Justice' (2008) 32 *Law and Human Behavior* 375 at 378.

of reparation on which all parties jointly agree. To meet these aims effectively, communication in restorative justice conferences is less formal than communication in trial settings, with a focus on concrete and imperfect persons taking different roles in the process of healing.

Regardless of their (somewhat vague) original aims, the less formal stance and the focus on concrete and essentially imperfect persons would further enhance critical self-reflection by the authority in the imposition of punishment. In less formal settings, not only the offender but also the victims and the punishing authority meet their own and one another's fallibility, change their emotional stance towards one another and towards themselves, and thereby develop and grow.

In concrete terms, taking a self-reflective stance at the sentencing stage might entail measures that construct the judge as a fallible human being rather than an infallible authority. These may include removal of gowns and wigs and more symmetrical sitting arrangements. In addition, victims may be allowed to present themselves in the courtroom as injured human beings rather than as mere witnesses giving an account of the incident for the benefit of the public or the state. This might entail incorporation of direct communication between victim and offender where appropriate, with the victim becoming more visible as a concrete person who has suffered; marginalising the role of legal representatives and engaging the offender, the victim, and the (fallible) judge in conversation. Such steps will allow the offender and the punishing authority to reflect on that which they share, and this reflection is part of a containing process of censure.

Nevertheless, it is not suggested that the sentencing stage would be turned into a restoration conference. Restorative justice, or at least some restorative practices like victim–offender reconciliation programs,[70] are often advocated as alternatives to punishment. The current proposal uses some of the techniques of restorative justice in order to make hard treatment justifiable and legitimate. But there are important differences. In restorative justice, the focus is on critical self-reflection by the offender;[71] in the current proposal, it is on critical self-reflection by the punishing authority. Restorative justice presumes – indeed, it must presume – that the offender admits to committing the crime and accepts responsibility. This is the basis on which mutual agreement with respect to appropriate

---

[70] For a discussion of such programmes in Canada, see JV Roberts and K Roach, 'Restorative Justice in Canada: From Sentencing Circles to Sentencing Principles' in von Hirsch et al (eds), above n 68, 237 at 239–40.

[71] See, for example, the 'Making Amends' model of restorative justice proposed by Andrew von Hirsch, Andrew Ashworth and Clifford Shearing ('Specifying Aims and Limits for Restorative Justice: A "Making Amends" Model?', in von Hirsch et al, above n 68, 21). The authors write: 'The "making amends" model, which resembles in important respects that sketched by Antony Duff ..., involves a response negotiated between the offender and his victim, which involves (1) the implicit or explicit acknowledgement of fault and (2) an apologetic stance on the part of the offender' (ibid at 25).

restoration is sought. In the current proposal, neither admission nor acceptance of responsibility is presumed or required; since agreement is not the aim of the process, punishment can be imposed in their absence. In more abstract terms, restorative justices suggests informality standing alone and facilitating private reconciliation; the current proposal is of informality complementing the formality of the trial stage and serving the interests of justice in the real world.

One consequence of this is that the process of positive punitive censure would not always end in robust and effective containment that includes the offender's significant growth. Just as psychological containment is not a guarantee for a child's (or a patient's) significant and demonstrable growth, containment in punishment is not a guarantee for the offender's significant and demonstrable growth. Moreover, full containment would normally require an ongoing process that the punishing authority cannot and should not take part in. The appropriate role of the punishing authority is limited to containment in one specific instance. Thus, it may well be the case that the offender would experience containment but would then regress to hostility. This, however, would not make punishment illegitimate. For punishment to be legitimate, its imposition must only provide the offender with the minimal conditions for significant growth and development and further include a moment of maturity and recognition. Whether the offender fully exhausts this opportunity or not can only be left for the offender. In this, the proposed account bears some resemblance to Duff's communicative account, which does not require the offender's transformation.[72]

It is noteworthy that research conducted by Joanna Shapland, Gwen Robinson and Angela Sorsby has provided evidence about the positive function of critical self-reflection in restorative sentencing.[73] These researchers examined, among other things, satisfaction and perceptions of legitimacy among offenders and victims who have taken part in restorative justice procedures, where some of the participating authorities present themselves as human and fallible. They further examined the frequency of reoffending among offenders who participated in restorative procedures. The outcomes were clear: such procedures tend to strengthen the parties' satisfaction and perceptions of legitimacy,[74] and they further lead to significant reduction in reoffending frequency[75] – a reduction that may indicate development and growth of offenders whose personality has been contained.

---

[72] Duff, above n 6 at 126 ('While offenders are forced to *hear* the message that punishment aims to communicate and to undergo a penal process intended to persuade them to accept it, they are not forced to *listen* to that message or to be *persuaded* by it – they are left free to reject it or to refuse to attend to it in the repentant spirit that it aims to induce.' Emphases in original).

[73] J Shapland, G Robinson and A Sorsby, *Restorative Justice in Practice: Evaluating What Works for Victims and Offenders* (London, Routledge, 2011).

[74] For satisfaction with outcome agreements, see ibid at 158. Satisfaction usually implies a strong perception of legitimacy.

[75] See summary of findings ibid at 196.

VII. OBJECTIONS

The analysis in this chapter breaks the boundaries of penology. Such a move can give rise to various objections, some of which I shall address here.

Some might object to the reliance on developmental theory on the grounds that such reliance assigns the state a parental role, and that this is neither correct nor desirable. This objection, however, would read too much into the reference to developmental theory. First, the only common denominator of the state and the parent is authority that is essential for the imposition of punishment. Authority is indeed crucial in developmental theory, and this makes developmental theory relevant for other authoritative spheres, including the legal sphere. But developmental theory is also shaped by other characteristics of parenthood that are irrelevant in the legal context. The proposed analysis acknowledges this fact and accounts for it by way of necessary modifications of developmental theory that reflect the non-parental position of the state in its relation with the offender. Second and relatedly, therefore, this objection would ignore undeniable differences between parents and the state – differences that, as a practical matter, do not allow the state to play a parental role. Parents are in constant and comprehensive interaction with their children. They respond to every aspect of their behaviour in ways that can be containing or repressive. This accounts for their crucial impact on the child's development. By contrast, the state is in limited interaction with the offender. It only responds to singular instances of behaviour that are alleged to constitute a crime, and accordingly its impact is limited. The proposed account does not suggest that it is, or that it should be, less limited.

Of course, it could be responded that even if the interaction between the state and the offender revolves only around singular instances of behaviour, the proposed account still assigns the state too extensive and intrusive a role in the life of the offender. According to this possible counter-argument, the interaction between the offender and the state in respect of such instances of behaviour must be as limited and unambitious as can be. Any attempt to engage the state in a loaded relationship with the offender is undesirable. This objection seems more persuasive. Arguably, it reaches many current communicative accounts of punishment, including Duff's, Maslen's, Du Bois-Pedain's, and the proposal made by Roberts and Dagan in this volume. It is an objection that lies at the heart of von Hirsch's preference for a unilateral expressive account of punishment.

How can the approach I have argued for in this chapter respond to this objection? To start with, it is hard to see how a requirement that the state engage in critical self-reflection when imposing sanctions can be intrusive from the point of view of the offender. Such a requirement does not prolong the interaction, nor does it require any active participation by the offender. It mainly changes the 'style' of the state's part in the interaction. It requires more from the state, with the expectation that the offender will benefit from the state's efforts and will more easily reintegrate in society. While the future outlook is indeed present, it does not impose anything on the offender. In addition, as already mentioned, liberal states already engage in critical self-reflection, even if mostly at a formal-structural level. Indeed, this is considered essential in a liberal state.

Moreover, I doubt whether a unilateral account of punishment is really possible. The offender who stands on trial and who is then convicted is undeniably in a relationship with the state – the state addresses him, makes demands and imposes punishment. In these circumstances, limiting the interaction to one expressive moment in which only the state participates actively arguably simply amounts to ignoring the offender's subjectivity in this bilateral relationship. Rather than respecting the offender and his liberty, it disrespects him.

VIII. CONCLUSIONS

Dissatisfaction with the realities of legal punishment, and especially with the prison system, has led penologists to rethink its justifications. Theorists have been developing justifications for legal punishment that entail more sympathetic procedures and more moderate and humane forms and amounts of punishment. This chapter is part of this theoretical effort.

My argument focuses on the condition of critical self-reflection by the punishing authority as a key to moderate and humane punishment. After tracing this condition to Hegelian penology, the chapter provides an alternative, naturalistic foundation for this requirement. For this purpose, it compares legal punishment with punishment in the school system, suggesting that both practices are to be analysed as developmental practices. The developmental analysis explains why critical self-reflection by the punishing authority is essential for the justification of punishment. This analysis, in turn, can be connected to a range of legal rules regulating the imposition of punishment. It can also demonstrate why some procedures using the tools offered by restorative justice should be adopted at the sentencing stage.

Breaking the boundaries of penology is by no means simple or straightforward. It is hoped that if such a move is taken with sufficient care, with awareness of its theoretical limits, and with reference to convincing and well-established similar moves that can be found in the literature, it can contribute to our understanding of legal punishment.

4

How Should We Argue for a Censure Theory of Punishment?

CHRISTOPHER BENNETT

A NDREAS VON HIRSCH was one of the first to defend an idea that has since become very popular: the idea that punishment can be justified, in part at least, as censure.[1] There are now many different types of censure theory – some labelled communicative; some called expressive; some hybrid and so on.[2] But many show the influence of von Hirsch's view. In this chapter I bring together some of the basic questions that a censure theory would have to answer – a number of which questions von Hirsch himself has brought to our attention and discussed in detail. I will ask what a censure theory has to be like in order to give satisfactory answers to these questions. I will then look briefly at von Hirsch's own version of the theory, and assess the answers that von Hirsch has previously given to the questions I have raised, and the answers that might be given on his behalf. I will suggest that thinking about the most adequate way to answer these questions delivers a censure theory that is different in some respects from the one that he puts forward.[3] Nevertheless, the theory that I will recommend can be seen to take inspiration from the important work that von Hirsch has done on censure theory over the past 40 years.

I. WHY A CENSURE ACCOUNT OF PUNISHMENT?

The turn to censure theory in the philosophy of punishment could be seen as having its genesis in two sources. First of all, there was growing suspicion of

---

[1] A von Hirsch, *Censure and Sanctions* (Oxford, Oxford University Press, 1993).

[2] T Metz, 'Censure Theory and Intuitions About Punishment' (2002) 19 *Law and Philosophy* 491.

[3] For the censure account that I have defended previously, see C Bennett, *The Apology Ritual: A Philosophical Theory of Punishment* (Cambridge, Cambridge University Press, 2008). For a recent re-statement, see my 'Punishment as an Apology Ritual' in C Flanders and Z Hoskins (eds), *The New Philosophy of Criminal Law* (Lanham, Rowman and Littlefield, 2016) 213.

the rehabilitative paradigm in punishment.[4] As well as increasing uncertainty about whether we possessed sufficient psychological knowledge to rehabilitate psychologically complex offenders, there were also ethical worries about open-ended punishments, about intrusive state intervention, and about coerced social conformity. In addition, there was a concern that purely rehabilitative responses to crime overlooked something that was an important part of human dignity and respect, namely that a person's actions are something for which he can be asked to answer. As a result of these concerns there was a turn towards responses to crime that were proportionate and external.

Secondly, there was the result of the Hart-Devlin debate.[5] In an important paper that could be thought of as dealing with what he would later call the 'unswept debris' of the Hart-Devlin debate,[6] Joel Feinberg suggested that punishment could be seen as a kind of authoritative collective condemnation of wrongdoing, and that there would be something missing in any view of punishment that left that out.[7] The result of these two sources was a view of punishment as an attempt to address the offender as a moral agent, responsible for his actions, with an authoritative judgement that his action was unacceptable.

Some would add a third, in some ways connected strand to these two sources of censure theory. This third strand had to do with a growing perception that a feature of modern societies is that major areas of social life are annexed by state bureaucracies in a way that alienates people from official forms of decision-making. This theme, associated in the UK with the New Left amongst other groups, emerges in phenomena such as the restorative justice movement, and in Nils Christie's famous paper, 'Conflicts as Property', in which he argues that the state has stolen conflicts from participants who would be better left to sort them out for themselves.[8] These views are often morally serious about crime, and are concerned with recovering a sense of the moral significance of wrongdoing for its main participants. The thought is that the moral seriousness of crime, its moral reality, can be lost when it is appropriated by a state concerned purely with the efficient solving of social problems. Some versions of this critique are explicitly anti-statist. But for others, it is not so much the state that is the problem, as the fact that the particular procedures the state deploys to deal with important areas of social life such as crime are concerned only with the efficient overall management of human resources, and thus distort their importance, emptying them of meaning. Important human dramas, Christie argued, become mired in procedures that fail to resonate with the significance their original participants would

---

[4] A von Hirsch, *Doing Justice: The Choice of Punishments* (Report of the Committee for the Study of Incarceration) (New York, Hill and Wang, 1976).

[5] See P Devlin, *The Enforcement of Morals* (Oxford, Oxford University Press, 1965); HLA Hart, *Law, Liberty and Morality* (Oxford, Clarendon Press, 1963).

[6] J Feinberg, 'Some Unswept Debris From the Hart-Devlin Debate' (1987) 72 *Synthese* 249.

[7] J Feinberg, 'The Expressive Function of Punishment' (1965) 49 *The Monist* 397.

[8] N Christie, 'Conflicts as Property' (1977) 17 *British Journal of Criminology* 1.

have ascribed to them. The state deals with these issues as problems of efficient social management, whereas for their 'stakeholders' they are problems about building and maintaining relationships, and taking seriously the values inherent in such relationships. I say that this is a possible source of censure theory, because theories that make censure central to their account of punishment might share this aspiration of 'humanising' state institutions by insisting that they need not be simply driven by technical matters of behaviour management, but can be a vehicle to reflect people's deep considered views about the moral significance of crime.

II. QUESTIONS THAT A CENSURE THEORY MUST ANSWER

However promising the turn to censure theory might be, any such theory will nevertheless have to give satisfactory answers to a number of questions. First, why is it important for the state to express censure, and in particular through punishment? Should censure be what Hart called the general justifying aim of punishment, and if so why?[9] Why is it worth setting up a huge and costly state apparatus in order to censure people? One sceptical view is that censure is all very well as a method of social control for small-scale groups, but that it will not do as an account of state punishment, where the job of defending individual and societal interests against threats of harm is far more urgent and people cannot always be expected to be stopped by a quiet word or an appeal to conscience. Another view, more accommodating of censure but nevertheless giving it only an instrumental and subsidiary role, might say that censure is all well and good because, in our particular social conditions, it is (one of) the best available means to reduce crime.[10] But this instrumentalist view does not give censure a distinctive justificatory role in its own right. That is, it is not committed to the claim that the state has sufficient reason, independently of crime-reduction aims, to operate an institution of censure. It does not see censure as a legitimate and important state aim in its own right. In this essay I will think of censure theories as those that *do* take censure to be a sufficiently important end for the state in its own right. Such theories need to explain why it is that (certain forms of) wrongdoing should be censured by the state.

Secondly, there are questions about the relation between the goal of censure and the form that such censuring takes in the operation of the system. Can censure be simply verbal? Or is the punishment itself required in order for

---

[9] HLA Hart, 'Prolegomenon to the Principles of Punishment' (1960) 60 *Proceedings of the Aristotelian Society (New Series)* 1; reprinted in HLA Hart, *Punishment and Responsibilty*, 2nd edn edited by J Gardner (Oxford, Oxford University Press, 2008).

[10] Cf J Braithwaite and P Pettit, *Not Just Deserts: A Republican Theory of Criminal Justice* (Oxford, Oxford University Press, 1993).

censure to be meaningful? If the latter, why is punishment the only, or the most adequate, way to express moral disapproval? These are questions in particular about the justification of the use of hard treatment in censure, and whether the need for hard treatment is internal to the goal of censure (so that a successful justification of censure will itself justify the use of hard treatment, perhaps as a condition of the meaningfulness of the censure), or whether the use of hard treatment needs its own separate justification in terms other than censure.[11]

Thirdly, what is the relation between state censure and our interpersonal moral practices of holding one another to account, of criticising unacceptable behaviour, of blaming, apologising and forgiving? One of the apparently attractive things about the censure view is that it treats the offender as a moral agent. But treating someone as a moral agent means treating him as someone whose acts have the moral consequences that we take them to have in everyday practice – that when you wrong someone you become liable to blame, anger, withdrawal and so on, to expectations that you will apologise, to requiring some kind of re-acceptance and reconciliation. So does the censure view seek to connect state punishment to those practices?

Fourthly, given that one of the apparent attractions of censure theory is its provision of determinate, proportionate punishments that fit the crime rather than the criminal, how does the censure theory deal with proportionality? There are perhaps two aspects to this question. One is what the censure theory's view is of the basis of proportionality judgements. And the other is how precise proportionality judgements are capable of being, if they are to do the work of censure, and to what extent precision matters. Connected with this point is the question whether censure theory is capable of providing determinate guidance for sentencing theory, and whether it should take itself to be in that business.

III. VON HIRSCH'S CENSURE THEORY

The spirit of von Hirsch's answers to these questions could perhaps be summed as follows (and here I draw largely on the account given in *Censure and Sanctions*).[12] The point of censure is that the institutions of social control must recognise our

---

[11] For engagement with the issues raised in this paragraph, see especially the chapters by Kleinig and von Hirsch in this volume.

[12] See von Hirsch, above n 1, esp at 9–19. It is important to note that, although this remains the canonical statement of it, von Hirsch's position has altered in subtle ways since this publication. An example is in his contribution to the present volume, where different levels of hard treatment are now treated as essential to being able to express different levels of censure (ie for more or less serious crimes). While acknowledging these alterations, I thought it important to set out and discuss the position in *Censure and Sanctions* in this part of my chapter. The canonical position is still so influential that is it worth discussing in its own right. But also it is in part through understanding the tensions in the canonical position that we can evaluate the subsequent alterations – that is, from the perspective of my own argument, we can see why eg giving hard treatment a tighter relation to the goal of censure, in order to accommodate proportionality, is a positive development.

identity as moral agents rather than just engaging in 'tiger control'. The importance of censure is not simply reducible to its being the best available means for social control, as on the instrumentalist view. Rather, censure has an important role in its own right. Censure recognises criminal action as wrongdoing and therefore also has the benefit that it vindicates victims, and acknowledges that what was done to them was unjustifiable. However, censure does not have to be expressed through punishment; it could equally well be expressed symbolically or verbally. The fact that we do express it through hard treatment is because we recognise the benefits of the threat of hard treatment in lowering crime. Were there no such preventive benefits this would not make the institution of censure redundant, since censure has an importance in its own right; but if this were to be the case there would be no reason for the expression of censure to involve hard treatment at all. However, the fact that the use of hard treatment is 'optional' does not prevent different levels of hard treatment expressing different degrees of censure (that is, for different degrees of seriousness of wrongdoing). The more serious the wrongdoing, the more severe the punishment. The gauging of the seriousness of crimes, however, is not simply a matter of intuition but a function of culpability and of the harm caused; and the harm component at least can be quantified to some extent on the basis that it concerns the impact of the crime on a person's 'living standard'. This is the basis of ordinal proportionality, or of the ranking of crimes from least serious to most serious, with sufficient spacing in between (and consistency across relevantly similar cases). We can make such ordinal judgements reasonably determinate. The living standard analysis also provides a basis on which we can make some quantification of punishments, and in such a way we can make judgements about punishments being excessive. However, cardinal proportionality – the correlation between a particular crime and a particular level of punishment – is conventional, though not without general moral limits such that we could recognise some punitive regimes as being excessively draconian.

How does von Hirsch's theory answer our key questions for censure theory? Let me leave the first question for last, since I think it is not straightforward to address. However, what is clearer is that in answer to the second question – what form does censure have to take – von Hirsch's answer is that the only necessary form that it has to take is something that will communicate a judgement of disapproval of wrongdoing. No other particular symbolic form is required. It is clearly possible, on von Hirsch's view, to communicate censure by proportionate punishment, and where varying the hard treatment varies the level of censure. But he thinks nothing morally important would be lost if we did not use hard treatment. On the third question, about the relation between punitive state censure and our practices of accountability (blame, apology and forgiveness), von Hirsch is largely agnostic. He certainly doesn't have the view that it is the perspective of these practices that is at the root of our sense that some actions require censure by the state. To answer the fourth question, about the basis of proportionality and the importance of precision, it seems clear that von Hirsch has always attempted to formulate his account in a way that will provide guidance for sentencing theory. This is an important and admirable goal. And clearly any theory of punishment has practical implications. Nevertheless, we should also recognise that this aspiration might push us to neglect the limitations of censure theory. It may be that censure theory *by itself* provides at best wide and indeterminate guidance about proportionality, and that, if precision is desired, it can only be achieved by supplementing the censure view, either explicitly or implicitly. So what is the basis of proportionality on von Hirsch's view? The official answer is that proportionality is required by the goals of censure.[13] That is all very well. But what the goals of censure are is not yet settled. To settle the issue we will really need to return to the first question, that of why we should have an institution of state censure in the first place. Without an answer to that question we don't really know what censure is doing and what demands it needs to satisfy. As a way of getting at this question, we might ask what is wrong, in von Hirsch's view, with disproportionate punishments. What is wrong with excessive, cardinally disproportionate punishments is clear: that the offender's interests are set back more than they needed to be. But what about failures of ordinal proportionality? If two offenders who have committed the same crimes are treated differently – if there is a failure of parity – then there is an unfairness done to (one of) the offenders. But what if there were insufficient spacing, or a mistaken rank ordering? We can't say what would be wrong with mistaken rank ordering until we have explained why proportionate censure is something the state is required to mete out. That takes us back to the first question.

So why does von Hirsch think that the state should be in the business of censuring crime? In one way the answer to this might seem obvious. Criminals are blameworthy – what they have done merits censure. However, that answer by itself is in fact insufficient, since there are blameworthy actions going on all the time that we don't censure, and don't expect the state to censure. Furthermore, it is not clear that this yet provides an answer to the question of what would be amiss if the state did not have an institution of censure. Does von Hirsch have an answer to that?

IV. WHY SHOULD THE STATE CENSURE WRONGDOING?

The idea of punishment as censure, particularly in von Hirsch's hands, could be seen as a way to recover and articulate something that was important in the retributive tradition of thinking about punishment, but which got lost in the blaze of criticism over retributivism's apparent commitment to the intrinsic goodness of the suffering of the morally bad. This important idea is that punishment responds to offenders (and suspects) as moral agents, that it treats

---

[13] And this is certainly the answer given in von Hirsch's chapter in the present collection.

them as accountable, as having acted for reasons, and therefore as having the kind of control over and responsibility for action that we take for granted in our everyday interpersonal dealings.[14] When I am trying to arrange a meeting with you, or write a paper with you, or run a family with you, or buy something from you, I am not just treating you as a system of inputs and behavioural outputs that I attempt to manipulate in order to bring about the best (for myself or for society as a whole).

One doesn't have to be a retributivist, of course, to agree that human agents are more than systems of inputs and outputs, and should be respected as such. However, the retributive tradition – at least in what has been called its positive strand – has sometimes drawn on this presumed fact about our responsiveness to reasons to argue that there is also some reason in its own right that wrongdoers should get their just deserts; and that by extension the state, if it is best placed to do so, should be the one to carry this out. The corollary of this in censure theory would be the view that wrongdoers should receive 'just censure' – and it is this view that I propose to consider here. On this view, there would be something lacking in a state that did not have an institution of censure, whether or not it was also an institution of punishment.

What could be the argument for this positive version of censure theory? The argument, very briefly sketched, might go something like this. In both our thinking and our action, we are responsive to reasons. This is not to say that we always comply with those reasons, but that those reasons state a standard to which our thought and action has to answer. Furthermore, our reason-responsiveness is not merely internal. We are the sort of reason-responsive creatures who are capable of engaging in interpersonal thought and discussion about which reasons we should take seriously and act on; and when we act on bad reasons, we can appropriately be held accountable, and subject to criticism in which our faulty thinking is pointed out. To be treated as one who cannot be subject to criticism would be to be treated as an agent who is not responsive to reasons. Assuming that moral reasons are amongst the reasons to which we are responsive, we can therefore be subject to moral criticism. Not all faults should be subject to criticism, of course – that would lead to a stultifying culture of judgementalism, and moralism in the pejorative sense. But in some contexts, and for some wrongs, it *can* be important to express moral criticism. And although

---

[14] The idea that this is an important part of the retributive tradition can be traced back to H Morris, 'Persons and Punishment' (1968) 52 *Monist* 475, and to the way Morris's view was taken up by eg JG Murphy, 'Marxism and Retribution' (1973) 2 *Philosophy and Public Affairs* 217 and J Finnis, 'The Restoration of Retribution' (1972) 32 *Analysis* 131. It was a Morris-type view of retribution as a restoration of a fair balance of benefits and burdens that informed von Hirsch's early work, such as *Doing Justice*, above n 4; however, this view was subjected to an influential set of criticisms by RA Duff in the development of his communicative theory of punishment in *Trials and Punishments* (Cambridge, Cambridge University Press, 1986). By the time of *Censure and Sanctions* (above n 1), von Hirsch had moved decisively to the censure model. It is a censure theory justification of the view that I sketch below, rather than a fair balance version.

sometimes we criticise people only when there is some further end we seek to achieve by doing so, sometimes the faults are such that their deservingness of censure itself, or the need to mark or acknowledge the gravity of the wrong, is sufficient reason to give expression to the criticism. Therefore it can sometimes be neglectful of the seriousness of wrongdoing, and of the perpetrator's identity as an agent competent to respond to moral reasons, if we do not subject him to moral criticism.

Now, von Hirsch doesn't advert explicitly to this positive version of the thesis. His way of making this point tends rather to be negative, arguing that wrongdoers are properly seen as blameworthy, and that on this basis punishment needs to be more than just 'tiger control'. This is a negative version of the thesis because it is to argue for respecting moral agency as a *constraint* on other goals rather than as a goal in its own right. It is to resist having to argue for what I earlier said was the characteristic claim of censure theory, namely, that censure is a sufficiently important goal of the state.

Nevertheless, for reasons that we shall now see, it seems wrong to classify von Hirsch as holding only the negative thesis. I will argue that von Hirsch *is* committed to the positive argument that the state has a sufficient reason to have an institution of censure, but that his writings have not addressed the justification for this claim that his position requires. The main reason for thinking that von Hirsch is committed to the positive thesis is that the negative thesis is compatible with all sorts of ways of respecting the offender as a moral agent, whereas von Hirsch's view emphasises censure, and takes it that only by having a censure aspect can a deterrent or protective institution of punishment be made compatible with respect for moral agency. The negative thesis is that respect for moral agency is only a constraint on goals such as that of social control. If von Hirsch held only the negative thesis then all he could consistently claim is that social control needs to be carried out in such a way as to respect moral agency, but where it is an open question in any situation what will be necessary to respect moral agency. However, that is not his view. Rather his view is that *censure* in particular is necessary as a response to certain kinds of wrongdoing. It is not an open question, for von Hirsch, what treatment *of offenders* is necessary to respect their moral agency, for he thinks the answer is that censure is necessary. Yet because von Hirsch does not explicitly give us something like the positive argument for censure that I sketched above, this claim goes undefended.

To press the point, consider the possibility that there might be ways in which social control could be carried out that would respect those involved as moral agents, but that would not involve the expression of censure. The burden of von Hirsch's criticism of pure deterrent or social control views is that being subjected to purely deterrent or incapacitative treatment would be insulting to the offender by ignoring his/her identity as a moral agent, that is, as one capable of understanding and reasoning practically about moral rules and values. But would it always be insulting to treat someone simply as a danger and not as a moral agent? For instance, say you are carrying an infectious disease, which you don't know about; but I know, and I urgently need to get you into quarantine. Is it not permissible for, or even required of, me to do everything within my power to stop you infecting other innocent people, even if I can't get you to understand the necessity for the quarantine?[15] In urgent situations where there is no time to explain the reasons, it seems that it might be quite proportionate simply to bundle you into quarantine. Would that be like tiger control? Well, maybe. But what is wrong or disrespectful in subjecting a person to what amounts to tiger control in such a high-stakes time-limited situation? Assuming that deterrent punishment could – at least in some cases – be precisely that kind of appropriate response to a high-stakes time-limited situation, what would be wrong or disrespectful in these cases in subjecting someone to deterrent punishment? Or maybe one thinks that in order for an intervention not to be tiger control there has to be at least some attempt to *justify* what one is doing to the other person; that there must be some attempt to explain to him the reasons for it, and why such treatment is necessary (since moral agents are precisely those who are amenable to grasping such justifications and seeing their force). But then, applied to punishment, if a person were punished purely for preventive or deterrent reasons, it surely wouldn't simply be tiger control if they had it explained to them why it was necessary to treat them in that way. Either way, then, it seems that persons could be punished for social control reasons, and yet at the same time be perfectly well respected as moral agents, but without their having to be subject to moral criticism for their behaviour.

The problem we are considering can be summarised as follows. If von Hirsch were to treat respect for moral agency merely as a constraint on otherwise warranted deterrent or preventive interventions, he would be unable to justify his conclusion that, in the context of criminal justice, such interventions would be disrespectful unless they also involved censure. For while there are ways of imposing deterrent or preventive treatment that *are* disrespectful, it seems that in certain circumstances such interventions might be perfectly compatible with the demands of respect. Yet it is clear from his writings that von Hirsch does believe that censure is a necessary component of to criminal justice measures, the component that redeems them and makes them compatible with respect for moral agency. To arrive at the conclusions von Hirsch defends, we need to show why it would be disrespectful to offenders not to subject them to censure, and not to mark the difference between cases of culpable and non-culpable harm-creation. Thus we need to fill the gap in von Hirsch's stated view by providing a positive account of the role of accountability relations in our interpersonal dealing. This, I believe, would be to argue that there are some contexts in which we

---

[15] In a joint paper with Antony Duff, von Hirsch argues in similar terms that the state may 'coercively quarantine a carrier of a dangerously contagious disease' and that in this, and certain other, contexts, 'the state's use of its coercive power is not constrained by responsibility requirements to the degree it is in the criminal law': see A Duff and A von Hirsch, 'Responsibility, Retribution and the "Voluntary": A Response to Williams' (1997) 56 *Cambridge Law Journal* 103 at 104.

owe it to a person to respond to him in ways that hold him to account for what he has done. If, in these contexts, one simply treated the offender as a danger to be neutralised one would then be failing to treat him as one should – one would be failing to see him and deal with him in the way that should have been most salient in that context, ie as an accountable agent. If one could make this positive argument one would have a way of articulating the intuition that adopting a purely deterrent or preventive approach would involve losing something of value, without being saddled with the implausible view that any action that has preventive or deterrent aims, and which leaves out censure, is impermissible and insulting.

In order to do that we would need a sympathetic articulation of the meaning and value of our practices of accountability: for example, of what underpins our sense that people ought to apologise for their wrongful actions; that they can stand in need of forgiveness before everyday business with them can be resumed; that reactions like distancing or, by contrast, angry confrontation, can be necessary when the wrongdoer is not prepared to apologise and try to put things right. By articulating the value of relating to people in the ways constituted by this set of accountability reactions, we would then have an explanation of what is wrong when these accountability reactions are ignored or displaced by the purely preventive – when the person is left out or excluded from the community defined by normative expectations and obligations to answer for one's conduct. This suggests that the way to plug the gap in von Hirsch's account is for censure theorists to think more carefully about my question number three: the link between state censure of crime and censure as it operates in our everyday practices of accountability, where liability to censure figures as a marker of inclusion within those practices. A successful censure theory needs some attempt to articulate the value of these practices and the value of inclusion within them.

V. ELEMENTS OF A POSITIVE VON HIRSCHIAN CENSURE THEORY

As I have understood it here, a censure theory that follows von Hirsch's lead has to articulate a positive role for censure that does not see it simply as a means to crime reduction goals, as the instrumentalist does, or as nothing more than a constraint on the pursuit of such goals, as the purely negative thesis does. However, such a censure theory also has to disprove the null hypothesis, as it were. It has to explain why in any situation there is something wrong with doing nothing. As we noted above in sketching the positive argument in favour of censure, it is too simple to think that we should criticise one another for all our failures of reasoning, or that morality requires us to censure all moral wrongdoing. If we are always on the look-out for one another's failings, and quick to call one another out, this would lead to a culture of mutual suspicion, mistrust, and a lack of individual privacy and room for authenticity, spontaneity and experimentation. Thus it is not always one's business to concern oneself with others' moral character, and not always even with the way they treat others (though there can be a point at which protecting the vulnerable trumps the need to respect others' rights to be left alone). My wrongdoing is not always your business. But this suggests that doing nothing in the face of wrongdoing is a real option, and perhaps often the right option. We therefore need some account of when it is wrong to do nothing in the face of wrongdoing, and why in those circumstances it is wrong; and we need an account specifically of why censure is necessary in those circumstances, and thus of why it would be wrong not to censure.

The kind of account that censure theory is looking for will therefore have to explain three things. First, it has to explain the character of the wrong involved in failing to censure. Secondly, it will have to explain something about the kinds of circumstances in which it is wrong not to censure, and what makes those circumstances special. And thirdly, it will have to explain how all this relates to punishment and the actual operation of sentencing in a criminal justice system.

If this is the right way for a von Hirschian account to proceed, we have to bear in mind that the account of what is wrong with failing to censure cannot be an instrumentalist one. According to the instrumentalist, the point of censuring is only to further certain independent goals to which censuring is the best available means. The instrumentalist therefore has an answer to the question of when it is wrong to fail to censure. It is wrong to fail to censure, on the instrumentalist view, whenever one's censure would have led to the production of benefits, or the avoidance of harms, which could not have been produced/avoided in any more cost-effective way. If censure is justified simply in terms of its tendency to inhibit harmful behaviour then it is wrong not to express censure in those circumstances in which it would have been cost-effective in doing so. While the censure theory we are thinking of here can avail itself of foreseen benefits such as this, the production of benefits and avoidance of harm cannot be the whole story in the justification of censure. To put it in terms of a well-known dichotomy, the instrumentalist account gives a purely forward-looking account of the explanation of what is wrong with failing to censure, appealing to benefits and harms that are independent of the offence but might be produced by various ways of responding to the offence; whereas the censure account is fundamentally backward-looking, and has to do, in some sense, with the offence itself.

Once we have put the matter this way, however, it might look as though the censure theorist has not left herself very much room for manoeuvre. What kind of story can we appeal to that will explain what is wrong with failing to censure, but where this explanation appeals simply to 'the offence itself'? In order to fill out this positive account, I think, we need to turn to another neglected aspect of the retributive tradition. Again, this has nothing to do with the supposed importance of making bad people suffer. Rather it has to do with the need not to acquiesce in the wrongdoing of others. In other words, the backward-looking view does not quite take its starting point from 'the offence itself,' but from the relation that the person censuring (or not) has to the offence, and whether that relation is a permissible one or not. Central to the retributive tradition is the thought that, as a non-contingent matter, it can be wrong not to make certain kinds of responses to wrongdoing. On a simple form of retributivism, this might be the view that it is somehow wrong not to pursue the suffering of the perpetrator, and to avenge oneself or the victim on him. But more sophisticated forms of retributivism will have the same structure: they simply involve more sophisticated views about what the appropriate responses to wrongdoing can be (for instance, distancing the wrongdoer or altering one's relationship with him; the wrongdoer feeling guilty, or making amends, etc). These more sophisticated forms of retributivism will still take it to be wrong, as a non-contingent matter, not to engage in those appropriate responses. But what kind of wrong can that be, which is not contingent on the harms or benefits that might stem from one's action or inaction? My thought is that it must be a wrong that involves a failure to stand in the right relation to the offence and to the offender: that sometimes when we fail to censure wrongdoing, we are effectively consenting to it, acquiescing in it, condoning it, and hence becoming complicit in it. The central thought on this aspect of the retributive tradition is that it is wrong to allow the original offence to persist, unanswered. When it does, we are implicated in the wrongdoing unless we do something to dissociate ourselves from it; and it is the act of censure that does the dissociating.

As we have seen, however, it is not *always* wrong not to censure wrongdoing; for it is not always the case that we are implicated in the wrongdoing unless we dissociate ourselves from it. Sometimes the null hypothesis is quite right. Indeed, the default position may well be that wrongdoing places us under no particular duty to dissociate ourselves from it. There is wrongdoing going on all over the place as I write and yet here I am blithely typing away. More plausibly, then, it is because of some special relation that one has to the circumstances of the offence and to those involved in it that one would be implicated in the wrongdoing if one were not to dissociate oneself from it. Yet sometimes there are such special relations, and in those cases one has reasons to dissociate.

The view that we have reasons to avoid complicity in the wrongdoing of others, and that these can be the most fundamental reasons that we have to censure others, to which instrumental reasons are additional, might raise some concerns. One likely worry is that this view sounds like moral self-indulgence.[16] Is the concern to have 'the right relation' to the offence not a self-centred matter of keeping one's hands clean? And does that not distract attention from the real matter of concern, which is how the victims have been treated?[17]

---

[16] Thanks to Antje du Bois-Pedain and Tatjana Hörnle for forcefully raising this concern.

[17] It is worth noting that this is the basic form of one influential criticism that consequentialists make of non-consequentialist ethics. It is characteristic of non-consequentialism that it demands that agents 'draw a line', as it were, and refuse to do certain things, no matter what the consequences. Maybe I think, for instance, that we should never launch a nuclear weapon that will kill indiscriminately even if doing so were the only recourse we had against an unjust attack that would

Although I agree that it is the victims that should be the central matter of concern, I find these criticisms unpersuasive. As I understand it, it is a fundamental moral task for each of us to determine where we stand on the things that go on around us, and whether we are prepared to live with them or not. The decision to censure can simply be an expression of revolt against some event, something in us that says that we cannot accept it, and that we stand against it. I think this is a familiar and morally important experience. Furthermore, it is not enough to see such reactions as simply our letting off steam. This would be an explanation of these reactions that was psychological rather than moral – that pointed to the quirks of our individual psychology, as if it would have been acceptable just to have been a bit more patient, or a bit less hot-headed. Of course, sometimes our reactions are simply letting off steam, or grandstanding, or signalling to those whose respect we desire. Sometimes, however, they are virtuous, and not self-absorbed: for instance, when we have to express our inability to tolerate even those things that we cannot change. More adequate, therefore, is the view that what is going on in such situations is that we are faced with some moral necessity not to treat wrongs as though they were permissible, and that it is constitutive of treating them as impermissible that we censure them. We withdraw our consent from those things, as it were, opposing them even when we cannot now change them, by expressing our censure.

Therefore the view that we can have weighty reasons to dissociate ourselves from wrongdoing by censuring it does not call on us to replace concern for the victim of wrongdoing with concern for one's own moral character. Rather the need for dissociation is an expression of revolt at the way the victim was treated, and an inability – a moral inability – to stand by and treat it as something that just happens, or is someone else's business. Therefore one's feeling of complicity in the offence, should one say nothing, is intimately bound up with the sense that, with one's silence, one would be letting the victim down.

Furthermore, it is also worth noting that there is an important sense in which a failure to censure can involve letting the wrongdoer down. To treat a wrongdoer as if her actions can cause us to be complicit is to treat her as someone whose actions can have an impact on us. We do not choose that others should do wrong, but sometimes they do; and on the view being put forward here,

---

kill, just as indiscriminately, an even larger number of victims on our side. Such weapons are so evil in their destructive power that I want nothing to do with them. My position is therefore non-consequentialist in the sense that it refuses to see the beneficial consequences as justifying the use of nuclear weapons. But, the consequentialist might say, when you say you want nothing to do with nuclear weapons, aren't you simply keeping your hands clean? Well, am I? Or is it rather that, as Bernard Williams thought, there is a virtue (of integrity) in standing for something, and that the consequence of having integrity is that one feel oneself unable to cross certain lines? (See B Williams, 'A Critique of Utilitarianism' in JJC Smart and B Williams, *Utilitarianism: For and Against* (Cambridge, Cambridge University Press, 1973) 77 at 93–118.) Because I don't find the consequentialist criticism of non-consequentialism very persuasive, I am not too troubled by the related criticism of my claims about complicity.

even though we cannot change the fact that they did what they did, we sometimes have an obligation to do the next best thing, which is to express our opposition to what they did, the result of which is that we can have duties, unbidden, to dissociate ourselves from those actions. That means that the actions of (some) others can have an impact on us, independently of whether we choose them to. To regard someone as one whose actions can have an impact on one in this way is to regard them as being in some kind of community with one; to disregard that, and to act as though there is not complicity in question, is to repudiate such community. This is the sense in which the failure to react to the offender by dissociating from her action can be to exclude her: for it is to treat her as though there was no community existing between you such that her actions would have any call on you.

I have argued that a successful censure theory – as we have understood it here as a positive but non-instrumental justification for a censuring response to crime – rests on an account of the need for dissociation from wrongdoing. Now readers who have followed the argument up to this point might agree that the phenomenon of complicity and dissociation that I have attempted to evoke is a recognisable part of the moral life. However, they might say, it seems a big step from this to the claim that this is also what is going on in the fundamental justification of a society's criminal justice system. Some might worry that claiming that the state, or its citizens, would be complicit in wrongdoing if they did not censure wrongdoing, might seem little better than metaphorical. How are we to make that conclusion plausible? Of course, one way to go would be to acknowledge that the criminal justice system as envisaged by the censure theory, although it makes sense, is not particularly important as a part of a modern polity. However, although I think we should always have that possibility before our eyes when dealing with any questions about the institution of punishment, it may be that this defeatist conclusion is too quick. So let us turn to our second question, that of the circumstances in which we can become complicit in others' wrongdoing. We are not always in the kind of community with others such that responsibilities arise for us to take a stand on their wrongdoing. But sometimes we are. One such case is worth briefly mentioning here, as it is directly relevant to the case of punishment, and to censure as the justifying purpose of punishment.

The worry might be that complicity can only come about from direct engagement with wrongdoing ('aiding and abetting, counselling or procuring', as the law has it), and therefore that the claim that the state or citizens would be complicit in wrongdoing were they not to censure cannot be sustained. Nevertheless, the law seems not to agree. At any rate, as Andrew Ashworth and Jeremy Horder note, the law does seem to recognise cases of what we might call complicity through normative control;[18] and I want to argue that such cases can

---

[18] J Horder, *Ashworth's Principles of Criminal Law*, 8th edn (Oxford, Oxford University Press, 2016) 440.

form a basis for a reasonable theory of the need for dissociation. In such cases, the wrongdoing of the complicit parties does not consist in their having direct control over an outcome – as one does who actually passes a murder weapon to the principal, or who distracts the security guard so that a crime can occur – but rather in their having authority over some domain in which the crime is committed, and hence control over whether the criminal act is done with their permission or not. An example is the case of a car owner who permits another to engage in reckless behaviour while driving the car.[19] It need not necessarily be the case that the owner could have prevented the reckless driving. Hence it is not necessary that the owner had physical control over whether the crime came about. The owner's wrong is not therefore a failure to exercise such physical control. The wrong rather centres on the fact that the owner could and should have made it clear that the reckless behaviour was not happening with his permission. He should have withdrawn his consent from it, a power he had as the owner of the car with normative control over the domain in which the crime was committed.

Now, we can draw a line between this kind of case and the claim that citizens and state can indeed be complicit in individuals' wrongdoing, as the same structural features are in place in both cases. One aspect of the circumstances of modern political community is that the state (or citizens as a whole where the state is a democratic one) has authority over the domain in which crimes are committed. This is not the case for every form of life, but applies to what are recognisably law-governed societies. What I mean by authority is simply that the state has a legal power through which it can determine whether some act is (legally) permissible or impermissible. The law is an apparatus by which the state can mark acts as impermissible, putting citizens under a legal obligation not to perform them. If we assume that the state does in fact possess authority in making such acts impermissible, then we can say that by virtue of these structures of legal regulation, the state now has a legal power to determine whether criminal actions are done with its permission or not. If this seems plausible, we can say that, wherever the state does not mark some act as impermissible, it regards it as permissible. It does not always have the power to prevent wrongdoing from occurring, but it has the power to determine whether the wrongdoing happens with its permission or not. Now, on the assumption that there are principles governing which acts it should mark as impermissible and which not, it can be complicit in allowing some acts to be permissible where it should have made them impermissible. In such a case there is something very much like complicity that comes about through a failure to criminalise, and the same argument applies (in principle at least) to a failure to censure violations of criminal law. The obligation to censure comes about as a result of the need to mark violations

---

[19] *Du Cros v Lambourne* [1907] 1 KB 40.

of the criminal law as cases of wrongdoing that were done without the state's permission: it would be complicity through the state's failure to make clear its attitude of disapproval of certain acts by marking them as impermissible. Here the state would indeed have duties to censure, and would be complicit in virtue of acquiescing in wrongdoing over which it had normative control. If the citizens of the state can intelligibly be seen as joint holders of the legal power to mark acts as impermissible, then they can also be seen as implicated in the failure to censure. If this sounds plausible, the idea of the state being under a duty to dissociate may at least be one that is worth further exploration.[20]

VI. SOME IMPLICATIONS OF RECONSTRUCTING VON HIRSCH'S VIEW

I have claimed that von Hirsch's view must be supplemented by an attempt to explain why there is a positive role for censure. The answer I have suggested is that censure is necessary because – but only insofar as – if there were no censure we would be complicit in the actions of others, and we must dissociate ourselves from them by marking those acts as wrong, and distancing ourselves from them. We are at risk of such complicity when we stand in certain kinds of relations of community with the wrongdoer, such that we would be acquiescing in her action if we were not to dissociate ourselves from it. Censure does that distancing. If this account is successful, it provides something lacking from, but needed by von Hirsch's account.

Some implications of the foregoing should quickly be noted, relating to the second, third and fourth questions raised in section II. First of all, in relation to the question of whether we should follow von Hirsch in thinking that the form that censure takes can be merely verbal, I think we have found reasons to dispute this. From the point of view of the theory developed in section V, the question is, 'What form does censure have to take if it is to dissociate the state from the wrongdoing?' Can a purely verbal expression of censure be enough? My reason for doubting this is that words are cheap, and that the crucial thing when expressing dissociation is to *show the way in which the wrongdoing matters*. It may be that for minor wrongdoing simply verbal censure would be enough, but more significant cases require something more to mark the moral breach involved. This relates to the question of the relation between state punishment and our everyday moral practices of accountability. Dissociation unavoidably takes place through action that is expressive and symbolic, and the state must find a symbolic language for marking the action as wrong: but where else could it find such a thing other than in our fundamental practices of accountability? Censure that does not appeal to the ways in which we understand dissociation to come about in our practices of accountability would lack meaning, will not

---

[20] C Bennett, 'Complicity, Legal Power and Normative Control' (unpublished manuscript).

be capable of showing the way in which the wrongdoing matters, and will not be capable of dissociating the political community from wrongdoing. State censure can therefore be seen ideally as an institutional expression of accountability practices that structure everyday life in the polity. In that way the reconstructed censure view whose contours I have sketched here can perhaps lay a greater claim to speak to what I called in section I of this essay the third source of motivation for censure views, that they should 'humanise' state institutions and restore a sense of the moral significance of crime. Nevertheless, despite this connection to moral practice, it is not clear to me that the censure view would be suitable only for a small-scale or rather homogenous society, and unsuitable for large-scale political societies: the account is suitable for a society whose members understand themselves to be bound closely enough that what one person does impacts on others, not just by directly affecting them, but in a sense that they have to take a stand on whether such actions are going to be acceptable.

What, then, should censure theory say about proportionality? As with the basic understanding of what dissociation involves, the censure view we are now imagining takes the root source of our understanding of proportionality to be the moral practices that structure the everyday life of the polity. I take it that we have some understanding of how to answer such questions – enough to structure a practice in which we deliberate about what to do, discuss with others whether some suggested response is enough, criticise people for not doing enough (or too much), and have regrets about not doing enough. But the understanding we have is likely to be highly context-sensitive and perhaps uncodifiable. It may come more in the shape of responses to examples than in general principles. Furthermore, proportionality in responses to wrongdoing is contestable, and no doubt subject to reasonable disagreement and cultural difference. I think censure theory has to be fairly open about the lack of determinacy in our judgements of proportionality. That's not the end of the story, however. It simply raises the question of what the pros and cons are of allowing discretion at the point of sentencing. Or perhaps one job of democratic politics is to formulate reasonably precise standards of 'what fits the crime' in the shape of sentencing guidelines. At any rate, concerns that a censure theory does not give us a clear account of proportionality do not seem to me to point to a fatal flaw in the account. Many questions about proportionality simply cannot be decided without detailed examination of cases, and it may be that they have to be left to the discretion of an appropriately constructed and supervised sentencing process.

VII. CONCLUSION

In this paper I have attempted to do justice to Andreas von Hirsch's fertile writings on the topic of censure theory. I have assessed von Hirsch's view in terms of the questions that a censure theory has to have answers for, and as a result I have found it necessary to supplement a von Hirschian approach in some important ways. I have argued that von Hirsch's view pays too little attention to the question of what the moral basis of an institution of censure is, and that as a result we are ultimately left unable to give full answers to the other questions that a censure theory has to deal with. I think that once we fill the gaps we have reason to draw some implications from censure theory that challenge some of the conclusions that von Hirsch himself draws. Nevertheless, the theory that we have ended up with is one that, I believe, recognisably takes inspiration from von Hirsch's seminal work.

Part II

Censure and Just Deserts Revisited: Issues for Desert Theory

5

Censure and Hard Treatment in the General Justification for Punishment: A Reconceptualisation of Desert-oriented Penal Theory

ANDREAS VON HIRSCH

PUNISHMENT, AS JOEL Feinberg asserts,[1] has two principal characteristics: censure and hard treatment. The censure element is extensively addressed in the recent literature of penal desert. The hard treatment element, however, has been less adequately explored. Here, I undertake a reassessment of the role of hard treatment, its relation to censure, and its bearing on why punishment should exist.

I. THE SCALING ROLE OF HARD TREATMENT

My earlier proposed rationale for the general justification of punishment can be characterised as a dual theory of 'censure plus deterrence'.[2] That model conceptualised the hard treatment element of punishment chiefly as furnishing a deterrent against injurious conduct.[3] I now think that this approach understated the role of hard treatment. In this chapter, I argue that hard treatment also has a salient role in the censure dimension of punishment's general justification: that is, as providing a scaling role that acts as the vehicle through which penal censure is expressed.

---

[1] J Feinberg, 'The Expressive Function of Punishment' in J Feinberg, *Doing and Deserving: Essays in the Theory of Responsibility* (Princeton NJ, Princeton University Press, 1970).

[2] This rationale is summarised in A von Hirsch, *Deserved Criminal Sentences: An Overview* (Oxford, Hart/Bloomsbury Publishing, 2017) ch 3.

[3] In that model, the censuring role of hard treatment was considered primarily when addressing the issue of quanta of punishment (the criteria for proportionality in sentencing) rather than as part of the general justification of punishment.

The scaling role of hard treatment has two aspects in the expression of penal censure: first, its amplifying function; and secondly, its grading function. Let me consider each in turn.

A. The Amplifying Function

The amplifying function of hard treatment was first addressed by John Kleinig in a 1991 essay.[4] His argument was that censure for criminal misconduct cannot adequately be conveyed purely through mere verbal or symbolic expressions of blame. The hard treatment embodied in the sanction is needed in order to convey the disapprobation with the requisite emphasis.

The amplification effect of hard treatment in expressing disapprobation is mirrored by the amplificatory effect of rewards in expressing approbation. The Nobel Prize would have less commendatory force, for example, were it merely expressed symbolically or verbally – say, by a plaque or a letter of congratulation from the Swedish Academy. In punishment, the amplifying function is served through hard treatment's 'reinforcement' feature, as Kleinig suggested. The hard treatment serves to augment the expressive force of the disapprobation conveyed. Where a serious offence is involved, for example, imposing a significant penal deprivation serves to express the requisite strong disapprobation – in a manner that mere words or symbols could not.

B. The Grading Function

Expressing censure through differing amounts of hard treatment serves also a *grading* function, of scaling the degrees of disapprobation expressed by the penal responses – so as to reflect crimes' varying degrees of seriousness, as a desert rationale requires. The communicative conventions of our culture provide insufficient resources for giving expression to differing degrees of reprobation through mere words or symbols. There exists no high priest who may credibly convey, through his words or ceremonies, how much more reprehensible robbery is than burglary. When censure is expressed through graduated doses of penal hard treatment, such grading effects can better be achieved.

Consider, here, the Swedish sentencing system. It provides for graduated levels of hard treatment for crimes of varying degrees of seriousness, ranging from small fines for minor offences; unit fines (measured by specified fractions of an offender's income) for intermediate crimes, and graded stints of imprisonment for more serious crimes – all depending on the degree of seriousness of

---

[4] J Kleinig, 'Punishment and Moral Seriousness' (1991) 25 *Israel Law Review* 401; also more fully Kleinig in this volume.

the conduct.[5] In a desert model, this grading function constitutes a critically important function of hard treatment in the penal system.

II. WHY LINK CENSURE TO HARD TREATMENT?

What is the rationale for this nexus between censure and hard treatment? *Why* should hard treatment thus be employed to express gradations of censure? Several matters should be considered here.

First, the link between censure and hard treatment is not straightforwardly analytic. No convincing philosophical argument is available that succeeds in deducing a purported entitlement to inflict penal hard treatment purely from conceptions of censure. Or at least, no such argument has occurred to me, nor have I seen a successful one in the recent literature on penal theory.[6] Using hard treatment to express censure constitutes, rather, a species of *symbolic action*: namely, doing something (imposing differing quanta of hard treatment) in order to express a judgement (of varying levels of disapprobation). So it constitutes the obverse of the performative utterance: instead of saying something to do something, we are doing something in order to express something. As with performative utterances, the criterion for success is not truth but appropriateness or 'fit'. With performative utterances, this is JL Austin's notion of 'felicitousness'.[7] For symbolic action, that norm might be termed 'symbolic appropriateness'.

Here, we also should invoke Peter Strawson's notion of *resentment*.[8] Hard treatment, in view of its unpleasantness, is suited to conveying (in addition to adverse normative judgements) such attitudes of resentment. In appropriate contexts (here, penalising wrongful conduct), such attitudes of resentment thus may be expressed through unwelcome treatment imposed on the perpetrator. Strawson's account of resentment – as expressing someone's warranted *animus* against another who has wronged him – may be traced back to Adam Smith's discussion of that conception in his *Theory of Moral Sentiments*.[9] Strawson's (and also Smith's) perspective is one of moral psychology – that certain feelings may be susceptible of normative analysis. Strawson's discussion of resentment refers chiefly to participants' reactions in everyday social interactions, when they feel they have been slighted or mistreated by others. Where a third party

---

[5] See N Jareborg, 'The Swedish Sentencing Reform' in C Clarkson and R Morgan (eds), *The Politics of Sentencing Reform* (Oxford, Clarendon Press, 1995).

[6] See further D Dolinko, 'Punishment' in J Deigh and D Dolinko (eds), *The Oxford Handbook of Philosophy of Criminal Law* (Oxford, Oxford University Press, 2011).

[7] JL Austin, *How to Do Things with Words* (Oxford, Oxford University Press, 1962). On Austin's notion of felicitousness, see further Kleinig in this volume.

[8] PF Strawson, 'Freedom and Resentment' (1962) 48 *Proceedings of the British Academy* 187, reprinted in PF Strawson, *Freedom and Resentment and Other Essays* (London, Methuen, 1974).

[9] A Smith, *The Theory of Moral Sentiments* [1759] (London, Penguin, 2010) part II, section I.

witnesses such behaviour, Strawson speaks rather of 'indignation'. In my discussion here, I am extending the term 'resentment' to include indignation. I am also extending the term further, to discuss disapproving attitudes expressed through social institutions: here, through legal punishment.[10]

But why should hard treatment be deemed a symbolically appropriate means for conveying censure? There are various possible reasons, including convention, historical use, and similarities between the means of expression and what is intended to be expressed. All three of these reasons appear to operate here. The use of hard treatment to express censure has a lengthy history and is a firmly established convention. Moreover, a degree of similarity exists between the means of expression and the normative judgement that is being conveyed. Censure is unpleasant and serves to discredit the conduct of the person involved. Hard treatment is likewise unpleasant, and thus may readily be used to convey such discredit. By contrast, granting a benefit is not unpleasant, and hence would not be an appropriate vehicle for expressing censure.[11]

Might we, however, replace hard treatment with an alternative means of expressing censure that does not involve its deprivations? A simple answer would be that no alternative vehicle comes to mind that would convey the disapprobation with sufficient clarity and emphasis. A long-established social convention, such as the use of hard treatment to express censure, would also be extremely difficult to alter. There is, however, a further reason for employing hard treatment as the vehicle for scaling penal censure: namely, its collateral function of deterrence – to which I turn next.

III. THE SUPPLEMENTARY DETERRENT ROLE OF HARD TREATMENT

In my previous writings, my analysis of the role of hard treatment gave principal emphasis to its crime-preventive function. I treated deterrence, along with censure, as two analytically separable (albeit linked) justifying reasons for supporting the existence of the criminal sanction.[12] Here, however, I am taking a different approach: this revised account gives primary emphasis to the function of hard treatment as the 'currency' through which penal censure is expressed. But might there still be supplementary reasons for utilising hard treatment?

It is here that deterrence comes into play. An element of deterrence is intrinsic to the criminal sanction itself. The sanction does not just convey

---

[10] For further discussion of Strawson's notion of resentment, and its bearing on the rationale for punishment, see also the essays by Jacobs and Kleinig in this volume.

[11] This brings to mind the ironic ending in Bertolt Brecht's and Kurt Weill's *Threepenny Opera*, where the robber Macheath purportedly is punished for his numerous crimes by being awarded a castle in Spain. This would be an inappropriate manner of expressing disapprobation (unless, conceivably, the castle were extraordinarily frigid and draughty, and residence in winter were compulsory).

[12] See most recently von Hirsch, above n 2 ch 5.

the message: 'desist please'. It *prohibits* certain conducts, and threatens unpleasant consequences for non-compliance.[13] Using graduated doses of hard-treatment as the means for expressing degrees of censure thus serves the further function of reinforcing the role of the sanction as a disincentive to crime. When hard treatment is used to express disapproval of criminal conduct, this not only helps to confront potential offenders with appropriately graded levels of disapprobation, but also introduces an additional prudential reason for desistance – in virtue of the unwelcome character of such treatment.

This resort to deterrence, however, would still require punishment's proportionality requirements to be observed. One should not be permitted to try to generate optimally efficient aggregate levels of deterrence – because the scaling requirements spoken of in section II above restrict the comparative doses of hard treatment that would be permissible in penalising crimes of differing seriousness.

Introducing the idea of deterrence, even in this limited fashion, permits us to invoke the Hobbesian argument that I have utilised in previous writings.[14] This argument is that, without an element of such compulsion, the constraints of law would be insufficient and this would thus render citizens' co-existence in society unbearably hazardous – in Hobbes' famous words, make human life 'nasty, brutish and short'. Verbal or symbolic censure is, of course, itself unpleasant – hence, its sole use could have some deterrent effect. The introduction of hard treatment, however, gives the penal response additional 'bite', not only making its use normatively appropriate for cases of more serious offending, but also making it less easily disregarded by those at whom criminal prohibitions are directed.

My just-stated quasi-Hobbesian argument assumes that the severity of the state's response does matter for crime prevention. But does that square with recent criminological research about deterrent effects? That research has tended to confirm Beccaria's thesis, that punishment's degree of severity matters less for deterrence than does the offender's likelihood of being punished.[15] My argument, however, addresses the severity of the penal response, not its likelihood.

Beccaria's thesis – concerning the limited deterrent impact of changes in punishments' severity – appears to reflect typical offenders' orientation towards the present rather than the remote future. When the standard penalty for

---

[13] See AP Simester and A von Hirsch, *Crimes, Harms, and Wrongs: On the Limits of Criminalisation* (Oxford, Hart Publishing, 2011) ch 1.

[14] For the role of the Hobbesian argument in my previous censure-plus-deterrence theory; see, eg von Hirsch, above n 2 at 37–43.

[15] C Beccaria, *On Crimes and Punishments* [5th edn 1766] edited by Richard Bellamy and translated by Richard Davies (Cambridge, Cambridge University Press, 1995). For a summary of empirical evidence on the deterrent effect of sentences see AE Bottoms and A von Hirsch, 'The Crime Preventive Impact of Penal Sanctions' in P Cane and HM Kritzer (eds), *The Oxford Handbook of Empirical Legal Studies* (Oxford, Oxford University Press, 2010).

robbery is raised from four years to six, this concerns deferred pains – what will in fact happen to the offender in the somewhat distant future. However, we are speaking here of severity increases that have their 'bite' at present. Instead of merely facing official disapprobation, the offender will be confronted *now* with unpleasant material consequences: the hard treatment of being confined in prison. He must confront, at present, not just official censure, but also hard treatment.

IV. CONCLUSION

The scaling role of hard treatment is not just something that just happens to arise in a desert-oriented penalty system. It provides the underpinnings for such a scheme. The two sub-functions of scaling spoken of in this chapter – amplification and grading – are crucial roles that are performed by the institution of the penal sanction. If hard treatment were deprived of its scaling function (say, if it were imposed for reasons largely unrelated to the seriousness of the offending behaviour), it is difficult to believe that the penal system could be perceived as one that seeks to penalise offenders justly and effectively.

6

Deserved Censure, Hard Treatment and Penal Restraint

ANDREW ASHWORTH

A LTHOUGH THEORIES OF punishment have long been debated by philosophers, theologians, lawyers and many others, the publication of Andreas von Hirsch's *Doing Justice* in 1976 undoubtedly marked a significant turn in the development of liberal penal theory. Since then, the 'justice model', the theory of deserved censure and proportionate sentencing have attracted increasing debate and, in some jurisdictions, have exerted a telling influence. Andreas himself has reworked his theory in subsequent publications, so that it is now known as a communicative theory that rests on censure and hard treatment and that prescribes proportionate sentences.

According to the von Hirsch theory,[1] a punitive response to wrongdoing can be said to be deserved, it being integral to everyday moral judgements involving praise or blame. The essence of conviction and punishment lies in the authoritative censure of an offender for an offence. The censure is thereby communicated to the offender, the victim and wider society: the amount of hard treatment involved in the sentence should be proportionate to the seriousness of the wrong, so conveying the degree of the censure. In relation to the offender, the censuring process treats him/her as a moral agent, recognising the element of fallibility in human nature and recognising also that offenders should be given an opportunity to amend their future conduct so as to avoid further wrongdoing. Thus the law should treat individuals as 'fallible agents capable of acting on moral reasons but possibly requiring some practical disincentives to aid them in resisting such temptation'.[2] The prudential disincentive is the hard treatment that punishment

---

[1] The brief account in this paragraph is based on A von Hirsch, *Doing Justice: the Choice of Punishments* (Report of the Committee for the Study of Incarceration) (New York, Hill and Wang, 1976) ch 2; A von Hirsch, *Past or Future Crimes: Deservedness and Dangerousness in the Sentencing of Criminals* (New Brunswick, Rutgers University Press, 1985) ch 5; A von Hirsch, *Censure and Sanctions* (Oxford, Oxford University Press, 1993) ch 2; and A von Hirsch and A Ashworth, *Proportionate Sentencing: Exploring the Principles* (Oxford, Oxford University Press, 2005) chs 2 and 9.

[2] Von Hirsch and Ashworth, *Proportionate Sentencing* (hereafter PS), above n 1 at 25.

involves (in the form of a financial penalty, community sanction or imprisonment). However, the prudential disincentive must not be disproportionate to the degree of the wrongdoing, and must therefore be 'tied to the normative reason conveyed by penal censure'. In his essay for this volume, von Hirsch retains the notion of hard treatment as a prudential disincentive, but he also emphasises the scaling or grading function of hard treatment. Thus, 'expressing censure through differing amounts of hard treatment serves also a *grading* function, of scaling the degrees of disapprobation expressed by the penal responses – so as to reflect crimes' varying degrees of seriousness, as a desert rationale requires'.[3]

Many of the propositions in the previous paragraph require a great deal of further discussion, and they receive it in the writings of von Hirsch. The purpose of this chapter is to focus on one particular aspect of theories based on deserved censure – their relationship with principles of penal restraint. Do these desert theories *require* penal restraint; or is it just that desert theories are usually held by liberals who also subscribe to principles of penal restraint? If the latter is true, could desert theories also be supported by those who believe that 'prison works'[4] and that more severe sentencing is called for?

The chapter begins with an exploration of the role played by 'underlying' deterrence in theories based on deserved censure. Section II goes on to examine four restraining arguments that appear in von Hirsch's theory: the 'drowning out' argument; progressive loss of mitigation for repeat offenders; the principle of parsimony; and decrementalism. Section III then confronts the question of whether von Hirsch's theory has adequate defences against those who believe that 'prison works' and who favour severity in sentencing.

I. THE ROLE OF 'UNDERLYING GENERAL DETERRENCE'

From the time of von Hirsch's earliest articulation of his theory in *Doing Justice*, it was already clear that deserved censure was not the sole foundation for his arguments. Chapter 5 of that book is entitled 'General Deterrence', and the role of general prevention is spelt out clearly:

> By means of the criminal law, the state proscribes various kinds of injurious conduct. But were the prohibition not backed by sanctions, violations might become commonplace. The threat and imposition of punishment is called for in order to secure compliance – not full compliance, but more compliance than there might be if there were no legal penalties at all.[5]

---

[3] A von Hirsch, in this volume at section I B (emphasis in original).

[4] The phrase used by British Home Secretary Michael Howard in 1993, when he started the movement that led to an escalation of English sentencing that almost doubled the prison population in the following decades: see Ministry of Justice, *Story of the Prison Population: 1993–2016 England and Wales* (London, Ministry of Justice, 2016).

[5] Von Hirsch, *Doing Justice* (hereafter DJ), above n 1 at 44.

A similar point is made in Hobbesian terms some years later: in a system that visited no painful consequences on offenders, 'it seems likely that victimizing conduct would become so prevalent as to make life nasty and brutish, indeed'.[6] The conclusion of the study of general deterrence by the Norwegian scholar Johannes Andenaes is also cited: 'it is still a fundamental fact of social life that the risk of unpleasant consequences is a very strong motivational factor for most people in most situations'.[7] Those particular words stand in need of some qualification, however. The risk must not be thought to be too low, and the quantum of the 'unpleasant consequences' must not be thought too low. Deterrence theory rests on a reluctance to run the risk of the consequences as subjectively perceived.

This reliance on general prevention is undoubtedly consequentialist, and von Hirsch acknowledged this from the outset – indeed, it is written in terms in *Past and Future Crimes*: 'On this issue, my argument has been consequentialist: the deprivation element in punishment helps prevent crime. The person is being made to suffer, rather than only being censured, in order to help safeguard others'.[8]

However, it appears that the nature of the argument from general prevention is simply that a criminal justice system with punishment is preferable to a system without punishment. The three-step reasoning used by von Hirsch remains relevant:

Step 1: Those who violate others' rights deserve punishment. That, of itself, constitutes a prima facie justification for maintaining a system of criminal sanctions.

Step 2: There is, however, a countervailing moral obligation of not deliberately adding to the amount of human suffering. Punishment necessarily makes those punished suffer. In the absence of additional argument, that overrides the case for punishment in step 1.

Step 3: The notion of deterrence, at this point, suggests that punishment may prevent more misery than it inflicts – thus disposing of the countervailing argument in step 2. With it out of the way, the prima facie case for punishment described in step 1 – based on desert – stands again.[9]

We will meet elements of this argument again in section II below. They are deployed by von Hirsch as part of his reasoning towards the central tenet of desert theory – that it rests on the 'interdependence of the twin concepts of deterrence and desert'.[10] The examples quoted in support of the indispensable

---

[6] Von Hirsch, *Past or Future Crimes* (hereafter PFC), above n 1 at 48.

[7] J Andenaes, *Punishment and Deterrence* (Ann Arbor, University of Michigan Press, 1974) 129; cited in von Hirsch DJ, above n 5 at 43, and von Hirsch PFC, above n 6 at 7–8.

[8] Von Hirsch PFC, above n 6 at 57. Note that this is not exclusively why the offender is 'made to suffer'. As von Hirsch argues in his chapter for this volume, penal hard treatment is, on account of its scaling function, also strongly intertwined with the censuring function of punishment.

[9] Von Hirsch DJ, above n 5 at 54.

[10] Ibid at 55.

role of underlying prevention include the 'natural experiments' involving the arrest of the entire Danish police force by the Nazis in 1944 (resulting in a tenfold increase in acquisitive crimes)[11] and the police strikes in Boston, USA in 1919, in Melbourne, Australia in 1923, and in Montreal, Canada in 1969 (all resulting in considerable lawlessness, mostly acquisitive crimes). Whilst each of these 'natural experiments' calls for careful dissection, in terms of their nature and effects, the similarity of their consequences tends to support the proposition that an operative system of criminal law enforcement that generally leads to the conviction and sentencing of offenders is an essential minimum.[12]

Matt Matravers has recently sought to challenge the orthodoxy that hard treatment is a necessary element in punishment.[13] Although there is insufficient space here to enter fully into the thought experiment he conducts, his reasoning includes the arguments that the incapacitative function of punishment can be achieved through non-punitive preventive measures, and that many lesser offences can be dealt with through non-punitive regulatory penalties (arguments that depend, as he acknowledges, on the definition of a punitive measure).[14] He then discusses two other difficult problems – that the prohibition on murder requires little reinforcement because there is a strong moral reluctance to kill, and that there may be many middle-range criminal prohibitions that people would be tempted to disobey if there were no hard treatment and no assurance that others would obey them – and his analysis of the latter group tends to support the implications of the police strikes and of the English riots of 2011.[15] While Matravers concludes that 'for many reasons it is unlikely we could abolish penal hard treatment here-and-now without unjustifiably increasing the risks of future criminal harms',[16] his essay raises serious questions about the justification for and claimed necessity of the infliction of human suffering as part of the criminal sanction.

We return, then, to von Hirsch's question whether 'deterrence is a reason for having *any* system of criminal sanctions at all'.[17] His answer, for the reasons articulated in the foregoing paragraphs, is that it is, with the emphasis on what we might term 'underlying general deterrence'. He is not concerned with

---

[11] Ibid at 42–43; see further Andenaes, above n 7 at 51.

[12] The same would not necessarily apply if the staff of the criminal courts were to go on strike, since the police and armed forces might be able to detain suspected offenders in the short term, whereas a police strike hits at the first step (arrest or summons) needed to initiate the criminal justice process.

[13] M Matravers 'Punishment, Suffering and Justice' in S Farrall, B Goldson, I Loader and A Dockley (eds), *Justice and Penal Reform: Reshaping the Penal Landscape* (Abingdon, Routledge, 2016).

[14] See further A Ashworth and L Zedner, *Preventive Justice* (Oxford, Oxford University Press, 2014) ch 1 and *passim*.

[15] See eg, LSE Social Policy Department, *Reading the Riots* (London, LSE and *The Guardian*, 2011), and J Treadwell, D Briggs, S Winslow and S Hall, 'Shopocalypse Now' (2013) 53 *British Journal of Criminology* 1.

[16] Matravers, above n 13 at 42.

[17] Von Hirsch DJ, above n 5 at 40.

marginal general deterrence, ie whether increasing the level of sentences for a given crime and publicising this will bring a corresponding reduction in the level of offending. He recognises that the findings of existing research do not tell strongly in favour of the marginal effect of increasing the penalty level for a given crime, although they do support the effect of increasing the believed probability of detection.[18] But von Hirsch insists on a separation between the underlying effect of deterrence in supporting the criminal justice system and the irrelevance of general deterrence to sentence levels for particular offences.[19] Even if it were to be established empirically that a certain increase in the penalty level for a given offence was highly likely to produce a significant reduction in the rate of commission of that offence,[20] a censure-based theory should not allow this factor to enter into calculations of the appropriate penalty level. That penalty level should be determined by taking account of the anchoring point of the whole sentencing system, the implications of cardinal proportionality, and (most emphatically on this issue) the dictates of ordinal proportionality. Thus:

> Suppose there are two kinds of offenses, A and B, that are of approximately equal seriousness; but that offence B can more effectively be deterred through the use of a severe penalty. Notwithstanding the deterrent utility of punishing offence B more severely, the objection remains that the perpetrators of that offence are being treated as if they are more blameworthy than the perpetrators of offense A – and that is not so if the crimes are of equivalent gravity.[21]

Thus, the two notions of reprobation and prevention are separate but inter-locking: reprobation for wrongdoing explains why the sanction should take a condemnatory form (censure), whereas prevention explains why the state should impose painful material consequences (hard treatment) on those culpable for

---

[18] A von Hirsch, AE Bottoms, E Burney and P-O Wikstrom, *Criminal Deterrence: an Analysis of Recent Research* (Oxford, Hart Publishing, 1999); and AE Bottoms and A von Hirsch, 'The Crime-Preventive Effect of Penal Sanctions' in PF Cane and HM Kritzer (eds), *Oxford Handbook of Empirical Legal Research* (Oxford, Oxford University Press, 2010). See also, eg, D Nagin, FT Cullen and CL Johnson, 'Imprisonment and Reoffending' in M Tonry (ed) *Crime and Justice: a Review of Research* volume 38 (New York, Oxford University Press, 2009); C Webster and A Doob, 'Searching for Sasquatch: Deterrence of Crime through Sentence Severity' in J Petersilia and K Reitz (eds), *Oxford Handbook of Sentencing and Corrections* (New York, Oxford University Press, 2012); D Nagin and JV Pepper (eds), *Deterrence and the Death Penalty* (Washington DC, National Academies Press, 2012).

[19] For further discussion, see A Bottoms, 'Five Puzzles in von Hirsch's Theory of Punishment' in A Ashworth and M Wasik (eds), *Fundamentals of Sentencing Theory* (Oxford, Oxford University Press, 1998) 89. Importantly, Bottoms distinguishes the quantum of punishment from its type, and goes on to argue (at 95–100) that preventive considerations, such as deterrent efficacy, could be relevant to making the appropriate choice of non-custodial alternative at the sentencing stage. Cf, M Wasik and A von Hirsch, 'Non-Custodial Penalties and the Principles of Desert' [1988] *Criminal Law Review* 555.

[20] For the necessary conditions, see the writings in n 18 above; for a more enthusiastic approach, see D Kennedy, *Deterrence and Crime Prevention* (Abingdon, Routledge, 2009), and cf A Braga and D Weisburd, *The Effects of 'Pulling Levers' Focused Deterrence Strategies on Crime* (Oslo, Campbell Systematic Reviews, 2012).

[21] Von Hirsch DJ, above n 5 at 72–73; see also von Hirsch and Ashworth, PS above n 2 at 136–37.

causing victimising conduct, and relative reprobation (not prevention) determines the appropriate quantum of hard treatment.[22] This reasoning connects well with von Hirsch's emphasis (in this volume) on the scaling or grading function of hard treatment.

II. PREVENTION AND PENAL RESTRAINT

Once it has been established that desert theory is partly about prevention and deterrence, what principles set the intensity of that pursuit? In particular, while many proportionality theorists are liberals who subscribe to an independent principle of penal restraint, does desert theory itself contain or refer to principles capable of exerting any downward thrust on punishment levels? In this section we consider four arguments deployed by desert theorists: the 'drowning out' argument; progressive loss of mitigation for repeat offenders; the principle of parsimony; and a decremental strategy.[23]

A. The 'Drowning Out' Argument

The claim of this argument is that the sentence prescribed for a given offence should not be so harsh as to 'drown out' the moral message of the law, turning the sentence into a 'naked demand' that would not be respectful of the individual's agency.[24] This connects the limits on punishment with the notion of respect for individual autonomy that underlies modern desert theory: proportionality theory regards the person censured as a moral agent, but also recognises that we are all 'morally weak and fallible' and that a prudential disincentive may need to be added to the moral appeal of the law if it is to be reasonably effective. That moral appeal includes treating offenders as persons, 'as individuals capable of choice, responsible for their actions, and punishable according to their degree of fault'.[25] But the 'hard treatment' should be kept at a moderate level; otherwise, 'the normative reasons for desistance supplied by penal censure could become largely immaterial, and the disincentive become much more than supplementary

---

[22] Von Hirsch PFC, above n 6 at 59; similarly Bottoms argues (above n 19 at 89) that 'the ultimate point of a *punishment system* is the prevention of undesirable behaviour, but that in any *specific instance of punishment* one initially looks back reprobatively to the act committed ("this is happening to you *because you did*" a certain deed)' (emphases in original).

[23] For a re-examination of these four arguments, with different conclusions, see the chapter in this volume by Matt Matravers.

[24] Von Hirsch, *Censure and Sanctions* (hereafter CS), above n 1 at 14; and RA Duff, *Punishment, Communication and Community* (New York, Oxford University Press, 2001) at 86–88. See also A Ashworth and L Zedner, 'Punishment Paradigms and the Role of the Preventive State', in AP Simester, A du Bois-Pedain and U Neumann (eds), *Liberal Criminal Theory* (Oxford, Hart, 2014) 3 at 11–14.

[25] Von Hirsch PFC, above n 6 at 171.

to the censuring message'.[26] Thus – and connecting the argument with respect for individual autonomy and with human rights (see below) – von Hirsch states that 'punished persons' vital interests are being trivialised when such drastic deprivations are used to convey merely a minor degree of censure'.[27]

Antony Duff argues that the drowning-out argument is particularly strong when considering punishment levels for ordinally minor crimes, such as speeding. 'If punishment (penal hard treatment) is to supplement rather than replace censure, it must not be so harsh that it effectively drowns out the law's moral voice'. Thus a financial penalty for speeding, viewed as a punishment conveying censure, 'could provide a useful and modest supplement to the moral appeal of the law – an appeal to which I am often not sufficiently attentive'.[28] However, Duff is reluctant to apply this reasoning higher up the scale, where the crime is more serious than 'ordinally minor' and the sanction is three to five years' imprisonment. This raises the question whether the drowning-out argument relies on an absolute notion of the limits of what may be regarded as a prudential disincentive, or on a relativist notion that compares the strength of the moral appeal embodied in the criminal law with the strength of the disincentive attached to breach of it. On the absolutist account that is implicit in Duff's discussion, prison terms of a certain length (more than three years, or at most more than five years) are simply incapable of being regarded as mere disincentives because they are too coercive. For Duff, the use of such coercive threats is unacceptable because they amount to deterrents that replace, not merely supplement, the law's moral appeal.[29] Is there room for an alternative, relativist account? The starting point here would be that the 'moral appeal' of the criminal law and the sentencing system is not general and constant but varies proportionately to the heinousness of the particular wrongdoing. On this view, the law against serious violence carries a stronger moral appeal than the law against theft from shops because serious violence is a much more egregious wrong; and this connects well with von Hirsch's emphasis on the scaling function of hard treatment (in this volume). Thus, the heightened social importance of preventing serious violence should surely mean that a more severe penalty can be attached to it without trenching so greatly on a person's autonomy as to cross the line between the merely prudential and the starkly coercive. Even if we were provisionally to accept this as a possibility, it would not displace the absolutist argument because the questions of cardinal proportionality and the permissibility of certain types of sanction would remain for debate. Capital punishment should be ruled out, but what limits should be placed on the scale of punishments for the ordinally most serious offences?

---

[26] Von Hirsch CS, above n 24 at 13.

[27] Ibid at 37.

[28] Duff, above n 14 at 87; see also RA Duff, 'Punishment, Communication and Community' in M Matravers and J Pike (eds), *Debates in Contemporary Political Philosophy: an Anthology* (London, Routledge and Open University Press, 2002) 394.

[29] Duff, above n 14 at 83.

According to what criteria should we assess the permissibility of 'life without parole', other forms of life imprisonment, and determinate prison sentences of 15 years or longer? If we are to assess this by reference to their effect on a person's autonomy and moral agency, would there not be a difference according to whether the target offence were murder or theft from a shop? Perhaps there are two barriers to be considered – one being the proper (absolute) limits on available sanctions (to be assessed on the degree of pain and collateral harms, on grounds of human rights, and on social acceptability), the other being the relative effect of the sanction on the strength of the moral wrongdoing to be prevented. We should note, however, that the very language of 'drowning out' is more apt to exclude extremely severe sentences than to generate prescriptions of appropriate punishment levels.

Clearly the question whether a sentence is so high as to 'drown out' the law's moral message, and yet necessary if the criminal law is to retain its preventive efficacy, may require a judgement that is both fine and adjusted to the particular social, political and legal context. In *Doing Justice* von Hirsch argued for a penalty scale that treated five years' imprisonment as the most severe available penalty for all but the most serious crimes.[30] Whether that was politically feasible in mid-1970s America remains for argument, but it would hardly be regarded as realistic in contemporary USA or the UK. Such has been the escalation of sentence levels in recent decades that it might take several years to reverse this trend, even to the extent of matching the German sentencing system that treats 15 years as its normal sentencing ceiling.[31] However, pessimistic as one might be about achieving a rapid reduction in sentence levels, there remains the argument that to impose a sentence of more than one year's imprisonment for theft from a shop would 'drown out' the law's moral message, and would fail to respect the scaling function of hard treatment (see von Hirsch in this volume). Such reasoning could be extended to many offences which lie towards the lower end of the ordinal rankings. The nub of the argument would be that the ordinal seriousness of the offence is comparatively low, and that the pains and deprivations of imprisonment are comparatively high, thus indicating that the penalty is relatively so severe that it could 'drown out' the moral message of the law.

B. Progressive Loss of Mitigation for Repeat Offenders

Many of the offenders who come up for sentence in the courts have a prior record of offending, and therefore a punishment theory's approach to such cases has a significant bearing on penal restraint or severity. Proportionality theory, as developed by Andreas von Hirsch, adopts a model based on progressive

---

[30] Von Hirsch DJ, above n 5 ch. 16.
[31] T Hörnle, 'Moderate and Non-Arbitrary Sentencing without Guidelines: the German Experience' (2013) 76 *Law and Contemporary Problems* 189.

loss of mitigation.[32] The sentence for the offence should be set by considerations of cardinal and ordinal proportionality; the first offender should receive a reduction in penalty; this discount should gradually diminish with subsequent convictions and then disappear. What is the justification for allowing the reduction in penalty?

> The discount provides recognition of the offender as a responsible actor, capable of altering his conduct on the basis of the critical judgement of his behaviour expressed through the previous sentence. It presumes that he will respond as he should, by making an effort of will to desist. It is only when he actually fails to desist that he gradually loses the discount.[33]

The connection between this justification and the conceptions of autonomy and moral agency underlying the 'drowning out' argument should be readily apparent. The reference to an 'effort of will' is to giving the offender an opportunity to exercise the self-restraint expected of him, through his moral agency. The theory is not precise about the number of previous convictions before the progressive loss of mitigation disappears and the proportionate sentence reasserts itself, but it seems that three previous convictions might be the appropriate stage – allowing the possibility of a few failed attempts at desistance, reflecting the human fallibility recognised by desert theory.[34] In the context of the present essay, the salient point is that the progressive-loss-of-mitigation approach conduces to penal restraint, since it disavows a deterrent or incapacitative strategy that would lead to ever more severe sentences for the repeat offender.

C. Penal Parsimony and Human Rights

At several points in his writings von Hirsch appeals to what he variously terms the principle of penal parsimony, the principle of least restriction, or the principle of sparing use of coercive state interventions: 'The state has the obligation of keeping the suffering of offenders to the minimum consistent with its penal objectives, and bears the burden of justifying why a given level of intrusion, and not a lesser one, is called for'.[35] The origins of this principle lie in liberal political theory. A more concrete application of the principle may be found in what we might term the human rights argument – that a fundamental right such as the right to liberty should not be taken away for an offence that amounts

---

[32] See A von Hirsch, 'Proportionality and Progressive Loss of Mitigation: Further Reflections' in JV Roberts and A von Hirsch (eds), *Previous Convictions at Sentencing: Theoretical and Applied Perspectives* (Oxford, Hart Publishing, 2010) 1. This volume also contains several other essays which develop or take issue with the basic desert approach.

[33] Ibid at 9–10.

[34] Ibid at 8–11.

[35] Von Hirsch PFC, above n 6 at 100; see also von Hirsch DJ, above n 5 at 5; von Hirsch CS, above n 24 at 44–45.

to the violation of a significantly lesser right, such as the right to personal property.[36] Before analysing this argument in detail, some remarks about the ranking of human rights are in order. As noted above, von Hirsch refers to offenders as 'those who violate others' rights',[37] and warns against 'punished persons' vital interests ... being trivialized'.[38] If we are to make progress with this argument for penal restraint, there is a need to consider how the various human rights might be ranked in terms of importance. One approach, implicit in the European Convention on Human Rights, is to separate those rights that may be qualified by the 'balancing' of other interests, from those that apply without such qualification.[39] The right to liberty falls into the latter category: the European Convention provides certain exceptions to the right, but does not allow this fundamental right to be qualified by 'balancing'.

In the context of desert theory the argument becomes one about prisons and proportionality. The prisons element in the argument emphasises that incarceration is a deprivation of the right to liberty, and moreover that this brings with it several 'pains of imprisonment' including loss of autonomy in everyday life, restrictions on freedom of movement, isolation from family and friends, loss of privacy and exposure to the risk of personal harm.[40] The consequential effect on partners and children should also be taken into account.[41] Deprivations of this magnitude should be reserved for the most serious of offences. Imprisonment should be regarded as too severe and disproportionate a response to what may be termed 'pure property offences', ie property offences not involving the threat of violence (robbery) or violation of the right to privacy (burglary). On this view the core offences from which the sanction of imprisonment should be taken away are thefts, frauds and offences of criminal damage. Even if these offences are committed persistently, the offenders should be sentenced without resort to imprisonment. English law already takes this approach with offences such as begging and soliciting for prostitution, which were made non-imprisonable in 1982.[42] The challenge is to devise community sentences aimed at changing the behaviour of persistent property offenders (which is likely to involve tackling drug and/or alcohol abuse), to combine this with compensation or reparation to the victim, and to have a sensitive regime for dealing with breaches.

[36] For elaboration, see A Ashworth, *What if Imprisonment were Abolished for Property Offences?* (London, Howard League for Penal Reform, 2012).

[37] Von Hirsch DJ, above n 5 at 54.

[38] Von Hirsch CS, above n 24 at 37.

[39] For fuller discussion, see A Ashworth and M Redmayne, *The Criminal Process*, 4th edn (Oxford, Oxford University Press, 2010) 30–38.

[40] For elaboration and references, see A Liebling and B Crewe, 'Prison Life, Penal Power and Prison Effects' in M Maguire, R Morgan and R Reiner (eds), *Oxford Handbook of Criminology*, 5th edn (Oxford, Oxford University Press, 2012) 895, at 898–901.

[41] R Condry, A Kotova and S Minson, 'Social Injustice and Collateral Damage: the Families and Children of Prisoners' in Y Jewkes, J Bennett and B Crewe (eds), *The Handbook of Prisons* (Abingdon, Routledge, 2016); S Wakefield and C Wildeman, *Children of the Prison Boom: Mass Incarceration and the Future of American Inequality* (New York, Oxford University Press, 2013).

[42] Criminal Justice Act 1982, sections 70–71.

The argument (focusing on individual rights, dignity and the impact on family life) does not necessarily lead to an all-or-nothing approach to sentencing: a middle way would be to allow the higher courts the discretion to use imprisonment for pure property offences where the offence is so extraordinarily serious that no sentence less than custody would meet the justice of the case (or some similarly restrictive wording). This would make the policy of the law clear – that in principle imprisonment is a disproportionate response to offences involving no violence, no threats and no sexual assault – while allowing the courts a circumscribed discretion to cater for exceptional circumstances. In this way the principle of penal parsimony might be given a more concrete application to the relationship between certain types of offence and certain types of sanction.

D. A Decremental Strategy

Although modern desert theory has a great deal to say about ordinal proportionality, it regards the anchoring point of the penalty scale (and therefore cardinal proportionality) as a matter of social convention that is culturally and politically determined.[43] Accepting that the anchoring point of sentencing levels in any particular country is likely to be a matter of convention, can it be changed? The experience of recent decades is that ordinal rankings can be changed upwards – for example, for drink-driving and causing death on the roads – and efforts are currently being made to change the ranking of driving whilst using a mobile phone. The question whether anchoring points can be changed downwards is more difficult to answer. Awareness of the pains and deprivations of imprisonment[44] has led many writers on punishment to support the principle of penal restraint or parsimony, even if they do not accept desert theory.[45] When John Braithwaite and Philip Pettit were developing their republican theory of criminal justice based on the preservation of 'dominion' they proposed that a major element in setting penalty levels should be a 'decremental strategy', according to which existing penalty levels should be gradually scaled down until the point is reached where there is evidence that measurable increases in crime are beginning to appear.[46] Within proportionality theory von Hirsch proposes a similar but more vigorous decremental strategy, starting from the proposition that the level of sentences should be set not as the primary means of crime-prevention but as a supplementary prudential disincentive. This indicates 'rather modest sanction levels' and 'changing existing censure-expressing

---

[43] Von Hirsch CS, above n 24 at 19: 'The amount of disapproval conveyed by penal sanctions is a convention'.

[44] See text at nn 41–42 above.

[45] A further example is N Morris, *The Future of Imprisonment* (Chicago, University of Chicago Press, 1974).

[46] J Braithwaite and P Pettit, *Not Just Deserts* (Oxford, Oxford University Press, 1990) 142.

conventions by moving the graded penalties down *pro rata*'.[47] Reasons for adopting the decremental strategy are to be found in the arguments already outlined above – keeping state-inflicted suffering to a minimum, not drowning out the law's moral message, and reducing reliance on incarcerative sanctions. Thus:

> The harsher a penalty system becomes, however, the less significant would be the normative reasons for desistance supplied by penal censure, and the more predominant would become the system's purely threatening aspects – that is, the more the system becomes, in Hegel's apt words, "a stick raised to a dog." This argument points towards keeping penalties at moderate levels. Indeed, it might even be possible, as far as proportionality is concerned, to scale down the sentencing system so that lengthy prison terms would be reserved only for the most serious violent offences.[48]

The difficulty with this, as von Hirsch and others have recognised, is that there are likely to be political obstacles to the pursuit of a decremental strategy in socio-economic systems such as the USA and the UK. The mass media are likely to campaign against any downward change; the families of some victims will weigh in; and some politicians will take up the cry.

However, the goal of pursuing a decremental strategy is attainable under certain conditions. In the Netherlands in the 1970s and 1980s penal moderation was assisted, possibly even generated, by close collaboration between senior judges, prosecutors and Ministry of Justice officials, many of whom had trained together and who exchanged jobs from time to time.[49] In Germany moderate sentencing levels are sustained by institutional features such as the form of German legal education (inculcating certain values) and the selection of career judges from the top law school graduates.[50] The same is true to some extent in Finland and Sweden, where the principle of proportionality is well established and prison use is relatively low.[51] These examples suggest that the anchoring point of a penalty scale can be changed downwards. Partly the ground is fertile where certain legal and judicial traditions prevail; partly the ground is fertile where at a deeper level certain forms of political and institutional conditions are to be found. As Tapio Lappi-Seppala concluded:

> Consensual politics lessen controversies, produce less crisis talk, inhibit dramatic turnovers and sustain long-term consistent policies. In other words, consensual democracies are less susceptible to political populism. While the consensus model is based on bargaining and compromise, majoritarian democracies are based on competition and confrontation. The latter sharpens distinctions, heightens controversies and encourages conflicts. This affects the stability and contents of policies, as well as the legitimacy of the political system as a whole. There is more crisis talk,

---

[47] Von Hirsch CS, above n 24 at 45.
[48] Von Hirsch and Ashworth, PS above n 2 at 142–43.
[49] D Downes, *Contrasts in Tolerance* (Oxford, Oxford University Press, 1988) 101.
[50] Hörnle, above n 31.
[51] See the discussion in von Hirsch CS, above n 24 ch 10 and in von Hirsch and Ashworth, PS above n 2 ch 6.

more criticism, more short-term solutions, more direct appeals to public demands, and a higher risk of exclusive populist penal policy.[52]

Thus 'consensual democracies' with coalition governments are likely to prove more fertile ground for decremental penal strategies, presumably supported by scholarly writings and adopted by judges and other practitioners.

III. PROPORTIONALITY AND PREVENTION

We have now seen that four sub-elements of von Hirsch's proportionality theory point distinctly in the direction of penal restraint: the 'drowning out' argument; progressive loss of mitigation for repeat offenders; penal parsimony and human rights; and a decremental strategy. The first two sub-elements are internal to desert theory, whereas the last two are situated more broadly in the background political theory of liberalism and are compatible with, but not exclusive to, desert theory. Having said that, the last two sub-elements have always been nested in von Hirsch's account of desert theory: as noted above, von Hirsch has insisted on the moral obligation of not deliberately adding to the amount of human suffering and on the state's obligation to keep the suffering of offenders to the minimum consistent with its penal objectives.[53]

While there are undoubtedly other arguments for penal restraint that do not depend on proportionality theory, enough has surely been done in Part II to demonstrate that proportionality theory conduces to penal restraint rather than to penal severity.[54] While there may be crude forms of retributivism that are used to increase the severity of penalty levels, none of them is consistent with the desert theory of von Hirsch. One cannot be a desert theorist and yet subscribe to the 'prison works' ideology, since that would be inconsistent with the four sub-elements of desert theory discussed in Part II above.

Two matters remain. First, it is important to examine one principle that is often put forward as the leading consideration when translating penal restraint into practical standards for sentencing, particularly imprisonment. This is the *ultima ratio* principle – that the criminal law and punishment should not be deployed if there are other less intrusive methods of responding to a wrong. The difficulty with this principle is that, although it rightly demands a justification

---

[52] T Lappi-Seppala, 'Imprisonment and Penal Demands: Exploring the Dimensions and Drivers of Systemic and Attitudinal Punitivity' in S Body-Gendrot, M Hough, R Levy and S Snacken (eds), *European Handbook of Criminology* (Abingdon, Routledge, 2013); see also the analysis by N Lacey, *The Prisoner's Dilemma: Political Economy and Punishment in Contemporary Democracies* (Cambridge, Cambridge University Press, 2008), identifying 'liberal market economies' as difficult terrain for penal moderation.

[53] See 'Steps 1–3' in section I of this chapter.

[54] For an examination of this issue in the light of recent penal history in England and Wales, see A Ashworth, 'Prisons, Proportionality and Recent Penal History' (2017) 80 *Modern Law Review* 473.

for deploying coercive responses such as the apparatus of the criminal law, and punishment especially, its proponents do not always recognise the full range of justifications. Efficiency and cost-effectiveness are not the only possible justifications for resorting or not resorting to the criminal law. The seriousness of the wrongdoing is a major justification: as Andrew Simester and Andreas von Hirsch argue, 'The public significance of enacting that some activity is a criminal offence can, on occasion, militate in favour of criminalization. If used selectively, criminal prohibition can be a tool for communicating to the public that the prohibited activity is wrongful and must not be done'.[55]

The same logic applies to sentencing: the public significance of making an offence imprisonable should be to draw special attention to its heightened wrongfulness, one of the communicative elements of proportionality theory. Even when it is intended as a principle of penal restraint, the principle of *ultima ratio* is not acceptable as usually formulated.[56] Thus, when it is expressed in terms such as 'imprisonment should only be used as a sanction of last resort', it fails to place sufficient emphasis on the seriousness of the wrongdoing and can instead be taken to suggest that it is justifiable to impose imprisonment simply because other, lesser sanctions have been used in the past. If a form of *ultima ratio* principle is to be retained, it should be expressed as the principle of the least restrictive *appropriate* response to wrongdoing – a formulation that heaps all the important normative debates on to the single word 'appropriate', but which at least signifies that one must decide whether the criminal law, or the sanction of imprisonment, or a substantial term of imprisonment, can be justified by reference to the seriousness of the wrongdoing. This returns the discussion to issues of proportionality, ordinal and cardinal.

When discussing the decremental strategy for penal restraint above,[57] we noted that the anchoring point of a sentencing system – and therefore the indicia of cardinal proportionality – is determined by social convention rather than by any form of objective calculation. It was argued that social conventions can be changed, and the possibility of downwards change was illustrated by reference to the Netherlands, Germany and the Scandinavian countries. However, ordinal proportionality plays a central role in people's understanding of the justice of punishments, largely through claims that certain punishments are unjust because disproportionate to others.[58] The underpinnings of such claims are analysed by von Hirsch in terms of three sub-requirements of ordinal proportionality:

(i)   *Parity*: 'when offenders have been convicted of crimes of similar seriousness they deserve penalties of comparable severity';

---

[55] AP Simester and A von Hirsch, *Crimes, Harms and Wrongs* (Oxford, Hart Publishing, 2011) 197.

[56] See the detailed arguments of N Jareborg, 'Criminalisation as Last Resort (*ultima ratio*)' (2005) 2 *Ohio State Journal of Criminal Law* 521, and D Husak, 'The Criminal Law as Last Resort' (2004) 24 *Oxford Journal of Legal Studies* 207.

[57] See Part II section D of this chapter.

[58] See the helpful discussion by Bottoms, above n 19 at 60–63.

(ii) *Rank-ordering*: because 'punishing crime Y more than crime X expresses more disapproval for crime Y', punishments should 'be ordered on the penalty scale so that their relative severity reflects the seriousness-ranking of the crimes involved'.

(iii) *Spacing*: 'suppose crimes X, Y and Z are of ascending order of seriousness, but that Y is considerably more serious than X but only slightly less so than Z. Then, to reflect the conduct's gravity, there should be a larger space between the penalties for X and Y than for Y and Z'.[59]

While these sub-requirements should not be taken as precise prescriptions for punishments, they indicate principled approaches to the calculation of ordinal proportionality which can be justified on grounds of justice, and which also exemplify the scaling function of hard treatment (as developed by von Hirsch in this volume). Clearly those approaches must be deployed in connection with a) the criteria for criminalisation (notably wrongdoing, harm and culpability),[60] and b) criteria for the use of sentences of imprisonment, generated by reference to the four arguments for penal restraint examined in Part II above. While details of these arguments and their implications await further development, there can be no doubt that they already establish a firm connection between proportionality theory and penal restraint, strong enough to mount a defence to those who argue that 'prison works' and who favour severity in sentencing.

---

[59] Von Hirsch CS, above n 24 at 18.
[60] See generally Simester and von Hirsch, above n 53.

7

Penal Censure, Repentance and Desistance

ANTHONY E BOTTOMS

THE PRINCIPAL PURPOSE of this chapter is to consider whether a liberal-democratic state that adopts a communicative theory of penal censure may reasonably incorporate within that theory a commitment to promote repentance among those who are punished.

From informal discussions with a few academic colleagues, I am aware that, for some readers, this will appear to be a very strange question – a strangeness that arises particularly from the use of the word 'repentance'. Such colleagues are not alone. A decade ago, an American periodical published an interview with a senior Greek Orthodox priest, in which he recommended repentance as the most effective weapon against 'the insidious human tendency towards self-satisfaction'. The interviewer candidly revealed his own initial reflections on this suggestion:

> *Repentance?* … Isn't it a wee bit extreme to drag that old moth-eaten language of shame and sin down from the musty attic of yesteryear? Seriously … we're on the cusp of a whole new *millennium*, man; this is the kind of thing you aren't supposed to say any more. Yet here he was saying it, and here [we were] publishing it with a straight face ….[1]

Yet in the context of this volume, a serious examination of repentance is anything but irrelevant. As is noted elsewhere, the workshop from which this book has arisen was convened to celebrate the fortieth anniversary of Andrew

---

[1] R Robertson, 'The Enemy Within: An Interview with Archimandrite Dionysios' (2006) 34 *What is Enlightenment?* 36, cited in A Torrance, *Repentance in Late Antiquity* (Oxford, Oxford University Press, 2006) 1 (emphasis in original). The interviewer later changed his mind, and decided that the use of this concept was 'cool'!

von Hirsch's *Doing Justice*,[2] which powerfully influenced a general shift in penal theory towards censure-based accounts of punishment.[3] Forty years after *Doing Justice*, one can therefore now identify several different communicative, censure-focused accounts of criminal punishment; and two of the most prominent of these – respectively by Antony Duff[4] and by John Tasioulas[5] – have explicitly proposed that repentance should play a significant role within the punishment systems of liberal-democratic states.[6] That proposal has been resisted by Andreas von Hirsch,[7] and this debate merits careful analysis, because it raises some crucial issues relating to contemporary punishment.

Against this background, the present chapter is structured in the following way. Section I draws on the work of Michel Foucault to emphasise that legal punishment must always be considered not simply in legal or philosophical terms, but also as a socio-political phenomenon.[8] It is further argued that one aspect of Foucault's analysis enables us to gain a fuller understanding of the character of the change in punishment practices that *Doing Justice* helped to promote. Section II turns more directly to what might be described as the 'repentance debate' within penal censure theory. It does so by, first, summarising the rich theory of punishment proposed by Antony Duff, in which repentance plays a significant role; and then by discussing two central topics relating to this theory, namely the definition of repentance, and the objections of some liberal penal theorists to the promotion of repentance within state systems of punishment. Section III develops the definitional issue by introducing the concept of repentance as 'turning around' – a recognised understanding within the Christian tradition which, it is argued, is less open than other definitions to objection by liberal penal theorists. Section IV examines relevant empirical research studies to assess what, if any, evidence there is that offenders repent, on any of the definitions previously discussed. Section V briefly considers some policy implications arising from the analysis of the chapter, and section VI concludes.

---

[2] A von Hirsch, *Doing Justice: The Choice of Punishments* (Report of the Committee for the Study of Incarceration) (New York, Hill and Wang, 1976).

[3] This is reflected in the title of one of von Hirsch's later books: A von Hirsch, *Censure and Sanctions* (Oxford, Clarendon Press, 1993).

[4] See especially RA Duff, *Punishment, Communication and Community* (Oxford, Oxford University Press, 2001).

[5] J Tasioulas, 'Punishment and Repentance' (2006) 81 *Philosophy* 279; J Tasioulas, 'Repentance and the Liberal State' (2007) 4 *Ohio State Journal of Criminal Law* 487.

[6] Repentance also features strongly in some other accounts of punishment that are less clearly in the mainstream of censure-based theory: see for example SP Garvey, 'Punishment as Atonement' (1999) 46 *UCLA Law Review* 1801.

[7] See especially von Hirsch, above n 3 at 72–77; A von Hirsch, 'Punishment, Penance and the State: A Reply to Duff' in M Matravers (ed), *Punishment and Political Theory* (Oxford, Hart Publishing, 1999) 43; A von Hirsch and A Ashworth, *Proportionate Sentencing: Exploring the Principles* (Oxford, Oxford University Press, 2005) ch 7.

[8] M Foucault, *Discipline and Punish: The Birth of the Prison* translated by A Sheridan (London, Allen Lane, 1977).

I. FOUCAULT ON PUNISHMENT

Michel Foucault's seminal text, *Discipline and Punish*,[9] famously begins with a horrific description of the public execution (in 1757) of the regicide Damiens. As Avishai Margalit has put it, this punishment had

> a public, theatrical, nature, featuring the torture wheel, the stake, the gallows, and dragging the bound victim through the city streets – all of which were intended to inflict the tortures of Hell on the condemned person before actually killing him. The profound cruelty of this form of punishment was also intended to humiliate the victim.[10]

Methodologically, however, Foucault claimed that it is a mistake 'to concentrate the study of the punitive mechanisms on their "repressive" effects [or] ... their "punishment" aspects alone'. Instead, a punishment system should be viewed as 'a complex social function' which includes various 'techniques possessing their own specificity in the more general field of ... ways of exercising power'; and this in turn means that one should always 'regard punishment as a political tactic'.[11] Thus, as Garland and Young have pointed out, a central merit of Foucault's work is that it addresses (as much previous writing on punishment did not) 'an abiding sociological problem'; namely, 'how to connect a special object, like penality, with ... general and central sociological concepts like social structure or power'.[12]

Empirically, Foucault was especially interested in the fact that, a century after Damiens' execution, the dominant form of punishment in France had changed completely, from public executions and other physical punishments to imprisonment. This new modality of penal power (which was administered in private, not in public) was characterised as subjecting the offender to various forms of exercise, or training, intended to produce behavioural compliance, and therefore constituting a form of 'discipline'. The move from the public ceremony of royal power (Damiens) to the private administration of disciplinary training exercises (the prison) was seen by Foucault to be of deep social scientific importance.

But Foucault also observed that in the late eighteenth century a third kind of mechanism of penal power was widely discussed,[13] especially in the writings of various 'reformers', notably the Italian Cesare Beccaria.[14] Beccaria's theoretical approach was based on a particular version of social contract theory, according

---

[9] Ibid.

[10] A Margalit, *The Decent Society* (Cambridge, MA, Harvard University Press, 1996) 263.

[11] Foucault, above n 8 at 23.

[12] D Garland and P Young, 'Towards a Social Analysis of Penality' in D Garland and P Young (eds), *The Power to Punish: Contemporary Penality and Social Analysis* (London, Heinemann Educational Books, 1983) 1 at 8. Garland and Young's essay was influential in encouraging the now widespread use of the term 'penality' to refer to punishment systems viewed as social institutions.

[13] Foucault, above n 8, Part Two, ch 2.

[14] C Beccaria, *On Crimes and Punishments* [5th edn 1766] edited by Richard Bellamy and translated by Richard Davies (Cambridge, Cambridge University Press, 1995).

to which each individual citizen sacrifices part of his or her freedom 'in order to enjoy what remains in security and calm'; and 'the sum of these portions of freedom ... makes up the sovereignty of the nation'.[15] The sovereign nation-state, formed on this basis, then creates various criminal offences in order to promote 'security and calm', and these crimes are backed up by punishments which provide 'tangible motives' against law-breaking.[16] Logically, however, a state based on these principles necessarily has limited powers, because its powers are restricted to those that the citizens have transferred to it. Accordingly, Beccaria concluded his treatise with the following 'general axiom' on punishment: 'In order that punishment should not be an act of violence perpetrated by one or many upon a private citizen, it is essential that it should be public, speedy, necessary, the minimum possible in the given circumstances, proportionate to the crime, and determined by the law'.[17]

A further consequence arising from this type of social contract approach is that, when a person's punishment has been completed, his/her full entitlements as a citizen are regained. Thus, even while an offender is being punished, he/she is, in Foucault's striking phrase when describing Beccarian-style punishment, a 'juridical subject in the process of requalification' as a full citizen.[18]

There are clearly some important differences between Beccarian punishment (described by Foucault as 'juridical') and disciplinary imprisonment – notably, the contractual, rights-based and minimalist dimensions of juridical punishment, and the much greater emphasis on coercive training in the carceral mode of penality. Foucault was therefore very much interested in the fact that, while the juridical model was briefly experimented with in various places in the late eighteenth century, historically speaking it quickly gave way, as a mainstream mode of penal practice, to the carceral model.

At the end of Part Two of *Discipline and Punish*, Foucault provides a very useful summary of various key features of the three ideal-typical mechanisms of punishment that he identified.[19] (These features include contrasts between these mechanisms in terms of the locus of the power to punish; the mode of penalty employed; and the imputed status of the offender within each mechanism). This important passage of text is set out in tabular form in Figure 7.1.[20] A contrast

---

[15] Ibid at 9.

[16] Ibid.

[17] Ibid at 113.

[18] Foucault, above n 8 at 131.

[19] The 'ideal type' is a methodological tool developed by Max Weber. It has been usefully characterised as a 'conceptual abstraction' that may be 'employ[ed] in trying to get to grips with the complexities of the social world ... Patterns of behaviour and institutional forms like capitalism, or Protestantism, or bureaucracy, are each composed of a large number of interconnected elements, both normative and structural. In order to comprehend [such an institution] ... it is necessary to reduce it to its core components. We do this by singling out and accentuating the central or basic features of the institution in question and suppressing or downgrading [other] ... features': F Parkin, *Max Weber* (London, Tavistock, 1982) 28.

[20] A version of Figure 7.1 was previously published in AE Bottoms, 'Neglected Features of Contemporary Penal Systems' in Garland and Young (eds), above n 12 at 177.

of perhaps particular significance is shown in the first row of the table, which concerns the 'locus of the power to punish'. As noted above, the main focus of *Discipline and Punish* is an attempt to understand the shift from the display of royal force (in the corporal mode) to the administrative training apparatus (in the carceral mode); significantly, however, in the juridical mode the locus of power is different, and resides in the 'social body' itself.

Figure 7.1 Foucault's characterisation of key features of three mechanisms of punishment

	Corporal	Juridicial	Carceral
(a) Locus of the power to punish	Sovereign and his force	Social body	Administrative apparatus
(b) Intended residual object of the power to punish	Ritual marks of vengeance	Signs (coded sets of representation)	Traces (behavioural habits of obedience)
(c) Mode of penalty	Ceremony of power	Representation	Exercise
(d) Status of offender	Vanquished enemy	Juridicial subject in process of requalification	Individual subject to immediate coercion

Source: Adaptation of passage in Foucault, n 8 at 130–31.

The analytical categorisation contained in Figure 7.1 has potential relevance in several ways for the questions addressed in this chapter. First, it demonstrates that there are different kinds of penal censure. Contemporary penal theorists tend to use the concept of penal censure to refer to the kind of punishment systems adopted in liberal-democratic states, yet the gruesome punishment of Damiens was clearly also a form of censure, albeit a very cruel one. This draws attention to the fact that what we ordinarily describe as 'penal censure theory' contains some important normative elements beyond mere 'censure'.

Secondly, Figure 7.1 shows that there are some radical differences (relating to power relations and the administration of punishments) in the social mechanisms utilised within the three ideal-typical modes of penality that Foucault describes: to use his words, each mode has 'techniques possessing their own specificity in the more general ways of exercising power'[21]. Since the seminal analysis of HLA Hart,[22] penal philosophers have usually followed him by distinguishing, within their analyses, the three distinct normative questions of: (i) what justifies a society in punishing wrongdoers (the *'General Justifying Aim'*

---

[21] Foucault, above n 8 at 23.
[22] HLA Hart, 'Prolegomenon to the Principles of Punishment' (1960) 60 *Proceedings of the Aristotelian Society (New Series)* 1 reprinted in HLA Hart, *Punishment and Responsibilty*, 2nd edn edited by J Gardner (Oxford, Oxford University Press, 2008).

of a punishment system); (ii) to whom may punishment justifiably be applied (the *distribution* of punishment); and (iii) what principles should determine the *amount* of punishment to be received by each offender? The strong implication of Foucault's work is that we need to add a fourth dimension to normative penal theorising by asking: 'what can be said about how a state should select the *modes of punishment* adopted within its criminal justice system?' Of the three penal theorists mainly considered in this chapter, Antony Duff has been the most alive to this issue,[23] and it is a topic to which we will return briefly in section V below.

Thirdly, in the context of the present chapter a matter of special significance concerns the detailed contrasts between Foucault's 'carceral' and 'juridical' modes (see Figure 7.1). This is because something akin to the carceral model had, by the 1960s, become very influential in many countries – and perhaps particularly in the United States, where many states had (in the alleged interests of 'treatment' and 'training') developed laws whereby the majority of custodial sentences were imposed for indeterminate amounts of time (for example 'five to ten years'). In such sentences, the prisoner's release date was determined primarily by whether he/she had – in the judgement of a parole board or equivalent body – sufficiently responded to the treatment or training offered; in other words, whether he/she had been sufficiently 'disciplined', in Foucault's language. Since this criterion bore no necessary relation to the seriousness of the crime committed, Beccaria's requirement that the amount of punishment should be 'proportionate to the crime'[24] was only rarely in evidence. As other chapters in this volume make clear, *Doing Justice* provided a stringent and effective critique of this kind of penal system, and to replace it, von Hirsch advocated a version of what Foucault described as the 'juridical model'. (Indeed, *Doing Justice* reports that 'to our surprise, we found ourselves returning to the ideas of such Enlightenment thinkers as ... Beccaria'[25]; and the main principles of the report are fully congruent with Beccaria's concluding 'general axiom', as previously cited). Andrew von Hirsch therefore enunciated a truly *liberal* theory of punishment, in both the technical and the popular sense of that word; and it was from this liberal standpoint that he was later to criticise the encouragement of repentance as an appropriate goal for a contemporary liberal-democratic state penal system. The question of whether the goal of promoting repentance is an appropriate aim for the penal system of a liberal-democratic state is therefore an important and live issue, to which we must now turn.

---

[23] Duff, above n 4 ch 3. See also Duff's later summary account of his theory, where he argues that we need to 'attend not just to the general meaning of punishment as a mode of censure, but to the distinctive meanings of different modes of punishment ... This is a dimension of punishment that has not received enough theoretical attention': RA Duff, 'Punishment, Retribution and Communication' in A von Hirsch, A Ashworth and J Roberts (eds), *Principled Sentencing: Readings on Theory and Policy*, 3rd edn (Oxford, Hart Publishing, 2009) 126 at 132.

[24] Beccaria, above n 14 at 113.

[25] Von Hirsch, above n 2 at 6.

II. THE REPENTANCE DEBATE IN PENAL CENSURE THEORY

At the beginning of a paper in which he went on to criticise Antony Duff's views on repentance and punishment, Andrew von Hirsch made clear that his critique was offered within a largely shared conceptual framework. As he put it, both he and Duff advocate the adoption of:

[A] *communicative* perspective on the criminal sanction's general justification: punishment, we both believe, should be conceptualized as a form of censure. Penal censure has important moral functions that are not reducible to crime prevention … What a purely "neutral" sanction not embodying blame would deny … is precisely this recognition of the person's status as a moral agent.[26]

John Tasioulas would also concur with this statement.[27] All three writers would also agree that, as Antony Duff once put it, 'whatever puzzles there might be about the general [retributivist] idea that crimes "deserve" punishment … there is surely nothing puzzling about the idea that wrongdoing deserves censure'.[28] However, expressions of censure can be merely verbal, so a censure theory of *punishment* (and, in particular, state punishment) needs also to explain what justifies the so-called 'hard treatment' element of state penalties. On this point, as well as on the possible role of repentance within a state punishment system, there are some divergences between the three theorists: all three agree that hard treatment can be justified, but their reasons for this conclusion differ.[29] However, this divergence is of only marginal significance to the main concerns of this paper, so I shall not develop it here.

To address the 'repentance debate' within penal censure theory, I shall first summarise some main features of the theoretical approach advanced by Antony Duff, who was the first major modern theorist to advocate a significant role for repentance within state penal systems.[30] Issues relating to the definition of repentance, and liberal objections to the promotion of repentance within punishment systems, will then also be explored.

---

[26] Von Hirsch in Matravers (ed), above n 7 at 69 (emphasis in original). Note that in this statement von Hirsch assumes that acts of censure necessarily 'embody' blame. Following the illuminating analysis of John Kleinig ('The Architecture of Censure', this volume) that censure is usually a formalised or institutionalised matter, I shall make the same assumption, while noting that the reverse statement is (on Kleinig's analysis) not true, since blaming can, and often does, take place more informally.

[27] Tasioulas, 'Punishment and Repentance', above n 5.

[28] RA Duff, 'Punishment, Communication and Community' in M Matravers (ed), above n 7 at 50.

[29] On this point, the most notable difference in the existing literature has been that von Hirsch, unlike the other two theorists, included crime prevention alongside censure as dual elements within the General Justifying Aim of a penal system: A von Hirsch, *Deserved Criminal Sentences* (Oxford, Hart/Bloomsbury, 2017) ch 3. However, von Hirsch modifies his view on this matter in his chapter in the present volume.

[30] Initially in RA Duff, *Trials and Punishments* (Cambridge, Cambridge University Press, 1986) ch 9; later in various texts, and most fully in Duff, above n 4.

A. Antony Duff's Theory of Communicative Punishment

A useful way to begin considering Duff's theory is to quote some words from the beginning and the end of the volume in which that theory is most fully elaborated, namely *Punishment, Communication and Community*.[31]

In the concluding paragraph of his book, Duff states that the task of theorising the justification of criminal punishment is 'not the task of finding a normative theory that will justify something like our existing penal practices'. Rather, it is the task of providing an in-principle normative justification for a defensible 'ideal' system of state punishment, in the light of which we can begin the task of 'so transforming the content and context of criminal punishment that it can become what it ought to be'.[32] In his writings, Duff frequently emphasises this 'ideal' feature of his theory, and it is a matter that must always be borne in mind by his readers.

In the introduction to the same volume, Antony Duff notes that there are reasonable grounds for being suspicious of anyone who offers 'a grand unitary "theory of punishment"'. Yet he immediately (and disarmingly) indicates that 'a unitary theory is what I offer'.[33] So what is this theory? Duff states it very succinctly: 'Criminal punishment ... should communicate to offenders the censure they deserve for their crimes, and should aim through that communicative process to persuade them to repent their crimes, to try to reform themselves, and thus to reconcile themselves with those whom they wronged'.[34]

Three points relating to this summary are of the greatest importance. First, the central justification of state punishment is the communication of *deserved censure*. Thus, Duff offers an explicitly retributive theory of punishment, focused on the traditional retributive concept of desert.

But secondly, Duff's theory is also centrally concerned with what he has elsewhere called 'the three "R"s of punishment'[35], namely *repentance, reform, and reconciliation*; and this has led Duff and others to refer to his theory, in shorthand, as a theory of 'punishment as secular penance'.[36] What has been

---

[31] Duff, above n 4.

[32] Ibid at 201.

[33] Ibid at xvii.

[34] Ibid. Duff qualifies his summary by saying that he does not imagine that any actual criminal justice system will ever be structured by a single unitary theory; however, he argues – consistently with the comments already quoted – that his account 'provides an ideal conception of what criminal punishment ought to be that deserves a central place, even if not the only place, in our normative understanding of punishment' (ibid at xvii–xviii).

[35] Ibid at 107.

[36] This analogy was most fully elaborated in Duff, *Trials and Punishments* above n 30; but see also, for example, 'Desert and Penance' in A von Hirsch and A Ashworth (eds), *Principled Sentencing*, 2nd edn (Oxford, Hart, 1998) 161. In later statements of his theory, Duff tends to give less prominence to the penance analogy; nevertheless, his 2009 summary paper restates the view that 'criminal punishment, on this account, can be seen as a species of secular penance': Duff, 'Punishment, Retribution and Communication' above n 23 at 131.

less often commented upon, but is in my view more important, is that his strong advocacy of 'the three Rs' shows that Duff, while clearly working within the retributivist tradition, nevertheless breaks with those versions of retributivism that are exclusively backward-looking (that is, whose accounts of punishment are focused solely on its appropriateness as a response to the wrong committed). For Duff as a retributive theorist, the offender's reform, and his reconciliation with society, are integral dimensions of the punishment process, even although they are future-oriented.[37]

This leads directly to the third point. A casual reader might interpret this future-oriented element in Duff's theory in instrumentalist terms (for example: 'the purpose of punishment is to induce repentance, reform and reconciliation'). Accordingly, Antony Duff has been at pains to emphasise that what makes punishment an appropriate way of pursuing 'the three Rs' is – in his words – 'not that it is likely to be instrumentally efficient in achieving them, but that it is *intrinsically appropriate* to them: [deserved punishment] is *the proper way to try to achieve those ends* if we are to show offenders (as well as victims) the respect and concern due to them, since only in this way do we address them as responsible moral agents in terms appropriate to the wrongs that they have committed and must now repair'.[38]

This important statement necessarily leads to a further question: how and why is punishment an 'intrinsically appropriate' way to achieve the three Rs? It is in response to this question that the communicative dimension of Duff's theory comes especially to the fore. For him, conviction and punishment 'communicate the censure that [the] wrongs deserve; internal to censure is the intention or hope that the person censured will accept it as justified; and to accept censure as justified is to accept that one did wrong, which entails *repenting that wrong and seeing the need to avoid such wrongdoing in future*'.[39] This last point is frequently repeated in Duff's work; thus, in an earlier essay he speaks of the role of punishment being 'to persuade [the offender] to accept as deserved the censure which punishment communicates – *an acceptance which must involve repentance*'.[40]

To assess fully the validity of this latter claim, we need some further explication of what Duff means by the term 'repentance'. And it turns out that his understanding of this concept is rather stringent:

> When I have done wrong, it is often tempting and all too easy to distract myself from that fact. I might say, to myself or to others, "Yes, I did wrong and I am sorry

---

[37] Indeed, Duff has said that his account 'offers a "third way" between retributivism and consequentialism: a way that does justice both to the retributivist thought that punishment must be focused on and justified by a past crime and to the consequentialist concern that punishment must aim to achieve some good': Duff, 'Punishment, Retribution and Communication' ibid.

[38] Ibid (emphasis added).

[39] Duff, above n 4 at 80 (emphasis added).

[40] Duff, above n 28 at 51 (emphasis added).

for it". I might think that I have now repented the wrong. But all too often I have not seriously repented, because I have not thought seriously enough about, that wrong. I allow myself to think that the matter is closed when I have merely papered it over. Repentance, at least with serious wrongs, cannot of its nature be something that is achieved and finished with in a moment ... It must go deep with the wrongdoer ... It must involve thinking through and seeking to understand what I did to the person I wronged and how I could have done it. ... [O]ne purpose of penal hard treatment ... is [to be] a way of trying to focus [the offender's] attention on his crime. It provides a structure within which, we hope, he will be able to think about the nature and implications of his crime, face up to it more adequately than he might otherwise (being human) do, and so arrive at a more authentic repentance. *As fallible human beings, we need such penances to assist and deepen repentance.*[41]

Given the comment, in this quotation, that repentance 'must go deep with the wrongdoer', I shall in the remainder of this chapter refer to this type of conceptualisation as a 'deep' understanding of repentance.

A final point to note in this summary account of Duff's theory is that he has often been asked how his approach would apply in circumstances where 'we have good reason to be empirically sure that our attempt to persuade an offender to repentance will fail'. His answer is that, in such a situation, 'we must still make the attempt', because if we did not do so we would have 'give[n] up on the offender as a moral agent – as someone within the reach of remorse – which is something we should never do'.[42]

Some aspects of Duff's theorisation will be discussed later in this chapter, but at this stage it seems appropriate to offer three interim comments, of a varied character.

First, Duff's statement that if an offender accepts censure, this acceptance 'must involve repentance'[43] (in the sense specified above) seems to be an empirical claim. However, as a later section of this chapter will show, this claim is not supported by the available empirical evidence.

Secondly, although as we have seen Duff has often used the term 'secular penance' as a shorthand description of his theory, this term seems to be not entirely appropriate. In religious usage, 'penance' is a hardship or exercise that a repentant sinner is ordered to undergo after having voluntarily confessed his/her wrongdoing, and declared an intention to avoid it in future; in response to this confession, the priest pronounces absolution and the appropriate penance. By contrast, Duff's theory of punishment, as stated in his summary quoted above, postulates that the purpose of a punishment system is to 'communicate to offenders the censure they deserve for their crimes', and that the system '*should aim through that communicative process to persuade them to repent their crimes*, to try to reform themselves, and thus to reconcile themselves with

---

[41] Duff, above n 4 at 107–08 (emphasis added).
[42] Duff, 'Punishment, Retribution and Communication' above n 23 at 131.
[43] Duff, above n 28 at 51.

those whom they wronged'.[44] There is a significant difference between these two kinds of social process, because true penance *follows* repentance, but in Duff's theory punishment *aims to encourage* repentance. (Even in pre-Reformation times, when penitential acts were often more material and 'punitive' than they are today, this difference was recognised by church authorities[45]). This might seem to be a weakness of Duff's theory, but I think that, ultimately, it is not. That is because the concept of 'penance' is not central to his theory – at least in its developed form[46] – in the way that 'the three Rs' are central. 'The three Rs', unlike 'penance', are concepts that appear in Duff's own summary of his theory (see above), and it is entirely possible to analyse the theory articulated in that summary in its own terms, and without reference to penance. That is how I shall proceed in the sections that follow.

Thirdly and much more positively, Duff's suggestion that a censure-based theory *intrinsically involves* a future-oriented dimension is extremely interesting. It is supported by the recent work of Miranda Fricker,[47] in which she argues that 'communicative blame' is the paradigmatic form of blame.[48] Blame, as we all know, can easily take harsh and socially destructive forms; but Fricker argues that well-directed *communicative* blame is essential to everyday life, and to 'the interpersonal normative energy that perpetually regenerates and develops shared moral consciousness'.[49] That is to say, every society depends to an extent on shared moral understandings; and the (usually minor forms of) praise and blame that are used in everyday communication will, if they are handled well, help to develop a well-functioning moral community.

Definitionally, communicative blame is seen by Fricker as 'a basic second-personal interaction of X blaming Y for an action, motive or attitude (or lack therof)'.[50] Using the terminology of JL Austin's speech-act theory[51] (the basic message of which is that 'in saying something, we do something'), Fricker goes on to argue two points. First, the 'illocutionary point' of any performance of

---

[44] Duff, above n 4 at xvii.

[45] See TN Tentler, *Sin and Confession on the Eve of the Reformation* (Princeton, Princeton University Press, 1977) at 122, commenting that there are people 'who admit they are inadequately sorry and unprepared to give up their favorite sins … Such a person cannot, of course, be absolved, even though he confesses his sins completely. On the other hand, neither is he to be sent away in despair. He should be admonished, encouraged, and told to perform a pious act, *not as a penance* but rather in the hope that its performance will lead him to eventual reform' (emphasis added). Compare the suggestion by Duff (above n 30 at 251) that, while penance is usually 'a *self-imposed* punishment through which [a sinner] can express his repentance and restore himself to the communion' there can also be 'an *imposed* penance' which can 'bring an initially unrepentant sinner to repentance' (emphases added).

[46] As noted above (n 36), the penance analogy was especially prominent in Duff's first statement of his theory: Duff, above n 30.

[47] M Fricker, 'What's the Point of Blame?: A Paradigm-Based Explanation' (2016) 50 *Nous* 165.

[48] On the relationship between the concepts of 'censure' and 'blame', see n 26 above.

[49] Fricker, above n 47 at 167.

[50] Ibid.

[51] JL Austin, *How to Do Things with Words* 2nd edn edited by JO Urmson and M Sbisa (Oxford, Clarendon Press, 1975).

communicative blame is, at minimum, to evoke in the wrongdoer a 'moral perception of the wrong one has done'[52] – and thereby better to align the moral perspectives of the blamer and the person blamed.[53] Then, secondly, Fricker argues that 'the perlocutionary point of Communicative Blame is to prompt a change for the better in the behaviour (inner and outer) of the wrongdoer'.[54]

Summarising her argument, Fricker says:

> By focusing on the interpersonal mechanism of Communicative Blame in its everyday functional mode, and by reference to its transformative illocutionary and perlocutionary points, I hope to have shown that blame need not, and does not basically, express any unworthy impetus such as vengeful retributive drive, moralistic high-handedness or anxious control-freakery; but is rather fueled by a transformative moral-epistemic energy towards shared moral sensibility, along with a candidly disciplinary hope. It is a communicative act that reprimands with feeling, in the hope of bringing the wrongdoer to better understand and perhaps correct her behaviour.[55]

It is clear from this summary that there are important similarities between Fricker's analysis of communicative blame and Antony Duff's analysis of communicative censure.[56] But Fricker, although mentioning remorse, does not explicitly discuss repentance; and so we now need to turn to aspects of the post-Duff 'repentance debate' within penal censure theory.

B. The Meaning of Repentance

One important issue in this debate concerns the meaning of the term 'repentance' itself. This is not considered in von Hirsch's writings; his discussion of 'repentance' and 'penance' is confined to a critique of Duff's work, and he therefore (and not unnaturally) takes for granted Duff's 'deep' concept of repentance (see previous discussion). In marked contrast, John Tasioulas has given detailed attention to the concept of repentance.[57] He identifies five 'elements' of this

---

[52] Fricker, above n 47 at 167. Austin (ibid at 98–99) explains that, in general, 'to perform a locutionary act' (that is, to speak) is also, at the same time, 'to perform an illocutionary act' such as 'giving some information', 'asking … a question' or 'pronouncing sentence'. Fricker's claim is that the illocutionary act of communicative blaming has *ipso facto* the aim of inducing in the person blamed the 'moral perception' described in the text.

[53] Fricker's text (ibid) actually goes further by saying that the illocutionary point is 'to inspire remorse in the wrongdoer, where remorse is understood as a pained moral perception of the wrong one has done'. But it can be argued that the inclusion of 'pained' and 'remorse' adds an emotional dimension that need not be present in every expression of communicative blame, for example as between parent and child.

[54] Ibid at 173. Austin (above n 51 at 101) explains the concept of a 'perlocutionary act' as follows: 'Saying something will often … produce certain consequential effects upon the feelings, thoughts or actions of the audience … and it may be done with the design, intention, or purpose of producing them'. Fricker's claim is that an act of communicative blaming is also a perlocutionary act, spoken with the aim of improving the wrongdoer's subsequent behaviour.

[55] Ibid at 174–75.

[56] This is briefly recognised by Fricker in a footnote: ibid at 183 n 15.

[57] Tasioulas, 'Repentance and the Liberal State' above n 5 section II.

concept, which can, he suggests, be 'schematically' stated as follows, in the 'rough temporal order in which they standardly appear':

(a)   The wrongdoer is assailed by guilt for his wrongdoing;

(b)   He comes to judge that what he did was wrong and to blame himself for his wrongdoing;

(c)   He confesses his wrongdoing and sincerely apologises for what he did;

(d)   He makes moral (and not only material) reparation for his wrong; this will 'typically involve publicly accepting deserved blame, including willingly undergoing … any punishment that is properly inflicted'; and

(e)   He resolves not to commit such a wrong again, and overcomes the 'moral defects' that led him to commit the crime.[58]

Although Tasioulas identifies these five separate elements of repentance, he also argues that it is not necessary for all the elements to be present in order to describe an offender as repentant: 'we need not deny the name, and any significance, to less full-blooded manifestations'.[59] Indeed, he suggests that one 'promising line of thought' affirms that the only 'necessary condition' for repentance is 'the presence of one or more of these elements, to some requisite degree'.[60] Accordingly, 'there are many cases of criminal wrongdoing in which the process of repentance, even if tolerably complete, need not sound a deep note in the offender's psyche'.[61] Also, when considering punishment, Tasioulas argues that 'the main point of contact with [the] schematic account of [the elements of] repentance is (d)'; this is because 'by accepting that his punishment is justified … and willingly undergoing it, the punishment operates as a public means of acknowledging his guilt and making moral reparation for it'[62] – even although (d) in itself does not include the self-blaming dimensions of elements (a), (b) and (c).

These brief quotations are sufficient to show that there is a degree of divergence between Duff and Tasioulas in their understanding of repentance, with the latter taking a significantly less stringent view of the requirements of repentance within a penal system.[63] This difference, and other definitional issues relating to repentance, will remain of importance as the discussion proceeds.

C. Objections to Repentance as a Goal within State Penal Systems

From an early date, Andrew von Hirsch has, from an explicitly liberal stance within political philosophy, contested Duff's view of the role of repentance within state punishment.[64] In a recent summary of his theoretical position, von

[58] Ibid at 488–89.
[59] Ibid at 491.
[60] Ibid.
[61] Ibid at 511.
[62] Ibid at 495.
[63] Although, perhaps strangely, Tasioulas does not draw attention to this difference.
[64] See the references cited at n 7 above.

Hirsch has stated that his most fundamental criticism of Duff's work is that he has doubts about 'the state's proper standing to delve so deeply into sentenced offenders' moral attitudes';[65] in the same source, he also explicitly reaffirms the arguments on this topic that he and Andrew Ashworth published in 2005.[66] Duff has on various occasions responded to these criticisms.[67] John Tasioulas has taken an intermediate position in this debate. He concedes that the concerns raised by liberal theorists such as von Hirsch are 'undeniably important'; nevertheless, he argues that these concerns should be read as 'constraining the character and fulfilment' of the role of repentance within state penal systems, rather than precluding any such role.[68]

In their chapter on this topic, von Hirsch and Ashworth rightly emphasise that punishment can have different connotations in different social contexts, and that state punishment is a special case, not to be too easily compared with punishments within other contexts such as professional organisations, schools, universities, or religious institutions. In discussing justifiable state punishments, they argue, we always need to bear in mind the 'constitutive grounds' (or raison d'être) of state penal systems, which focus on 'the character of the minimum norms for peaceable co-existence, and their enforcement'.[69] Where punishments are properly sustainable on these grounds, 'these coercive institutions might also be given certain supplemental functions, perhaps concerned in part with the offender's "reform" – but the latter functions cannot alone support the existence of the criminal sanction'.[70]

It is interesting that, in the passage just cited, von Hirsch and Ashworth explicitly endorse 'reform' as a supplemental (and, clearly, future-oriented) feature of state penal systems – a view that is also supported by Duff (see above on 'the three Rs'). Unfortunately, this point of congruence is missed by von Hirsch and Ashworth, who never refer to Duff's 'three Rs', but always – when discussing his theorisation – to an undifferentiated concept of 'the penance perspective', within which Duff's deep version of repentance is by implication granted the dominant role. It is this that leads von Hirsch and Ashworth to object to the potential intrusiveness of state actions in pursuit of hoped-for repentance (see above). They argue that a novice monk would not be entitled to say to an abbot 'it's none of your business what I feel', but that a convicted citizen could very reasonably, in a liberal state, say exactly that in response to intrusive inquiries by state officials about deep aspects of his/her personal life.[71]

A slightly different way of expressing this point is to distinguish, as von Hirsch did in some earlier writings, between penal censure that 'deals with

---

[65] Von Hirsch, above n 29 at 43.

[66] Von Hirsch and Ashworth, above n 7.

[67] Perhaps most notably in the direct exchange of views between von Hirsch and Duff in Matravers (ed), above n 7.

[68] Tasioulas, 'Repentance and the Liberal State' above n 5 at 510.

[69] Von Hirsch and Ashworth, above n 7 at 100.

[70] Ibid at 101.

[71] Ibid at 104.

the person *externally*' (as advocated by von Hirsch) and penal censure that 'is meant to elicit certain *internal* states' (including the promotion of repentance, as advocated by Duff).[72] Expanding on this distinction, von Hirsch indicates that, in his view, 'the disapproval conveyed by the sanction gives the actor the opportunity to reconsider his actions and to feel shame or regret. However, it is left to him to respond: censure, on my analysis, need not specially be fashioned to elicit certain sentiments in him – whether those be shame, repentance or whatever'.[73]

As becomes clear from quotations such as these, the von Hirsch-Ashworth critique of repentance has theoretical linkages to two other relevant debates. The first concerns theories of the liberal state, and in particular the view that such a state must remain neutral as between competing conceptions of the good life (for example, by people of different faiths). By advocating censure for the offender's crime, but then postulating that the punishment simply gives him 'the opportunity to reconsider his actions' (without any particular steer from the state about *how* he should reconsider), von Hirsch and Ashworth locate themselves firmly in this liberal tradition.

Then, secondly, there is the historical contrast between the 'juridical' and the 'carceral' traditions of penality, to which Foucault drew attention, and which in more recent times was a key issue after the publication of *Doing Justice*. An important part of the goal of the 'carceral model' (and of the 'rehabilitative ideal' as it had developed in the United States by the mid-twentieth century[74]) was precisely to seek to rehabilitate the 'whole person', which meant a degree of probing into his inner life: he/she was, in Foucault's language, the subject of *discipline*, imposed by the state. The 'juridical tradition', as Foucault described it, was much more limited in its aims; and both *Doing Justice* and the earlier critique of the rehabilitative ideal by the American Friends Service Committee,[75] sought to remove some of the injustices that had arisen from the implementation of the vision underpinning this 'ideal'. In light of this background, von Hirsch and Ashworth's caution about state intrusiveness is both understandable and justified. Equally justified is their anxiety about the likely ineffectiveness of possible side-constraints against excessive intrusiveness within a basically disciplinary system: as they put it, 'if the very point of the penal process is to induce certain attitudes ..., it will be far more difficult to develop adequate restrictions on scrutiny of offender attitudes'.[76]

In the face of substantial objections such as these, how does a theorist such as John Tasioulas seek to defend the inclusion by a liberal state of a goal of repentance within its penal system? He begins by helpfully distinguishing

---

[72] Von Hirsch, above n 3 at 72.

[73] Ibid.

[74] FA Allen, *The Decline of the Rehabilitative Ideal: Penal Policy and Social Purpose* (New Haven, Yale University Press, 1981).

[75] American Friends Service Committee, *Struggle for Justice* (New York, Hill and Wang, 1971).

[76] Von Hirsch and Ashworth, above n 7 at 105.

two separate features of the liberal critique: one relating to the citizen's *autonomy*, and the other to the dangers of *moral perfectionism*. In both cases, he spells out well the liberal objection, which in the former case is as follows:

> The problem with trying to engineer repentance through hard treatment ... is that it is a gross interference with the offender's autonomy. This sort of intrusion into his innermost self fails to respect his status as a responsible moral agent: it is an attempt coercively to manipulate his deepest moral feelings and convictions, pre-empting his own decision-making about how it is best for him to live. [Even if] the process succeeds, the resultant condition will have been achieved heteronomously and, as in indoctrination or domination, the offender's rational capacities will have been overcome.[77]

In response to this objection, however, Tasioulas reasonably suggests that it is 'full-blown repentance, of the character-transforming ... variety' that is particularly in focus in the objection.[78] As we have seen, his own approach to repentance in penal systems by no means requires that this 'full-blown' version of the concept be adopted. Accordingly, he believes that his theory is not vulnerable to the critique, not least because the repentance he seeks to promote is one that will be chosen autonomously.

Turning to the second objection, that of moral perfectionism, the liberal anxiety here is that the inclusion of repentance as a goal within penal systems might seem to put 'the state in the business of trying to foster healthy moral responses and improved moral characters among its citizenry'; and this is contrary to the standard liberal view that it is not appropriate for a state to deploy its power in order to promote a particular version of the good.[79] Tasioulas has a lengthy and complex response to this objection, which cannot be fully summarised here.[80] One crucial point, however, is his suggestion that:

> The state's authority to concern itself with repentance stems ... from the fact that doing so enables ... citizens better to comply with the values that they already have reason to comply with. In particular, it facilitates criminal wrongdoers in atoning for their wrongs by reintegrating themselves with those values. And here it must be stressed that the correct values are to be understood as objectively correct, rather than whichever values happen to be highly prized by a given community[81] ... Atonement ... is first and foremost reintegration with objective values that apply to the offender whether he identifies with them or not.[82]

---

[77] Tasioulas, 'Repentance and the Liberal State' above n 5 at 509.

[78] Ibid at 511.

[79] Ibid at 513.

[80] Ibid at 513–18.

[81] Consistently with this view, Tasioulas (ibid at 514) explicitly contrasts his position with that of 'some defenders of the importance of repentance in legal punishment' (including Duff) who show a 'tendency ... to articulate their theory under the auspices of a general political communitarianism'.

[82] Ibid at 513–14.

On Tasioulas' view, therefore, while in general a liberal state is committed to neutrality with regard to competing visions of the good, its criminal law is of necessity committed to upholding certain core values ('objective values', as Tasioulas puts it) that are necessary for the basic preservation of the public peace. It is, so the argument goes, therefore not 'moral perfectionism' to try to persuade offenders to reconnect with such values through repentance/atonement.

D. Overview of the Repentance Debate

Where, then, are we left as a result of the repentance debate, as developed in the existing literature? Different commentators might well offer differing responses to this question, but one reasonable interpretation would seem to be as follows:

 (i) Antony Duff's suggestion that a future-oriented dimension is intrinsically appropriate to a retributive, communicative censure-based theory of punishment is a proposal of great interest and importance, and is congruent with Miranda Fricker's theory of communicative blame;

 (ii) However, Duff's proposal that state punishment should aim to promote a 'deep' version of repentance (as the first of his 'three Rs') is difficult to reconcile with justifiable liberal objections that this will breach the offender's autonomy, and run the risk of aiming at an inappropriate moral perfectionism;

(iii) As John Tasioulas has shown, less 'full-blown' versions of repentance can more easily be defended as part of a liberal penal system; and the debate between his approach and that of von Hirsch and Ashworth seems to be finely balanced. However, Tasioulas' defence seems to lack precision about what exactly might count as a justifiable version of 'repentance' within a penal system.[83] In the practical world of criminal justice, this seems likely to lead to a lack of clarity among managers and practitioners about how they might reasonably be expected to promote such an imprecise goal.

If this interpretation has merit, then a first step towards unlocking some of the puzzles would seem to be to return once again to the meaning of 'repentance', to see whether it can be clarified in ways that might make it more viable within penal systems, without falling foul of reasonable liberal objections.

---

[83] See his comment, previously quoted, that, on one 'promising line of thought', the only necessary condition for the characterisation of a response as one of repentance is 'the presence of one or more of' the various elements of repentance, 'to some requisite degree': ibid at 491.

III. REPENTANCE AS 'TURNING AROUND'

In this section, I shall introduce a fresh theoretical understanding of 'repentance' which can, I believe, help to take the debate forward. The central feature of this understanding is well captured in the opening words of the entry for 'repentance' in a 1967 *Dictionary of Christian Ethics*: 'Christian thought about sin and repentance can be represented by the figure of a man with his back turned to God and moving away from him; the figure stops still, and then turns to face God and begins to move towards him'.[84] The author adds, perhaps unnecessarily, that this is not intended as a literal or allegorical description of sin and repentance; rather it is meant as 'an indication of the way to think about' such matters.

In the present context, it is of course necessary to translate this suggestion into secular terms. On this basis, its particular interest lies in the fact that the 'way of thinking' it suggests is in some ways significantly different from the accounts of repentance offered by Antony Duff and John Tasioulas. In each of those accounts, self-blame plays a prominent role;[85] by contrast, in the cited dictionary description, primacy is given to the act of turning away from a less good towards a better path. Self-blame is of course not precluded, but it is not the dominant motif.

A characterisation of repentance as 'turning around' is certainly not the only interpretation available within the Christian tradition; but, equally, it is not an eccentric understanding within that tradition. To illustrate this point, consider the Greek words *metanoeō* (a verb) and *metanoia* (a noun), which in English versions of the New Testament are usually translated 'to repent' and 'repentance'. There is a consensus in modern scholarship that the core meaning of *metanoia* is simply 'a change of mind or purpose'.[86] To take a prominent example of how the word is used, in the Gospel of Mark the first words attributed to Jesus at the beginning of his ministry are: 'The time is fulfilled, and the kingdom of God has come near; repent [*metanoeite*], and believe the good news'.[87] As the context suggests, the main action for which this statement calls is a change of mind or purpose in response to the radically new situation described.

---

[84] RFC Browne, 'Repentance' in J Macquarrie (ed), *A Dictionary of Christian Ethics* (London, SCM Press, 1967) 295.

[85] More obviously so in Duff's theorisation; but note the wording of elements (a), (b) and (c) in Tasioulas' 'schematic' understanding of the concept of repentance, previously discussed.

[86] A modern edition of a classical Greek-English Lexicon offers definitions as follows: *metanoia*: 'change of mind or heart', 'repentance', 'regret', and possibly 'afterthought'; *metanoeō*: 'to perceive afterwards or too late', 'to change one's mind or purpose' and 'to repent [of]': H G Liddell, R Scott and H S Jones (eds) *A Greek-English Lexicon*, 9th edn (Oxford, Clarendon Press, 1968) at 1115. See also the definitions in FW Danker (ed), *A Greek-English Lexicon of the New Testament and Early Christian Literature*, 3rd edn (Chicago, University of Chicago Press, 2000) at 640: *metanoia*: primarily 'a change of mind', also 'repentance, turning around, conversion'; *metanoeō*: (i) change one's mind, (ii) feel remorse, repent, be converted.

[87] *Mark* 1:15 (translation from the New Revised Standard Version). All the main English translations since the 1611 Authorised Version have used the word 'repent' when translating this verse.

Before the Reformation, however, repentance was understood primarily in relation to the Western church's sacrament of penance – a view that was enhanced by the fact that most bibles were in Latin, and *metanoia* was translated as *poenitentia*. This 'penitential' interpretation was forcefully challenged by Luther in his Ninety-five Theses of 1517.[88] However, in everyday contemporary understandings of repentance, the 'penitential' view remains powerful, as is attested by the extract from an American periodical quoted at the beginning of this chapter. It is also, of course, this version of the concept that is adopted in Duff's theory of punishment.

Given this background, some contemporary scholars have, when writing in English, chosen to use the word *metanoia* instead of 'repentance, penance, penitence and so on', on the grounds that 'the former means something entirely different from the latter'.[89] However, an alternative view is that this is an exaggeration: while '*metanoia* as a "change of mind" is a broader term compared with repentance, it nevertheless contains within its semantic range … the concepts of regret, sorrow for sin and moral amendment associated with "repentance" … To completely dissociate the words, then, would be unwise'.[90] On this view – which I shall follow – the core meaning of *metanoia* is indeed a 'turning around', but that does not preclude 'turning around' sometimes including regret and remorse. In light of these definitional issues, in the remainder of this chapter I will explore the application to punishment theory of an understanding of repentance as primarily 'turning around' (as in the dictionary metaphor) or 'a change of mind or purpose' (that is, as *metanoia,* as standardly translated in English bibles). I will further propose that, on this understanding of repentance, it is justifiable for the penal system of a liberal state to encourage a commitment to repentance among those who are punished.

This proposal can be elaborated as follows. All three main theorists considered in this chapter (Duff, Tasioulas and von Hirsch) concur in adopting a censure-based, communicative theory of punishment. Miranda Fricker's theorisation of communicative blame in effect endorses and develops an aspect of Duff's theory by suggesting that communicative blame ('a basic second-personal interaction of X blaming Y for an action') of course conveys moral disapproval, but that it also has a (future-oriented) 'perlocutionary point', namely, 'to prompt a change for the better in the behaviour (inner and outer) of the wrongdoer'.[91] This is not quite what von Hirsch has in mind for punishments as censure: on his analysis, it will be recalled, 'the disapproval conveyed by the sanction gives the actor the opportunity to reconsider his actions and to feel shame or regret.

---

[88] Torrance, above n 1 at 10. Luther's second thesis (as translated by Torrance) states that the word repentance 'cannot be understood to mean sacramental penance, i.e. confession and satisfaction, which is administered by the priests'.

[89] Ibid at 31.

[90] Ibid.

[91] Fricker, above n 47 at 167, 173.

However, it is left to him to respond …'[92] – with, it seems, no particular recommendation as to how he should respond to the censure. But Tasioulas is surely right in arguing that the criminal offences proscribed by a justified liberal penal code will be based on 'objective values'. On that basis, it is hard to see why there should be any objection in principle to a liberal state seeking to shape its penal system so that the perlocutionary point of the censure is to prompt a change for the better in the behaviour of the offender, in relation to the proscribed offences. That does *not* mean making deep intrusions into the life of the offender against his will – the objections of liberal theorists to this kind of practice are theoretically sound, and the known excesses during the period of the 'rehabilitative ideal' offer a salutary warning about this kind of practice. A liberal state will therefore seek to encourage a 'turning around' by the offender, but not the adoption of deep contrition – that will be left as the private concern of the punished citizen.[93]

By comparison with the rather complex concept of repentance within punishment systems advocated by Tasioulas, a further advantage of the notion of 'repentance as turning around' is its simplicity. Staff within prison services, probation services and the like can easily see the point of a penal theory that permits the imposition of some deprivations on offenders as a punishment, yet simultaneously suggests that an important feature of this punishment is that it should encourage those punished to think about changing their behaviour in the future. That simplicity should also be apparent to offenders – and, as we shall see in the next section, it is highly congruent with how they often currently respond to being punished.

We should also note a subtle difference in the temporal focus as between Duff's 'deep' understanding of repentance and 'repentance as turning around'. As we have seen, Duff has commented that 'all too often' people who think they have repented have not truly done so, because they 'have not thought seriously enough about that wrong'.[94] This is a primarily backward-looking understanding of repentance, although, as Duff has made clear, it naturally leads to a determination to behave differently in the future.[95] By contrast, the primary focus of 'repentance as turning around' is the future state, or future relationship, to which the person repenting aspires. It is recognised that one needs to move on from – and deal with – the past, but it is the future that is of central significance. The difference is one of focus, not of absolutes; but it is a significant difference.[96]

---

[92] Von Hirsch, above n 3 at 72.

[93] There remains, however, the potential objection, previously discussed, that side-constraints against intrusiveness in this kind of system will be ineffective. This issue will be considered in the next section, after relevant empirical evidence has been summarised.

[94] Duff, above n 4 at 107.

[95] Duff, 'Punishment, Retribution and Communication' above n 23 at 131.

[96] A further and related difference is that the 'deep' version of repentance is focused initially on the wrong act that has been committed, whereas the 'turning around' version focuses primarily on the broader issue that Bernard Williams has described as 'Socrates' question', namely, 'how one should live': B Williams, *Ethics and the Limits of Philosophy* (London, Routledge, 2006; originally

In a penal theory context, the consequence of this point is that communicative censure is theorised as *intrinsically including* an illocutionary message that the action in question was wrong, and a perlocutionary message to the wrongdoer to change his/her behaviour. There is, however, no explicit focus on remorse or regret. Those emotions might well emerge when and if the wrongdoer alters his/her behaviour, but they are not themselves the illocutionary or perlocutionary point of the censure.[97] That being the case, this approach arguably offers a more convincing answer to the often-asked question concerning the punishment of the recalcitrant offender. Duff's response to this issue, it will be recalled, is that we must attempt to persuade such a person to repent, because not to do so would be to 'give up on the offender as a moral agent – as someone within the reach of remorse'.[98] But on the 'turning around' concept of repentance, the illocutionary and perlocutionary point of the censure is to prompt not remorse, but a 'change of mind or purpose' towards the behaviour required by the 'objective values' enshrined in a justifiable criminal code. For a state non-coercively to encourage an apparently recalcitrant offender to adopt such a goal is surely neither controversial nor pointless.

IV. EMPIRICAL EVIDENCE ON REPENTANCE

What empirical evidence is available as regards the extent to which offenders repent – in any of the senses previously discussed in this chapter? To tackle this question, I shall consider separately long-term prisoners (those who have been convicted for serious crimes) and those convicted of less serious offences (many of whom might also have been imprisoned at some point in their careers).

A. Long-term Prisoners

Relatively little research has been conducted on the specific question of how long-term prisoners respond to their punishment, *qua* punishment. Extensive literatures exist on issues such as power and social relationships in high-security prisons, but much less attention has been paid to how prisoners in such institutions make sense (including moral sense) of the sentence that the court has imposed upon them, in the context of their having to live in confinement for an extended period of time, and eventually to return to society. Fortunately,

---

published by Fontana, 1985) 1, referring to a remark that Plato attributes to Socrates in *Republic* Book 1 section 352D. As with the backward-looking/forward-looking contrast, this difference is one of focus, not of absolutes.

[97] Compare also n 53 above on Fricker's discussion of the illocutionary point of communicative blame.

[98] Duff, 'Punishment, Retribution and Communication' above n 23 at 131.

however, a recent small study by Marguerite Schinkel focuses on exactly these questions.[99] This research was based on narrative interviews with 27 men who either were currently, or had recently been, serving prison sentences of four years or more in Scotland. In her main text, Schinkel analysed what the men had said about the purposes perceived in the sentence; their perceptions of the legitimacy of punishment in light of their experience of the prison environment; and (at the end of their sentence or beyond) their thoughts about desisting from crime.[100] In the context of the present chapter, it is particularly helpful that Schinkel also published a separate paper in which she attempted to examine how her findings related to the ideals set out in Antony Duff's theory of punishment as moral communication.[101]

In this paper, Schinkel reported little congruence between Duff's theory and the men's experiences. In the courtroom, for example, their attention was focused almost exclusively on the length of the sentence that the judge would impose. Given this cognitive focus, and the fact that they were 'often overwhelmed by emotion', respondents simply 'did not interact with the court as a moral arena'.[102] Later, in prison, two matters in particular militated against moral communication, as presented in Duff's theory. First, 'most interviewees commented that the only time that their offence, their sentence and questions of morality were discussed within the prison was during cognitive behavioural courses'; moreover, the impact of these (limited) interactions was blunted by the fact that the courses were in effect mandatory if one wished to progress towards release, which frequently led to formal rather than substantive attention to the course content.[103] Secondly, and perhaps more importantly, the need to cope – for a lengthy period – with the well-documented pains of imprisonment led many men to adopt a strategy of 'getting your head down'. This meant that they tried to limit their thoughts to events within the prison, rather than issues of moral communication about offences and offending.[104]

Elsewhere in Schinkel's work, however, there are some indications of less negative findings. First, she reports that nine of the men she interviewed (one-third of the sample) mentioned 'having time to think' as a purpose or effect of imprisonment; as one of them said, 'You do an awful lot of thinking in prison'.[105] The content of this thinking was not explored in the research, but presumably it could include thinking about one's offence and/or where one's life is heading,

---

[99] M Schinkel, *Being Imprisoned: Punishment, Adaptation and Desistance* (Basingstoke, Palgrave Macmillan, 2014).

[100] Ibid chs 2–4.

[101] M Schinkel, 'Punishment as Moral Communication: The Experiences of Long-Term Prisoners' (2014) 16 *Punishment and Society* 578.

[102] Ibid at 578.

[103] Ibid at 590. On substantive and formal compliance see G Robinson and F McNeill, 'Exploring the Dynamics of Compliance with Community Penalties' (2008) 12 *Theoretical Criminology* 431.

[104] Ibid.

[105] Schinkel, above n 99 at 40–41.

given the fact of a long sentence. If so, this must surely count as an element within a communicative process, even though the prison authorities rarely engaged in explicit moral dialogue (see above).[106] Then, secondly, it is important to note that, in this sample 'desistance was almost universally desired'.[107] Schinkel does not emphasise this finding, but – in light of the previous discussion in this chapter – it is very significant, because it means that repentance in the sense of a wish to 'turn one's life around' was very common.

More recent research also suggests that Duff's theory of punishment, in its full form (that is, including 'deep' repentance) does have real-life applicability for a minority of serious offenders. Alice Ievins conducted an interview-based and ethnographic study in an English prison for adult male sex offenders.[108] Amongst other topics, she studied prisoners' adaptations to their sentence, and found that these were very varied, not least because some men strongly contested their guilt. One group, however, 'felt extreme guilt and shame for their offence, and saw the sentence as both a deserved punishment and an opportunity to transform themselves into the responsible citizens they felt themselves truly to be'.[109] This group (described as 'the redeemed') comprised about a fifth of Ievins' interview sample of 42 cases. They were serving long terms (almost all had received sentences of ten years or more), and most were first offenders. This profile (a serious offence committed by a person with no previous contact with the criminal justice system) is, perhaps, particularly likely to lead to Duff's ideal response to punishment (ie deep repentance, and a commitment to reform and reconciliation); but it is certainly of interest that a response of this kind is found among an identifiable minority of prisoners.[110]

B. Offenders Committing 'Volume Crimes'

In the previous subsection, we noted Schinkel's finding that, among her sample, a wish to desist was almost universal. That finding has been widely replicated in the many studies of desistance from crime that have been completed in the

---

[106] On this see also a Californian study referenced by Schinkel: M Comfort, 'The Best Seven Years I Could'a Done: The Reconstruction of Imprisonment as Rehabilitation' in P Carlen (ed) *Imaginary Penalities* (Cullompton, Willan, 2008) 252. In the conclusion to this essay, Comfort includes a quotation from one of the prisoners that she studied: he commented that in prison 'you got a perfect chance to really find *you*. [Having that chance] was refreshing Not in the sense of being in jail ... [but to] really be able to just think' (at 273 emphasis in original).

[107] Schinkel, above n 99 at 120.

[108] A Ievins, 'Adaptation, Moral Community and Power in a Prison for Men Convicted of Sex Offences', unpublished PhD thesis, University of Cambridge (2017). I am most grateful to Alice Ievins for permission to refer to her findings.

[109] Ibid at 76.

[110] Sex offenders now comprise nearly a fifth of the daily average population of sentenced male prisoners in England and Wales. If (which is not certain) the proportion of 'the redeemed' in Ievins' sample is representative of all male sex offenders in English prisons, then 3–4% of the male sentenced prison population would come into this category.

last two decades,[111] most of which have focused on groups of offenders who have committed what are often called 'volume crimes'.[112] Research samples of this kind often include recidivist offenders, so it is worth emphasising that even the majority of such offenders also wish to stop. For example, the sample of young men (aged 19–22) recruited for the Sheffield Desistance Study had, at first interview, an average of eight convictions for 'standard list' (ie non-motoring) offences, yet 56 per cent of this group said they had made 'a definite decision to try to stop', while a further 37 per cent said they 'would like to stop, but I'm not sure if I can'.[113] The second of these categories highlights the difficulties of achieving full desistance if one has been a repeat offender – a point to which we shall return. But, as in Schinkel's study and many others, the wish to desist was very widespread. Long-term statistical studies further show that, eventually, almost all such offenders do end their criminal careers, and that the fastest deceleration of offending rates (even among recidivists) occurs in the early twenties.[114]

In an earlier section, it was claimed that empirical evidence does not support Antony Duff's statement that 'to accept censure as justified is to accept that one did wrong, which entails repenting that wrong and seeing the need to avoid such wrongdoing in future'.[115] To substantiate that claim, we need some precision about the evidence. At least in England and Wales, the great majority of convicted offenders (including those sent to prison) do in fact accept their punishment as justified,[116] and – as we have just seen – they also wish to avoid further criminality. Sometimes, of course, the wish to desist develops largely

---

[111] For overviews of such studies see JM Shapland and AE Bottoms, 'Desistance from Crime and Implications for Offender Rehabilitation' in A Liebling, S Maruna and L McAra (eds), *Oxford Handbook of Criminology*, 6th edn (Oxford, Oxford University Press, 2017) 744; M Rocque, *Desistance from Crime* (New York, Palgrave Macmillan, 2017).

[112] The phrase 'volume crimes' is not a technical term, but is used loosely by the police and criminologists to refer to the most common non-motoring offences. Examples of such offences are thefts, burglaries, taking cars, handling stolen goods, criminal damage, drugs offences, less serious assaults and unarmed street robberies.

[113] AE Bottoms and JM Shapland, 'Steps towards Desistance among Male Young Adult Recidivists' in S Farrall, M Hough, S Maruna and R Sparks (eds), *Escape Routes: Contemporary Perspectives on Life after Punishment* (London, Routledge, 2011) 43 at 57. Other analyses within this study confirm that these figures do represent the men's genuine wishes.

[114] See for example: A Blokland, D Nagin and P Nieuwbeerta, 'Life Span Offending Trajectories of a Dutch Conviction Cohort' (2005) 43 *Criminology* 919; A Piquero, DP Farrington and A Blumstein, *Key Issues in Criminal Career Research: New Analyses of the Cambridge Study in Delinquent Development* (Cambridge, Cambridge University Press, 2007) ch 9.

[115] Duff, above n 4 at 80.

[116] Direct empirical evidence on this point is hard to find, simply because acceptance of sentences is so widespread. The best evidence is therefore indirect – in empirical studies, the few who do not accept their sentences as justified are normally highlighted as exceptional. There are, however, a few specific groups where researchers have identified a higher-than-average proportion of those contesting the justice of their sentence: these groups include sex offenders; those convicted of 'joint enterprise' offences; and persons recalled to prison for a breach of licence conditions not involving a fresh offence.

for instrumental reasons, rather than the normative concerns that Duff has primarily in mind. But even where desistance has a clear normative element, it is rare for volume-crime offenders to 'repent their wrong', in the 'deep' sense of repentance that Duff stipulates, at the beginning of their journey towards desistance. Thus, it is not the case, empirically speaking, that 'accepting one has done wrong' *entails* deep repentance.

These points can be illustrated by evidence from the so-called 'Tracking Progress on Probation Study', a longitudinal study of desistance among a sample of probationers, carried out in England by Stephen Farrall and colleagues. In this research, interviews with the same research sample took place at three distinct time periods: in 1997–99 (three 'sweeps' of interviews); in 2003–04 ('Sweep Four') and in 2010–13 ('Sweep Five').[117] In Sweeps Four and Five, very interesting analyses were reported concerning the 'emotional trajectories' of those sample members who, at those dates, were classified as 'desisters'.[118] In these analyses, desisters were classified along a 'broad range of travel' that was arranged temporally (at the time of the interview) from 'early hopes' to 'normalcy', although – since people can and do relapse – some had previously reached a later stage in this journey before beginning again, after a setback, with 'early hopes'. This 'desistance range' was then cross-tabulated with a specified set of emotions.[119] For the purposes of this chapter, the most significant emotions studied were 'regrets about the past' and 'guilt, shame or disgust'; and Table 7.1 shows the reported results for these emotions, using a simplified classification of 'earlier' and 'later' phases of desistance.[120]

One important finding in this table concerns the overall total of respondents who reported feeling emotions of *either* regret about the past *or* guilt/shame. As will be seen, nearly two-thirds of desisters at Sweep Four, and just over half at Sweep Five, reported such emotions. In other words, regrets, guilt or shame are often, but not always, associated with journeys towards desistance.

---

[117] The main results of the study are reported in three books: S Farrall, *Rethinking What Works with Offenders* (Cullompton, Willan, 2002) (Sweeps 1–3); S Farrall and A Calverley, *Understanding Desistance from Crime* (Maidenhead, Open University Press, 2006) (Sweep 4); and S Farrall, B Hunter, G Sharpe and A Calverley, *Criminal Careers in Transition* (Oxford, Oxford University Press, 2014) (Sweep 5).

[118] See Farrall and Calverley, ibid ch 5, and Farrall et al, ibid ch 7. The original sample in the 'Tracking Progress' study comprised 199 persons (male and female) who were commencing probation orders in one of six probation areas. At Sweep 4 (approximately six years later), 51 of these respondents were re-interviewed, of whom 33 were classed as desisters. At Sweep 5 (approximately 13 years after the first interviews), 105 respondents were re-interviewed, of whom 71 were classed as desisters. Interviewees classed as desisters at Sweeps Four and Five constitute the samples for the analyses of emotional trajectories.

[119] The desistance categories, and the list of emotions, were reported in slightly different ways at Sweeps Four and Five. For details see Farrall et al, above n 117.

[120] The researchers identified four temporal categories in Sweep Four, and five in Sweep Five. For each Sweep, Table 7.1 combines categories 1 and 2 as 'earlier desistance' and the remainder as 'later desistance'.

Table 7.1 Tracking Progress on Probation Project: Selected Emotions at Earlier and Later Stages of Desistance Trajectories

	Earlier desistance stage	Later desistance stage	All interviewees
Sweep Four:			
N	14 (100%)	19 (100%)	33 (100%)
Regrets about past	4 (29%)	9 (47%)	13 (39%)
Guilt, shame or disgust	5 (36%)	12 (63%)	17 (52%)
Either emotion	6 (43%)	15 (79%)	21 (64%)
Sweep Five:			
N	30 (100%)	41 (100%)	71 (100%)
Regrets about past	16 (53%)	13 (32%)	29 (41%)
Guilt, shame or disgust	15 (50%)	9 (22%)	24 (34%)
Either emotion	20 (67%)	16 (39%)	36 (51%)

Source: Data extracted from Farrall et al, n 115, Figs 7.1 and 7.2.

Turning to more detailed results, a striking feature of Table 7.1 is the contrast between the temporal patterning at the two time periods: in Sweep Four there were higher levels of regret or guilt in the later stages of desistance, whereas in Sweep Five the reverse was true. Why the difference?

To begin with the Sweep Four pattern (more regrets/guilt at later stages), a case study of 'Jamie' illustrates the some of the factors in play:

> There was a BMW convertible with the engine running sat in a car park. Back when I was seventeen I would probably have jumped straight in there and gone. I would have loved that … [But] I wouldn't steal a car now because I know [that] the mortgage don't get paid and things like that. … When I was seventeen I thought it weren't harming no one. It was only a fifty pound Metro [car that I stole], it wasn't worth anything. But now I realise that fifty pound Metro is probably someone's wages for a week to get to work in, and then you know, the kids don't get fed and shit like that.[121]

The attitude that Jamie describes from when he was 17 is clearly not one that would lead to repentance in Duff's sense, even if he were caught. But now that he is older and has a partner, he sees things differently – and it is this kind of change that explains the fact that the age-range at which there is the fastest deceleration of offending among persistent offenders is the early twenties (see above). The evidence relating to desistance by persistent offenders at this age is that it usually comes about gradually: as researchers in the Sheffield study

---

[121] Farrall and Calverley, above n 117 at 119.

have put it, desistance, if taken seriously, means learning to lead a law-abiding life when one has previously led a criminal life – and this takes time.[122] Various factors have been shown to influence this kind of change, such as a relationship with a romantic partner, satisfactory employment, a strong wish to avoid further imprisonment, a determination to come off drugs, deliberately avoiding meeting criminal friends or going to risky places, and improved relationships with a parent or parents, who provide(s) needed support. Very frequently, journeys of this kind encounter obstacles, and sometimes there is a relapse and then a fresh attempt to desist. But many are eventually successful. When they are, it is not uncommon for people to look back and realise, as Jamie did, that in one's earlier life people have been hurt by the crimes that were committed, and to regret this. To return to the language of repentance, trajectories of this kind are clearly attempts to repent by turning around; and, as in Jamie's case, it can frequently happen that people develop a deeper sense of regret/guilt/repentance at a later point in the journey. But, contra Duff, what does not usually happen is deep repentance at the start of a process of change.

Turning now to the Sweep Five pattern shown in Table 7.1 (more regrets/guilt at the earlier stages of the desistance journey), how is this different pattern to be explained? In answering this question, it is important to recognise that the interviews at Sweep Five took place more than a decade after the respondents were first placed on probation. So at least an important part of the answer is that many of those who now expressed regret or guilt in the 'earlier' stages of desistance were in fact those who had previously tried to desist, but had experienced setbacks.[123] Accordingly, it was often the case that 'their guilt [was] rooted in reminiscences of their previous betrayals of trust that others ... had placed in them', and/or a realisation that to get the money that they felt they needed, they have had to steal from someone and that such an act is 'really bad'.[124]

In summary, therefore, deep repentance of the kind that Duff defends as part of the purposes of punishment does exist among offenders. But it does not exist universally or near-universally, and its distribution (among different people, and at different times in a desistance journey) is somewhat unpredictable. By contrast, the wish to repent by 'turning around' is almost universal. Thus, the theoretical and the empirical analyses in this chapter can be seen to coalesce. Together, they support the view that 'repentance as turning around' is not only a normatively defensible stance for a liberal penal system to adopt, it is also one that is supported by most people who are punished.

There remains, however, the 'side-constraint' issue rightly raised by von Hirsch and Ashworth. To recapitulate, if a state includes encouragement to repent within its censure-based penal system, will it still be possible to 'develop

---

[122] AE Bottoms and JM Shapland, 'Learning to Desist in Early Adulthood: The Sheffield Desistance Study' in JM Shapland, S Farrall and AE Bottoms (eds), *Global Perspectives on Desistance* (London, Routledge, 2016) 99.
[123] Farrall et al, above n 117 at 194.
[124] Ibid at 197.

adequate restrictions on scrutiny of offender attitudes', to ensure that the penal intervention does not become overly intrusive?[125] In light of the empirical evidence, the impact of this objection is in practice less significant than it might seem theoretically, since the great majority of offenders wish to 'turn their lives around' – and it is actually more common for them to complain that criminal justice workers have provided *insufficient* help towards 'going straight', than that the state has been too intrusive.[126] A reasonable assessment is therefore that this is an important issue for a state to guard against, but it is not such a serious problem as to require a rejection of the view that 'repentance as turning around' is an intrinsically appropriate element within a censure-based state punishment system.

V. IMPLICATIONS FOR STATE POLICY

In the first section of this chapter, it was suggested – on the basis of an examination of the work of Foucault – that there is a strong case for adding the question 'what mode of punishment is desirable?' to HLA Hart's famous three questions (which relate to punishment's general justifying aim, its distribution, and its amount). Given the subsequent analysis, it should be even more evident why this 'fourth question' is necessary. It has been argued here that, following Duff, it is intrinsically appropriate for retributive (censure-based) punishment not only to look backwards towards the offence, but also to promote the forward-looking aims of reform and reintegration, in the pursuit of which the offender's repentance – in the sense of 'turning around' – may be properly sought by the state. The analysis has required little attention to Hart's questions, yet it has probed some difficult and controversial issues, thus demonstrating that the question of 'the mode of punishment' is fully worthy of serious attention by penal philosophers.

If the argument of this chapter has merit, it carries two important implications for state policy as regards modes of punishment. First, the state needs to consider what forms of punishment practice will best take forward the aims of reform and reintegration, within the framework of censure-based punishment. Secondly, the state also needs to try to ensure that, at the end of the punishment, the offender is given appropriate opportunities to resume his/her life as a citizen of the society in question.

---

[125] Von Hirsch and Ashworth, above n 7 at 105.

[126] For example, Schinkel carried out her study in a prison that had been 'praised for the positive relationships between staff members and prisoners', yet there was 'anger and frustration' among prisoners because they felt that 'they needed greater individual attention and support to be able to move away from offending upon release' (Schinkel, above n 99 at 128, 131–32). See also JM Shapland, AE Bottoms and G Muir, 'Perceptions of the Criminal Justice System among Young Adult Would-Be Desisters' in F Lösel, AE Bottoms and DP Farrington (eds), *Young Adult Offenders* (London, Routledge, 2012) 128.

Whole essays have been written on each of these topics, and it is not possible here to tackle them in any detail. Accordingly, I shall focus only on the second question ('what happens at the end of punishment?'), and I shall offer only some brief theoretical and some brief practical comments.

As regards theory, it is appropriate to return to Foucault's analysis of modes of penality (Figure 7.1), and in particular to recall that, in the 'juridical model' (the model closest to liberal penal censure theory) the status of the offender is that of a 'juridical subject in process of requalification'. In other words, according to this model, it has been necessary to punish the offender in order to bring home to him/her the fact that he/she has done wrong; but when the punishment is completed, he/she is again a full citizen, and even during the punishment he/she was a person 'in process of requalification' towards that status.

We saw in section I that Foucault's analysis of 'juridical punishment' was drawn largely from Beccaria's social contract theory. It is therefore of great interest that a recent essay by Antje du Bois-Pedain draws upon the work of a different social contract theorist (Johann Gottlieb Fichte[127]) in developing the case for what she memorably calls 'punishment as an *inclusionary* practice' (emphasis added).[128] The basic point is simple: except for the very few people whose crimes are so heinous that we, as a society, cannot again tolerate their becoming free citizens of our polity, the point of punishment is to censure, with the hope of better moral alignment between the offender and society (Fricker's 'illocutionary and perlocutionary points'). Therefore, at the end of the punishment, the person punished resumes his/her status as an included citizen (in some cases, with some reasonable conditions of reintegration). These are theoretical ideals, but they are not utopian; and in pursuing them, we can be encouraged by the recognition that the great majority of offenders eventually want, above all, to become law-abiding citizens.

But that brings us to the practical point, because in real life there can be severe structural obstacles facing those who wish to desist from crime. This point is well illustrated by some results from Schinkel's study, where some depressing contrasts were identified as between those men who were interviewed towards the end of their sentence, and those interviewed after release ('on licence'). The licence group were – as a result of their post-release experiences – less optimistic about the future, having, for example, found severe difficulties in obtaining employment, so that many 'no longer felt in charge of their own destiny in the way that those … within the prison did'.[129] This emphasises the point that

---

[127] JG Fichte, *Foundations of Natural Right According to the Principles of the Wissenschaftslehre* [1797] edited by F Neuhouser and translated by M Baur (Cambridge, Cambridge University Press, 2000).

[128] A du Bois-Pedain, 'Punishment as an Inclusionary Practice: Sentencing in a Liberal Constitutional State' in A du Bois-Pedain, M Ulväng and P Asp (eds), *Criminal Law and the Authority of the State* (Oxford, Hart Publishing, 2017) 199.

[129] Schinkel, above n 99 at 106. As the author acknowledges (at 6), a longitudinal research design would have been methodologically stronger than the cross-sectional study actually conducted; however, there seems no reason to doubt the validity of these reported contrasts.

if punishment is to be an 'inclusionary practice', or a way of 'requalifying a juridical subject', then this places obligations on society, as well as on the person punished. As Stephen Farrall and colleagues put the matter, at the end of their chapter on 'emotional trajectories':

> Failure to find sufficiently well paid and satisfying work, to find and fund adequate housing, as well as reminders of their perceived 'criminal' status may all prevent the evolution of initial hopes [of desistance] … Structural impediments can lead to feelings of frustration, even among the enthusiastic and well-intentioned, requiring them to fall back on individual resources of determination and willpower. The danger is that … these [resources] will be extinguished, leading to despondency, disillusion and possibly reoffending. If feasible and realistic pathways that would-be desisters may travel do not exist or are blocked, then feelings of hope … run the risk of turning into *false* hopes.[130]

VI. CONCLUSION

This chapter has focused upon the debate on 'repentance' within penal censure theory, but it has necessarily also considered wider issues. Within the context of the volume as a whole, perhaps the most important aspect of the chapter has been to draw attention to a sometimes neglected feature of Antony Duff's version of censure theory, namely his claim that censure intrinsically involves a forward-looking dimension – a claim that is now also supported by Miranda Fricker's paper on communicative blame.

Early in the discussion, Duff's own summary of his theory was quoted: 'Criminal punishment … should communicate to offenders the censure they deserve for their crimes, and should aim through that communicative process to persuade them to repent their crimes, to try to reform themselves, and thus to reconcile themselves with those whom they wronged'.[131] At various points in the chapter, aspects of Duff's theory have been criticised. However, at the conclusion of the relevant debates, what has emerged – at least so far as the penal censure element of punishment is concerned[132] – is a theoretical claim very close to the core of Duff's concerns:

> Criminal punishment should communicate to offenders the censure they deserve for their crimes. That communicative process will intrinsically convey the message

---

[130] Farrall et al, above n 117 at 216 (emphasis in original).

[131] Duff, above n 4 at xvii.

[132] Recall that Duff himself stated that his ideal conception of punishment, as summarised here, 'deserves a central place, even if not the only place, in our normative understanding of punishment' (see n 34 above). This hint of pluralism has, in my view rightly, subsequently been taken further by other scholars: see for example M Matravers, 'Is Twenty-First Century Punishment Post-Desert?' in M Tonry (ed), *Retributivism Has a Past: Has it a Future?* (New York, Oxford University Press, 2011) 30; M Tonry, 'Solving the Multiple-Offense Paradox' in J Ryberg, JV Roberts and JW de Keijser (eds), *Sentencing Multiple Crimes* (New York, Oxford University Press, 2018) 241.

that the state encourages them to repent (in the sense of *metanoia*), to try to reform themselves, and thus to reconcile themselves to the society whose rules they have broken. The state in turn has a duty to help those who are punished to reintegrate within mainstream society.

Yet, as a concluding thought, we need once again to return to the work of Foucault. A central feature in the analysis of *Discipline and Punish*[133] is that, for socio-political reasons, the proposals of eighteenth-century reformers such as Beccaria were not implemented, and instead the 'carceral' mode of disciplinary punishment came to dominate penal systems in most Western countries. This chapter has argued that there are strong theoretical reasons to advocate the kind of punishment system encapsulated in the summary set out above, and that such a policy is congruent with relevant empirical evidence. However, as Fricker has rightly pointed out in the conclusion of her paper on blame, 'whether blame promotes good or ill ... is troublingly contingent', and there is always an 'on-going risk that ... the moral outlook of ... the morally misguided may gain the ascendancy'.[134] Translating that thought to the specific sphere of criminal punishment, we can affirm, with Antje du Bois-Pedain, that there are compelling normative reasons why, in liberal-democratic states, governments should promote the concept of 'punishment as an inclusionary practice';[135] but it would be foolish to deny that, both in the recent past and in the present, there have been strong social and political forces that have caused governments in many countries to adopt policies based instead on the idea of 'punishment as an exclusionary practice'.[136] That fact leaves us with a final question, which will have to remain unanswered here: why might a liberal-democratic state knowingly tolerate the existence of social conditions in which it is very hard for an offender to turn his/her life around?

[133] Foucault, above n 8.
[134] Fricker, above n 47 at 181.
[135] Du Bois-Pedain, above n 128.
[136] I Loader and R Sparks, 'Penal Populism and Epistemic Crime Control' in A Liebling et al (eds), above n 111, 98; J Pratt, *Penal Populism* (London, Routledge, 2007).

8

The Evolution of Retributive Punishment: From Static Desert to Responsive Penal Censure

JULIAN V ROBERTS AND NETANEL DAGAN*

T HE FORTIETH ANNIVERSARY of the seminal penal theory volume *Doing Justice*[1] is an opportune time to reconsider the current state of retributive sentencing. The landscape of retributive justice has changed in recent decades.[2] There has been an evolution in retributive theorising, reflected in a terminological shift from 'desert' to 'penal censure'. This shift in conceptual emphasis – and its consequences for legal punishment – is the subject of this essay. Our discussion examines the implications for sentencing practices, particularly the administration of sentences of imprisonment and lengthy community orders.

This chapter proceeds as follows. In section I we distinguish the relatively *static* version of desert articulated in *Doing Justice* (and other early writings by von Hirsch) from a more *dynamic* concept in which penal censure is expressed in a way that permits a positive reaction from the offender (and subsequent response from the state). We note that a more recent, quasi-retributive[3] version of penal desert generates a wider ambit of circumstances considered relevant to the deserved sentence. Section II explores at greater length the consequences of this transformation for the administration of sentences. We argue that

---

*The authors contributed equally to the chapter. We thank the editors of this volume for comments on previous drafts of this essay, and we are also are grateful to the participants at the Cambridge seminar, the Robina Institute scholars, and participants at the criminal law workshop at the Hebrew University for their feedback on the ideas discussed here.

[1] A von Hirsch, *Doing Justice: The Choice of Punishments* (Report of the Committee for the Study of Incarceration) (New York, Hill and Wang, 1976).

[2] For a collection of essays exploring the future of retributivism, see M Tonry (ed), *Retributivism Has a Past: Has it a Future?* (New York, Oxford University Press, 2011).

[3] We term this model 'quasi-retributive' because, unlike other desert theorists, we argue that the amount of punishment an offender deserves is affected by his subsequent conduct with respect to his crime and his sentence.

censure-based considerations are not exhausted with the imposition of sentence in court; they remain alive throughout the administration of the sentence. From this position we conclude that there is a need to conduct a 'second look' sentence review, particularly for lengthy terms of custody.

I. DISTINGUISHING STATIC DESERT FROM DYNAMIC CENSURE

According to the traditional desert-based approach to sentencing, severity is determined solely by reference to the seriousness of the crime. In *Doing Justice*, von Hirsch notes that seriousness 'has two major components: harm and culpability'.[4] Once these have been determined, a court imposes a commensurate sanction. Harm and culpability are generally invariant, fixed at the time the crime is committed. Although the full impact of the offence may not be immediately apparent, courts routinely calibrate the seriousness of the crime at the point of sentence. The determination of an offender's culpability for the crime is even more time-limited. Consideration is generally restricted to his immediate circumstances at the time of the offence, the offender's mental state, his capacity for reflection and his ability to comply with the law and so forth. In *Past or Future Crimes*, von Hirsch explicitly addresses the components of seriousness and their temporal limits: 'Let me begin … with the two components of seriousness: harm and culpability. Harm refers to the injury done or risked by the criminal act. Culpability refers to the factors of intent, motive and circumstance'.[5] This quotation makes it clear that the determinants of seriousness are well established once the crime is committed. Under this model, at sentencing a court is reconstructing the events and mental state at the time of the crime, and the sentence then reflects this reconstruction.

According to this approach, a court should not inquire beyond the circumstances of the offender's life at the time of the commission of the crime. Once a court has determined these two elements, logic requires that the sentence also becomes immutable: If the determinants of sentence are fixed, so too is the sentencing outcome. This reality has important consequences for sentences of imprisonment, as the following example illustrates.

Consider an offender sentenced to three years' imprisonment. After two years in custody he may have addressed the causes of his offending, and reduced his risk of recidivism. While laudable, this conduct is unrelated to the offence, and so a classic desert-based approach would have no reason to modify the sentence to reward this kind of behaviour in prison. The elements which determined the length of sentence remain fixed until the last moment of imposed

---

[4] Von Hirsch, above n 1 at 79. See also RA Duff, *Punishment, Communication and Community* (New York, Oxford University Press, 2001) 135.

[5] A von Hirsch, *Past or Future Crimes?* (New Brunswick NJ, Rutgers University Press, 1985) 64.

prison time has been served. Indeed, making significant changes in the sentence length would actively undermine the principles of proportionality and parity in sentencing.[6] From this vantage point, early release from prison necessarily has to be based on considerations external to desert theory. If such considerations were to be recognised as legitimate, this would require conceding that the imprisonment regime is not purely desert-based. In addition, any modification of sentence based on desert-external considerations changes the nature of the message regarding the seriousness of the offence.

Our contention is that a different logic applies when the sentencing model reflects a dynamic and *responsive* penal censure rather than *static* desert. According to the dynamic model, the amount of censure that an offender deserves for his crime may change in response to certain acts of the offender. Sensitivity to some post-offence and, particularly, post-sentence behaviour thereby becomes internal to assessments of (continuing) deservedness of punishment.

According to what we term 'static' desert, post-offence conduct does not affect the seriousness of the crime or the offender's culpability for the offence. Under a purely desert-based sentencing rationale, the focus of the sentence is, therefore, tightly drawn upon the culpable act or omission. The offender's general lifestyle and his actions after the commission of the crime should carry no weight. They are not seen as affecting an offender's culpability and are therefore excluded from the sentencing equation.[7]

A responsive censure-based approach, however, necessarily expands the ambit of inquiry at sentencing. Penal censure engages the offender in a more clearly communicative manner. Andreas von Hirsch and Andrew Ashworth capture the essence of the concept in this way: 'The punishment conveys to the actor a certain critical normative message concerning his conduct … this message treats him as a moral agent – that is an agent capable of moral deliberation'.[8] These authors further note that 'When the offender is thus censured, a moral response on his part is deemed appropriate', but then suggest that 'The censure, however, serves only to give the actor the opportunity to make such a response'.[9] Yet does it make sense to provide offenders with an opportunity but to then remain oblivious to whether they avail themselves of the opportunity? We argue that the censuring authority should be attentive to the fruits of the offender's moral deliberation, as they may affect the degree of censure that is (or remains) appropriate.

Even more importantly, a responsive censure approach draws the sentence administration phase into the purview of desert-based punishment. Desert theory contains restraining arguments for the punitiveness of the state, such as

---

[6] A von Hirsch, *Censure and Sanctions* (Oxford, Oxford University Press, 1993).

[7] A von Hirsch and A Ashworth, *Proportionate Sentencing: Exploring the Principles* (Oxford, Oxford University Press, 2005).

[8] Ibid at 17.

[9] Ibid at 17–18.

the 'drowning out' argument, progressive loss of mitigation for repeat offenders, the principle of parsimony, and related decremental penal strategies.[10] However, desert theory fails to offer any restraints on the severity of punishment after sentencing, no matter what offender does thereafter. The punishment phase itself – which can last for years and even decades, sometimes for an offender's entire natural lifespan – creates a normative 'vacuum' for desert theory. In contrast, we argue that a responsive censure-based account offers an important resource for evaluating the degree of deserved punishment into the administration of the sentence.

Communicative punishment theory provides a starting framework for our purposes. Antony Duff has developed the communicative meaning of the punishment.[11] For Duff, punishment communicates the censure that an offender deserves as a kind of secular penance and provides a means by which the offender can focus on the wrongfulness of the offence.[12] The 'hard treatment', which is intrinsic to communicative punishment, serves both to promote repentance by focusing the offender's attention on his crime and its implications, and also as a vehicle for the reparation owed to the victim and the community. Duff describes the penal communication as a rational and reciprocal act that aims to engage another person 'as an active participant in the process who will receive and respond to the communication, and it appeals to the other's reason and understanding'.[13]

Duff emphasises, however, that while hard treatment conveys an expression of the apology that is owed and the prisoner's response to the penal dialogue, it does not *require* the offender to be repentant. For Duff, the moral possibility of punishments does not depend upon their actual success in making wrongdoers engage in the communicative enterprise, or to answer for, to repent, or to make amends for their crimes: 'The value and importance of the attempt to engage him in a penal dialogue does not depend on its actual or likely success'.[14] Prisoners may be forced to *hear* the penal message, but they may not be forced to *listen* to that message or, for that matter be persuaded by it. Regardless of the prisoner's conduct during imprisonment, once he has completed his sentence 'we treat him as (as if) reformed'.[15]

---

[10] These are fully discussed by Ashworth, in this volume.

[11] Duff, above n 4; RA Duff, L Farmer, S Marshall and V Tadros, 'Judgment and Calling to Account' in RA Duff, L Farmer, S Marshall and V Tadros (eds), *The Trial on Trial: Volume 2* (Oxford, Hart Publishing, 2006) 1 at 6 noted that: 'calling to account is a two-way process'.

[12] For further discussion and critique of Duff's model, see Bottoms in this volume.

[13] Ibid at 79.

[14] Ibid at 28–29; RA Duff, 'Can We Punish the Perpetrators of Atrocities?' in T Brudholm and T Cushman (eds), *The Religious in Responses to Mass Atrocity: Interdisciplinary Perspectives* (Cambridge, Cambridge University Press, 2009) 79 at 91.

[15] RA Duff, 'Who Must Presume Whom to be Innocent of What?' (2013) 42 *Netherlands Journal of Legal Philosophy* 170, at 190; Duff, above n 4 at 118–19.

A. Weaknesses of 'Static' Desert

A static approach to penal censure suffers from several deficiencies.[16] First, it assumes a narrow, stimulus-response model of state sentencing. The court assesses the harm caused and the offender's level of culpability and then imposes a proportional sentence to be discharged by the offender. This resembles for example a fixed penalty scheme for parking offences, whereby the sentencing authority imposes fines to be paid in full. Having paid the fine, there is no further engagement until another parking violation arises. There is no interactive capability; the state is indifferent to the reaction of the offender.[17] The criminally recalcitrant and the morally reformed are treated alike. This indifference on the part of the censuring authority disrespects the offender's agency and moral standing which should be of central concern to a retributive sanction.[18] Second, a static approach offers no incentives for the moral transformation which the sentence is ultimately seeking. Yet moral awakening does not necessarily occur spontaneously or as a reflexive response to the experience of punishment.

If the degree of censure appropriate to a particular offender changes during the administration of the sentence, so too should the stringency of the sanction. That a sentencing system should respond to post-sentence developments is obvious when the justification of a sentence (unlike in desert theory) partly hangs on the level of risk posed by an offender. In such a system, it would make no sense to insist on the full sentence being served regardless of the offender's changing level of risk during his confinement. A prisoner who reduces his level of risk while in prison should not be treated throughout his sentence as posing the risk he originally represented years earlier, upon admission to custody. An invariant approach becomes particularly self-defeating since imprisonment is imposed to reduce the offender's risk level. If risk determined the original sentence, and if that risk level changes, so too should the sentence.

We are of the view that the same logic applies to penal censure. If the degree of appropriate censure changes during the course of the sentence, cleaving to the original sentence results in retributive over-punishment. The key question we need to address, of course, is why the appropriate level of censure might diminish in response to new developments.

---

[16] Tonry argues in his contribution to this volume that retributive theories cannot by themselves provide adequate normative frameworks for just sentencing. We share this critique as it applies to the static form of desert that we describe here. Our concept of responsive censure is offered as one way retributivists may rise to the challenge by adopting what Tonry describes as 'new premises'.

[17] This approach is acceptable for minor transgressions where harm and culpability are both more uniform and limited.

[18] Limitations on space prevent us from elaborating on the point, but it is worth noting that the static approach to censure is clearly at odds with judicial practice and also responses to wrongdoing in everyday life. In both of these very different contexts the censuring authority is responsive to the actions of the 'offender', and not simply at the point of first confrontation over the 'offence'. In everyday life, what kind of a person expresses condemnation, imposes punishment and is ever thereafter oblivious to the reaction of the transgressor?

B. The Case for Dynamic Censure

We recognise that the offender's culpability for the offence is immutable. If the sentencing process is concerned exclusively with the offender's blameworthiness *at the time of the crime*, this obviously cannot change as a result of subsequent actions. What may change, however, is the degree of *censure* appropriate to the case, a rather different matter. Penal censure conveys a message of moral disapproval and this can be viewed as something more dynamic than simply a snapshot of condemnation. An offender's actions after the crime, including his conduct post-conviction, may affect the degree of censure that is warranted, and hence the nature of the sentence as it is experienced by the offender. The sentencing process should not remain blind to the offender who achieves or progresses towards his own moral transformation. This reasoning suggests that *some* actions by the offender should trigger a response from the state. For example, the prisoner who undertakes reparative steps to address the harm caused should benefit from a mitigation of punishment on the grounds that the degree of censure deemed appropriate at the time of sentencing is no longer necessary.

We advocate a model of penal censure which is dynamic and reciprocal, not static and unidirectional. In everyday life,[19] we express censure in a way that responds to the actions of the censured person.[20] Imagine that Jack, in his first year of university, has spent all his weekly allowance – given to him by his parents to buy books and pay academic fees – on champagne. Jack's parents express their strong disapproval, and their 'hard treatment' entails cancellation of his allowance for the next academic year. Yet is it appropriate to exact every week's 'penalty' for the whole forthcoming year if Jack has spent the summer working to reimburse his parents? This is not unearned mitigation; it is retributively significant conduct. As we shall argue in the next section, the actions which serve to mitigate the degree of censure necessary are of a particular nature; *they must be related to the offence for which censure was originally expressed.* State censure should also engage the censured offender, and respond to his conduct, if appropriate. John is rude to his colleagues at the end of term faculty meeting and they decide to suspend his attendance for the whole of the next term. Yet at the first termly meeting, John expresses his regret and apologises for his conduct. He commits himself to a more collegial course of action. Should his colleagues enforce the full suspension regardless of his response to the censure?

---

[19] The link to daily life is noted in von Hirsch, above n 1 at 82, where he states that proportionality 'uses a commonly understood concept employed in everyday life: the notion of censure'.

[20] Third parties: we do not have the space to discuss the issue further, but victims clearly have an interest knowing the offender's response to censure. Many victims express satisfaction when the offender responds positively, and the unresponsive offender can create even more resentment and possibly suffering among victims. Victims are relevant because, as von Hirsch, above n 6 at 10, notes: 'Censure addresses the victim'. See also von Hirsch and Ashworth, above n 7 at 19: 'Penal censure also has the role of addressing third parties'.

Responsive penal censure thus creates a dialogue, albeit a limited one, with the offender.[21] It is important to note that harm and culpability remain the primary determinants of sentence, rather than prevention of reoffending. The central difference between static and responsive censure is the recognition of the offender as a responsive agent. Hannah Maslen argues that the concept of dialogue is responsive – one is not involved in dialogue if one ignores the other participant's response.[22] A censure that ignores the offender's responsive communication would fail to legitimately appeal to the offender's moral reasoning because it does not address him in his present state of understanding. Instead, it would deafly seek the response it should have already heard.

II. CONSEQUENCES OF A DYNAMIC CENSURE MODEL FOR SENTENCING DECISIONS AND SENTENCE ENFORCEMENT

The practical consequences of moving from static desert to dynamic censure involve the range of factors considered at sentencing,[23] and thereafter the administration of sentences.

A. Expanding the Range of Sentencing Factors

A static desert approach such as the one taken in *Doing Justice* insists that, at sentence, 'only those circumstances that affect the seriousness of the offender's crime qualify' for consideration.[24] A communicative, censure-based approach expands the ambit of circumstances relevant to sentencing. A number of factors which traditionally have been regarded as unrelated to blameworthiness become relevant to the degree of censure deemed appropriate. Dynamic censure rejects the proposition that actions by the defendant after the commission of the crime

---

[21] Again, from von Hirsch, above n 1 at 82: 'One visits censure or reproof on people, not acts'.

[22] H Maslen, *Remorse, Penal Theory and Sentencing* (Oxford, Hart Publishing, 2015). Maslen also argues that responsive censure consists of three parts: one in which the punishing authority develops a preliminary response to the offence; a second in which the offender communicates her own response to the offence and/or to the punishing authority's preliminary response; and a third where the punishing authority responds to the offender's communication. See also Levanon in this volume for other applications of the responsive censure model.

[23] There may be consequences for sentencing procedure as well. The conventional approach involves holding the sentencing hearing as soon as possible after conviction is recorded, or once pre-sentence reports have been prepared. Yet if sentencing is deferred for a period this creates an opportunity for the offender to reduce the degree of censure expressed, through the kinds of actions we later describe in this chapter. Many jurisdictions including England and Wales now permit deferred sentencing in order to create such opportunities, although these provisions are usually conceptualised in terms of restorative justice.

[24] Von Hirsch, above n 1 at 101.

are irrelevant, and offers a new, desert-based argument for why such actions should be considered by the sentencing court.[25]

Remorse is a factor generally regarded as irrelevant to desert-based sentencing. If a sentencing court is concerned only with the offender's mental state at the time of the offence, then it is hard to see a role for remorse. Desert-based sentencing regimes which nevertheless mitigate sentence severity when the offender is remorseful do so in recognition that the sentencing equation should permit some room for non-retributive factors such as remorse or plea. A responsive censure-based approach will approach remorse differently.[26]

Plea is another similar factor. Leaving aside concerns about the truthfulness of the remorse, or the true motivation underlying a plea,[27] both remorse and plea can be easily accommodated within the sentencing equation. The remorseful offender has internalised the message (or censure). The guilty plea may be taken as evidence that the offender has taken steps to minimise the harm of the offence: victim impact has been mitigated by obviating the need for testimony, and the state – the 'official' party in the prosecution – has been spared the time and cost of the trial; the guilty plea is thus a reparative gesture. Both remorse and plea support a claim for diminished censure and hence mitigated punishment. Von Hirsch and Ashworth acknowledge that 'acknowledgment of wrongdoing' and 'an effort at better self-restraint'[28] are examples of the appropriate moral response to censure, yet they do not recognise these as grounds for any diminished censure and therefore of the punishment. Our view is that if these are examples of an appropriate positive response to censure they should result in a diminished punishment.

With respect to such forms of conduct, von Hirsch and Ashworth adopt an approach which involves the expression of state sympathy: 'we should show some sympathy towards a person who seems already to have taken a message of punishment to heart and to have started to mend his ways'.[29] We advocate a

---

[25] For an earlier argument that some actions taken after the crime carry retributive significance, see JV Roberts and H Maslen, 'After the Crime: Retributivism, Post-Offence Conduct and Penal Censure' in AP Simester, A du Bois-Pedain and U Neumann (eds), *Liberal Criminal Theory: Essays for Andreas von Hirsch* (Oxford, Hart Publishing, 2014) 87. Post-conviction conduct is recognised in sentencing statutes and guideline schemes in many jurisdictions, including England and Wales, New Zealand, Israel and Sweden, all countries where the legislature has placed proportionality on a statutory footing as the fundamental principle at sentencing. This is itself an indication that there may be some retributive significance to these behaviours.

[26] We do not regard remorse as a one-shot claim in mitigation to be recognised only at sentencing; an offender may become remorseful only at some point later during the administration of the sentence. There is therefore a need to recognise remorse, even if it appears later at the time of the second look at the sentence.

[27] Was the plea entered simply in order to secure a more lenient sentence, or does it reflect a genuine desire to mitigate the harm of the offence and limit the impact of the crime on the victim and the state?

[28] Von Hirsch and Ashworth, above n 7 at 18.

[29] Ibid at 171.

more principled justification than mere sympathy: on our reading, the offender is *entitled* to some mitigation if the criteria for post-offence conduct as a mitigator have been met.[30]

B. Dynamic Censure and Late Sentence Reviews[31]

Responsive censure requires a court to consider, within limits, circumstances beyond the crime which can affect the appropriate level of censure and which may justify a less punitive sanction. If the censure is to be responsive, it must consider developments occurring after sentencing, including during the administration of the sentence. A responsive censure model means that the censuring authority does not abandon the offender following sentencing. At a later point in the sentence, there is a need to evaluate whether the degree of censure expressed at sentencing remains appropriate. If sentencing consisted solely of the imposition of modest fines, there would be no need (or indeed opportunity) for the offender to respond to censure. For many offenders, however, sentencing results in a court order which may last for years, even a lifetime. When this occurs, it creates an opportunity for the offender to respond, and an obligation on the state to consider this response.[32] One such response consists of the court taking a second look at the original sentence. The need for a 'second look' sentence review is particularly pressing in jurisdictions like the US, where prison terms can account for substantial proportions of an individual's natural life. We shall shortly distinguish a late sentence review from a traditional parole hearing. First however, we clarify the concept of 'second look' or late sentence reviews.

i. Late Sentence Reviews

A truly dynamic censure model would involve repeated interactions between the state and the offender. This is clearly not feasible. However, there is no reason why the state cannot revisit the original censuring decision once years have passed. Late sentence reviews exist in many American jurisdictions.[33]

---

[30] There are parallels with the first offender sentencing discount. This should be regarded as a culpability-based entitlement: see discussion in JV Roberts, 'Re-Examining First Offender Discounts at Sentencing' in JV Roberts and A von Hirsch (eds), *Previous Convictions at Sentencing: Theoretical and Applied Perspectives* (Oxford, Hart Publishing, 2010).

[31] We restrict our discussion to sentences of imprisonment, but note that lengthy community penalties should also attract a second look review late in the life of the order.

[32] This suggests that penal cultures affect the sentencing model; the need for sentence reviews becomes particularly pressing in sentencing regimes which impose harsh and lengthy sentences.

[33] See KR Reitz, 'The 'Traditional' Indeterminate Sentencing Model' in J Petersilia and KR Reitz (eds), *The Oxford Handbook of Sentencing and Corrections* (New York, Oxford University Press, 2012) 270 at 329; see also Reporter's Note for Model Penal Code: Sentencing (Tentative Draft No 2) (Philadelphia, PA, American Law Institute, 2011) 94–95.

After 15 years in prison, for example, a hearing will often be held to determine whether there are grounds to release the prisoner early.[34] The justifications for revisiting a prisoner's sentence are traditionally founded upon non-retributive considerations.[35] These are usually related to ill-health, and reflect 'subjective retributivism', humanitarianism or mercy-based considerations.[36] Responsive censure, however, justifies a sentence review to determine whether there are censure-related reasons to justify release.

A number of grounds have been proposed to justify early release following a late sentence review. The Model Penal Code notes that: 'The passage of many years can call forward every dimension of a criminal sentence for possible re-evaluation. On proportionality grounds, societal assessments of offense gravity and *offender blameworthiness sometimes shift* over the course of a generation or comparable periods'.[37] Leaving aside circumstances relating to risk and rehabilitation (see below), the grounds for release proposed in the Code thus include:

- Physical or mental infirmity, related to old age or other causes;
- Terminal or incapacitating illness;
- Exigent family circumstances; or
- A shift in societal attitudes to the offence of conviction.

Prisoners can therefore point to several potential factors that support early release. It is paradoxical, however, that these do not engage the offender as an autonomous *active* agent. Moreover, arguably none relate to retributivism – as a deserved sanction for the *past* crime. Rather, in order to be released early, one of a number of adverse circumstances has to befall the prisoner; alternatively, she must passively await an evolution in public attitudes to secure her early release. A responsive censure model offers a different reason to justify a second-look sentence review: the need, on grounds of censure, to engage the offender as an autonomous *active* agent, which may then result in early release from prison.

---

[34] The Model Penal Code, ibid at s 305.6 includes a provision for sentence modification by a judicial decision-maker after serving 15 years of a long prison sentence.

[35] As the Model Penal Code drafters, ibid at 79–80, note: 'On this principle, determinate prison sentences are least justifiable when they last years or decades. *Both moral and consequentialist judgments* become suspect when their effects are projected so far forward into a distant future' (emphasis added).

[36] As the Model Penal Code drafters for s 305.7, ibid at 99, also suggest: 'The purposes of sentencing that originally supported a sentence of imprisonment may in some instances become inapplicable to a prisoner who reaches an advanced age while incarcerated, or a prisoner whose physical or mental condition renders it unnecessary, *counterproductive, or inhumane* to continue a term of confinement' (emphasis added). For an argument that considerations of human dignity should lead to a taking into account of the likely effects of punishments on offenders and their prospects for living satisfying lives post-release, see Tonry in this volume.

[37] Model Penal Code, ibid at 80 (emphasis added).

Early release has long been regarded as anathema to a retributive sentencing regime.[38] The desert-based case against parole runs this way. At sentencing, a court determines sentence in accordance with the twin components of a proportional sentence – harm and culpability. If a nine-year prison sentence is imposed it should not be disturbed (ie, reduced and rendered less proportionate) by a releasing authority which allows the offender to serve half the sentence in the community, on parole. If two co-accused sentenced to nine years' imprisonment serve very different periods in custody because one of them has progressed towards his rehabilitation in prison, retributive parity has been lost. Their punishments would fail to reflect the seriousness of the same offence. Rehabilitation has trumped retribution. The retributive opposition to parole is made clear by von Hirsch and Hanrahan who write that: 'the desert model … requires that the duration of the individual offender's confinement be based only on an assessment of the gravity of his criminal conduct'; also, 'An offender's desert is normally just as well ascertainable at the time of sentence – when the nature of his crimes can already be known – as at a later date'.[39]

The one exception to this rule offered by these authors – one of the same exceptions we already cited above from the Model Penal Code – is curious. They argue that if societal attitudes to the reprehensibleness of the offender's crime change, the prison sentence should be reduced.[40] This means that a prisoner must live in hope of a change in social attitudes as the only way to secure early release, and removes from him any ability to modify his sentence. In addition, when the offender committed the offence he was intentionally committing a crime 'worth' x years in prison. A downward shift in societal attitudes cannot retrospectively reduce his retributive liability to 'half of x' years, so it is unclear exactly why the offender should be the adventitious beneficiary of shifts in public opinion.[41]

---

[38] The desert-based arguments against parole had practical implications in recent history. Retributive opposition to parole was a primary factor in the elimination of parole across the United States since the 1970s. Canada also offers an illustration. In 1987, the Canadian Sentencing Commission proposed a desert-based sentencing reform in which proportionality would be the guiding principle. Under the new regime, parole would be abolished. See Canadian Sentencing Commission, *Sentencing Reform: A Canadian Approach* (Ottawa, Department of Justice, Canada, 1987).

[39] A von Hirsch and K Hanrahan, *The Question of Parole: Retention, Reform, or Abolition?* (Cambridge, MA, Ballinger Publishing, 1979) 28–29; and, further at 29: 'Judgments about seriousness are judgments about past events … By waiting longer one learns nothing new'. See also RA Bierschbach 'Proportionality and Parole' (2012) 160 *University of Pennsylvania Law Review* 1745 at 1759: 'From the standpoint of retributive culpability, a constitutional requirement that we draw out the time frame of sentencing by years or decades does not make much sense. If we know everything we need to know about culpability now, then a parole board does not need to take a second look later on'. See also KR Reitz, 'Reporter's Study: The Question of Parole-Release Authority' in *Model Penal Code: Sentencing* (Draft No 2) Appendix B (Philadelphia, PA, American Law Institute, 2011) 121.

[40] See also von Hirsch and Hanrahan, ibid at 108: 'Such a procedure might have the advantage of allowing the case to be considered in a calmer atmosphere, when it has lost some of its notoriety and a more detached assessment of the crime can be made'.

[41] Attitudes towards the crime may harden over time too, yet this does not justify increasing the amount of time the offender spends in prison for the offence now regarded as being more serious than at the time of conviction. Such an approach would, among other things, contradict the principles of legality and fairness in sentencing.

Early release from prison has therefore been understood by desert theorists as a primarily risk-based decision, devoid of any retributive considerations. In contrast, we argue that the prisoner's conduct may carry retributive significance. During the trial, an offender may well be limited in his ability to respond to the penal censure because he is either overwhelmed by the legal process, or has yet to internalise the wrongfulness of his crime. However, during the administration of the sentence prisoners have the opportunity to do so and the period of punishment should be seen as a proper phase for responding to censure.

The claim for early release therefore does not rest solely on grounds of risk to the community and offender rehabilitation. There are two justifications for allowing prisoners to serve part of their sentence in the community. First (and traditionally), after a period of confinement the prisoner may not represent the same level of risk as when he entered prison, possibly years earlier. His likelihood of reoffending and his potential for rehabilitation may be very different. Second, his conduct post-conviction and post-admission to prison may diminish the need for the degree of censure originally expressed at sentencing. On either ground, continued detention of the prisoner may be unjustified.

ii. Distinguishing Second Look Sentencing from Parole

The question arises: is our argument simply relabelling parole: old, rehabilitative wine now decanted into new, quasi-retributive bottles? It is important therefore to distinguish this censure-based claim for a review from the parole release model. Several features separate second look reviews from rehabilitative parole.

First, the criteria for release are very different. A rehabilitationist grants release for reasons which carry no retributive significance. For example, the offender has secured employment upon release. This may reduce his propensity to reoffend and promote reintegration, but does not justify any less penal censure. Similarly, a parole board may consider, on risk grounds, to release a genuinely repentant prisoner who has experienced a religious conversion and broken with his former way of life.[42] However, on a retributive account, the state should not diminish the stringency of censure for just any kind of worthy conduct. The actions of the prisoner *must relate to the offence for which censure was originally expressed*. The degree of penal censure necessary should not be affected by actions unrelated to the offence. The sentence is not adjusted to encourage the offender to lower risk to the community. Diminished censure is not a reward for positive behaviour but rather a recognition that the full stringency of the sanction is, in light of the prisoner's actions, not proportionate.[43]

---

[42] MK Miller, SC Lindsey and JA Kaufman, 'The Religious Conversion and Race of a Prisoner: Mock Parole Board Members' Decisions, Perceptions, and Emotions' (2014) 19 *Legal and Criminological Psychology* 104 at 106 noted that: 'Parole board members may consider an inmate's religious conversion or non-religious (secular) lifestyle change when deciding whether to release the inmate'.

[43] As Kleinig in his contribution to this volume explains: 'To the extent that censure is a performative, an act that has 'social' consequences of some kind, it is not removed or withdrawn by a change

Second, under a rehabilitation justification there is no theoretical limit to the intrusion into a sentence of imprisonment. A prisoner admitted for nine years but who makes great progress in lowering his risk of recidivism may safely be granted parole within a couple of years, or even earlier. Indeed, the more liberal parole regimes allow an offender to apply for release as early as one-sixth of the way into the sentence.[44] In contrast, if the grounds for release are quasi-retributive, there are important limits to the degree to which censure may be diminished without the sentence losing its focus on the offence of conviction. This is one of several issues in retributive sentencing for which there is no ready answer.[45] A reasonable limit may be one-third of the total custodial term.[46]

Third, although we have used the term 'dynamic' to describe a responsive censure model, this is inaccurate in the sense that there is no ongoing dialogue between the state and the offender. With respect to terms of imprisonment, for most offenders, the recalibration of the degree of censure will[47] occur only once, hence the term 'second look' sentencing. Parole, however, involves potentially many hearings following successive (but unsuccessful) applications. During the course of their sentences, long-term and life prisoners may make many applications for parole.

'Second-look' sentencing at a point deep into the sentence carries dangers, the principal being the threat to parity and ordinal proportionality. If two comparable offenders sentenced to serve six years are treated differently after three years (one benefitting from release), important procedural safeguards need

of heart (or the will of the person censured), *but only as a result of some determination by the censurer or authority that oversees the act of censure*' (emphasis added).

[44] In some US states, release eligibility in some cases is set immediately upon admission to prison with no minimum stay other than determined by the parole board. See Reitz, above n 33 at 275.

[45] There are others. For example, in discussing the number of convictions which may be acquired before an offender loses his 'first offender' status and is denied the associated mitigation, von Hirsch above n 5, at 87 responds: 'How many repetitions may occur before the discount is lost entirely? I have no ready answer, as this seems a matter of judgment even in everyday acts of censure'.

[46] In fixing this limit we concur with Rhine et al, who advocate dividing judicial and paroling discretion by a ratio of 3:1 or 2:1. The difference between our positions is that, for Rhine et al, the judicial decision reflects proportionality and the releasing decision utilitarianism, while we favour a model in which the two stages are more integrated. See EE Rhine, J Petersilia and KR Reitz, 'The Future of Parole Release: A Ten-Point Reform Plan' in M Tonry (ed), *Crime and Justice: A Review of Research* volume 46 (Chicago, University of Chicago Press, 1992) 279. The Model Penal Code, above n 33 at s 305.6(5), however, authorises judicial authority to 'modify any aspect of the original sentence, so long as the portion of the modified sentence to be served is no more severe than the remainder of the original sentence. The sentence-modification authority under this provision shall not be limited by any mandatory-minimum term of imprisonment under state law'. The drafters of the Model Penal Code explain, ibid at 87–88, that: 'Subject to the ceiling on prospective severity, this is intended to be as broad an authority as possible to craft a modified sentence. Any lawful sanction or combination of sanctions that would have been available to the original sentencing judge should be among the options permissible at sentence modification.'

[47] Lifers and long-term prisoners may benefit from more than a single review. It may be appropriate for a life prisoner to be evaluated every ten years. Again, s 305.6(2) of the Model Penal Code, ibid, offers a model: 'After first eligibility, a prisoner's right to apply for sentence modification shall recur at intervals not to exceed 10 years'.

to be implemented. One important distinction between incorporating censure-related conduct into a late sentence review, on the one hand, and conventional risk-based parole, on the other hand, is that the censuring authority should also serve as the releasing authority. Rather than a parole board applying nebulous risk-related criteria, the decision is to be taken by a judicial body with all the due process considerations of a sentencing court. Such a perspective also provides the censuring authority with a better sense of 'ownership' and responsibility over the punishment.[48] Indeed, in some jurisdictions the paroling authority is chaired by a judge, while in others the sentencing judge has the opportunity for a second look on the sentence.[49]

A retributive punishment without any possibility of early release means that the punishment is a passive 'quantitative' process rather that an active 'qualitative' one. Years may pass and the prisoner may change in almost every respect – but the punishment the prisoner deserves remains the same. Under a static desert regime, a prison sentence fails to reflect the complexity of the experience of serving a (sometimes lengthy) period of imprisonment. The future is always open to change; 'nothing is written'. If the state imposes a sentence which accounts for a significant portion of an individual's life, it should reassess the original censuring message in light of the prisoner's conduct. A prison sentence conveys a powerful message of censure and communicates to the prisoner that he should focus on the wrongfulness of the offence. On a proper conceptualisation of censure, it is unjustifiable to ignore the prisoner's response to such a message.

The censuring message is directed to the offender as well as the offence. Different persons may not 'need' the same degree of censure.[50] An invariant approach signals to the prisoner that his moral reform, when it occurs, is always irrelevant to the penal dialogue. It expresses the community's scepticism regarding his ability to change and to repair his relationships with the victim and the community. It disrespects his efforts and fails to recognise his individual sense of agency. It also conveys a message him that he is no different from his unresponsive cellmate, and accordingly should be treated no differently.[51]

---

[48] Such an approach also reflects a greater responsibility of the judicial authority on the implementation of the legal punishment. See also RM Cover, 'Violence and the Word' (1986) 95 *Yale Law Journal* 1601.

[49] As explained by the drafters of the Model Penal Code, above n 33 at 82: 'The judicial model for sentence modification is also consistent with the institutional philosophy of the Code … that judges should be the central authorities in the system, with a greater share of sentencing discretion than other official actors'.

[50] J Ryberg, *The Ethics of Proportionate Punishment: A Critical Investigation* (Dordrecht, Kluwer, 2007) 29.

[51] The American Supreme Court has explicitly rejected such an 'irrevocable judgment' about the offender in *Graham v Florida* 130 S Ct 2011, 2027 (2010). When holding that a life without parole sentence for juvenile non-homicide offenders is unconstitutional, the court explained that such a sentence, 'means denial of hope; it means that good behavior and character improvement are immaterial; it means that whatever the future might hold in store for the mind and spirit of [the convict], he will remain in prison for the rest of his days … no matter what he might do to demonstrate that

Other authors have also advanced retributive bases for sentence modifications. In particular, they have suggested that such changes should be made on retributive grounds based on (1) post-sentencing character changes over time,[52] and (2) post-sentencing changes in the subjective experience of the prisoner's suffering.[53] Neither of these would be 'retributive grounds' that our 'second look' responsive sentence model would recognise. Under the responsive censure model, the fact that a prisoner's suffering increases due to infirmity, old age or illness, or that he 'becomes a different person' through some change in his personality or outlook, would not justify release since these factors do not relate to the offence for which censure was originally expressed. Such factors could well fall to be considered in the context of parole, but not in a 'second look' sentencing hearing.

iii. Identifying a Responsive Prisoner

We now address the question of who should be considered a responsive prisoner. Although we cannot offer an exhaustive list of responsive actions, we can distinguish between groups of factors which may be relevant:

a. Responsive Offence-related Factors

Some actions are related directly to the offence. If a prisoner mitigates the seriousness of the past offence, he directly addresses the harm inflicted and the state should consider him as responsive and deserving of some censure mitigation. In fact, many offenders have the opportunity to mitigate the offence's harm in some way. Rehabilitation and restorative justice programs in prison share the common goal of raising offender awareness of the victim's harm and allowing prisoners to making amends for their crime.[54] Compensating the financial loss of the victim through paid prison-work programme or other means; showing sincere empathy, apologising, taking responsibility for the harm inflicted are also relevant.[55] As noted in our earlier discussion of sentencing factors,

---

the bad acts he committed as a teenager are not representative of his true character, even if he spends the next half century attempting to atone for his crimes and learn from his mistakes'.

[52] BD Robbins, 'Resurrection from a Death Sentence: Why Capital Sentences Should be Commuted upon the Occasion of an Authentic Ethical Transformation' (2001) 149 *University of Pennsylvania Law Review* 1115 at 1164, with respect to capital sentences notes: 'The transformed offender downgrades his desert and changes in character is ways radical enough to call for the prorating of punishment under the maxim of proportionality'. See also C Flanders, 'The Supreme Court and the Rehabilitative Ideal' (2014) 49 *Georgia Law Review* 383.

[53] AJ Kolber, 'The Subjective Experience of Punishment' (2009) 109 *Columbia Law Review* 182.

[54] DW Van Ness, 'Prisons and Restorative Justice' in G Johnstone and DW Van Ness (eds), *Handbook of Restorative Justice* (New York, Willan Publishing, 2007) 312.

[55] JV Roberts, 'Listening to the Crime Victim: Evaluating Victim Input at Sentencing and Parole' (2009) 38 *Crime and Justice: A Review of Research* 347; N Padfield and JV Roberts, 'Victim Input at Parole: Probative or Prejudicial?' in A Bottoms and J Roberts (eds), *Hearing the Victim: Adversarial Justice, Crime Victims and the State* (Cullompton, Willan Publishing, 2010) 255.

sincere remorse – a common but controversial parole factor – may also diminish the level of appropriate censure.[56]

In practice, there is overlap between rehabilitative and offence-related responsive actions. For example, 'second look' mitigation can be granted or denied based on remorse, which may be taken to indicate both responsive insight into the wrongfulness of the offence, and a reduced likelihood of further offending. However, this may not always be the case. A recidivist property offender who is willing to compensate his victim and is remorseful, may deserve release on responsive censure grounds even though his risk of reoffending remains high based on his long history of drug addiction. On the other hand, a first-time fraudster who rejects any opportunity to effect moral reform does not deserve second look mitigation on responsive grounds, even if his risk of reoffending is negligible.

b. Responsive Non-offence-related Factors

A second group of actions provide evidence of responsivity to state censure for the crime even though they do not directly relate to the offence's harm or culpability. Consider voluntary self-reform programmes in prison that address the causes of the offending behaviour (such as substance addiction and certain mental or psychological states).[57] A prisoner may undergo such a programme because he has been receptive to the state's message that the behaviour which landed him in prison is wrong and that the programme may help him learn to avoid it. Such factors are among the most common risk factors considered at parole and so there is even greater overlap between risk and responsive censure. However, our focus is on the prisoner's responsiveness to censure and conduct relating to the crime and not on the risk of reoffending. Therefore, some cases will not overlap. An exemplary prisoner may still pose a risk, as may a prisoner who has completed extensive drug treatment.

c. Non-responsive (Excluded) Factors

A third group of actions is unrelated to the censure. Risk assessment tools take into account any factor which proves to be a good risk predictor, subject only to any constitutional limits. In practice, although many different risk prediction

[56] Roberts and Maslen, above n 25.
[57] See MM O'Hear, 'Beyond Rehabilitation: A New Theory of Indeterminate Sentencing' (2011) 47 *American Criminal Law Review* 1247 at 1268. For O'Hear, quoting Duff, 'The inmate's efforts to comply with this regime can be seen as a secular penance – burdensome work that "expresses to those concerned the offender's repentant recognition of the wrong she has done". On the other hand, persistent, wilful violations of prison rules warrant backup sanctions for the same reason that violations of probation conditions warrant such sanctions. (Additional) imprisonment seems no less appropriate a sanction in the prison than the probation context'. However, conduct such as keeping prison rules is not focused on the *wrongfulness of the past offence* and therefore, on our model, does not deserve responsive censure-based mitigation.

instruments are in use, they all rely heavily on *static* risk factors that a prisoner is unable to alter during a prison stay. These static factors include: prior convictions; past failures on probation or parole; a history of drug use or addiction; age; gender; pre-incarceration marital status and employment history.[58] Such factors may predict risk, reduce the prisoner's propensity to reoffend or promote reintegration after release, but they are unrelated to the past offence and therefore to the deserved degree of censure. Hence, such circumstances are *irrelevant* for a sentence review based upon retributive considerations.

iv. Should Responsive Censure Increase Punishment at the Late Sentence Review?

If the penal censure for responsive prisoners can be mitigated by the prisoner's conduct, some may argue it also should be aggravated: the unresponsive prisoner should have his sentence extended accordingly.[59] However, a responsive second-look model, as part of a liberal penal regime, should not allow sentencing enhancements. Extending the punishment for the unresponsive prisoner forces him to listen to the penal message, while coercing his co-operation. It violates his freedom to remain unpersuaded by the communicative dialogue which left the prisoner free to reject the penal message.[60] Of course, it could be said that the prisoner is not entirely free to reject the penal message either: after all, release from prison constitutes such a powerful incentive to accepting the 'penal message' that it could be seen as form of coercion.[61] Even if one were to accept that argument, however, there would be another reason why extending the censure for an unresponsive prisoner is unacceptable: doing so loses the focus of the censure for the past offence in favour of prison conduct.

v. Limitations on Dynamic Censure during the Sentence Enforcement Stage

We began this chapter by noting the limitations of a static approach to determining the appropriate level of censure. It is important to now acknowledge the limitations on the degree to which the state should mitigate punishment to recognise diminished censure at the second-look hearing. First, a very significant

---

[58] Reitz, above n 33 at 278.

[59] O'Hear, above n 57 at 1265 has proposed a different normative communicative model for indeterminate sentencing. His model conceives of 'delayed release' within the indeterminate range as a retributive response to persistent, wilful violations of prison rules.

[60] Duff, above n 4.

[61] J Hampton, 'The Moral Education Theory of Punishment' (1984) 13 *Philosophy and Public Affairs* 208 at 232, while discussing her moral education theory, argues: 'The parole board uses the threat of refusal of parole to get the kind of behavior it wants from the criminal, and the criminal manipulates back – playing the game, acting reformed, just to get out. In the process, no moral message is conveyed to the criminal, and probably no real reformation takes place'. See also J Ryberg, 'Is Coercive Treatment of Offenders Morally Acceptable? On the Deficiency of the Debate' (2015) 9 *Criminal Law and Philosophy* 619.

modification of the sentence would undermine the original message of censure. Second, there are practical limits on the offender's ability to respond to censure. An offender who has defrauded his clients of their savings may be able to compensate them for their loss, but compensation will be impossible for most crimes. Yet the claim is not that offenders can perform responsive miracles, and still less that the state should repeatedly recalibrate the degree of censure necessary. Rather, our aim is more modestly to argue that censure is not immutably fixed at the time of sentencing. Offenders whose lives are radically affected by a lengthy term of imprisonment *deserve* reconsideration.

Finally, incorporating post-conviction conduct into the determination of the appropriate degree of censure carries obvious dangers as well as benefits. At sentencing this practice may differentially favour the defendant who is able to mobilise the necessary resources to support a claim for diminished censure. For example, white-collar defendants may more easily be able than other categories of offender to provide evidence that less censure is appropriate. If the opportunities to respond to censure are unequally distributed, this may create a threat to sentencing equality.[62] We cannot address these concerns here fully. However, two important remedial steps are the following. First, the nature of censure-related conduct and the limits on the extent to which it may affect the sentence must be clear. Second, for sentences of imprisonment, the releasing authority and the censuring authority need to be amalgamated. A releasing authority composed of professionals involved in predicting risk and rehabilitation would be replaced by a judicial body, and preferably the court which imposed sentence in the first instance. The second-look review is conducted in a judicial rather than an administrative tribunal.

III. CONCLUSION

Responsive censure retains the retributive focus on the crime of conviction and the offender's culpability but also recognises, as a dynamic concept, a temporal element to the determination of the appropriate level of censure. During the period between the commission of the crime and the end of the sentence, the state remains responsive to the offender. Her actions in response to the offence and the subsequent censure have the potential to diminish the appropriate degree of censure, and hence the stringency of the punishment imposed. There are, however, clear limits on the degree to which the offender may reduce the level

---

[62] Or does it? Two bank robbers make off with £20,000 each. A year later both are finally charged with the robbery. Offender A, who had buried his loot, now disinters the funds and provides it to the authorities, along with some additional money of his own, as compensation. Offender B lost all his ill-gotten gains, along with his personal savings, in a weekend in the casino. Can he claim it is unfair if offender A receives some mitigation which is denied to him? Offenders committing crimes for which compensation is impossible are assuming this consequence when they commit the crime.

of censure (and hence mitigate the punishment). It may well be the case that few prisoners would benefit from the second-look review. The point, however, is not merely to liberalise a punitive carceral regime, but rather to recognise the agency of the offender and to ensure a more accurate calibration of the offender's deserved censure.

A dynamic, responsive censure model therefore has consequences both for the determination of sentence and its administration. In determining the level of censure (and the stringency of the sanction) a court should recognise offence-related conduct following the crime. Once sentence is imposed, there should be an opportunity for the offender to bring to the attention of the censuring authority any post-sentence behaviour which may justify recalibration of the amount of censure which is appropriate. The longer the sentence imposed – whether served in prison or the community – the stronger the censure-based reasons are for allowing the offender an opportunity to demand some reconsideration. Life prisoners have the strongest claim to a court revisiting their censure level and their time in detention. After, say, 30 years in prison, such prisoners may ask whether the degree of censure expressed all those years ago is still necessary. As noted earlier, this reconsideration is independent of the issues of risk and rehabilitation. For prisoners, this 'second look' can result in earlier release based on diminished censure; with respect to lengthy community sentences, it can result in their modification through relaxation of the conditions imposed. Responsive penal censure as articulated in this essay focuses on the crime yet also rejects the tightly drawn limits placed upon a sentencing court by early desert writings; in this sense, it reflects the evolution of desert-based sentencing which began shortly after publication of *Doing Justice*.

9

Dealing with Potential Terrorists within a Censure-based Model of Sentencing

ALESSANDRO CORDA*

I N PHILIP K Dick's *Minority Report*, John Anderton describes the work of the Precrime Division he leads: 'we get them first, before they can commit an act of violence ... We can claim they are culpable. They, on the other hand, can eternally claim they're innocent. And, in a sense, they *are* innocent'.[1] In Dick's vision of the future, major violent crimes are prevented. Yet the toll is harsh punishment of 'would-be criminals'.[2]

In this chapter, I address the issue of whether and, if so, to what extent, increases in sentences beyond the censure-based deserved amount can be justi- fied by the offender's alleged dangerousness. This topic raises issues concerning censure, proportionality and dangerous offenders that go beyond traditional analyses of whether and when predictions of dangerousness arguably justify use of disproportionately severe punishments. The focus is on preparatory terrorist offences recently enacted in many Western jurisdictions as a response to attacks carried out by terrorist groups or organisations. Unlike traditional criminal laws, two elements are distinctive: first, reductions in what must be proved to convict (merely preliminary acts suffice to hold defendants criminally liable and subject to punishment); and second, disproportionately severe punishments in relation to the act proved.

Stiff above-desert sentences for dangerous offenders have usually been seen as permissible only for very serious violence, actual or threatened. Present-day reality, however, confronts sentencing scholars with cases in which desert limits

* I am extremely grateful to Michael Tonry, Anthony Bottoms and Julian V Roberts for their comments on earlier drafts of this chapter. I also want to thank Andrew Ashworth, Antje du Bois-Pedain, John Kleinig and Marlen Vesper-Gräske for helpful discussion.
[1] PK Dick, *Minority Report and Other Classic Stories* (New York, Citadel Press, 2002) 7 (empha- sis in the original).
[2] Ibid.

are exceeded with regard to pre-inchoate activities that may never result in harmful conduct or a credible threat of violence. My arguments are based on, yet go beyond, Andreas von Hirsch's analysis to date of sentence enhancements on account of dangerousness.

Section I discusses von Hirsch's perspective in regard to dangerousness-based deviations from a just deserts model of punishment conceived as a censuring response proportionate to the perpetrator's blameworthiness. Section II describes one of the most distinctive features of recent anti-terrorism legislation: the dramatic shift towards extremely severe punishment for potential terrorists convicted of preparatory offences. Section III briefly discusses UK and US models and developments. Section IV introduces and discusses four arguments that, either in a compatibilist or non-compatibilist way, are aimed at finding grounds for coexistence between principles of proportionality in sentencing and punitive schemes targeting would-be terrorists. Finally, section V offers proposals to safeguard as much as possible a desert-based notion of censure in relation to the punishment of 'terrorists in the making'. I argue that the potential impact of the ultimate harm sought by the perpetrator of merely preparatory acts cannot alone justify the imposition of extremely severe sentences. Judges should instead carefully assess whether in practical terms the preparatory acts increase the likelihood of terrorist acts; they should also pay greater attention to the defendant's strength of intention.

I. CENSURE, DESERVEDNESS AND DANGEROUSNESS
IN ANDREAS VON HIRSCH'S WRITINGS

Andreas von Hirsch has progressively developed and refined an account of sentencing in which penal censure conveying reprobation is the foundation stone for the imposition of proportionate, deserved sentences. Offenders deserve to be censured for the acts they commit, and punishment is justified because it delivers a unique message of reprobation to the wrongdoer. The proportionality principle dictates the severity of the punishment to be imposed.

Proportionality between the severity of the penalty and the seriousness of the offence has been central to von Hirsch's theory. In *Doing Justice*, the magnitude of the punishment inflicted is described as signifying 'the degree of blame ascribed' to the offender.[3] Over time, the notion of censure has become more explicit and central to the von Hirschian account of desert, culminating in *Censure and Sanctions*. There, he asserts the primacy of 'the blaming function' of punishment.[4] Hard treatment thus becomes the vehicle through which censure is conveyed: the community's degree of disapprobation for the wrongdoing is

---

[3] A von Hirsch, *Doing Justice: The Choice of Punishments* (Report of the Committee for the Study of Incarceration) (New York, Hill and Wang, 1976) 72.

[4] A von Hirsch, *Censure and Sanctions* (Oxford, Oxford University Press, 1993) 14.

expressed to the perpetrator 'through the visitation of hard treatment'.[5] In a system of sentencing primarily seen as a censuring process:

> [F]airness requires that penalties be ordered consistently with their blaming implications. The severity of the punishment, and hence its degree of implied censure, should thus comport with the seriousness (i.e., the extent of wrongfulness) of the defendant's criminal conduct. Disparate or disproportionate punishments are unjust, because they impose a degree of penal censure on offenders that is not warranted by the reprehensibleness of their criminal conduct.[6]

Thus, a censure-based account of punishment justifies but also demands proportionality in sentencing. Von Hirsch offers a predominantly censure-based view of criminal sanctions in relation to the appropriate 'amount' of punishment. At the level of the 'general justifying aim' of a system of punishment,[7] however, after distancing himself from the so-called 'benefits and burdens' theory endorsed in *Doing Justice*, he has more explicitly advocated an 'account that includes both deontological features and those concerned with consequences'.[8] Moreover, within this 'mixed' approach, when speaking of the reasons for the state's involvement in punishment, 'consequences may matter more' than censure, because 'the state's primary concerns relate to the consequences of its measures for its citizenry'.[9] These remarks certainly open the door to consequentialist concerns even within a censure-oriented architecture.

Proportionality lies at the core of desert theory, but since *Doing Justice* von Hirsch has reluctantly allowed for deviations in limited cases. Increased punishments on account of dangerousness are one of them, but are to be considered exceptions comprising 'a small class of especially fearsome cases: namely, defendants who stand convicted of serious assault crimes and who have extensive records of violence'.[10] In later works, he returns to the issue. The question

---

[5] Ibid.

[6] A von Hirsch, 'Punishment Futures: The Desert-model Debate and the Importance of the Criminal Law Context' in M Tonry (ed), *Retributivism Has a Past: Has It a Future?* (New York, Oxford University Press, 2011) 256 at 256.

[7] For this terminology, see HLA Hart, 'Prolegomenon to the Principles of Punishment' in his *Punishment and Responsibility: Essays in the Philosophy of Law* (New York, Oxford University Press, 1968) 1. Hart famously distinguishes three justificatory issues: (a) the issue of the 'general justifying aim' of punishment; (b) the 'distribution' issue (who should be punished?); and (c) the issue of the 'amount' of punishment to be imposed.

[8] A von Hirsch and A Ashworth, *Proportionate Sentencing: Exploring the Principles* (Oxford, Oxford University Press, 2005) 32.

[9] Ibid at 32n. Counterbalancing this statement, von Hirsch and Ashworth (ibid) also argue that 'when speaking of the question of the justification of punishment's impositions on those punished, emphasis should be given to treating persons as moral agents ... which suggests ... a primacy of the censuring element'. See also A Ashworth and L Zedner, 'Punishment Paradigms and the Role of the Preventive State' in AP Simester, A du Bois-Pedain and U Neumann (eds), *Liberal Criminal Theory: Essays for Andreas von Hirsch* (Oxford, Hart Publishing, 2014) 3 at 5–6; RL Lippke, 'Mixed Theories of Punishment and Mixed Offenders: Some Unresolved Tensions' (2006) 44 *Southern Journal of Philosophy* 273 at 283–88.

[10] Von Hirsch, above n 3 at 126.

is whether and, if so, to what extent, to allow stiff enhancements in penalties beyond the censure-based deserved amount, in order to prevent future crimes predictable because of the offender's dangerousness.[11]

In *Past or Future Crimes*, von Hirsch expressed concern about sentencing schemes that make room for preventative measures at the expense of proportionality on grounds of future dangerousness. He rejected the validity of selective incapacitation that conceives sentencing policy mostly as 'a device for the control of undesirables' irrespective of their past criminal history.[12] To von Hirsch, such a theory 'downplays the condemnatory features of punishment and reflects little concern for offenders as autonomous persons, whose liability should depend on their choices'.[13]

Later, von Hirsch and Ashworth criticised the use by Anthony Bottoms and Roger Brownsword of Dworkin's competing rights theory. Dworkin famously restricted the use of detention against a person's will to cases in which an individual poses a 'vivid danger' of serious harm to others,[14] but left the concept undefined. Bottoms and Brownsword elaborated on 'vivid danger' and applied it to sentencing. They argued that a vivid danger has three distinct elements: *seriousness*; *temporality* (which in turn is constituted by *frequency* and *immediacy*); and *certainty* of one or more future criminal conducts.[15] The degree of harm and the temporal framework of future offending (how often and how soon) do not for them count as much as the certainty component: 'if there is a very low score in the certainty factor, then whatever the danger it is hardly vivid'.[16] Only as the likelihood of offending increases may the harm threatened be considered as a basis for departures from fairness at sentencing. In such a case, violating the offender's right to a proportionate sentence may be justified by the protection of potential victims' rights not to be seriously harmed. Von Hirsch and Ashworth rejected this model: 'An offender's entitlement to fair treatment ... could readily be "trumped" by crime prevention concerns' relabelled as 'purported "rights" of potential victims'.[17]

However, von Hirsch and Ashworth were less negative about the second of Dworkin's criteria for derogation from fairness. This 'permits a requirement of

---

[11] For a discussion of the contemporary tendency to adopt an excessively broad concept of the 'dangerous offender', see K Harrison, *Dangerousness, Risk and the Governance of Serious Sexual and Violent Offenders* (New York, Routledge, 2011) 7–8.

[12] A von Hirsch, *Past or Future Crimes: Deservedness and Dangerousness in the Sentencing of Criminals* (New Brunswick NJ, Rutgers University Press, 1985) 170.

[13] Ibid at 170–71.

[14] R Dworkin, *Taking Rights Seriously* (Cambridge, MA, Harvard University Press, 1978) 11.

[15] AE Bottoms and R Brownsword, 'Dangerousness and Rights' in JW Hinton (ed), *Dangerousness: Problems of Assessment and Prediction* (London, Allen and Unwin, 1983) 9 at 15–21. See also AE Bottoms and R Brownsword, 'The Dangerousness Debate after the Floud Report' (1982) 22 *British Journal of Criminology* 229.

[16] 'Dangerousness and Rights' at 17.

[17] Von Hirsch and Ashworth, above n 8 at 52. For a different critique of the competing rights theory, see RS Frase, 'Can Above-desert Penalties Be Justified by Competing Deontological Theories?' in Tonry (ed), above n 6, 169 at 184–86.

fairness to be overridden when harmful consequences of an extraordinary character otherwise would occur … [that is, where] abiding by a fairness constraint (here, proportionality of sentence) might involve evil consequences of such exceptional magnitude as to warrant deviating from that constraint'.[18] This said, von Hirsch also recognises the difficulties and dangers of implementing such a policy. In particular, there is the problem that even when the likelihood of the future occurrence of extraordinary harmful consequences can be predicted to a high degree of accuracy,[19] the seriousness of the offence of conviction cannot be disregarded in the determination of the punishment to be imposed on the 'dangerous' offender.[20] In order to avoid grossly disproportionate sentences for offenders classed as dangerous, von Hirsch and Ashworth argue that the current offence(s) must include 'a grave act of violence'. 'The less serious the conviction offence is … the more blatantly disproportionate' the extension of the criminal sentence would be.[21]

In von Hirsch's account of sentencing, therefore, prevention and incapacitation play only limited roles. While he accepts prevention as an important part of the general justifying aim of a penal system, that does not justify relegating the condemnatory function of criminal penalties to the margins. The censure expressed by punishment is to be primarily commensurate to the perpetrator's conduct and culpability. Doing otherwise amounts to a version of '"beast control" … that would not address the actor as a moral agent'.[22]

Preventive sentencing schemes regarding dangerous offenders represent a clear departure from retributive principles. However, certain limits are generally proposed. In order to be classified as dangerous and sentenced accordingly, substantial requirements must be met. Typically, the seriousness of the current offence alone cannot trigger a judgment of dangerousness. For example, the extended determinate sentence (EDS) introduced in 2012 in England and Wales balances proportionality concerns and crime prevention considerations in a special sentencing scheme targeting violent dangerous offenders.[23] In the EDS, there are various limiting factors: commission of a specified violent or sexual offence; substantial evidence of past or current criminality; individualised assessment of the risk posed to the public; and a statutory cap on the maximum length of the custodial sentence and any extension period.[24]

---

[18] Von Hirsch and Ashworth, above n 8 at 52–53.
[19] That is, a significantly high score in the *certainty* factor under the Bottoms–Brownsword model.
[20] Von Hirsch, above n 4 at 51–52.
[21] Von Hirsch and Ashworth, above n 8 at 56.
[22] Ibid at 26.
[23] Cf Section 124 of the Legal Aid, Sentencing and Punishment of Offenders Act 2012, inserting a new section 226A into the Criminal Justice Act (CJA) 2003. EDSs consist of a custodial term that must reflect the seriousness of the offence of conviction, followed by an extended licence period – a term of supervised release in the community – which is determined by the court based on what it considers 'necessary for the purpose of protecting members of the public from serious harm'.
[24] Under new section 226A CJA 2003, extended sentences for adults can only be imposed where *all* the following conditions are met: (1) an adult offender is guilty of a specified violent or sexual

Dangerousness, while important, therefore does not completely trump proportionality, for it is incapable of triggering harsher sentences absent, at least, evidence of actual harm.

Statutory specifications of the dangerous offender usually include commission of serious violent offences and assessment of the offender's likelihood of committing further serious crimes. Such requirements restrict use of overly severe sentences based on vague notions of future dangerousness. Pre-inchoate terrorist offences are different, which illustrates von Hirsch and Ashworth's warning against the possible 'vulnerability … to erosion toward a wider and less defensible scope of use' of sentencing policies allowing, under certain conditions, for departures from desert on grounds of dangerousness.[25] In the next section, I describe this system of radical departures that makes other structured forms of deviation from the just desert model seem modest.

II. WOULD-BE TERRORISTS AND DISREGARD
OF PROPORTIONALITY CONSTRAINTS

Above-desert sentencing schemes for dangerous offenders, like the EDS in England and Wales, tend to anchor deviations from proportionality to appreciable measures of risk of re-offending,[26] and thereby justify consequentialist departures from desert principles in light of ostensibly reliable indicators of future criminality. Punishment policies regarding potential terrorists have, however, decisively severed any link between the severity of the punishment and the inherent seriousness of the current offence, the offender's criminal record, and other significant status factors.

In the post-9/11 world, criteria of fairness in punishment have been increasingly undermined in many Western jurisdictions. A new class of offences has been enacted to prevent individuals from committing acts capable of generating large-scale harm. Such newly created crimes belong to the category of preparatory offences, a sub-category of pre-inchoate offences. The filing of charges can trigger extremely harsh penalties on defendants (whether or not they have any

---

offence; (2) the court assesses the offender as a 'significant risk' to the public of committing further specified offences; (3) a sentence of imprisonment for life is not available or justified; and (4) the offender has a previous conviction for an offence listed in Sch 15B to the CJA 2003 or the current offence justifies an appropriate custodial term of at least four years. The extended licence period is limited to up to five years for a violent offence, and eight years for a sexual offence. Furthermore, the sum of the prison term and the extended licence must not exceed the maximum penalty provided for by the law for the offence of conviction. See, eg, F Emmerich and D van Zyl Smit, 'England and Wales' in K Drenkhahn, M Dudeck and F Dünkel (eds), *Long-Term Imprisonment and Human Rights* (New York, Routledge, 2014) 119 at 124–25.

[25] Von Hirsch and Ashworth, above n 8 at 60 (discussing the application criteria of the Bottoms–Brownsword model).

[26] On which see, eg, N Morris and M Miller, 'Predictions of Dangerousness' (1985) 6 *Crime and Justice: A Review of Research* 1.

criminal history) who commit acts that do not entail violence per se. Disequilib-
rium exists between the severity of sentences generally imposed and the harms
caused by offenders. Proportionality concerns are sacrificed to the prevention of
possible future harms of greater or lesser magnitude.

Pre-inchoate offences comprise 'conduct that may constitute the initial stage
of a complete offence or of a dangerous act, but does not constitute a dangerous
act in its own right'.[27] Traditional inchoate offences like attempt, conspiracy and
encouragement[28] are intrinsically dangerous for they entail 'conduct in which
the actor loses control of the effects of his criminal intentions',[29] which has to be
proved by the prosecutor. Pre-inchoate anticipatory offences by contrast impose
criminal liability and punishment for acts that are harmless in themselves and
pose no present danger or threat. The relationship to actual harm chiefly rests
upon the offender's longer-term intentions.[30] The actor is not convicted and
punished for carrying out an attempt to cause harm, but for planning or intend-
ing to do so.

Neither are pre-inchoate offences '*in themselves* dangerous acts' nor do they
'*in themselves* make eventual harm more likely'.[31] Furthermore, 'If the would-be
terrorist's intentions should change, any [possible] danger associated with the
preparatory act disappears'.[32] The eventual harm would occur only 'upon the
making of an intervening choice'[33] by the actor. Nonetheless, certain conducts
are made subject to criminal punishment whether that choice is made or not,
even when statistically the feared future decision occurs only in a minority of
cases. The alleged magnitude of the remote harm to be prevented therefore
takes precedence over the likelihood component, generally taken into account in
deciding whether to punish a conduct of remote harm.[34]

Pre-inchoate crimes are not something new. Criminal codes and statutes
in common and civil law jurisdictions have long criminalised and punished
crimes of possession (ranging from possession of toy guns, fake IDs, and graffiti

---

[27] P Ramsay, 'Democratic Limits to Preventive Criminal Law' in A Ashworth, L Zedner, P Tomlin
(eds), *Prevention and the Limits of the Criminal Law* (Oxford, Oxford University Press, 2013) 214
at 215.
[28] On which see generally MT Cahill, 'Inchoate Crimes' in MD Dubber and T Hörnle (eds), *The
Oxford Handbook of Criminal Law* (New York, Oxford University Press, 2014) 512.
[29] Ramsay, above n 27 at 215.
[30] Ibid at 216. See also P Ramsay, *The Insecurity State: Vulnerable Autonomy and the Right to
Security in the Criminal Law* (Oxford, Oxford University Press, 2012) 142–43.
[31] P Ramsay, 'Preparation Offences, Security Interests, Political Freedom' in A Duff, L Farmer,
S Marshall, M Renzo and V Tadros (eds), *Structures of Criminal Law* (Oxford, Oxford University
Press, 2011) 203 at 211 (italics in the original).
[32] Ibid (adding: 'Merely preparatory acts only make eventual first-order harms more likely in so far
as the preparer's criminal intentions persist').
[33] A von Hirsch, 'Extending the Harm Principle: "Remote" Harms and Fair Imputation' in
AP Simester and ATH Smith (eds), *Harm and Culpability* (Oxford, Oxford University Press, 1996)
259 at 264.
[34] Ibid at 261–63.

instruments, to offensive weapons, drugs and child pornography)[35] or preparation (eg, obtaining certain materials and tools)[36] and also status offences
(eg, public drunkenness or vagrancy) that do not inevitably precede or necessarily trigger a subsequent harm.[37] Historically, pre-inchoate crimes not involving
any substantial step towards the commission of a serious offence have existed as
easy-to-prove sentinels deployed at the outer borders of the criminal law. They
are enforcement-oriented exceptions to an approach to criminalisation and
punishment premised on actual or threatened harm.[38] Precisely because they
are exceptional, such offences usually receive comparatively small penalties.[39]
Their sentencing has traditionally been informed by a proportionality maxim:
the remoter the harm, the lighter the punishment.

Preparatory pre-inchoate terrorist offences enacted following high-profile
terrorist attacks typically contradict that maxim. Such crimes are often punished
with penalties that rival in harshness those imposed for conduct traditionally at
the core of criminal codes such as murder, aggravated assault or robbery. Terrorist preparatory offences are also often subject to the same maximum penalties
as completed acts of terrorism. All of this is at odds with the rank-ordering
component of ordinal proportionality in which punishments 'are to be ordered
on a penalty scale so that their relative severity reflects the seriousness rankings
of the crime involved'.[40] Furthermore, for such offences no inquiry is required
concerning factors that are material to the defendant's dangerousness. Rather,
would-be terrorists are punished on the basis of an irrefutable presumption
of future dangerousness. Put differently, any person found guilty of a terrorist
preparatory crime is by definition deemed dangerous in regard to the infliction
of serious bodily harm to other people.

It must be noted that judgments of dangerousness are statements of a
present condition. A person may be deemed 'dangerous' now even if the danger
in a predictable percentage of cases will not be manifested in future bad acts.

---

[35] See, eg, MD Dubber, 'Policing Possession: The War on Crime and the End of Criminal Law'
(2001) 91 *Journal of Criminal Law and Criminology* 829; D Husak, *Overcriminalization: The
Limits of the Criminal Law* (New York, Oxford University Press, 2008) 44.

[36] See, for example D Ohana, 'Desert and Punishment for Acts Preparatory to the Commission
of a Crime' (2007) 20 *Canadian Journal of Law and Jurisprudence* 113; B McSherry, 'Expanding
the Boundaries of Inchoate Crimes: The Growing Reliance on Preparatory Offences' in B McSherry,
A Norrie and S Bronitt (eds), *Regulating Deviance: The Redirection of Criminalisation and the
Futures of Criminal Law* (Oxford, Hart Publishing, 2009) 141.

[37] For a vehement critique of the proliferation of such easy-to-prove crimes in the US context,
see WJ Stuntz, 'The Pathological Politics of the Criminal Law' (2001) 100 *Michigan Law Review*
505 at 510.

[38] MD Dubber, 'Legitimating Penal Law' (2007) 28 *Cardozo Law Review* 2597 at 2605–06 argues
that pre-inchoate offences are a critical device in the programme to 'eliminate threats,' representing
'tools in the detection and control of the offensive'.

[39] It would not be accurate to state they are also few in numbers. On the contrary, pre-inchoate
offences are part of the so-called 'over-criminalisation' phenomenon, on which see generally Husak,
above n 35.

[40] A von Hirsch, 'Proportionality in the Philosophy of Punishment' (1992) 16 *Crime and Justice:
A Review of Research* 55 at 79.

Thus, from such a perspective speaking of would-be terrorists as 'potentially dangerous' offenders makes little sense.[41] Rather, one might speak of 'abstract' and 'actual' dangerousness to identify the opposite ends of a spectrum of the likelihood of committing future serious crimes. Systems like the EDS in England and Wales trigger enhanced sentences for offenders who, on the basis of the gravity of the current offence and other factors (mostly, prior convictions), are deemed very likely to commit serious crimes in the future. By contrast, perpetrators of preparatory terrorist offences routinely receive severe sentences even though they have committed no acts of serious violence and often have no prior criminal history and present no other risk factors. According to traditional models of dangerousness prediction, would-be terrorists often fall at the low-risk end of the spectrum of predicted serious acts of violence. Rather, 'risks and stakes' considerations apply, as we shall see.[42]

III. TREATMENT OF POTENTIAL TERRORISTS: A COMPARATIVE OVERVIEW

In response to recent terrorist attacks, many European countries have enacted laws punishing preliminary conduct not involving any direct threat or harm; such offences typically carry remarkably severe maximum penalties. In the United States, individuals merely plotting to travel abroad and join specified terrorist groups have been charged with conspiracy to provide material support to a listed terrorist organisation, and have faced extremely harsh penalties. These developments represent paradigmatic approaches.

A. UK Developments in a European Context

The Terrorism Act 2006 (TA 2006), enacted after the bomb attacks in London in 2005, introduced three examples of the new category of 'prophylactic crimes'[43] aimed at 'authorizing police action at a relatively early stage' before any terrorist attacks have occurred.[44] These offences target individuals, not groups, at a stage when no inchoate, uncompleted criminal plan has yet been developed.

---

[41] For the use of the expressions 'potential dangerousness' and 'potentially dangerous' in the criminal justice context, see for example respectively M Matravers, 'Is Twenty-first Century Punishment Post-desert?' in Tonry (ed), above n 6, 30 at 42; SJ Morse, 'Preventive Confinement of Dangerous Offenders' (2004) 32 *Journal of Law, Medicine and Ethics* 56 at 58.

[42] See below, section V.

[43] The expression is borrowed from AP Simester, 'Prophylactic Crimes' in GR Sullivan and I Dennis (eds), *Seeking Security: Pre-Empting the Commission of Criminal Harms* (Oxford, Hart Publishing, 2012) 59.

[44] A Ashworth and L Zedner, *Preventive Justice* (Oxford, Oxford University Press, 2014) 98. See also V Tadros, 'Justice and Terrorism' (2007) 10 *New Criminal Law Review* 658 at 670 (arguing that such criminal offences have been enacted primarily to give the police new, powerful investigative tools).

Most importantly, section 5 provides a very broad definition of the *actus reus* for preparation of terrorist acts. It is an offence punishable by up to life imprisonment for a person with intent to commit an act of terrorism, or to assist another to do so, to engage in 'any conduct in preparation for giving effect to' that intention. Ashworth explains that the conduct may well be 'perfectly normal and non-dangerous of itself: buying a map or a railway timetable or obtaining a price list for chemicals may fulfil the *actus reus*. The essence of the offence is the intention, coupled with a preparatory act of some kind'.[45] Despite being enacted only in 2006, section 5 has become the most frequently charged provision of counter-terrorism legislation since 9/11.[46]

In 2016, in the absence of sentencing guidelines issued by the Sentencing Council, the Criminal Division of the Court of Appeal in *R v Kahar* provided detailed guidance concerning sentences that should be imposed for preparation of acts of terrorism under section 5.[47] The court listed six levels of offending, determined in relation to (a) 'the culpability of the offender principally by reference to proximity to carrying out the intended act(s) measured by reference to a wide range of circumstances including commitment to carry out the intended act(s)'; and (b) the potential harm that could be caused, measured in terms of impact on immediate victims and the wider public. The guidance provided on levels of seriousness and appropriate sentences covers any preparatory conduct from the most to the least serious.[48]

Life imprisonment with a minimum term of 30 to 40 years or more (level 1) is considered an appropriate sentence for an offender who has taken steps that nearly amount to attempted multiple murder, or conspiracy to commit similar acts that were likely to succeed. The lowest sentences, from 21 months to five years (level 6), are prescribed for offenders who never got far in their plans or were never likely to get far, and for minor roles in intended acts at the lowest end of seriousness. Sentences of five to ten years are often imposed (level 5) on offenders who make extensive preparations with real commitment, but do not get very far in carrying out the plan.[49]

The Sentencing Council issued guidelines for terrorist offences only in early 2018. Most notably, these guidelines are likely to result in harsher punishment in

---

[45] A Ashworth, 'Attempts' in J Deigh and D Dolinko (eds), *The Oxford Handbook of Philosophy of Criminal Law* (Oxford, Oxford University Press, 2011) 125 at 127. See also C Walker, *Terrorism and the Law* (Oxford, Oxford University Press, 2011) 224–25.

[46] 125 principal charges out of 588, slightly more than 21% of the total. See Home Office, Operation of Police Powers under TA 2000 and Subsequent Legislation: Arrests, Outcomes and Stops and Searches, Quarterly Update to 31 December 2015 (March 2016), Table A.05a.

[47] *R v Kahar and others* [2016] EWCA Crim 568. The Sentencing Council for England and Wales was created in 2009 in order to produce 'definitive sentencing guidelines' which courts are required by statute to follow, unless the interests of justice dictate otherwise. The Sentencing Council is gradually issuing definitive guidelines for all the main types of offence.

[48] Ibid at paras 29–34.

[49] For a summary of successful prosecutions by the Counter-Terrorism Division of the Crown Prosecution Service (CPS) since 2006, and related sentences imposed, see www.cps.gov.uk/publications/prosecution/ctd.html#a02 (accessed 12 September 2017).

cases at the lowest end of the seriousness scale. The guidelines call for a sentencing range for the lowest-level forms of preparation of between three to six years, compared to 21 months to five years under the guidance provided for in *Kahar*.

Section 6 TA 2006 prohibits training others in terrorist activities or receiving training. It covers any person who 'provides instruction or training' in enumerated skills to other persons and, at the time of providing such instruction or training, knows that the trainee intends to use such newly acquired skills for terrorist purposes.[50] A person who merely receives instruction or training in the enumerated skills is also covered if he/she intended to use such new knowhow for terrorist purposes. The intention component again plays a key role. Until 2015, the maximum penalty for training for terrorism under section 6 was ten years' imprisonment. The Criminal Justice and Courts Act 2015 raised the maximum to life imprisonment.[51]

The third section, section 8, punishes attendance at a place used for terrorist training. It need only be shown that the accused knew or believed that the place attended is used for instruction or training in connection with the commission or preparation of acts of terrorism, or sought to receive training for terrorist purposes.[52] The offence is punishable by imprisonment for up to ten years, or a fine, or both.

The UK is not alone in Europe in authorising extremely severe criminal sanctions for nearly harmless conduct as long as the offender acts with a terrorist intention as part of the fight against terrorism. Germany,[53] Italy[54] and France,[55] for example, also punish preparation for committing terrorist acts, and providing or receiving terrorist training, with significant penalties. A few jurisdictions have also criminalised travelling or attempting to travel abroad 'for the purpose of the perpetration, planning, or preparation of, or participation in, terrorist acts, or the providing or receiving of terrorist training' in order to limit the growing number of so-called 'foreign fighters'.[56] In Spain substantial penalties

---

[50] See Walker, above n 45 at 206 (noting that s 6 expanded on s 54 of the UK Terrorist Act 2000 by including techniques other than specified weapon training such as, for example, the making, handling or use of a noxious substance).

[51] In order to address the challenge posed by foreign fighters, section 81 of the Serious Crime Act 2015 also extended extra-territorial jurisdiction to section 5 (preparation of terrorist acts) and extended the existing scope of extra-territorial jurisdiction in respect of section 6 (training for terrorism).

[52] K Roach, 'Terrorism' in Dubber and Hörnle (eds), above n 28, 812 at 825 (observing that journalists or others legitimately visiting a training camp might be subject to punishment).

[53] B Weißer, 'Prevention of Terrorist Crimes – Prosecution before the Fact?' in E Salygin and E Ivanov (eds), *Development of International Justice for Purpose of Countering International Terrorism* (Moscow, National Research University Higher School of Economics, 2013) 53 at 58–63. New amendments expanding preparatory offences entered into force in mid-2015, criminalising travelling abroad to receive terrorist training.

[54] F Fasani, *Terrorismo Islamico e Diritto Penale* (Padua, CEDAM-Wolters Kluwer, 2016) at 339 ff.

[55] F Galli, *The Law on Terrorism: The UK, France and Italy Compared* (Bruxelles, Bruylant, 2015) at 64–67.

[56] See point 6 of Resolution No 2178 of the UN Security Council of September 24, 2014, S/RES/2178 (2014) at 4–5. A 'foreign fighter' is defined as an individual who leaves his or her country

are even provided for the habitual access of websites that allegedly promote terrorism, if done with the intention to carry out terrorist acts.[57]

B. Developments in the US

Since 9/11, the statute chiefly used in the United States for prosecuting would-be terrorists has been 18 USC § 2339B(a)(1). It criminalises the provision of 'material support or resources' to designated foreign terrorist organisations (FTOs), or attempting or conspiring to do so.[58] The current penalty is imprisonment of up to 20 years. The Federal Sentencing Guidelines Manual indicates for this crime a base offence level of 26, triggering, with no or negligible criminal history (criminal history category of I), a recommended custodial sentence between 63 and 78 months.[59] The harshness of the guidelines for material support to terrorist organisations is apparent. Consider, for example, that in the case of a repeat offender with a criminal history category of V who committed an aggravated assault causing serious bodily injury to the victim (offence level 19) the applicable guideline range would be between 57 and 71 months in prison. Furthermore, in material support cases terrorism enhancement is generally nearly automatically applied, thus increasing the base offence level by 12 points and the criminal history category up to category VI (the highest level).[60] In this scenario, the applicable sentence would range from 360 months to life imprisonment.[61] However, a Guidelines sentence cannot exceed the statutory maximum. Since the maximum term of imprisonment for violation of § 2339B is 20 years, courts must impose the statutory maximum.[62]

---

of origin or habitual residence to join a non-state armed group in an armed conflict abroad, and who is primarily motivated by ideology and religion. See, eg, T Mehra, 'Foreign Terrorist Fighters: Trends, Dynamics and Policy Responses' (2016) *The International Centre for Counter-Terrorism*, https://icct.nl/wp-content/uploads/2016/12/ICCT-Mehra-FTF-Dec2016-2.pdf.

[57] M Cancio Meliá, '11/3 and 7/7 ten years on: Terrorismusstraftaten im spanischen Strafrecht' (2015) 10 *Zeitschrift für Internationale Strafrechtsdogmatik* 538 at 543.

[58] §2339B is the most commonly used provision of the so-called material support statutes (§§ 2339A–D) aimed at preventing 'the development of terrorist capabilities' by terrorist and extremist groups. See F Laguardia, 'The Nonexceptionalism Thesis: How Post-9/11 Criminal Justice Measures Fit in Broader Criminal Justice' (2016) 19 *New Criminal Law Review* 544 at 550 (§ 2339A punishes providing material support to terrorists; § 2339C prohibits financing of terrorism; § 2339D criminalises receiving military-type training from a foreign terrorist organisation).

[59] US Sentencing Guidelines Manual § 2M5.3 (2016).

[60] The terrorist enhancement does not necessarily attach to any prosecution of a listed federal crime of terrorism, but only when the offence is specifically 'calculated to influence or affect the conduct of government by intimidation or coercion, or to retaliate against government conduct' (§ 2332b(g)(5)). On the genesis and evolution of the terrorist enhancement see WE Said, 'Sentencing Terrorist Crimes' (2014) 75 *Ohio State Law Journal* 477 at 499–503; GD Brown, 'Punishing Terrorists: Congress, the Sentencing Commission, the Guidelines, and the Courts' (2014) 23 *Cornell Journal of Law and Public Policy* 517 at 533–34.

[61] US Sentencing Guidelines Manual § 3A1.4 (2016).

[62] US Sentencing Guidelines Manual § 5G1.1 (a) (2016).

Material support prosecutions are mainly intended to aid in preventing terrorist activity in the future.[63] Since its enactment in 1996 as part of the Anti-terrorism and Effective Death Penalty Act (AEDPA), § 2339B provides a 'readily available charge' for such a purpose,[64] though its use has been adapted in recent years to fight non-conventional terrorist groups. Since ISIS[65] became the main global terrorist organisation, the number of aspiring foreign fighters planning to migrate to terrorist hotspots has grown exponentially. The media increasingly report stories of young people planning or plotting with others to travel to Syria in order to join the self-proclaimed caliphate.[66] In all recent reported cases, the individuals trying to join ISIS themselves represented the only 'material support or resources' to be provided to the foreign terrorist group for the purposes of § 2339B; no currency, monetary instruments, lethal substances, weapons or false IDs were involved. The material support or resources element was described as 'personnel', which may include the charged person herself.[67]

Section 2339B is not technically a pre-inchoate offence. However, as routinely applied, it closely resembles a thought crime, or little more than that, in which the conduct requirement has been significantly diluted. Most of the young defendants charged never used arms, travelled outside the country or planned to murder anyone. They merely intended or plotted with others to travel abroad and join ISIS, and in some cases assisted each other with planning and funding their efforts. The severe prison terms that can be imposed thus raise serious proportionality concerns in relation to the harm actually caused or threatened, especially when one considers that § 2339B was enacted having primarily in mind individuals such as arms traffickers, document forgers, money launderers and people with weapons and combat skills who had the capability of significantly contributing to the success of a terrorist group or organisation.

Currently, prosecutions mostly concern people in their late teens or early twenties who plotted to join ISIS but had no money, connections, previous training, special skills or other strategic assets to offer the caliphate. People charged are often only abstractly dangerous, frequently being caught after

---

[63] WE Said, 'The Material Support Prosecution and Foreign Policy' (2011) 86 *Indiana Law Journal* 543 at 556.

[64] R M Chesney, 'Beyond Conspiracy? Anticipatory Prosecution and the Challenge of Unaffiliated Terrorism' (2007) 80 *Southern California Law Review* 425 at 436. See also WE Said, *Crimes of Terror: The Legal and Political Implications of Federal Terrorism Prosecutions* (New York, Oxford University Press, 2015) ch 3.

[65] The acronym stands for 'Islamic State of Iraq and Syria'.

[66] See, eg, S Shane, '6 Minnesotans Held in Plot to Join ISIS', *The New York Times*, 20 April 2015; J Berlinger and CE Shoichet, 'Mississippi Woman Pleads Guilty on Charge That She Tried to Join ISIS', 30 March 2016, www.cnn.com/2016/03/30/us/mississippi-isis-guilty-plea-jaelyn-young.

[67] Previously, cases like that of John Phillip Walker Lindh – a US citizen who was captured as an enemy combatant in 2001 during the war in Afghanistan – were deemed rare and exceptional. The 2002 Lindh case was the first in which a federal court ruled, with precedential status, that it is possible to indict someone under § 2339B based on the theory that the accused was attempting to provide 'personnel' (his/her own body) to a foreign terrorist organisation (*United States v Lindh*, 212 F Supp 2d 541 (ED Va 2002)).

a few exchanges on social media with undercover federal agents who test their willingness to leave the country and join an FTO abroad. Furthermore, in the exercise of their discretion, prosecutors frequently charge the same defendant with conspiring and attempting to leave the country to join and fight for a terrorist organisation abroad, thus pushing the length of the punishment dramatically upward. To sum up, in the US aggressive practices reshaping traditional boundaries of conspiracy and material support liability have allowed the prosecution, conviction and extremely harsh sentencing of merely potential terrorists, 'even in the absence of any specificity as to violent acts that they might commit'.[68]

IV. DESERT, CENSURE AND PUNISHMENT FOR TERRORIST OFFENCES: IS A COMPATIBILIST EXPLANATION POSSIBLE?

The offences and related sentencing provisions described in the previous section concern non-harmful behaviours that cause no direct harm and involve no use of violence. Nor do they entail establishment or maintenance of a terrorist group or organisation (so-called general preparation).[69] They involve preparatory conduct that is punished with harsh prison sentences based mostly on the intentions of the offender. The centre of gravity shifts from actions to mere inclinations.

In just deserts theory, the censuring response entails and requires a proportionate punishment. Where no imminent danger is involved, the likelihood of future grievous harm is merely theoretical, and the offender has no history of violence, how can extremely severe penalties be justified? In this section, I discuss and evaluate four attempts to provide such a justification.

A. Punishing Would-be Terrorists as an Offshore Penal Sub-system

A first argument is that notions of desert and censure are radically *incompatible* with the criminalisation and punishment of terrorist offenders. There is no possibility of adapting or stretching a censure approach to deal with such cases.

---

[68] See RM Chesney, 'Optimizing Criminal Prosecution as a Counterterrorism Tool' in B Wittes (ed), *Legislating the War on Terror: An Agenda for Reform* (Washington, DC, Brookings Institution Press, 2009) 98 at 101.

[69] See S Wallerstein, 'Criminalizing Remote Harm and the Case of Anti-democratic Activity' (2007) 28 *Cardozo Law Review* 2697 at 2722 who distinguishes between *general* and *specific* preparatory stages of 'anti-democratic' acts. In her view, the former is less controversial a case from a desert perspective for, unlike preparations with regard to specific harmful conduct, 'Further danger is found in general preparations which create and maintain the structure – the organization – that would eventually carry out direct harmful acts'. Thus, unlike sporadic acts, 'general preparations at the organizational level add up to the probability that harmful activity will follow'.

Terrorist preparatory offences are therefore best characterised as an *offshore penal sub-system* concerning proscribed conduct and related penalties.[70] In the wake of the 9/11, German criminal law scholar Günther Jakobs famously called for a differentiation between a 'criminal law for the enemy' (*Feindstrafrecht*) and a 'criminal law for the citizen' (*Bürgerstrafrecht*).[71] That bifurcation would require the introduction of a binary code not only for procedural guarantees, but also for substantive criminal law and sentencing; there would be safeguards against arbitrary and unfair governmental actions for the citizen, and repression for the enemy.

The premise of this approach seems to be that there is 'something additional and intrinsically wrong about being a certain kind of person, engaged in a certain kind of activity' justifying a 'special' criminalisation and punishment regime.[72] This represents a *sui generis*, subjective characterological argument entirely detached from objective assessments based on evidence about a defendant's past behaviour, including in the form of prior convictions.[73]

Potential terrorists are thus seen as traitors to the democratic state. Harsh penalties serve an incapacitating function, but also provide 'an effective deterrent against future treason'.[74] In order 'To prevent enemies from violating citizens' "right to security", they must be incapacitated'.[75] The inability of the censuring message to perform its function in relation to certain offenders leads

---

[70] The term 'offshore penal system' in both a physical and legal meaning has been first utilised to describe offshore systems of 'justice' such as Guantanamo or Abu Graib. See also CE Paliero, 'L'agorà e il palazzo. Quale legittimazione per il diritto penale?' (2012) 7 *Criminalia* 95 at 115 (using this term to refer to sub-systems which deny basic principles of what should be a cherished 'democratic criminal law', first and foremost in regard to the violation of harm principle constraints).

[71] See G Jakobs, 'Bürgerstrafrecht und Feindstrafrecht' (2004) 5:3 *HRRS* 88; G Jakobs, 'On the Theory of Enemy Criminal Law' in MD Dubber (ed), *Foundational Texts in Modern Criminal Law* (Oxford, Oxford University Press, 2014) 415. See also MD Dubber, 'Citizenship and Penal Law' (2010) 13 *New Criminal Law Review* 190 at 201.

[72] N Lacey, 'The Resurgence of Character: Criminal Responsibility in the Context of Criminalisation' in RA Duff and SP Green (eds), *Philosophical Foundations of Criminal Law* (Oxford, Oxford University Press, 2011) 151 at 164.

[73] On which see generally M Redmayne, *Character in the Criminal Trial* (Oxford, Oxford University Press, 2015) 2–8; also N Lacey, *In Search of Criminal Responsibility: Ideas, Interests, and Institutions* (Oxford, Oxford University Press, 2016) 102, where she describes s 5 of the UK Terrorism Act 2006 (criminalising the mere preparation of terrorist acts) as a crime rooted in an approach to criminal liability based on 'a combination of risk and character'.

[74] KE Eichensehr, 'Treason in the Age of Terrorism: An Explanation and Evaluation of Treason's Return in Democratic States' (2009) 42 *Vanderbilt Journal of Transnational Law* 1443 at 1482. To a significant extent, the treatment of anarchists represented the precursor, in nineteenth-century criminal law, of the current situation. For example, CL von Bar, *A History of Continental Criminal Law* (Boston, Little Brown and Co, 1916) 373–74 observes that 'German Governments lived under the obsession that political unrest was to be ascribed to the mildness of the deterrent criminal law; and thus, in spite of the jurists' protests, the spirit of official terrorism gained ground more and more. The most innocent and well-disposed citizen might now come into the grasp of the law for acts and utterances which a suspicious government and a facile judiciary chose to interpret as offenses under the new definitions'.

[75] MD Dubber, 'Paradigms of Penal Law' in Dubber and Hörnle (eds), above n 28, 1017 at 1038.

the legal system to adopt a quarantine approach[76] in which any concern for individual desert and proportionality is abandoned in favour of segregation from the general population.[77] Under this model, the pursuit of safety at all costs has expanded and distorted the criminal law. Criminalisation and penalties 'are justified not on grounds of retributive justice but rather on grounds of criminal security'.[78] In developing penal policies for terrorism, legislatures do not much care about the (allegedly) enhanced blameworthiness of the offender. Instead, they are primarily concerned to address the public's increased anxiety.[79]

This analysis is incompatible with concern for censure and proportionality. Sentences are unrelated in any conventional sense to the reprehensibility of acts committed. The primary goal is to send a message that has little to do with the behaviour charged. By importing the unrelenting struggle against terror into the domestic criminal justice system, courts are deployed to fight terrorism at home pre-emptively.[80]

B. Culpability at Centre Stage for Censure-based Considerations

In addition to the incompatibilist 'offshore' thesis, three compatibilist explanations can be put forward. The first of these centres on the absolute primacy of the offender's culpability – 'the factors of intent, motive, and circumstance that bear on the actor's blameworthiness'[81] – in relation to calculation of the deserved punishment to be threatened and imposed in regard to terrorism offences. When harm, even if very remote, is hugely serious, it may be reasonable to characterise the suspect as hugely culpable. Under this account, desert considerations are skewed towards the subjective side of culpability. The objective component, represented by the harmful conduct, becomes almost irrelevant compared with a disruptive intention to use terrorism to dismantle key principles and values of the democratic order. Put differently, the offender's intention is so evil that even

---

[76] See M Foucault, *Discipline and Punish: The Birth of the Prison* translated by A Sheridan (New York, Vintage Books, 1977) at 195–97 for the description of the quarantine practices in a seventeenth-century town stricken with plague.

[77] See K Huigens, 'What Is and Is Not Pathological in Criminal Law' (2002) 101 *Michigan Law Review* 811 at 812. The same logic of quarantine has favoured the enactment of 'three strikes' laws, mandatory minimum sentences, rigid determinate sentencing systems – ironically 'often described as a triumph of retributivism in punishment' (ibid at 820).

[78] Tadros, above n 44 at 679.

[79] B Ackerman, 'Terrorism and the Constitutional Order' (2006) 75 *Fordham Law Review* 475 at 475.

[80] 'Terrorism has to become a zero-tolerance crime. … It is the court's responsibility to fashion a sentence that takes any and all steps to minimize … any risk that you might pose in the future' (US District Judge J Mendez, quoted in N Hong, 'ISIS Sentences Pose Challenge for Judges', *The Wall Street Journal*, 23 December 2016, www.wsj.com/articles/isis-sentences-pose-challenge-for-judges-1482489003).

[81] A von Hirsch, 'Commensurability and Crime Prevention: Evaluating Formal Sentencing Structures and their Rationale' (1983) 74 *Journal of Criminal Law and Criminology* 209 at 214.

harmless preparatory acts falling within its long shadow would justify extremely severe penalties. Intention to cause, or contribute to causing, a grievous harm in an uncertain future takes a preponderant role in censuring considerations. The degree of harm intended is constitutive of the actor's blameworthiness, regardless of the actual amount of harm caused or already risked.

What is to be severely punished is therefore, on this account, the offender's contemplation of committing very serious violent crimes. The actor's manifested disposition stands out as the key element. The *mens rea* represents the crucial 'marker of dangerousness, or offensiveness': 'The "higher" the *mens rea*, the more offensive the offender, and the more in need of penal discipline', regardless of the inherent harmfulness of the offence.[82] At first glance, this approach seems unjustly and excessively focused on culpability at the expense of harm, actual or threatened. Yet at a closer look, considering the often elusive nature of the *actus reus* in preparatory terrorism offences, a careful assessment of the defendant's *mens rea* could represent the key element for calibrating the penalty in a way that is more respectful of proportionality considerations.[83]

C. Being Threatening as a Serious Wrong

A second compatibilist argument is that 'to be threatening or terrifying is to deserve severe punishment' and that 'to cause fear is a blameworthy wrong'.[84] From this perspective, threatening and dangerous individuals may be punished with lengthy sentences because generating fear is in itself a serious wrong that deserves severe punishment and justifies enhanced censure. A harsh penalty should thus be regarded as proportional to the harm threatened.[85]

In my view, this argument cannot justify heavy sentences for pre-inchoate terrorist offences. This is because such acts 'incorporate elements of risk and an intelligence mindset' focusing more on 'suspicious activities' and 'statuses' than 'on acts that are dangerous in themselves'.[86]

Even a person fully trained in guerrilla warfare does not necessarily constitute a source of actual and serious danger, ie at the maximum level in the spectrum of likelihood. Those skills may never be put to use. The same line of reasoning applies, *mutatis mutandis*, in regard to someone preparing a terrorist act who does not get far in his plans, or the aspiring foreign fighter who is arrested

---

[82] Dubber, above n 38 at 2605.

[83] See below section V.

[84] A Ristroph, 'Terror as a Theory of Punishment' in Tonry (ed), above n 6, 155 at 159–60.

[85] Fear is a very subjective emotion, extremely hard to measure and quantify. Thus I will not address the issue of the deserved amount of punishment in relation to the fear that the offender causes or intends to cause.

[86] Roach, above n 52 at 827. See also Ashworth and Zedner, above n 44 at 180 ('Terrorism offences create a sphere of operation in which police and security officials may monitor, stop and search, interrogate, and detain would-be terrorists with the aim of forestalling the consummate harm').

before he can leave his home country. The case law demonstrates that, in a vast number of cases, the preparatory acts the criminal justice system punishes are not solidly linked to a substantial likelihood of future dangerousness.[87] Rather, the existence of a serious danger that triggers severe sentences is inferred from the '*abstract* existence of risks ... one wishes to prevent'.[88]

In many cases, the alleged grave dangerousness rests almost entirely upon the defendant's intent to commit a terrorist act in a more or less distant future. Yet intention alone does not provide solid grounds for departures from proportionality on account of dangerousness in case of individuals who '*might* engage in violent acts in the future' but who have not 'engaged in conduct constituting [even] an attempt'.[89] Conduct such as preparing for carrying out a terrorist act prior to an attempt being made, receiving terrorist training, or travelling abroad for terrorist purposes does not automatically constitute a vivid and present danger. And the proved willingness to act is not enough. Being willing to cause harm is conceptually different from being highly likely to do so.[90]

Think of someone who travels abroad to join a terrorist organisation but then changes his mind after reaching the destination; or who, after receiving weapons training, desists from carrying out a terrorist attack; or who buys explosive materials and a map of the London underground with the intent to place a bomb, but then repents and aborts his plans. Under current laws, all these people are punishable by harsh penalties for pre-inchoate terrorist crimes. Repentance or voluntary withdrawal will not affect issues of liability and punishment. Those actions do not constitute attempts to commit a terrorist attack; no substantial step has been taken, so repentance and voluntary withdrawal will not affect issues of liability and punishment as they would on a charge of attempt.

Punishing with harsh sentences preparatory behaviours that would be legal absent a terrorist intent challenges the viability of the argument that making people fearful is a serious wrong that deserves severity. This is because, for

---

[87] A clear pattern of behaviour is yet to be established. See G Mythen and S Walklate, 'Criminology and Terrorism' (2006) 46 *British Journal of Criminology* 379 at 391 (noting that 'The new techniques of counter-terrorism do not seem to be based around reliable quantitative judgments about the probabilities of offending').

[88] R Castel, 'From Dangerousness to Risk' in G Burchell, C Gordon, and P Miller (eds), *The Foucault Effect: Studies in Governmentality* (Chicago, University of Chicago Press, 1991) 281 at 287–88.

[89] Chesney, above n 68 at 103 (emphasis in the original). Furthermore, and more generally, it can be observed that some risks, regardless of how likely they are to materialise, are perceived as less acceptable than others. For example, an analogy could be made between ISIS recruitment and street gang recruitment, yet no specific offences and related draconian penalties exist for the latter.

[90] Ramsay above n 31 at 212 argues that the would-be terrorist 'has demonstrated that he has a will to commit dangerous acts. It is not the act but the actor that is dangerous. The actor is dangerous by virtue of his willingness to act on his criminal intentions'. The author thus seems to adopt a one-dimensional notion of dangerousness, without acknowledging the width of the spectrum of likelihood that has as its opposite poles abstract and actual dangerousness. See above, section II.

pre-inchoate offences, the punitive response generally occurs very early in situations of merely abstract dangerousness, while a rational fear is usually defined as something that occurs in response to a clear and present danger.

D. Penal Policy 'on Steroids'

A third compatibilist explanation starts from the observation that external factors may reshape the notion of deserved punishments. The political construction of certain offences can sometimes influence and, ultimately, change moral assessments of a specific type of behaviour. Given this, a useful parallel can be drawn between the rhetoric and lexicon of the 'war on terror' and those of the American 'war on drugs'.

In 1971, President Nixon launched what he called a national 'war on drugs', naming drug abuse 'public enemy number one'. Some states also acted with an iron hand. Most notably, in 1973 New York State passed the Rockefeller Drug Laws, 'the most severe in the nation at the time',[91] that provided for extremely harsh sentencing for drug-related offences. In the early 1980s, the war on drugs rhetoric gained greater intensity when President Ronald Reagan declared illicit drugs to be 'a threat to US national security'.[92]

The 'war on drugs' rhetoric legitimised legislative initiatives viewed by many as just responses to something that, allegedly, put some of the basic foundations of society at risk. With the drug problem characterised as something much worse than a 'simple' public health issue, legislatures enacted severe laws as ostensibly proportionate responses to the threat. Harsh new laws governing low-end drug crimes were promoted as proportionate to their blameworthiness.

The same political psychology has been used to justify harsh measures in the war on terror's approach to pre-inchoate offences.[93] The shift in moral assessment leads not only to a new consensus of what can be deemed justifiable. Rather than justifying excessive punishments on consequentialist grounds (deterrence and incapacitation), the 'discourse of war' makes harsh penalties

---

[91] M Mauer, 'Why Are Tough on Crime Policies So Popular?' (1999) 11 *Stanford Law and Policy Review* 9 at 10.

[92] On the role of political rhetoric in shaping the discourse on the 'war on drugs' in the US, see AB Whitford and J Yates, *Presidential Rhetoric and the Public Agenda: Constructing the War on Drugs* (Baltimore MD, Johns Hopkins University Press, 2009) 74–94. The tough drug laws enacted in the US during the 1970s and 1980s represent, to a significant degree, the precursor to a more comprehensive 'get-tough' approach: see J Simon, *Governing Through Crime: How the War on Crime Transformed American Democracy and Created a Culture of Fear* (New York, Oxford University Press, 2007) 102–06.

[93] See for example J Forman, 'Exporting Harshness: How the War on Crime Helped Make the War on Terror Possible' (2009) 33 *NYU Review of Law and Social Change* 331 at 373–74. The discourse of security and risk surrounding the enactment and implementation of Israeli extreme anti-terrorism laws may represent an interesting reference point: see M Ajzenstad and B Ariel, 'Terrorism and Risk Management: The Israeli Case' (2008) 10 *Punishment and Society* 355 at 369.

seem appropriate and proportionate. Altered perceptions of dangerousness have decisively modified the community's understanding of desert.[94]

Penal policies 'on steroids' thus not only redefine sentencing tools, but also, and most importantly, may reshape popular intuitions about proportionality and desert. When the stakes are raised, what under different scenarios would be seen as disproportionate and undeserved punishments become appropriate also from a retributivist perspective. This way, a new standard of deservedness is created, one that has nothing to do with a normal evolution in the perceived gravity of a certain conduct. The recalibration of the public discourse redefines the co-ordinates and boundaries of desert. Hence, the abstract concept of proportionality seems to 'have little limiting potential'[95] when the caps that anchor the severity of the punishment to the seriousness of the crime are reset. Inter-offence comparisons are not ignored; rather, new assessments of seriousness are assigned to certain crimes, and the relative severity of the punishments that their commission justifies increases accordingly.

V. SENTENCING POTENTIAL TERRORISTS: WHERE DO WE GO FROM HERE?

This chapter has examined the radical challenges that the expansion of anti-terrorism law poses to the account of punishment based on censure for blameworthy behaviour. Many Western countries are seemingly going down the same path. In response to high-profile terrorist attacks, a significant number of jurisdictions have applied the logic of 'punitive prevention' to the realm of criminal penalties.[96] Significant political and media pressure has been put on courts 'to hand down severe sentences to denounce and deter terrorism'[97] even though many of the newly criminalised preparatory acts are in themselves not 'worthy of moral criticism, let alone condemnation'.[98]

In the current political climate, prosecutors are not likely to become more selective in bringing charges. New laws make it easy to prove the few and tenuous elements of pre-inchoate terrorist offences. Sentencing judges might be expected

---

[94] See FE Zimring and G Hawkins, 'Dangerousness and Criminal Justice' (1986) 85 *Michigan Law Review* 481 at 500. Ristroph, above n 84 at 155, argues that 'Desert is not an antidote to public sensibilities, but a vehicle for their expression'.

[95] N Lacey and H Pickard, 'The Chimera of Proportionality: Institutionalising Limits on Punishment in Contemporary Social and Political Systems' (2010) 78 *Modern Law Review* 216 at 227 (noting that in today's societies appeals to proportionality may be useful with regard to *ordinal* proportionality but not so much in terms of *cardinal* proportionality).

[96] See, eg, AM Dershowitz, *Is There a Right to Remain Silent?* (Oxford, Oxford University Press, 2008) 137 ('The preventive state seeks to anticipate and stop harms before they occur. The threat of mass-casualty suicide terrorism is pushing democratic societies, and especially those more vulnerable to this threat, away from exclusive reliance on a deterrence or punitive model and toward a more preventive model').

[97] Roach, above n 52 at 831.

[98] Tadros, above n 44 at 675–76.

to play a major role in moderating the effects of the new regime by evaluating pleas reached by the parties and exercising discretion at sentencing. However, a recent comparative analysis focusing on the US, the UK, Canada, Australia and New Zealand cheerlessly concluded that:

> Courts seem sympathetic to the sentiments that underlie the legislature's decision to impose heavy maximum sentences for precursor terrorism offences. They attach little weight to the fact that a defendant was arrested before having had an opportunity to give effect to his or her terrorist intentions. What matters are defendants' intentions prior to their arrest.[99]

Offenders are to be punished and censured harshly not for what they have done, but mostly for what they might do in the future. The proportionality inquiry does not attend to the offender's intrinsic blameworthiness. Rather, it chiefly focuses on 'the putatively catastrophic, but necessarily uncertain harm in prospect',[100] generally without rigorous analysis regarding 'the degree of harm sought to be averted and the likelihood that the harm would occur'.[101] The tension with Andreas von Hirsch's views in *Doing Justice* is apparent: 'An offender does not *deserve* to be punished more severely on account of a crime he is predicted to commit, however likely its occurrence. ... to the extent that his behavior is merely forecast, there is no such action for which he can be held to blame'.[102]

It is certainly not enough to justify the new regime with simple and vague claims that the stakes are high since 'Provided the stakes are high enough, potentially anything goes'.[103] When stakes are high most people believe that even low risks justify considerable limitation of personal autonomy. This applies to sentencing,[104] but not only to sentencing.[105] The vast majority of persons charged with preparatory terrorist offences are low-risk but high-stakes offenders; most judges seem willing to sentence them harshly without much anxiety.

These developments parallel the morally suspect 'enemy law' paradigm, which justifies the use of a 'separate track' for dealing with the wrongs committed by what is characterised as a class of intrinsically evil *outsiders*. This paradigm

---

[99] R Douglas, *Law, Liberty, and the Pursuit of Terrorism* (Ann Arbor, University of Michigan Press, 2014) 160 (also noting that courts 'do not attach much weight to the fact that most of those convicted of terrorism offences have had no prior convictions or to the fact that some of them would have been people of excellent character but for their involvement in terrorism').

[100] L Zedner, 'Terrorizing Criminal Law' (2014) 8 *Criminal Law and Philosophy* 99 at 117.

[101] CS Steiker, 'Proportionality as a Limit on Preventive Justice: Promises and Pitfalls' in A Ashworth, L Zedner, and P Tomlin (eds), *Prevention and the Limits of the Criminal Law* (Oxford, Oxford University Press, 2013) 194 at 196.

[102] Von Hirsch, above n 3 at 125 (emphasis in the original).

[103] Simester, above n 43 at 66.

[104] See, eg, DM Gottfredson et al, 'Stakes and Risk: Incapacitative Intent in Sentencing Decisions' (1989) 7 *Behavioral Sciences and the Law* 91.

[105] Think of various facets of everyday life where measures are used even with no reason to believe individuals represent threats (eg, metal detectors and frisking at public meetings; security screening at airports). See generally Morris and Miller, above n 26 at 22–26.

must be rejected, for it is completely disconnected from traditional notions of proportionate justice. The argument according to which 'being threatening is a serious wrong' is similarly unpersuasive; this is because it fails to fully capture the substantial difference between abstract and actual dangerousness. Nor can the malleability of societal notions of desert and proportionality reconcile the severe sentencing of aspiring terrorists with desert theory. Von Hirsch conceived, developed and defended censure theory as a framework for penal moderation, not as an architecture for accommodating escalating spirals of punitiveness for the latest pressing threats.

To conclude, here is my view of whether and when severe punishments are justified for pre-inchoate actions related to terrorism:

First, a generic risk of future offending alone cannot justify imposition of undeservedly severe sentences on grounds of 'abstract' dangerousness. Sentences for preparatory terrorist offences should be 'tied more closely to the gravity of the conduct actually done than to necessarily speculative assessments of prospective risk of harm, however grave'.[106] The judge should take account of whether preparatory acts meaningfully increased the likelihood of future harm.

Second, the offender's personal culpable mental state should be a primary focus. Current sentencing practices tend to lead to extremely harsh penalties both for those who acted 'out of foolishness' and for those who were actually motivated by a mass-murderous aim. A closer focus on the defendant's strength of intention to bring about a particular consequence or result would produce greater correspondence between the severity of punishment and the threats genuinely posed by the offender's behaviour (ie, the 'actual significance' of the preparatory act).[107]

Third, significant sentence enhancements for preparatory terrorist offences should be limited to cases in which the extraordinary magnitude of the eventual harm intended – for example, an act of serious violence endangering the state – substantially increases the offender's blameworthiness and, consequently, justifies the censure expressed by the severe punishment imposed. Such cases do not include preparatory acts coupled with vague intentions of committing generic acts of terrorism.[108] Rather, the court should ascertain

---

[106] Zedner, above n 100 at 119.

[107] See Chesney, above n 68 at 128.

[108] It must be noted that no internationally-agreed definition of terrorism exists to date. See, eg, 18 US Code § 2331, s 1 of the UK Terrorism Act 2000, and Article 1 of the EU Framework Decision 2002/475/JHA. Especially difficult is to find common ground in regard to the notions of *terrorist action* (what counts as an act of terrorism?), *terrorist purpose* (what aims amount to a terrorist goal?), *terrorist target* (who can be a target of a terrorist action?), *terrorist method* (do terrorist acts necessarily have to terrorise?) and *terrorist agent* (who can commit an act of terrorism?). Sometimes definitions of terrorism at the national level are very broad, including nearly all types of attacks on the state and its officials committed with the intent to spread fear among the population and/or influence or coerce the government to some degree. On the problems of defining terrorism, including risks of over-inclusiveness, see in particular JS Hodgson and V Tadros, 'The Impossibility of Defining Terrorism' (2013) 16 *New Criminal Law Review* 494.

that the defendant sought to further something that is commonly referred to as an 'existential threat to the state', something whose occurrence would put into question the continued existence of a nation, its people, or its government, would threaten its territorial integrity, or would pose a manifest challenge to a nation's core values or interests.[109] Furthermore, to justify the imposition of a substantial and severe sentence, the prosecutor should also provide evidence of the adequacy of the preparation to further actions aiming at extremely serious harms that would endanger the state (a concrete 'materiality threshold').

VI. CONCLUSION

Ashworth and Zedner have observed that:

> The more catastrophic the potential consummate offence, the greater the imperative to prevent, and the more it can justly be said that prosecution and punishment of the completed offence comes too late, which is why a significant feature of terrorism offences is that they criminalise pre-inchoate, preparatory, facilitative, and associative offences.[110]

Elsewhere, Lucia Zedner rightly comments that, in today's anti-terrorism policies, 'the possibility of forestalling risks competes with and even takes precedence over responding to wrongs done'.[111]

The need to pre-empt and prevent acts of terrorism, including by means of the criminal law, certainly exists. It would be naïve to argue for the blanket abolition of pre-inchoate terrorist offences and for dealing with would-be terrorists exclusively at the intelligence level and by means of preventive removal. Yet limiting principles like those passionately and rigorously developed over the past four decades by Andreas von Hirsch should not be sacrificed or obliterated. The arguments and modest proposals I have put forward in this essay attempt to shape a more just sentencing framework for the growing realm of pre-inchoate terrorist offences, one that some seem eager to transform into a punitive dystopia that Philip K Dick might have imagined, in which concepts of desert and proportionality can hardly aspire even to second-class citizenship.

---

[109] Only few extremely serious acts would qualify as such. See J Wolfendale, 'The Narrative of Terrorism as an Existential Threat' in R Jackson (ed), *Routledge Handbook of Critical Terrorism Studies* (Abingdon, Routledge, 2016) 114 at 117–19 (criticising the 'destructive effects' of the catch-all existential threat narrative in shaping counterterrorism legislation).

[110] Ashworth and Zedner, above n 44 at 180.

[111] L Zedner, 'Pre-Crime and Post-Criminology?' (2007) 11 *Theoretical Criminology* 261 at 262.

Part III

Censure, Desert and the Jurisprudence
of Punishment

10

Rootless Desert and Unanchored Censure

MATT MATRAVERS

Although *Doing Justice* is careful to warn that the notion of decarceration is central to the model ... [the] blatant and unembarrassed defense of desert by those concerned about the present severity of punishment may become perverted by those who think present punishment too lenient.[1]

THIS CHAPTER SETS out from a puzzle: Andrew von Hirsch's *Doing Justice* (*DJ*) argued passionately for reductions in punishment in general and in incarceration in particular.[2] Indeed, in the Preface to the book, one of the other members of the Committee (of which *DJ* is the report) comments that 'it would be better to ignore the recommendations of the Committee entirely than to accept any part of them without that focus on decarceration about which all its other arguments pivot'.[3] Yet, what followed (in the USA, UK and elsewhere) was in a sense the worst of all worlds. The recommendations of the Committee to reduce punishment were largely ignored, but the underlying language of 'desert' was taken up by theorists and politicians alike and used to drive an enormous expansion of criminalisation, punishment, and incarceration.

To be clear, my claim is not that the arguments of *DJ* – or von Hirsch himself – caused or were responsible for the subsequent rise in punishment. Any complex social phenomenon such as mass incarceration will have many causes, most of which are likely to be entirely unrelated to the appearance of an academic text, or even the report of a commission.[4] Rather, this chapter examines whether the

[1] MR Gardner, 'The Renaissance of Retribution – An Examination of Doing Justice' (1976) 3 *Wisconsin Law Review* 781 at 791.

[2] A von Hirsch, *Doing Justice: The Choice of Punishments* (Report of the Committee for the Study of Incarceration) (New York, Hill and Wang, 1976).

[3] W Gaylin and DJ Rothman, 'Introduction' in ibid at xl.

[4] For contrasting accounts of how to understand the rise in punishment, see N Lacey, *The Prisoners' Dilemma: Political Economy and Punishment in Contemporary Democracies* (The Hamlyn

ideas of *DJ* (and related work) had to be – as Gardner suggested – 'perverted' in order to fit with policies inimical to those recommended in the book,[5] or whether they were consistent with those policies and, indeed, with many others. Lest this be thought either of quaint historical, or narrow parochial, interest, the chapter goes on to argue that the reasons underlying the absence of a necessary fit between 'just deserts' and reduced punishment indicate something about the nature of liberalism in what might be described as a 'post-anthropomorphic, post-theocentric, post-Nietzschean world';[6] and thus can inform our response to mass incarceration.

The chapter has five sections: section I gives a brief outline of the desert-based position posited by von Hirsch. Sections II and III consider desert and entitlement, and the relations between entitlements and hard treatment. Section IV considers the implications of the absence of desert for setting the anchoring points of the sentencing scale before, finally, section V concludes.

I. 'JUST DESERTS'

The history of the emergence of the 'just deserts' movement is well known and will not be dwelt on at any length here, but it is important to emphasise the degree to which it was a *critical* project. Prior to the mid-1970s, punishment in the USA (and elsewhere[7]) was primarily rehabilitative in character and delivered through 'individualised' and largely indeterminate sentences. For example, in California and Washington, convicted offenders condemned to state prison could only be sentenced to a period of between one year and the statutory maximum for the offence. The decision as to when the offender should be released lay entirely with the Parole Board. The aim was to 'fix' the offender and, as *DJ* puts it, 'just as we did not tell doctors when to pronounce a patient cured, we were not, in the guise of fixed sentences to tell wardens or parole boards when to release an inmate'.[8]

Lectures 2007) (Cambridge, Cambridge University Press, 2008) and D Garland, *The Culture Of Control: Crime And Social Order in Contemporary Society* (Oxford, Oxford University Press, 2001). For a sophisticated discussion of the role of proportionality theory in the expansion of punishment, see A Ashworth, 'Prisons, Proportionality and Recent Penal History' (2017) 80 *Modern Law Review* 473.

[5] Gardner, above n 1.

[6] The quotation is adapted from David Gauthier's description of the project he undertook in his *Morals by Agreement* (Oxford, Clarendon Press, 1986). Writing in 1988, he said that this book 'is an attempt to challenge Nietzsche's prescient remark, "As the will to truth ... gains self-consciousness ... morality will gradually perish." It is an attempt to write moral theory for adults, for persons who live consciously in a post-anthropomorphic, post-theocentric, post-technocratic world. It is an attempt to allay the fear, or suspicion, or hope, that without a foundation in objective value or objective reason, in sympathy or sociality, the moral enterprise must fail': D Gauthier, 'Moral Artifice' (1988) 18 *Canadian Journal of Philosophy* 385 at 385.

[7] For example, Sweden: see A von Hirsch, *Deserved Criminal Sentences: An Overview* (Oxford, Hart Publishing, 2017) 4–7.

[8] Gaylin and Rothman, above n 3 at xxxi.

Although support for this system was not unanimous in the post-war period,[9] it came under sustained attack from the mid-1960s, coinciding with a more general theoretical rejection of consequentialist moral theory that climaxed in John Rawls's hugely influential *A Theory of Justice*.[10] In punishment, the attack was in part motivated by similar theoretical concerns, but it was also specific in challenging whether rehabilitation worked; whether it was equitable in its treatment of like cases; and whether it was racially and politically biased. In short, the rehabilitative ideal rested on notions of humanitarianism, science and progress, all of which were shown to be (at best) problematic. The system was therefore unscientific, discriminatory and, given the many offenders kept in prison because of their skin colour or political beliefs, deeply reactionary.[11]

Although *DJ* contains a positive argument from so-called 'fair play' theory, it is fundamentally a work of criticism.[12] The committee is described as 'suspicious' of the claims of rehabilitation; 'skeptical'; free of the 'heady optimism and confidence of reformers in the past'; and as proposing a solution of 'despair, not hope'.[13] In this, the structure of the book is revealing. Ignoring the preface, introduction and a final chapter on doing penal justice in circumstances of distributive injustice, it contains sixteen chapters. Chapter one is on scope, Chapters two through four concern the system as it then existed, Chapter five deals with general deterrence, and Chapters seven to sixteen take up the articulation of a 'commensurate-desert' ('proportionality') system of sentencing. There is a single chapter, Chapter six, dedicated to the theoretical defence of desert, which takes up a mere ten pages (just under seven per cent of the substance of the book). That chapter borrows heavily from what was then a leading retributivist theory – the 'balance of benefits and burdens theory' pioneered by Jeffrie Murphy and Herbert Morris[14] – but nothing in the rest of the book depends on this. Rather, chapter six has two functions: first, to put the language of blameworthiness at the centre of the discussion; and second, following Rawls, to highlight the general failings of consequentialist moral theory as a means to establishing 'commensurate-desert' as a requirement of fairness or justice.

---

[9] See for example CS Lewis, 'The Humanitarian Theory of Punishment' (1949) 3 *The Twentieth Century: An Australian Quarterly Review* 5.

[10] J Rawls, *A Theory of Justice* (Cambridge, MA, Harvard University Press, 1971).

[11] On the effectiveness of such schemes, see RL Martinson, 'What Works? Questions and Answers About Prison Reform' (1974) 35 *The Public Interest* 22; on procedural unfairness and inequities, see KC Davis, *Discretionary Justice: A Preliminary Enquiry* (Baton Rouge, Louisiana State University Press, 1969); on racial bias, see American Friends Service Committee, *Struggle for Justice: A Report on Crime and Punishment in America* (New York, Hill and Wang, 1971).

[12] Reflecting some years later on *DJ*, von Hirsch describes it as a 'response' to rehabilitative and incapacitation-based thinking. 'The principle of proportionality,' he writes, 'was offered as a means for *restricting* the state's authority to punish'. Von Hirsch, above n 7 at 108 (emphasis in the original).

[13] Gaylin and Rothman, above n 3 at xxxiv, xxxix.

[14] H Morris, 'Persons and Punishment' (1968) 52 *Monist* 475; J Murphy, 'Marxism and Retribution' (1973) 2 *Philosophy and Public Affairs* 217.

It is indicative of how little rests on the benefits and burdens account that von Hirsch went on first to question it in *Past or Future Crimes* (*PFC*) – where he writes that he has 'come to doubt the force of this and similar arguments'[15] – and then, in *Censure and Sanctions* (*CS*), to describe himself as 'convinced of its deficiencies'[16] all whilst remaining a staunch advocate of 'commensurate-desert'. However, as will be argued below, it is the absence of a sound theoretical account of desert that allows the scale of punishments to float free and thus be compatible with *both* more and less punitive regimes.

Although the details, and in particular the emphasis, of von Hirsch's account has changed over time, the core argument around what I will now call 'proportionality' (rather than 'commensurate-desert') has remained remarkably consistent. It consists of two claims. First, that punishment expresses blame (later rephrased as censure). Second, that the degree of punishment must be proportionate to the degree of blameworthiness; it must express the appropriate degree of censure. In *DJ* these claims take the form: 'Someone who infringes the rights of others ... does wrong and deserves blame for his conduct. It is because he deserves blame that the sanctioning authority is entitled to choose a response that expresses moral disapproval: namely punishment', and 'the severity of the penalty – connoting as it does the degree of blame ascribed – ought to comport with the gravity of the infraction'.[17] Forty years later, in *Deserved Criminal Sentences* (*DCS*), the two claims remain: the 'conceptual basis' is that punishment conveys 'censure or disapprobation of a convicted person for his or her criminal misconduct', and 'a sentence's severity should be made fairly proportionate to the seriousness of the defendant's criminal conduct'.[18] Two questions arise. One concerns the nature of the desert claim; the other, the 'hard treatment' and its place in a censure-based theory.

II. DESERTS AND ENTITLEMENTS

The English word 'desert' is problematic in that it can be used both to describe the outcome of some rule or social practice and a more brute claim that is not dependent on any such thing. To illustrate this, Feldman and Skow give an example of a wealthy grandfather and his two grandchildren: 'One grandchild is vicious and rich; the other is virtuous and poor. The vicious grandchild never treated his grandfather with respect. The virtuous grandchild was always respectful and caring. Suppose the grandfather leaves his entire fortune to the

---

[15] A von Hirsch, *Past or Future Crimes: Deservedness and Dangerousness in the Sentencing of Criminals* (Manchester, Manchester University Press, 1986) 58.

[16] A von Hirsch, *Censure and Sanctions* (Oxford, Oxford University Press, 1993) 7n.

[17] Von Hirsch, above n 2 at 48.

[18] Von Hirsch, above n 7 at 1.

vicious grandchild'.[19] In these circumstances, many people might say something like, 'Of course, the vicious grandchild deserves the money given the will, but really his other (virtuous) grandchild deserved it given his conduct'.

This distinction has been marked by different philosophers in a variety of ways. For example, John Kleinig distinguishes between 'raw' and 'institution-alised' desert claims,[20] others between 'pre-' and 'post-' institutional desert or sometimes 'pre-' and 'post-' justicial desert, but the most common way is probably to distinguish 'deserts' and 'entitlements'.[21] On this account, the vicious grandchild is entitled to, but does not deserve, the inheritance and vice-versa for the virtuous grandchild.

The point is that 'raw' desert claims 'are not dependent on any legal or quasi-legal system of rules'.[22] With respect to punishment, a desert theorist of this kind is committed to the idea that, other things equal, we have reason to bring into existence systems that (aim to) punish appropriate wrongdoers to realise 'the good that punishment achieves', which is that 'someone who deserves it gets it'.[23]

More fully,

> it is pre-institutionally *pro tanto* just, in and of itself, for those who culpably engage in moral wrongdoing to be deliberately made to suffer some type of loss in return for their wrongdoing. Being deliberately made to suffer a loss is deserved by wrong-doers in and of itself – i.e., simply as the deliberate imposition of some type of loss – as what, prior to any institution, constitutes a just requital for moral wrongdo-ing. It is what moral wrongdoers positively have coming to them in return for their wrongdoing.[24]

This idea of 'desert' can be contrasted with an account of 'entitlements' such that, 'if some social or legal institution is in place in your social group, and that institution has a rule that specifies some treatment for those who have some feature, and you have the feature, then you are entitled to that treatment'.[25] Although it seems odd to describe someone as being *entitled* to punishment – entitlements are usually to things that are good – the distinction is sufficiently

---

[19] F Feldman and B Skow, 'Desert', in EN Zalta (ed), *The Stanford Encyclopedia of Philosophy* (revised entry Winter 2016), available at https://plato.stanford.edu/entries/desert.

[20] J Kleinig, 'The Concept of Desert' (1971) 8 *American Philosophical Quarterly* 71.

[21] See, for example, J Feinberg, 'Justice and Personal Desert', reprinted in J Feinberg, *Doing and Deserving: Essays in the Theory of Responsibility* (Princeton, Princeton University Press, 1970) 55; S Scheffler, 'Justice and Desert in Liberal Theory', reprinted in S Scheffler, *Boundaries and Alle-giances: Problems of Justice and Responsibility in Liberal Thought* (Oxford, Oxford University Press 2001) 173; M Matravers, 'Mad, Bad, or Faulty? Desert in Distributive and Retributive Justice' in C Knight and Z Stemplowska (eds), *Responsibility and Distributive Justice* (Oxford, Oxford University Press, 2011) 136.

[22] Kleinig, above n 20 at 71.

[23] M Moore, *Placing Blame: A General Theory of the Criminal Law* (Oxford, Oxford University Press, 1997) 87.

[24] KE Boxer, *Rethinking Responsibility* (Oxford, Oxford University Press, 2013) 111.

[25] F Feldman and B Skow, above n 19.

vital that, in the absence of an appropriate alternative word, this is the usage that will be adopted below.[26]

Despite the title, *Just Deserts*, and the association of that book with the revival of retributivism in the 1970s, it is clear that von Hirsch is an 'entitlement' and not a desert theorist. Consider, for example, the following passages:

> There are … certain institutions that by their very nature connote approbation or disapprobation. Prime examples are grades, prizes, and punishments. *If one establishes such things at all*, then they ought, given their implications of praise or blame, to be distributed according to the degree of praiseworthiness or blameworthiness of the actor's conduct.[27]

And

> If one asks why punishment ought to be apportioned to the gravity of the criminal conduct, therefore, the answer is not that this would create optimum deterrent or pedagogical influence, for it may or may not do so. The requirement of proportionate punishment is, instead, derived directly from the censuring implications of the criminal sanction. *Once one has created an institution with the condemnatory connotations that punishment has*, then it is a requirement of justice, not merely of efficient law enforcement, to punish offenders according to the degree of reprehensibleness of their conduct.[28]

The conflation of the language of desert and entitlement that is common in the literature on punishment arises because von Hirsch (rightly) insists that the institutions of criminal justice need to respect two demands of proportionality. Cardinal proportionality concerns the absolute limits on punishment (the anchoring points of any sentencing scale). Ordinal proportionality requires that 'persons convicted of crimes of comparable seriousness should receive punishments of comparable severity … Persons convicted of crimes of differing gravity should suffer punishments correspondingly graded in their onerousness'.[29]

Given these requirements, the language of desert easily slips in: Say defendant D1 receives a sentence of x for crime y, then one can say that, other things equal, defendant D2, who is guilty of a crime z of comparable seriousness, similarly deserves x. Or, more critically, when responding to indeterminate sentences that mean that D2 in fact ends up with a sentence far more onerous than D1

---

[26] In an anonymous report on a paper of mine, a referee criticised my use of 'entitlement' in relation to punishment on the grounds that 'there is something odd about focusing on the "legitimate expectations" of someone liable to punishment. This is because talk of "expectation" at least pragmatically implicates some desire for what is being expected. But generally people don't desire to be punished'. I am happy to concede the implication, but if the distinction between 'desert' and 'entitlement' is genuine, then we need a word for 'entitlement' when it comes to blame, punishment, and so on. In the absence of an alternative, all I can do is specify the meaning as here.

[27] Von Hirsch, above n 15 at 35 (emphasis added).

[28] Ibid (emphasis added).

[29] A von Hirsch, 'Proportionality in the Philosophy of Punishment' (1992) 16 *Crime and Justice: A Review of Research* 55 at 76.

(perhaps because D2 is more resistant to rehabilitation than D1), it is easy to think that D2 is getting far more than he justly deserves. The language of entitlement – D2 is getting more than that to which he is entitled – lacks equivalent rhetorical force, but is nevertheless correct.

III. ENTITLEMENTS AND HARD TREATMENT

Before considering the issue of hard treatment, it is perhaps appropriate to offer some recapitulation. On this reconstruction of the von Hirschian account, the overall purpose of the criminal justice system is two-fold: first, it has a preventive purpose because 'criminal behaviour is profoundly threatening to citizens' vital interests: to their physical safety and to their living resources'.[30] Second, it allows for the expression of appropriate censure in response to some kinds of wrongdoing. The censure in punishment 'conveys to victims the acknowledgement that they are *wronged* by criminal conduct … [and] addresses the offender as a moral agent'.[31] The demands of censuring appropriately generate the need for cardinal and ordinal proportionality, and these constrain the pursuit of criminal justice's preventive purpose.

Given that one puzzle addressed in this chapter concerns the explosion of hard treatment that followed the publication of *DJ*, two questions need to be addressed. First, how do the two parts – prevention and censure – fit together, and what is the role of hard treatment in this? Second, to what hard treatment, if any, is a given offender entitled; that is, how is the cardinal scale to be fixed?

A. Censure and Hard Treatment

In one way or another, then, punishment both expresses censure and discourages criminal behaviour. However, in von Hirsch's theorisation, in all instances where there might be a tension between these two functions, it is the expression of appropriate censure that is given priority (as a demand of justice and/or as a means of respecting the agent as a moral person). Put differently, it is censure to which the offender is entitled and hard treatment has to be fitted around that (if it has to be fitted at all).[32]

What is the connection, then, between censure and hard treatment and what follows for cardinal proportionality? To answer this, we can use an adaptation

---

[30] Von Hirsch, above n 7 at 37.

[31] Ibid.

[32] It is possible that 'censure' is *deserved* (as understood above) in that one might claim that the idea that 'moral failure deserves moral criticism' is internal to what we mean by morality. However, that would not change the argument here (and the particular form of censure for breaking codified criminal laws that is under discussion is clearly post-institutional).

of a distinction owed to Feinberg between 'basic' and 'derivative' entitlements.[33] The basic entitlement owed to the offender is the responsive attitude of disapproval and the expression of censure. The derivative entitlement is the form of treatment that is 'fitting' as an expression of that which is basic; in this instance, censure.[34]

Feinberg himself comments that the forms – the 'mode[s] of treatment' – of any such derivative entitlement are the 'natural or conventional means of expressing the morally fitting attitudes'.[35] This, then, invites the question of which of these – 'natural' or 'conventional' – properly characterises penal hard treatment.

One possible argument for the claim that hard treatment is the 'natural' means of expressing penal censure is that a desire to impose suffering (hard treatment) on offenders as a response to being wronged is a psychological predisposition shared by human beings. This predisposition is then 'tamed' or 'institutionalised', but must nevertheless retain the form of imposed suffering. For reasons I have given elsewhere, the premise on which the argument relies is false. It might be true that human beings have a psychological predisposition that inclines to fairness, and so to *some* response to wrongdoing, but whether restoring fair relations requires hard treatment is precisely what is in question.[36]

Perhaps we might give a slightly different meaning to 'natural' to avoid the stark dichotomy of 'natural' or 'conventional'. That is, we might claim that hard treatment – as the appropriate 'mode' of expression – is conventional, but that the convention is a result of the (unique) fit between the basic entitlement of penal censure and the derivative entitlement through which that censure is expressed (at least in serious cases).

Retributivists of various kinds have tried to fill out this argument in diverse ways: the language of penal hard treatment is necessary, it has been argued, to vindicate the value of the victim; to defeat the wrongdoer; and/or to focus the attention of the wrongdoer on his wrongs so as to aid his reform.[37] Although these arguments have been rightly criticised, the claim persists that 'mere' verbal denunciations will not suffice.[38] John Kleinig puts the point as follows:

> But for the most part our sensitivities are too dull, our hypocrisy too common, for mere face-to-face blaming to make its point. The childhood retort: 'Sticks and

---

[33] Feinberg, above n 21. Note, Feinberg is discussing 'deserts'.

[34] Ibid at 82.

[35] Ibid.

[36] See further, M Matravers, 'Punishment, Suffering and Justice' in S Farrall, B Goldson, I Loader and A Dockley (eds), *Justice and Penal Reform: Reshaping the Penal Landscape* (Abingdon, Routledge, 2016) 27.

[37] RA Duff, *Punishment, Communication, and Community* (Oxford, Oxford University Press 2001); J Hampton, 'Correcting Harms versus Righting Wrongs: The Goal of Retribution' (1992) 39 *UCLA Law Review* 1659; J Kleinig, 'Punishment and Moral Seriousness' (1991) 25 *Israel Law Review* 401.

[38] M Matravers, *Justice and Punishment: The Rationale of Coercion* (Oxford, Oxford University Press 2000) 12; RA Duff, 'Penal Communications: Recent Work in the Philosophy of Punishment' (1996) 20 *Crime and Justice: A Review of Research* 1.

stones will break my bones, but names will never hurt me', is as much part of our adult communal experience as it is of our childhood learning. Indeed, many of us become less rather than more sensitive to the import of words as we get older. We inure ourselves against their impact. Unless we see or experience some form of hard treatment, we are likely to remain anaesthetized to the significance of our actions. In the case of moral wrongdoing, that is likely to require an empathetic appreciation of what our conduct constituted for someone else. Hard treatment may register where words fail.[39]

I have my doubts that this argument tells us very much – witness the 'may' in the final sentence – but let us grant for the moment that hard treatment is either non-contingently connected to the expression of serious blame or so deeply embedded in the cultural meanings and social practices of the societies under discussion as to be unavoidable; a mere verbal admonition will not do. However, even when this is granted, it only establishes a non-contingent connection between censure and some form of hard treatment. The theory so far has nothing to say about what, or how much, hard treatment ought to be associated with crime, and crimes of different degree. This is a point that was made forcefully by van den Haag in a review of *DJ*:

> Just deserts fails even more fundamentally to tell us what is deserved for any crime. Suppose we agree that murder is a serious crime and burglary a less serious one. Thus murder deserves more punishment than burglary, though nothing tells us how much more. But what does murder deserve in the first place? Execution? Life in prison? Twenty years? Ten? Just deserts theory cannot tell.[40]

This point is largely conceded by von Hirsch who admits that when it comes to 'the issue of cardinal magnitude … desert theory must play a more restricted role'.[41] In 1985, he considered the possibility of using 'prison population constraints' to help guide the setting of the cardinal scale,[42] but given the argument for penal hard treatment as (at least in part) a means to express censure, von Hirsch (like others) has rightly come to regard the cardinal scale – and so the answer to van den Haag – as being a matter of social convention.[43] As von Hirsch's sometime co-author, Andrew Ashworth, puts it, 'whereas proportionality theory has some determinacy in relation to ordinal proportionality, it regards the anchoring point of the penalty scale (and therefore cardinal proportionality) as a matter of social convention that is culturally and politically determined'.[44]

---

[39] Kleinig, above n 37 at 417.

[40] E van den Haag, 'Punishment: Desert and Crime Control' (1987) 85 *Michigan Law Review* 1250 at 1254.

[41] Von Hirsch, above n 7 at 59.

[42] Von Hirsch, above n 15 at 95.

[43] Von Hirsch, above n 7. Cf Kleinig, above n 37 at 417: 'We are dealing here with cultural meanings, with the significance for us of speech acts and other forms of conduct'.

[44] Ashworth, above n 4 at 483. Cf N Lacey and H Pickard: 'What has been thought of as proportionality, in short, is not a naturally existing relationship, but a product of political and social construction, cultural meaning-making, and institution-building': 'The Chimera of Proportionality: Institutionalising Limits on Punishment in Contemporary Social and Political Systems' (2015) 78 *Modern Law Review* 216 at 219.

The problem – discussed further below – is that ceding the cardinal scale to social convention whilst tying together censure and hard treatment, and giving primacy to the former, renders the theory entirely compatible with changes in social meanings that ratchet punishments up rather than down. In the USA and UK from the end of the 1970s onwards, and for a variety of reasons, penalty levels went up, prison came to express even mild levels of censure, and considerations of ordinal proportionality – as well as other factors that were disproportionate – moved the anchoring points upwards and so delivered mass incarceration.[45] Von Hirschian 'desert' theory did and does not have the resources to counter this because, as argued above, it is not in fact a 'desert' theory, but an 'entitlement' one, and that to which one is entitled (the translation of the appropriate moral disapproval into the appropriate hard treatment) is largely a matter of social convention.

Against this, both von Hirsch and Ashworth have argued that proportionality theory does have the resources to exert 'downward thrust on punishment levels'.[46] In this volume, Ashworth offers a number of arguments to this end.[47] The most powerful of these depend on the relationship between the elements of censure and hard treatment, so it is to this that we now turn.

B. Anchoring the Scale and Increased Punishments

Over the course of his career thus far, von Hirsch's account of how the two elements of his theory fit together has evolved. In *DJ*, it is clear that as a demand of justice, commensurate-desert has priority: 'the commensurate-deserts principle should have priority over other objectives in decisions about how much to punish. … For the principle … is a requirement of justice, whereas deterrence, incapacitation, and rehabilitation are essentially strategies for controlling crime'.[48] However, as the text acknowledges, this is little more than an assumption and in general the account of hard treatment in the book is focused much

---

[45] Note, the argument is *not* that proportionality theory was responsible for the increase in punishment. As Andrew Ashworth (ibid) has shown, despite reference to 'just deserts' (notoriously misspelled as 'desserts') in the 1991 UK Criminal Justice Act, adherence to proportionality demands played very little, if any, role in the subsequent increase in punishment. And, of course, some of the most notorious policies of the age – notably 'three strikes and you're out' – violate (ordinal) proportionality. Thus I agree entirely with Ashworth's conclusion that 'proportionality theory … is certainly not doomed to lead to escalating [penal] severity' (at 488). The point is rather two-fold: that proportionality theory was consistent with the increase in punishment and that (more speculatively), the danger identified at the start of this chapter – that the 'blatant and unembarrassed' language of desert would play into the hands of those bent on increasing punishment – was in part realised. Ashworth is sceptical about the second of these claims, although he is careful to limit his scepticism to the influence of the language of proportionality theory properly understood. Ibid.

[46] Ibid; also von Hirsch, above n 7.

[47] Ashworth in this volume.

[48] Von Hirsch, above n 2 at 74.

more on the questions of 'how much?', and 'of what kind?' in relation to hard treatment and different offences, than it is on the theoretical place of hard treatment in the overall account.

Although punishment's role in blaming – censuring – is present in *DJ* (following Feinberg's influential paper),[49] hard treatment is identified in the main with the need to secure order. As von Hirsch puts it, 'the threat and imposition of punishment is called for in order to secure compliance – not full compliance, but more compliance than there might be were there no legal penalties at all.'[50]

As von Hirsch describes in *DCS*, this position survived into *PFC* where a 'bifurcated' account was given, such that the criminal law is described as performing two 'interlocking functions'. By 'threatening unpleasant consequences, it seeks to discourage criminal behaviour' while 'through the censure thereby expressed, the sanction also registers disapprobation of the behaviour'.[51] However, it did not quite survive into *CS*. Here, the criminal prohibition and the censure for its violation appeal to the moral reason of citizens. The role of hard treatment is as a 'prudential supplement' that provides an additional (prudential) reason for compliance; an additional reason that might be needed given that human beings are for the most part neither fully saints nor fully sinners.[52] The two functions of punishment – contributing to compliance and censuring – are not separate objectives to which one must be given priority, but are rather 'intertwined'. 'A penal measure provides that a specified type of conduct is punishable by certain onerous consequences. Those consequences both constitute the hard treatment and give concrete expression to the censure.'[53]

This argument seems to be compatible with a range of penalty schemes (with cardinal anchoring points) ranging from the lenient to the severe, given the possibility that harsh penalties might be required for general deterrence in a society in which the social meanings of such penalties accords with appropriate levels of censure.[54] However, von Hirsch and Ashworth (as well as others such as Duff) argue that this is not the case for a number of reasons to which we now turn.

i. 'Drowning Out'

Given that the moral message of the law is to be accompanied by a prudential supplement, von Hirsch and Ashworth argue that the level of hard treatment must not 'drown out' the moral message conveyed by censure.[55] As Ashworth

---

[49] J Feinberg, 'The Expressive Function of Punishment', in Feinberg, above n 34 at 95.

[50] Von Hirsch, above n 2 at 44.

[51] Von Hirsch, above n 7 at 37.

[52] Von Hirsch, above n 16 at 12–13.

[53] Von Hirsch, above n 7 at 37.

[54] It is worth repeating that this is not to say that the theory is not consistent with low levels of hard treatment understood in a different context to express appropriate censure.

[55] Ashworth above nn 4 and 47; von Hirsch, above n 16; A von Hirsch, 'Proportionality in the Philosophy of Punishment: From "Why Punish?" to "How Much"' (1990) 1 *Criminal Law Forum* 259;

puts it in this volume, 'the sentence prescribed for a given offence should not be so harsh as to "drown out" the moral message of the law, turning the sentence into a "naked demand" that would not be respectful of the individual's agency'.[56]

I have argued elsewhere that the drowning out objection rests on an implausible understanding of (moral) agency with respect to both minor and more significant offences.[57] With respect to minor offences, it is of course entirely plausible that the threat of hard treatment is operative in the practical reasoning of most agents. In advance of committing some criminal infraction, the risk of the penalty is likely to weigh in the reasoning of the agent and it is for this reason that, say, speed cameras and fines are effective in slowing down motorists. Now imagine that the fine was doubled or quadrupled. In such circumstances, presumably most people would pause and think the risk was not worth it. However, should they then feel that they have been treated in a way incompatible with the respect owed to them as agents? That seems wildly overdramatic; prudential reasoning is as much an aspect of agency as moral reasoning.

In the case of more serious offences, one might wonder – as Duff does and as Ashworth discusses – whether, beyond some fairly low baseline, increases in penal hard treatment have a rapidly diminishing capacity further to drown out the moral message. But, as with the argument as a whole, that discussion seems alien to lived experience. It is just implausible to think that someone contemplating armed robbery will attend to the moral message prohibiting the conduct and, were he to find himself tempted, be swayed by the risk of attracting the prudential supplement of three years in prison, but that his reasoning would be entirely different were the sentence likely to be six years.

The point is that most citizens do not think about the moral reasons not to commit armed robbery. For these people, the reasons not to do so are inert since there is never an occasion in which they need to figure in their mental life. For those who are sorely tempted, it is hardly plausible that the absence of overwhelming prudential reasons not to do so would help them to focus on the moral reasons not to do so. As I put it elsewhere, 'for the core criminal offenses, we are not – in Andrew von Hirsch's terms – neither saints nor sinners, but something in between .... We are actually saints or sinners (in the relevant senses) for whom the threat is either inert or (we hope) sufficient'.[58]

RA Duff, 'Punishment, Communication and Community' in M Matravers (ed), *Punishment and Political Theory* (Oxford, Hart Publishing, 1999) 48.

[56] Ashworth in this volume, at section II A.

[57] M Matravers, 'Is Twenty-First Century Punishment Post-Desert?' in M Tonry (ed), *Retributivism Has a Past, Has it a Future?* (Oxford, Oxford University Press, 2011) 38. The argument of the next several paragraphs borrows heavily from this account.

[58] Ibid at 39. It is worth noting that on the drowning out account, the extraordinary punitiveness of the UK and USA should mean that the moral message of the criminal law is entirely deafened. I am not sure quite what this means, or how it could be empirically verified, but whilst the moral message of the criminal law does indeed seem to me to be lost for some people in some communities, the root causes of that lie in wider questions of justice of the kind discussed in Matravers, above n 36.

ii. Progressive Loss of Mitigation

Ashworth calls on the same conception of agency in the second argument he offers in defence of proportionality theory having a 'downward thrust' on penalty levels. Given that we are all fallible – 'neither saints nor sinners' – von Hirschian theory allows a reduction in the otherwise prescribed ordinal penalty for first offenders. Having been censured once, the sinner is meant to respond 'by making an effort of will to desist'. Should he fail to do so, then the reduction in sentence for future offences is progressively lost.

Although it is true that 'progressive loss of mitigation' will be less punitive than a theory that provides for an increased sentence for each repeat offence, this is not enough to show that proportionality theory 'conduces to penal restraint' for two reasons.[59] First, progressive loss of mitigation is one possible way of dealing with repeat offenders within proportionality theory. It is entirely – indeed, arguably more – consistent with the theory to argue that offenders should receive the proportionate sentence for each offence on each occasion. An argument might even be made that repeat offenders manifest increased culpability and so should, properly and proportionately, receive increased penalties. Second, even if one grants progressive loss of mitigation as an aspect of proportionality theory, this only shows that with respect to repeat offenders the account is less punitive than some possible alternatives; not that it necessarily requires parsimony in sentencing overall and is thus incompatible with the punitive turn that followed the publication of *DJ*.

iii. Weighing Rights

Ashworth's third argument explicitly appeals to a principle of parsimony that is independent of proportionality theory. The principle of parsimony holds that the suffering imposed on offenders ought to be the minimum required to meet the state's penal objectives. However, not only is that principle independent of proportionality theory, it is (as Ashworth recognises by omission as he makes no further use of the principle) empty until the 'penal objectives' are specified. More specifically – and damagingly for proportionality theory – *if* the objective is to express the appropriate degree of censure *given that* (as Ashworth and von Hirsch agree) the cardinal scale will be determined by social meanings and conventions, then the minimal imposed suffering needed to achieve that objective will be considerable where those meanings and conventions are punitive.

Although described under the heading of the principle of parsimony, the substance of Ashworth's argument in this section appeals to a different claim: 'that a fundamental right such as the right to liberty should not be taken away

---

[59] Ashworth in this volume, at section II B.

for an offence that amounts to the violation of a significantly lesser right, such as the right to personal property'.[60]

Ashworth has used this argument elsewhere to make an admirable case for limiting the use of imprisonment.[61] It is in one sense an argument from proportionality, in the sense in which lawyers and courts sometimes use the term when weighing questions of rights (as in, for example, whether extending the scope or length of pre-charge detention is a proportional response to an increased threat of terrorist attack). But, note, this is not the same sense of proportionality as deployed in proportionality theory as discussed here. If it relates at all, it is a contribution to the discussion over the anchoring points of the scale (to issues of cardinal proportionality), which as we have seen, is itself something on which proportionality theory is silent.

Given that the argument from parsimony turns into an argument about the appropriateness of imprisonment for some offences – and so a contribution to the debate over cardinal proportionality – it is perhaps unsurprising that Ashworth's fourth argument is not concerned with whether proportionality theory exerts a 'downward thrust' on penalty levels, but rather with whether the theory is consistent with a 'decremental strategy' (should one be adopted) and with the political circumstances that relate to the adoption of such a strategy.

iv. Proportionality Theory and Punishment Levels

As we have seen, Ashworth – reading von Hirsch – offers four arguments to align proportionality theory and penal moderation: arguments from drowning out; progressive loss of mitigation for repeat offenders; weighing rights; and a general decremental strategy. As he admits, the first two 'are internal to desert theory, whereas the last two are situated more broadly in the background political theory of liberalism and are compatible with, but not exclusive to, desert theory'. Nevertheless, he concludes, enough has been done 'to demonstrate that proportionality theory conduces to penal restraint rather than penal severity'.[62]

Ashworth's conclusion seems to be over-optimistic. As argued above, it is only the drowning out argument that is properly 'internal' to proportionality theory. It, like the other three arguments, may 'always have been nested in von Hirsch's account', but they are not necessary features of that account. The other three arguments are, as Ashworth writes, compatible with proportionality theory, but the question posed here is whether proportionality theory is *also* compatible with penal severity. Only the drowning out argument would suggest that it is not and, for reasons given above, that argument is not persuasive. Moreover, the next section will argue that proportionality theory, whilst not responsible

---

[60] Ashworth in this volume, at section II C.

[61] A Ashworth, *What if Imprisonment were Abolished for Property Offences?* (London, Howard League for Penal Reform, 2013).

[62] Ashworth in this volume, at section III.

for the massive increase in punishment that followed, is not only compatible with that increase, but does not have the resources to respond in part because it (rightly) eschews any commitment to desert.

IV. IN DESERT'S ABSENCE: PROPORTIONALITY THEORY AND SOCIAL CONVENTIONS OF CENSURE

What turned out to be fatal to the enterprise of developing a theory consistent only with reducing incarceration was two things: (1) tying together censure and hard treatment ('It is because he deserves blame that the sanctioning authority is entitled to choose a response that expresses moral disapproval: namely punishment'[63]); and (2) not recognising that once one does that, then the theory can no longer control the cardinal scale because the translation of the appropriate moral disapproval into the appropriate hard treatment is a matter of social convention. Moreover, just as proportionality theory can offer a decremental strategy – in which as the 'meanings' of imposed sufferings change, so considerations of ordinal proportionality push down punishments along the whole scale – incremental increases have the 'equal and opposite' effect. For example, once imprisonment is established as expressing the appropriate censure for comparatively minor offences, so more serious offences must be met with greater suffering to ensure that the appropriate censure is delivered. And so it is that we are led to circumstances in which purely expressive – indeed, meaningless – penalties are imposed to indicate seriousness of offence (consider, for example, the 150-year sentence given to the fraudster Bernie Madoff, or the 30,000 year sentence – six sentences each of 5,000 years – handed down to the rapist Charles Scott Robinson).

Of course, one can argue against the system of mass incarceration (and worse) on grounds of humanity, parsimony, cost and even deterrence, but so long as censure trumps deterrence and censure is dictated by social convention, proportionality theory has lost control of the baseline, and one's arguments are just those of one citizen amongst many. Although perhaps those first responses to *DJ* that worried about the unembarrassed use of the term 'desert' were right to worry about the ways in which language can contribute even indirectly to social and political culture, this is not to say the proportionality theory caused the massive inflation of punishment levels that followed, but that it was powerless to resist it when it happened.

One question that arises is why this danger was (and is) not foreseen by the advocates of proportionality theory as it was (and is) by its detractors. One can only offer conjectures. One is that the overall arguments – of *DJ* and all subsequent work in the tradition – were critical of the use of punishment and

---

[63] Von Hirsch, above n 2 at 49.

decrementalist in tone. Another, is that the elision of desert and entitlement was (and is) misleading. This is because some accounts of (pre-institutional) desert offer guidance as to the appropriate levels of punishment and so to the anchoring of the scheme. Consider the most famous (or notorious) of these, the *lex talionis*: 'an eye for an eye, a tooth for a tooth'.[64] Whilst this principle is subject to well-known objections,[65] it does purport to establish a scale, and so limits, to punishment. In another form, the same principle is taken not to require equivalence, but some notion of 'fittingness'; something eye-like for an eye and tooth-like for a tooth.[66] Although less clear, even this might be taken to offer determinate guidance on what is deserved.

As Michael Moore and others have emphasised, *lex talionis* is not a theory of desert or of retributive punishment. It is an account of how much of what kind of thing is deserved that can be put in place once an account has been given that punishment should be inflicted *because* deserved. But, even then the language is deceptive because retributivism is committed to the claim that 'punishment should be graded in proportion to desert', so some account of what is actually deserved is internal to retributivism.[67]

Given that proportionality theorists like von Hirsch and Ashworth are not retributivists of this sort, this discussion might seem irrelevant. The claim that it is not rests on the idea that the linguistic confusion of desert and entitlement might have provided a (false) sense of a scale. For example, as we have seen, Ashworth calls on an argument about the relative weight of rights violated (by the offender) and taken away in punishment (by the state) in determining the appropriate use of imprisonment: 'for an offence that amounts to no more than a deprivation of property, it is difficult to justify a deprivation of such a funda-mental right as that to personal liberty'.[68] I happen to agree, but not because property offenders do not deserve imprisonment, which is the sentiment that seems to haunt this part of Ashworth's text.

The problem with both the fully retributive and, shall we say, 'latent' desert accounts is not the difficulty of establishing what is deserved or the right 'balance' – clearly, that is something that is in practice a matter of social convention, and so no help in providing a principled limiting of punishments.[69]

---

[64] *Exodus* 21:23–25; *Leviticus* 24:17–20.

[65] In his *Philosophy of Right* – not a book noted for its witty asides – Hegel proffers a one-eyed, toothless criminal: GWF Hegel, *Philosophy of Right* [1821] translated by T M Knox (Oxford, Oxford University Press, 1952) 72 (Remark to Paragraph 101).

[66] For example, 'The *lex talionis* is fundamentally qualitative rather than quantitative. Its "like for like" instruction indicates ... that the wrong-making features of a crime should be countered with a punitive response that partakes of cognate features'. M Kramer, *The Ethics of Capital Punishment: A Philosophical Investigation of Evil and its Consequences* (Oxford, Oxford University Press 2011) 77.

[67] Moore, above n 23.

[68] Ashworth, above n 61 at 4.

[69] Clearly some societies have thought there to be a particular 'fittingness' between crimes of theft and loss of a hand. Documents found after the retreat of ISIS stated that 'thefts of a value higher

The problem is rather that – absent a great deal of metaphysical baggage of the kind embraced by Kant and, in a very different way, by Moore – the account simply makes no sense.[70] In a disenchanted world, claims that murderers deserve to suffer or that property offenders do not deserve to go to prison are not wrong, but as nonsensical as the claim that 'a writer who spends ten years working on a novel … deserves to write a good novel'.[71] As one reviewer of the book in which that final claim appeared put it, 'perhaps the most valuable aspect of Sher's book is that it explains why desert has not played a significant role in any major [contemporary] moral theory'.[72]

The argument (or perhaps, hypothesis) above is that 'the desert thesis' – the claim that 'when a person has done something that is morally wrong it is morally better that he or she should suffer some loss in consequence'[73] – was not an official part of von Hirschian proportionality theory, but that the intuitions on which it rests play, and played, a role in reassuring proportionality theorists that the theory could resist increases in punishment levels of the kind we have seen in the USA and UK. Sadly, the intuition that, for example, no one deserves to go to prison for life for mere possession (not production or distribution) of

---

than a quarter dinar will result in your right hand being chopped off; the consumption of alcohol will give you 40 lashes; and thieves who also assault people shall be killed by crucifying, get their hands and feet severed, or, be thrown into exile. Those who are of age and engage in extramarital affairs shall be stoned to death … [and] the punishment for homosexuality is death through burning, stoning or being thrown from the highest point of the village or town' (available at www.blankspot. se/the-bureaucracy-behind-the-death-cult-of-is/#). For that matter, Kant described 'homosexual sex, bestiality and masturbation "the most disgraceful and the most degrading [conduct] of which the human being is capable"': see L Denis, 'Kant on the Wrongness of "Unnatural" Sex' (1999) 16 *History of Philosophy Quarterly* 225 at 232.

[70] For discussion, see Matravers, above n 38 at 81–86. Lacey and Pickard make a similar claim in arguing that agreement over the content of proportionality – in my terms, the anchoring of the penalty scales – in the eighteenth and nineteenth centuries depended on what they call a '*broader cosmology of authority and right*' that encapsulated status hierarchy, an account of penal authority tied to the sacred, and a shared symbolism (all of which are, thankfully, unavailable to late modern societies such as the contemporary USA and UK). Lacey and Pickard, 'The Chimera of Proportionality', above n 44 at 228–29.

[71] G Sher, *Desert* (Princeton, Princeton University Press 1987) 63. 'Disenchanted' is borrowed from Max Weber, who in turn borrowed 'Disenchantment of the World' from Schiller, to capture not merely the decline in the belief of sacramental magic, but an understanding of the world as, at least in principle, subject to knowable scientific laws and without 'meaning'. As Weber writes, 'the fate of our times is characterized by rationalization and intellectualization and, above all, by the "disenchantment of the world"' (M Weber, 'Science as a Vocation' in HH Gerth and CW Mills (eds), *From Max Weber: Essays in Sociology* (London, Routledge, 2009) 129 at 155. As Alasdair MacIntyre recognised more than 30 years ago (although in his case to lament the situation), in a disenchanted world, 'notions of desert and of honor become detached from the context in which they were originally at home. Honor becomes nothing more than a badge of aristocratic status, and status itself, tied as it is now so securely to property, has very little to do with desert. Distributive justice cannot any longer be defined in terms of desert either, and so the alternatives become those of defining justice in terms of some sort of equality … or in terms of legal entitlements': A MacIntyre, *After Virtue: A Study in Moral Theory* 2nd edn (Notre Dame IN, University of Notre Dame Press, 1984) 232.

[72] B Gert, 'Review of Sher, *Desert*' (1989) 99 *Ethics* 426 at 427–28.

[73] TM Scanlon, *What We Owe to Each Other* (Cambridge, MA, Harvard University Press, 1998) 274; see also TM Scanlon, 'Giving Desert Its Due' (2013) 16 *Philosophical Explorations* 101.

child pornography is impotent in a world in which that is the sentence to which they are entitled given a punitive cardinal scale.

V. CONCLUSION: OR WHERE DO WE GO FROM HERE?

In trying to explain why moral philosophers (and others) have not converged on the substance of morality, the realist scholar Michael Smith comments that moral argument has not 'had much of a history in times in which we have been able to engage in free reflection unhampered by a false biology (the Aristotelian tradition) or a false belief in God (the Judeo-Christian tradition)'.[74] Although I do not think he is right in his expectation of what a period of concentrated reflection unhampered by enchantment will bring, perhaps Smith is right about the long shadow cast by false beliefs in general and by the deep Judeo-Christian commitment to pre-institutional desert in relation to punishment in particular. Certainly, Nietzsche seems to have thought so:

> Today, we immoralists have embarked on a counter movement and are trying with all our strength to take the concepts of guilt and punishment out of the world – to cleanse psychology, history, nature, and social institutions and sanctions of these ideas. And there is in our eyes no more radical opposition than that of the theologians, who continue to infect the innocence of becoming by means of the concepts of a 'moral world-order', 'guilt', and 'punishment'. Christianity is religion for the executioner.[75]

Nietzsche's argument is addressed in particular to the idea of responsibility (and derivatively to desert), and it is no accident that the greatest current push-back against the idea of deserved punishment has come from incompatibilists (those who think that responsibility is incompatible with the claim that human actions are caused).[76] However, the argument in this chapter does not depend on any claim about responsibility. Rather, what I have tried to establish is that 'just deserts' was never about desert and that the absence of desert contributed to the loss of control of the cardinal scale. Finally, I have offered a speculative suggestion that, despite its absence, the language and shadow of desert may have contributed to the advocates of 'just deserts' being blind to the danger of their account underwriting penal expansion.

If this is right, then (as noted earlier in this chapter) we need to engage in penal theory as people 'who live consciously in a post-anthropomorphic,

---

[74] M Smith, 'Moral Realism' in P Singer (ed), *A Companion to Ethics* (Oxford, Basil Blackwell, 1991) 399 at 409.

[75] FW Nietzsche, *The Anti-Christ, Ecce Homo, Twilight of the Idols, and Other Writings* [1899] edited by A Ridley and J Norman and translated by J Norman (Cambridge, Cambridge University Press, 2005) 181.

[76] For example, D Pereboom, 'Free Will Skepticism and Criminal Punishment' in T Nadelhoffer (ed), *The Future of Punishment* (Oxford, Oxford University Press, 2013) 49.

post-theocentric, post-technocratic world ... without a foundation in objective value or objective reason, in sympathy or sociality'.[77] That is not easy, and not within the scope of this chapter.[78] The point is that any such account will have to draw on resources from outside proportionality theory; for example, arguments from efficacy, parsimony, cost, deterrence and so on.

In rough form (and borrowing liberally from Andrew Ashworth), we might say the following:

> The purposes of the criminal law are: to announce (some sub-set of) what ought not to be done (more rarely, some sub-set of what ought to be done); to censure (in accordance with ordinal proportionality) those who (under certain conditions) do what has been announced as what ought not to be done; to deter by threat of sanc-tion those who would otherwise do what has been announced as what ought not to be done; and to do this in ways that meet certain other criteria (such as efficacy, parsimony, value-for-money, etc.).[79]

This is not a mixed account; rather, it is a plural one. In particular, censure and deterrence are independent. The results may well be counterintuitive (one might end up threatening more severe hard treatment for less serious, but harder to detect, crimes than for more serious, more easily detected crimes).[80] But, perhaps we should welcome conclusions that run counter to intuitions shaped by a system as deplorable as the criminal justice system. The important thing is that the argument is not inconsistent so long as censure and deterrence are inde-pendent. Indeed, in many other respects it is more intuitive than most theories of punishment in that it recognises that we condemn criminality (whether or not we have caught the criminal), but we impose hard treatment on those we catch in order to reduce crime.

Of course, this leaves a great deal to be done, including providing an expla-nation of how the different parts of the account fit together under an overall account of liberal justice. Censure (proportionality) theory will be an essen-tial part of the account – indeed, once uncoupled from hard treatment censure might provide the room that remains for desert[81] – and its contribution to penal theory will thus continue to be seminal.

---

[77] Gauthier, 'Moral Artifice', above n 6.

[78] I hope to offer such an account in a future monograph.

[79] The passage from Ashworth from which this is adapted reads: 'the rationale for the criminal law is to provide for the conviction and punishment of those who culpably do serious public wrongs, the distinctive technique being to declare those wrongs, to provide for the public censure of those who commit them (by means of conviction under a procedure that satisfies due process or human rights principles), and to provide for punishment up to a proportionate maximum': A Ashworth, 'Attempts' in J Deigh and D Dolinko (eds), *The Oxford Handbook of Philosophy of Criminal Law* (Oxford, Oxford University Press, 2011) 129.

[80] See Matravers, above n 57. For discussion, see A Bottoms, 'Exploring an Institutionalist and Post-Desert Theoretical Approach to Multiple-Offense Sentencing' in J Ryberg, J Roberts and J de Keijser (eds), *Sentencing Multiple Crimes* (Oxford, Oxford University Press 2018) 31 at 43–46.

[81] Cf Scanlon, 'Giving Desert Its Due', above n 73.

11

The Role of Victims' Rights in Punishment Theory

TATJANA HÖRNLE

I N THIS CHAPTER, I will argue that victims should be given a more prominent role within punishment theory. Answers to the question why the state is justified in censuring and punishing offenders should include references to the rights of victims. Victims in this context are the individuals whose rights have been violated through crimes – not a group of unspecified persons who might be victimised in the future. This needs to be emphasised because punishment theories that point to deterrence or other methods of crime prevention use the term 'victims' in the latter sense, referring not to actual but to potential future victims.

Punishment theories have neglected the interests of victims because well-established explanations of punishment, most notably preventive theories, focus on collective interests (see section I below). My arguments presuppose that justifications of punishment must vary depending on the kind of crime. Emphasising the interests of victims in contrast to collective interests only makes sense for a limited group of offences, that is, crimes against persons, their households and their property. The main thesis in this chapter is that victims of such crimes have a right to obtain a statement about the wrong done to them, not only in the form of compensation for material losses (that can be left to tort law) but in the form of a criminal court's condemnatory message (section III below). In addition to warnings and norm-affirming messages to the general public (which are important, too, but will not be discussed here), the formal declaration that a wrong was done serves victims' interests. I do not assume that victims have an absolute right that the state conveys this message, that is, a right that must be fulfilled under all conditions. Victims' rights should be conceived as prima facie rights. Public interests can be more important than victims' rights, but the more serious the criminal offence was, the less it is justifiable to forego criminal punishment. The broader framework for the punishment theory proposed here is provided by expressive theories of punishment, however, I draw some distinctions with regard to moral philosophers' approaches that rely on a more demanding paradigm of moral communications (section II below).

Writing about victims' rights is often understood as a plea to empower individual victims and to grant them greater influence in trials, pre-trial procedures and sentencing. This is not my aim. Arguing for a stronger role of victims in punishment theory does not necessarily mean proposing a stronger position of victims in procedural contexts. State punishment and criminal procedures have to comply with public values and principles such as the principle of equality that demands the equal treatment of offenders who have committed similar crimes. With regard to the plurality of values and goals that have to be accommodated,[1] the individual victim's interests can only be one consideration to be taken into account, but not the only one (see section IV below).

I. COLLECTIVE INTERESTS AND VICTIMS' INTERESTS

Traditional punishment theories point exclusively to collective interests rather than to the interests that the victim of the crime may have. This is even true for some approaches that are called 'retributive theories'. Consider, for instance, Kant's famous picture of a *Blutschuld* (blood guilt) that sticks to people leaving their island and dispersing themselves before having executed the last murderer in the island's prison.[2] His (otherwise unintelligible) reference to 'blood guilt' would make sense against a background of collective interests grounded in religion, that is, if the islanders expect God's punishment for not distancing themselves from the sinner in their midst.[3] The focus on collective interests is most obvious with regard to preventive theories of punishment. Preventive theories are based on the notion that it is in our collective interest to keep the number of future crimes as small as possible. On the question how this collective interest can be served, there are numerous variations: through modifying the dispositions of the particular offender, through deterring other potential offenders, or, in a more indirect and long-term way, through influencing the general public by reaffirming norms of conduct and supporting public trust in their validity.[4]

It is not my intention to challenge preventive theories in a fundamental way. To the contrary, crime prevention and affirming legal norms of conduct *must be* building blocks for a comprehensive punishment theory that has to cover all kinds of criminal wrongs. Many offences do not violate the right of an individual person but endanger genuine collective interests. We share a collective interest

---

[1] See for this point also J Tasioulas, 'Punishment and Repentance' (2006) 81 *Philosophy* 279 at 279.

[2] I Kant, *Metaphysik der Sitten* [1787] in *Werkausgabe* edited by W Weischedel volume VIII (Frankfurt, Suhrkamp, 1977) 455. English translation available in *Kant's Political Writings* edited by H Reiss (Cambridge, Cambridge University Press, 1970) 131 at 156.

[3] This is not to claim that Kant made this assumption.

[4] For the considerations that are categorised as 'positive general prevention', see M Dubber, 'Theories of Crime and Punishment in German Criminal Law' (2005) 53 *American Journal of Comparative Law* 679 at 699–703; C Roxin, 'Prevention, Censure and Responsibility: The Recent Debate on the Purposes of Punishment' in AP Simester, A du Bois-Pedain and U Neumann (eds), *Liberal Criminal Theory: Essays for Andreas von Hirsch* (Oxford, Hart, 2014) 23 at 28–29.

in criminalising and punishing behaviour such as, for example, tax evasion, the counterfeiting of money, corruption, and incitement to crimes via the internet. The relevance of collective interests has grown over time and continues to do so: the more complex and spatially extended social and economic relations are, the more important become institutions that protect external and internal security, a distributive state with dependable tax revenue and a non-corrupt administration, and other infrastructures such as a reliable currency system. Victim-related arguments only apply to a subset of criminal offences, that is, offences against persons. Punishment theory must inevitably accommodate different rationales. Criminal law theorists should not nurture the illusion of a one-size-fits-all punishment theory.

Scholars sometimes oppose this conclusion and the messiness that comes with it, and strive for the beauty of a holistic punishment theory.[5] However, justifying complex and highly intrusive institutions such as the criminal law and the criminal justice system cannot be convincing *and* adhere to an aesthetic ideal of simplicity at the same time.[6] Thinking about punishment theories can only lead to a box of bricks, and for different offences, these building blocks have to be arranged differently. Even for the subset of serious crimes against persons, it would not be convincing to disregard preventive purposes entirely. All criminal laws strive to deter persons, and actual punishments are necessarily connected to this preventive purpose (a law not applied would be an empty law). Acknowledging preventive purposes should, however, not be a reason to ignore victims' interests.

II. THE VICTIM IN EXPRESSIVE THEORIES OF PUNISHMENT

Contemporary punishment theories emphasise expressive functions, as the central component[7] or one important feature[8] of criminal punishment. The latter

---

[5] See, for instance, M Pawlik, *Person, Subjekt, Bürger: Zur Legitimation von Strafe* (Berlin, Duncker & Humblot, 2004) 53.

[6] For the need of multiple justifications G Stratenwerth, *Was leistet die Lehre von den Strafzwecken?* (Berlin, De Gruyter, 1995) 20–22; J Gardner, 'Crime: In Proportion and in Perspective' in A Ashworth and M Wasik (eds), *Fundamentals of Sentencing Theory: Essays in Honour of Andrew von Hirsch* (Oxford, Clarendon Press, 1998) 31 at 32–33.

[7] J Feinberg, 'The Expressive Function of Punishment' reprinted in M Tonry (ed), *Why Punish? How Much?: A Reader on Punishment* (Oxford, Oxford University Press, 2011) 111; A von Hirsch, *Censure and Sanctions* (Oxford, Clarendon Press, 1993) ch 2; RA Duff, *Punishment, Communication, and Community* (Oxford, Oxford University Press, 2001); C Bennett, *The Apology Ritual: A Philosophical Theory of Punishment* (Cambridge, Cambridge University Press, 2008); Tasioulas, above n 1; K Günther, 'Criminal Law, Crime and Punishment as Communication' in AP Simester, A du Bois-Pedain and U Neumann (eds), above n 4, 123; U Kindhäuser, 'Zu einem "kommunikativen" Straftatmodell' in T Rotsch, J Brüning and J Schady (eds), *Strafrecht – Jugendstrafrecht – Kriminalprävention in Wissenschaft und Praxis: Festschrift für Heribert Ostendorf zum 70. Geburtstag* (Baden-Baden, Nomos, 2015) 483; B Wringe, *An Expressive Theory of Punishment* (Basingstoke, Palgrave, 2016).

[8] V Tadros, *The Ends of Harm* (Oxford, Oxford University Press, 2011) ch 5; Roxin, above n 4 at 39–41.

view (important feature but not the singular rationale) is preferable. I share Victor Tadros' assessment that the task of justifying criminal punishment cannot be shouldered *solely* by emphasising its expressive role, even if one takes expressive functions and particularly their meaning for victims seriously.[9] Criminal justice systems are expensive, even if overall sentence severity is kept within reasonable limits.[10] Arguments to defend criminal punishments need to address different audiences. Justifications are not only owed to offenders for the serious infringements of their liberties, but also to the public for the usage of resources, and to other persons on whom the criminal justice system imposes personal hardship (for instance, if the trial corroborated the accused's innocence). For these reasons, a justification of criminal punishment as an institution must include *benefits for all* in the form of crime prevention. However, this does not commit us to crime prevention as the only goal. The aim of this chapter is to adjust the spotlight on victims' interests without denying the relevance of other elements for the complex task of justifying criminal punishment.

With regard to crimes that seriously victimise individuals, my version of a mixed punishment theory emphasises the expressive features of criminal punishment. In the following sections, I will explain what I mean by expressive features, and why victim-centred arguments are important. Before coming to these details, some differences between my approach and contemporary theories of expressive punishment are worth mentioning. The first difference is that most expressive theories do not pay enough attention to victims. Proponents of expressive theories do mention that penal censure also speaks to the victims, in addition to the public and the offender; however, they do not elaborate much on this point.[11] If the underlying question is: 'Who is the addressee of penal censure?', it is convincing to put offenders in first place. Defendants are the main characters in a criminal trial and the censuring message must be addressed primarily to them. But if the question is: 'Why should the practice of penal censure be upheld?', victims' interests deserve more attention than they receive in contemporary expressive theories of punishment.

Secondly, expressive theories of punishment have been developed mainly by moral philosophers who assume that penal communications should simulate moral communications. They focus on moral blame and interpersonal moral dialogues to explain penal censure.[12] This is, however, not the best approach to

---

[9] Tadros, ibid at 103–05.

[10] Unlike the situation in, for example, the US: see M Tonry, *Sentencing Fragments: Penal Reform in America, 1975–2015* (Oxford, Oxford University Press, 2016) ch 1.

[11] Von Hirsch, above n 7 at 10; Duff, above n 7 at 114; Tasioulas, above n 1 at 284; Günther, above n 7 at 127. See for an exception J Hampton, 'Correcting Harms Versus Righting Wrongs: The Goal of Retribution' (1992) 39 *UCLA Law Review* 1659 at 1692–94.

[12] For a more critical view of the dialogue as a model for state punishment, see K Brownlee, 'The Offender's Part in the Dialogue' in R Cruft, MH Kramer and MR Reiff (eds), *Crime, Punishment, and Responsibility: The Jurisprudence of Antony Duff* (Oxford, Oxford University Press, 2011) 54 at 66.

conceptualise state punishment. Criminal punishment takes place in a specific legal and institutional context, that is, within the relations between the state and citizens (in their specific role as citizens). Theories of criminal punishment should therefore take the rights between citizens and between state and citizens as a starting point. The difference between the moral philosophy perspective on criminal punishment, on the one hand, and the political philosophy perspective, on the other hand, manifests itself, for example, if one considers the intensity of desirable communication. For moral philosophers, it seems natural to expect a moral dialogue with defendants, while for the view taken here moral requirements of this kind are too ambitious.

Moral philosophers draw, of course, some distinctions between the content of moral communications and the content of messages in criminal convictions. Antony Duff and Sandra Marshall, for instance, argue that criminal censure must refer to public wrongs and that the scope of conduct to be labelled 'public wrongs' must be narrower than what can be considered a moral wrong.[13] Nevertheless, in their view, the structures of penal censure resemble moral communications in crucial aspects. The idea is that accused persons have to give answers to a community to which they belong prior to the crime.[14] One pole in this communication is the offender, whose qualities as a moral agent are emphasised;[15] the other is the community to which the offender belongs. Justifications of punishment that borrow heavily from moral philosophy undervalue the most important feature: it is of crucial importance that the state administers criminal punishment.[16]

Political philosophers, on the other hand, might be accused of overemphasising the role of the state at the cost of victims. Matt Matravers argues that it would be wrong to see criminal offences as conflicts that are the property of the parties. To support this thesis, he points to the state's monopoly on the use of violence.[17] I agree with most of what he says, but would come to a somewhat different conclusion. In my view, justifications of punishment need to take the framework of vertical relationships between the state and citizens into account, but also horizontal relationships between persons in their role as citizens.[18]

---

[13] SE Marshall and RA Duff, 'Criminalisation and Sharing Wrongs' (1998) 11 *Canadian Journal of Law and Jurisprudence* 7; RA Duff and SE Marshall, 'Public and Private Wrongs', in J Chalmers and F Leverick (eds), *Essays in Criminal Law in Honour of Sir Gerald Gordon* (Edinburgh, Edinburgh University Press, 2010) 70.

[14] RA Duff, 'Responsibility, Citizenship, and Criminal Law' in RA Duff and S Green (eds), *Philosophical Foundations of Criminal Law* (Oxford, Oxford University Press, 2011) 125 at 131–32.

[15] Duff, above n 7 at 80–82; Tasioulas, above n 1 at 284, 294.

[16] See for this point also M Matravers, 'The Victim, the State, and Civil Society' in A Bottoms and J Roberts (eds), *Hearing the Victim: Adversarial Justice, Crime Victims and the State* (Cullompton, Willan, 2010) 1; M Thorburn, 'Criminal Law as Public Law' in RA Duff and S Green (eds), above n 14, 21.

[17] Matravers, above n 16 at 8–10.

[18] The term 'citizen' does not refer exclusively to citizenship in a formal legal sense. Citizens in a wider sense are persons who live together in a given jurisdiction as residents, and a complete picture

Once we think of the relationship in which agents in a constituted legal order stand to each other, it would be misguided to frame that relationship as a moral relationship between two individual human beings. Rather, the horizontal relationships between such agents are constituted by rights that citizens have against each other (typically rights to non-intervention,[19] but also limited rights to protection and assistance, relevant for crimes of omission). The rights to non-intervention that persons as citizens have against each other are much simpler and less demanding than the rich web of moral rights between them.

The basic relations that underpin state punishment can be depicted graphically in the form of a triangle (Figure 11.1). The three corners represent the state, the offender, and the victim,[20] the three sides the relational structures that are characterised by rights. The base of the triangle is formed by the victim's right to non-intervention that the offender disregards. The state, at the apex of the triangle, stands in rights-relations to both offenders and victims *qua* citizens. Rights of victims against the state will be discussed in the following sections. The rights of offenders against the state during criminal proceedings and sentence enforcement are just as important, but are not addressed in this chapter.

Figure 11.1 Rights-relations relevant to state punishment

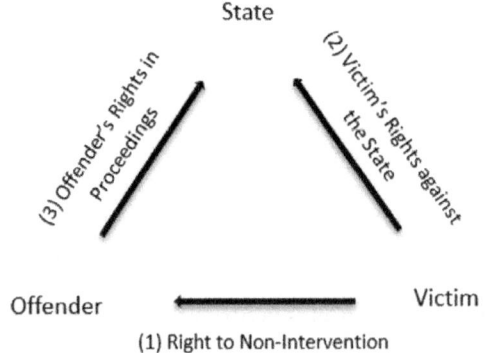

My approach deviates from moral philosophers' assumptions concerning offenders' appropriate reactions to censure. If one models penal censure according to the paradigm of a moral exchange, communication rather than the mere expression of censure is required, including offenders' responses. Reactions are expected such as they would be appropriate in moral communications, for example, that offenders respond to justified censure by acknowledging that

---

must also accommodate the fact that some rights are extended to all human beings. See for questions regarding persons who are in a technical, public law-sense non-citizens Duff, above n 7 at 141–48.

[19] In German constitutional terminology: *Abwehrrechte* (literally: defensive rights).

[20] In the case of offences against public interests, the collective that shares the violated interest takes the space of the individual victim.

they have done wrong[21] and with repentance.[22] I do not wish to challenge this for moral contexts where it seems indeed appropriate that wrongdoers react to justified blame with repentance. My point rather is: for the purpose of criminal law, the communicative messages should not be seen exclusively or primarily as a moral dialogue with the offender. The multifaceted messages that are part of criminal convictions should not be distorted by giving offenders' amendments, repentance, etc the same significance as in moral dialogues. In criminal law contexts, the expressive functions are more important than the communicative features.[23] This is not to claim that the criminal justice system must ignore post-crime meritorious behaviour. It can be taken into account in favour of offenders under certain conditions, provided it is possible to do so without distorting the accurate description of wrongdoing that is owed to the victim. A solution might be to consider offenders' post-crime and post-conviction achievements for decisions about early release or a partial waiver of payments during the enforcement stage.

III. REASONS TO INTEGRATE VICTIMS' INTERESTS IN THEORIES OF PUNISHMENT

So far, I have only sketched the basic idea that victims of crimes have a right against the state to obtain a statement about the wrong done to them. It is still necessary to give reasons why such a right should be acknowledged.

A. The Desire for Retaliation

A straightforward answer to the question why victims' interests should matter could point to psychological needs. Human beings' desire for revenge and retaliation might be sufficient reason to ground state punishment.[24] My version of the victim-centred aspects within punishment theory is more complex than such a straightforward reference to the emotions that trigger retaliation. As a starting point, however, the thesis is convincing that we should not ignore or deny the emotions that people typically experience once another person has intruded into their personal sphere without a legitimate reason. 'Personal sphere' includes the

---

[21] Von Hirsch, above n 7 at 10.

[22] See Duff, above n 7 at 79–82, 106–12; Tasioulas, above n 1; Bottoms, in this volume.

[23] On this see also von Hirsch, above n 7 at 10; Bennett, above n 7 at 193–97; Wringe, above n 7, chs 4 and 5.

[24] J Murphy, 'Hatred: A Qualified Defense' in JG Murphy and J Hampton, *Forgiveness and Mercy* (Cambridge, Cambridge University Press, 1990) 88 at 94–95; K Levy, 'Why Retributivism Needs Consequentialism: The Rightful Place of Revenge in the Criminal Justice System' (2014) 66 *Rutgers Law Review* 629; T Walter, *Strafe und Vergeltung – Rehabilitation und Grenzen eines Prinzips* (Baden-Baden, Nomos, 2016).

body (in the case of injuries, sexual offences, restrictions on freedom of movement), spatial structures and objects assigned to the victim's use with the right to exclude others (dwelling, property), and intangible components such as human dignity. If the violation of a right to non-intervention is not trivial, victims typically experience anger and resentment, and often the desire that offenders should suffer for what they have done.[25] Social psychologists and criminal law theorists point out that a desire for retaliation is a strong and widespread emotion,[26] which can, for example, be witnessed in movies and other narratives.[27] This does not imply that every human being will experience a similarly strong desire under all circumstances – obviously, a lot depends on both individual personality and social and cultural background. But if one looks at a sufficiently large number of persons, such as in experiments of the Ultimatum Game-type, they show a consistent tendency to punish others in response to behaviour that is perceived as unfair. Persons do this even if they have to pay the costs, that is, if they lose potential gain by withdrawing funds from the unfair opponent.[28] It is debated how the outcome of these experiments should be interpreted. Do participants who punish enforce social norms of fairness in a way that *is* rational and socially valuable in the long run? Or do they succumb to impulsive urges? There are indications that the latter, that is, the 'mere emotion' explanation, plays an important role: if participants are intoxicated, they are even more prone to punish at higher costs for themselves.[29] JL Mackie has offered a plausible explanation why not only emotional reactions to one's own suffering are widespread but also shared feelings of resentments and the corresponding moral convictions concerning retribution. During the history of mankind, strong emotional reactions and retaliatory acts by the victim and supportive others must have been beneficial to survival because such responses decrease the likelihood of future attacks. It seems plausible that evolutionary processes have moulded our contemporary emotional responses and cooperation in resentment.[30]

Describing the roots and the persistence of retributive emotions does not commit us to approve of them without any further questioning. From a psychologist's point of view, the impact of retributive emotions on future well-being would require some scrutiny. To what degree is acting out anger and resentment

---

[25] J Holroyd, 'The Retributive Emotions: Passions and Pains of Punishment' (2010) 39 *Philosophical Papers* 343 at 344–45.

[26] N Vidmar, 'Retribution and Revenge' in J Sanders and VL Hamilton (eds), *Handbook of Justice Research in Law* (New York, Kluwer, 2001) 31 at 41–55; Levy, above n 24 at 651–52; Walter, above n 24 at 10.

[27] J Murphy, 'Two Cheers for Vindictiveness' (2000) 2 *Punishment and Society* 131 at 132–33.

[28] See for instance the experiments by E Fehr and U Fischbacher, 'Third-Party Punishment and Social Norms' (2004) 25 *Evolution and Human Behavior* 63.

[29] CK Morewedge, T Krishnamurti and D Ariely, 'Focused on Fairness: Alcohol Intoxication Increases the Costly Rejection of Inequitable Rewards' (2014) 50 *Journal of Experimental Social Psychology* 15.

[30] JL Mackie, 'Morality and the Retributive Emotions' in M Tonry (ed), above n 7, 271 at 278–81.

helpful for dissolving negative emotions?[31] Does retaliation promote mental stability and maintain the victim's self-respect?[32] Or are we dealing with more ambivalent emotions that might sometimes lead into a destructive cycle? The most likely answer seems to be: it depends (mainly on the personality of the persons involved and the details of the offence). For our purpose, that is, for the justification of state punishment, we can leave further scientific inquiries aside. Beyond evolutionary explanations and psychology, we need reasons why the state ought to address victims' emotions and why an institution such as criminal punishment with its high monetary and non-monetary costs could be justified on this basis. To this end, the moral argument that a wrongdoer deserves that others respond with resentment[33] is not sufficient, either. 'Morally deserved' in interpersonal relationships is not the same as 'permitted or required' as a task for the state.[34] Two sets of arguments for the necessity of state punishment can be developed: consequentialist reasons that shift the arguments from psychology and moral philosophy to sociology, and rights-based based reasons that are part of a normative theory that focuses on the role of the state. Each will be examined in turn.

B. Consequentialist Reasons to Take Emotions Seriously

Consequentialist reasoning points to collective interests: the state needs to institutionalise what would otherwise occur as private retaliation, driven by victims' emotions and the emotions of persons close to them. State punishment serves to channel and absorb anger and retaliatory urges in order to avoid harmful consequences for the public.[35] Such harmful consequences are spirals of mutual violence between groups that might have spillover effects and undermine the state's monopoly on violence. If private retaliation is not suppressed and the underlying emotions not dealt with in an institutionalised form, the results can be eruptions of violence and lengthy blood feuds.[36] John Gardner speaks of the criminal law's 'displacement function'.[37] Pointing to possible aggressive reactions

---

[31] Murphy, above n 27 at 133–34; Levy, above n 24 at 652.

[32] For the connection with self-respect, see J Murphy, 'Forgiveness and Resentment' in JG Murphy and J Hampton, above n 24, 14 at 16–17.

[33] See for this argument Z Cogley, 'Basic Desert of Reactive Emotions' (2013) 16 *Philosophical Explorations* 165.

[34] Holroyd, above n 25 at 369.

[35] Murphy, above n 27 at 132; Gardner, above n 6, 31; N MacCormick and D Garland, 'Sovereign States and Vengeful Victims: The Problem of the Right to Punish' in A Ashworth and M Wasik (eds), above n 6, 11 at 27.

[36] For anthropological views on blood feuds, see KF Otterbein and CS Otterbein, 'An Eye for an Eye, A Tooth for a Tooth: A Cross-Cultural Study of Feuding' (1965) 67 *American Anthropologist* 1470.

[37] Gardner, above n 6.

is, however, only half of the story. If individual victims repress their emotional reactions but see no one else responding to the violation of their rights, resignation and social withdrawal have to be expected. Both retaliatory reactions and the silent retreat into disappointment ought to be prevented.

These functional explanations why the state must respond to crimes against individuals are likely to gain increased importance in societies shaped by migration. Cultural contexts and socialisation influence the prevalence and intensity of retaliatory emotions.[38] If citizens or their families have migrated from states with a history of ineffectiveness and/or corruption, they are adapted to environments that promote responding to crimes with retaliation. It would be misleading to label traditions of private reactions to crime exclusively as eruptions of archaic emotions. In dysfunctional states, victims' retaliation can be rational. It cannot be expected that migration will quickly dissolve all prior patterns of behaviour. Older modes of response might resurface after families have moved to a more efficiently and more fairly organised state. Under such conditions, it becomes even more important that the state takes its duty to respond to crimes seriously.

C. Victims' Rights to a Response by the State

The conclusion that the state has to interfere on behalf of the victim cannot only be drawn on the basis of functional reasoning, but also be defended with a rights-based approach to theories of punishment and criminalisation. Victims of crimes may not only report feelings of anger and resentment, but also point to the fact that the crime violated their rights. This argument is not dependent on the actual occurrence of negative emotions. Even if victims react in a calm, well-adjusted way, they have a right that the state responds to the incident. Criminal law acknowledges and protects citizens' rights to non-intervention – shown above in Figure 11.1 as the base of the triangle. These rights to non-intervention are rights that citizens have against each other. After an offender has violated a fellow citizen's right, its meaning and scope should be reaffirmed and the offender censured. If the law acknowledges a right in a general and abstract way, this entails the duty to confirm and specify the scope and meaning of a rights violation in an individual case. Having a right in the abstract would be pointless if its violation were simply ignored.

One might consider that the task of affirming the right could be left to an institution other than the state. However, this idea meets several objections. First, statements must come from someone with a high degree of authority. Our societies and their constitutional framework are egalitarian, which clashes with any view that judicial authority is derived from social status, religious leadership or personal charisma. Judges' authority must be based in a formal and egalitarian

---

[38] Vidmar, above n 26 at 45–46.

way on either the will of the people (in the case of elected judges) or be granted by a meritocratic system of appointments. Secondly, we have developed high epistemic standards that make it necessary to base judgments on facts corroborated by evidence. This requires professionalisation of criminal justice activities including high levels of education and complex structures of review and control. For these reasons alone, there is no alternative to the state as the provider of institutions that meet these standards. And, thirdly, within the modern constitutional state, the central notion that individuals have rights that are protected by the state implies that it is a genuine task of the state to reaffirm these rights after violations.[39]

What is the content of the victim's right that the state should respond to the incident? It would be misleading to argue straightforwardly that it is a right to see the offender punished. Primarily, the individual victim has a right that the state examines the events and, if supported by evidence, affirms that the victim has been subjected to a legal wrong. This judgment about wrongdoing – which is an essential component of any criminal conviction – goes beyond the reaffirmation of an abstract and general norm of conduct. Judicial statements about wrongdoing are more specific than the judgments to be found in criminal laws. They break down the abstract messages about prohibited conduct into a statement about a particular interaction. The wrong is described in a more detailed way and the degree of wrong in the specific case is evaluated.

These judgments about wrongdoing should not be one-sided assessments that focus exclusively on the offender's acts and his *mens rea*. Offenders also have rights, including the right that victims' wrongdoing in the specific interaction, and victims' obligations, will also be taken into account. This is evident in cases involving prior attacks by the victim or other forms of provocation. Beyond wrongful behaviour, there is the additional question of whether a victim has perhaps violated an obligation to protect his/her own interests and thus whether the offender's wrongdoing was less serious. This topic is neglected in criminal law theory, perhaps because a strong tradition in our mode of moral assessment tends to focus on the offender's guilty mind rather than on mutual duties in the interaction between citizens. However, for many crimes the conclusion that the offender did wrong, and how much, necessarily depends on assumptions about what the victim should have done. Consider, for example, sexual offences. Both the norms of conduct and the retrospective judgments involve some assumptions about how victims ought to behave, for instance concerning modest dress, resistance, escape and verbal expressions of disapproval. Only the latter (expressing lack of consent) is a defensible obligation,[40] however, courts have explicitly or implicitly assumed a wide range of victims' obligations. The crucial point is to

---

[39] A Harel, 'Why Only the State May Inflict Criminal Sanctions: The Case Against Privately Inflicted Sanctions' (2008) 14 *Legal Theory* 113.

[40] For my defence of a 'no means no' model, see T Hörnle, 'Wie § 177 StGB ergänzt werden sollte' (2015) 162 *Goltdammer's Archiv für Strafrecht* 313 at 319–22.

make such underlying assumptions explicit and scrutinise them. Such considerations are not restricted to sexual offences but apply to all offences with individual victims.[41] In cases of fraud, for example, one could argue in favour of an obligation to be critical in the eye of evidently implausible stories. Whatever the position taken on the specific content of victims' obligations in different contexts, the general point is that criminal courts should trace the mutual rights and obligations between citizens.

The victim's right should be described as a multi-faceted right. First, it is a right to have the case examined – unless the alleged rights violation was of a trivial kind, in which case the public interest in a sensible allocation of limited resources can be the decisive factor. Secondly, if the evidence supports the conclusion that the accused indeed has committed a criminal wrong, the victim has the right to obtain confirmation that her right to non-intervention (for instance, her right to physical integrity) has been violated. Thirdly, this includes the right to have the degree of wrongdoing assessed. The fourth component is that the offender is addressed with a censuring message. If wrongdoing has been established, the person who has committed the wrongful act should be confronted with a condemnatory judgment.

Another question is whether victims also have a right that the offender is punished, that is, a right that he has to undergo some kind of unpleasant or hard treatment in addition to the censure expressed. A requirement of this sort could be supported with a functional argument, contending that retaliatory emotions must be absorbed in order to avoid spirals of violence. It seems obvious that to this end the state must inflict a certain degree of suffering on the offender. John Gardner argues that 'the criminal law's medicine must be strong enough to control the toxins of bitterness and resentment which course through the veins of those who are wronged'.[42] If the starting point is not a reference to emotions and the need to displace retaliatory responses, but victims' right to obtain a statement about the degree of wrongdoing, one might be more inclined to consider verbal reactions without more tangible sanctions attached.[43] The crucial question from this perspective is whether the relationship between censure and hard treatment is contingent.[44] Our long-standing traditions of punishments could be mere conventions (see Joel Feinberg's definition of the expressive function: 'punishment is a conventional device for the expression of attitudes of resentment and indignation'[45]).

Speaking of conventions and contingencies implies that they are open to be replaced with other devices.[46] If one reconsiders the forms and details of

---

[41] T Hörnle, 'Die Obliegenheit, sich selbst zu schützen, und ihre Bedeutung für das Strafrecht' (2000) 156 *Goltdammer's Archiv für Strafrecht* 626.

[42] Gardner, above n 6 at 33.

[43] See for such an argument Günther, above n 7 at 133–38.

[44] See for this claim Günther, above n 7 at 135.

[45] Feinberg, above n 7 at 113.

[46] T Scanlon, *The Significance of Choice: The Tanner Lectures on Human Values* (Salt Lake City, University of Utah Press, 1988) 149 at 214 ('we could just as well "say it with flowers"'), and the

sanctions, it is of course possible to modify them. However, the more fundamental question whether hard treatment in general *could be given up* in the context of an expressive theory requires the answer: perhaps in theory, but hardly in societies that resemble ours. The first obstacle is of the linguistic kind. Merely verbal censure would require both exceptional verbal skills on the part of the censuring person or body and high sensitivity to the minutiae of verbal censure on the part of the audience. It is quite difficult to communicate a quantitatively fine-tuned degree of censure *only* through words. Secondly, in order for merely verbal censure to be taken seriously, one would require a high degree of authority and standing of those who express censure. This might work if offender, victim and the general audience share a high degree of respect for the institution expressing it (imagine a 'high priest' in religious environments), but in our contemporary secular and egalitarian states, judges cannot be expected to have this kind of authority *qua* their office. It is a common feature of legal systems to work with visible signs of distinction (such as robes and court room architecture) but such efforts will be increasingly less suited to impress contemporary audiences.[47] Solemn words will usually not be sufficient to convey the seriousness of censure.[48] They need to be accompanied by some kind of token in the form of unpleasant treatment to underline the message. This does not mean that the strong expression 'suffering' is appropriate in all cases, but the unpleasant treatment must go beyond the demand to pay financial compensation for the costs the victim had incurred due to the crime.[49] And the more serious the crime was, the stronger become functional arguments that require 'bitter medicine' for the offender to soothe retaliatory emotions.

IV. CONSEQUENCES FOR CRIMINAL TRIALS

Proposals to integrate victims' rights into a complex theory of punishment have to address the objection that this might have far-reaching consequences for criminal procedure and sentencing (for sentencing, see section V below). After all, for decades,[50] or even centuries,[51] state criminal procedures have displaced victims. Victims have to stand back and let the state, that is, public prosecutors, dominate the proceedings. My intention is not to challenge in a fundamental way the displacement or neutralisation of victims in criminal proceedings.

poignant reply by M Matravers, *Justice and Punishment* (Oxford, Oxford University Press, 2000) 257 n 9: 'flowers typically say something else'.

[47] Gardner, above n 6 at 50–52.

[48] J Kleinig, 'Punishment and Moral Seriousness' (1991) 25 *Israel Law Review* 401 at 417–18.

[49] For the view that payment of court costs and compensation could be sufficient, see N Hanna, 'Say What? A Critique of Expressive Retributivism' (2007) 27 *Law and Philosophy* 123 at 138.

[50] For the implementation of public prosecution in England, see J Spencer, 'The Victim and the Prosecutor' in A Bottoms and J Roberts (eds), above n 16, 141.

[51] See for the history of public prosecution in Germany, W Wohlers, *Entstehung und Funktion der Staatsanwaltschaft. Ein Beitrag zu den rechtshistorischen und strukturellen Grundlagen des reformierten Strafverfahrens* (Berlin, Duncker & Humblot, 1994).

Criminal law theorists disagree whether the state prosecutes cases on behalf of the victim or on behalf of the public.[52] The point to be made here is: a preference for the first option does not necessarily entail the conclusion that individual victims must be granted more extensive powers in criminal procedures.

If one categorises victims' interests and (potential) rights, they can be divided into five groups. The first group consists of *service rights*.[53] Victims share an interest to be treated well in their encounters with criminal justice agencies and when they have to appear in court. Normative claims referring to service rights will not raise principled objections. It seems obvious that victims should be treated in a respectful and considerate way and that proceedings should be designed to make vulnerable persons feel as comfortable as possible. The second right can be called *a right to be heard*. Victims should be able to present all the facts about the crime known to them. Public interests and victim interests overlap: if victims are sources of information about facts relevant for conviction, they ought to be encouraged to share their knowledge with the prosecution and with courts. (For the questions that arise with regard to sentencing and victim statements, see section V below).

A third facet of victims' interests deserves more scrutiny. Should we acknowledge *a right to participation in trials*? Some victims feel the desire to become part of the proceedings beyond their role as witnesses. German law allows victims to appear in court as ancillary prosecutors (*Nebenkläger*) in the case of serious crimes against persons.[54] In recent times, very large numbers of ancillary prosecutors have participated in trials for heinous crimes, such as the trial against supporters of the German terrorist cell called the National Socialist Underground (NSU).[55] If parents and other relatives of murder victims feel that it is important to be present in the courtroom or at least to be represented by an attorney, this is not because they could report relevant facts. Involvement obviously serves *expressive needs*,[56] needs that might perhaps be described as being visible rather than invisible. Such expressive needs are understandable, but they raise some serious questions about the feasibility and duration of trials with more than 100 participants, the position of the accused who is confronted with a wall of opponents, and negative side-effects that a booming business for attorneys (paid by the state) might have.[57]

---

[52] See for the latter view Matravers, above n 16 at 6.

[53] For the distinction between service rights and procedural rights, see C Hoyle, 'Victims, the Criminal Process, and Restorative Justice' in M Maguire, R Morgan and R Reiner (eds), *The Oxford Handbook of Criminology*, 5th edn (Oxford, Oxford University Press, 2012) 398 at 407.

[54] §§ 395–402 StPO (German Code of Criminal Procedure).

[55] Ninety-five accessory prosecutors and 60 lawyers representing them, see www.nsu-watch.info/2017/09/facts-figures-about-the-nsu-trial.

[56] See for expressive functions P Rock, 'Hearing Victims of Crime: The Delivery of Impact Statements as Ritual Behaviour in Four London Trials for Murder and Manslaughter' in A Bottoms and J Roberts (eds), above n 16, 200.

[57] In the NSU trial, non-existing victims were represented (and the state paid fees), see www.spiegel.de/panorama/justiz/phantom-opfer-meral-keskin-ermittlungen-gegen-nsu-anwalt-a-1057393.html.

The fourth and most controversial category consists of conceivable procedural rights that would give victims *the power to make decisions* such as whether a case should be dismissed, plea bargaining with the defendant should take place, what kind of evidence should or should not be heard, etc. The phrase 'neutralisation of victims' means that victims are denied such rights in contemporary trials. Public prosecutors, and not victims, decide about beginning, conducting and ending criminal proceedings. For instance, victims who would prefer that no trial takes place usually do not have the power to terminate proceedings.[58] If one focuses on victims' prima facie right to obtain a condemnatory statement regarding the wrong done to them, this might seem counterintuitive – after all, the notion of a right implies the power to waive this right. But again, an adequate concept of criminal procedure must take *a wide range of other considerations* into account: offenders' rights,[59] public values and public policy considerations. If one assumes, as I do, that it is not convincing to develop *all* details of justifying and organising criminal punishment in a neat way from one master principle,[60] it follows that acknowledging victims' rights within punishment theory does not entail neglecting other principles. Some of the reasons that support the institution of public prosecutions and the displacement of victims are actually related to victims' interests. Even from a victim's perspective, it makes sense to see public prosecutors as fiduciaries. Most actual victims could not or would not want to shoulder the burden of deciding themselves about procedural issues and offenders' fates. The fiduciary role of state agencies also protects socially or personally weak persons who might not be able to assert themselves against pressures by more powerful defendants and/or their peer groups. Other reasons to be cautious about individual victims' power in criminal proceedings are based on collective interests and shared values reflected in constitutions and fundamental procedural principles. Powerful public institutions such as criminal justice systems must treat offenders who have committed similar crimes equally. Equality and fairness require that criminal trials follow uniform rules rather than being guided by individuals' idiosyncratic preferences and powers of self-assertion.

It is also legitimate to take the limits of public resources into account. The claim that victims have a prima facie right to have their case examined does not

---

Also, at least in cases with political dimensions, the dynamics within large groups of attorneys might promote conspiracy theories: for the conspiracy theory in the NSU trial see A von der Behrens, 'Kontrolle als Gestaltung. Der Verfassungsschutz und der NSU-Komplex' (2017) 50 *Kritische Justiz* 38 at 46–47 (hinting at involvement of the state in the murders).

[58] There are exceptions (German law demands a formal application of the victim for certain misdemeanours such as simple assault, insult and trespassing, §§ 123 II, 194, 230 German Penal Code) but the general rules disenfranchise victims.

[59] See A Ashworth, 'Victims' Rights, Defendants' Rights and Criminal Procedure' in A Crawford and J Goodey (eds), *Integrating a Victim Perspective Within Criminal Justice* (Aldershot, Ashgate, 2000) 185.

[60] See for the difference between neat and messy theories RA Duff and S Green, 'Introduction: Searching for Foundations' in RA Duff and S Green (eds), above n 16, 1 at 8–9.

mean that every single criminal complaint must trigger full efforts to gather evidence and to continue the case until a formal verdict is reached. At the early stages, the label 'victim' must anyhow be understood as 'alleged victim', and it is obviously legitimate to dismiss a case if there are serious doubts concerning facts. And even if it is very likely that indeed the accused has violated a right of the complainant, in the case of a minor rights violation there must be some leeway to discontinue the proceedings. A victim's right that the state does not ignore the incident should not be understood as an absolute right that must prevail under all circumstances. Only if serious violations of important individual rights are at stake, a case must not be dismissed if there is the possibility to obtain the necessary evidence.

A fifth category of potential victims' rights could consist of *control rights*. Advocating against extensive participatory rights does not entail arguing against victims' right to apply for judicial review if state prosecutors terminate proceedings without good reasons. If one views state prosecutors as fiduciaries who have to protect victim interests as well as public interests, in individual cases the question can arise whether conflicting interests have been balanced adequately. Procedural theory must consider whether victims should be able to initiate reviews of crucial decisions taken by the public prosecutor such as the right to challenge dismissals[61] – but again, public policy considerations, such as the costs of such reviews, may also be taken into account.

V. CONSEQUENCES FOR SENTENCING

A final question concerns what rights victims might have at the sentencing stage. This is a particularly controversial topic. Authors who focus on the politics of criminal justice have argued that conservative politicians have exploited the topic of victims' rights and have thereby contributed to higher levels of punitiveness.[62] One must, however, distinguish two different issues: the use and abuse of victim rhetoric in political agendas, and the question of victims' rights within theories about criminal procedure. Political campaigns typically refer to hypothetical or future victims, either based on concerns about social problems or justice, or as a strategy to attract punitively minded voters. This is not my subject.

Criminal law theorists should consider three types of possible victims' rights with regard to sentencing: a right to be heard; the power to be involved

---

[61] See for victims' access to judicial review in England Spencer, above n 50 at 148–51; in Germany the remedy for victims is called 'Klageerzwingungsverfahren', see § 172 German Code of Criminal Procedure.

[62] See for instance L Henderson, 'The Wrongs of Victim's Rights' (1985) 37 *Stanford Law Review* 937 at 948–53; M Dubber, *Victims in the War on Crime: The Use and Abuse of Victims' Rights* (New York, New York University Press, 2002); M Tonry, 'Rebalancing the Criminal Justice System in Favour of the Victim: The Costly Consequences of Populist Rhetoric' in A Bottoms and J Roberts (eds), above n 16, 72.

in decision-making; and control rights. Again, it needs to be emphasised that proposing a victim-centred punishment theory does *not* mean automatically endorsing all of these options. The most far-reaching approach entitles victims to participate in sentencing, for instance, by giving them the right to recommend a sentence or to veto courts' decisions. Countervailing reasons are, however, overwhelmingly strong. Such an approach clashes with important principles such as the principle of equality: these decisions should be left to judges. Similar considerations apply to control rights. German law denies the right to appeal against sentences even for those victims of serious crimes who became accessory prosecutors.[63] There are good reasons to be restrictive with control rights regarding sentencing outcomes: pragmatic reasons (keeping the number of appeals within reasonable limits), but also principled reasons. The right to appeal would be used selectively and thus could undermine the principle of equality, and it would become a source for widespread disappointment because victims' perceptions of the just sentence would often clash with the equality principle.

A right to be heard is the subject of intense discussions. In Britain, the US, Canada and Australia, for instance, victims are entitled to make personal statements or victim impact statements.[64] Advocates of victim participation in sentencing argue that 'sentencing without victim input is impoverished sentencing'.[65] Criminal law theorists have expressed objections,[66] even those who give victims space in punishment theory.[67] A crucial point is what exactly a right to speak would encompass. A thin concept points to facts known to the victim. If public prosecutors take their role as fiduciaries for victims seriously, they must gather information about the impact of the crime – provided that this information is necessary to evaluate the violation of rights the victim has suffered. The latter restriction is important. If, for instance, an attack has violated the right to bodily integrity, the seriousness of injuries matters, but it is not necessary to take further consequences (for instance, falling into a depression and thus losing one's job) into account to describe the violation of rights.

Advocates of victim statements usually have a thicker concept in mind. Most victims will not (or not exclusively) sort the events into the category 'violations of my rights'. They will focus on harm and personal suffering in a broader sense. If a right to be heard at the sentencing stage is meant to fulfil expressive functions,[68] at least in trials for serious crimes one has to expect narratives with

---

[63] Accessory prosecutors can appeal (§ 400 German Code of Criminal Procedure), but the right to appeal sentencing decisions is excluded.

[64] Hoyle, above n 58 at 412–13. German law does not grant a right to speak but leaves it to the presiding judge's discretion to collect evidence regarding the impact of crimes on victims' lives.

[65] J Shapland and M Hall, 'Victims at Court: Necessary Accessories or Principal Players at Centre Stage?' in A Bottoms and J Roberts (eds), above n 16, 163 at 186.

[66] A Ashworth, 'Victim Impact Statements and Sentencing' (1993) *Criminal Law Review* 498.

[67] Gardner, above n 6 at 52; Murphy, above n 27 at 137.

[68] E Erez, 'Who's afraid of the Big Bad Victim? Victim Impact Statements as Victim Empowerment *and* Enhancement of Justice' (1999) *Criminal Law Review* 545 at 550–53; P Cassell, 'In Defense of Victim Impact Statements' (2008) 6 *Ohio State Journal of Criminal Law* 611 at 621–23;

wide temporal extensions rather than information tailored to the violation of rights. This invites two kinds of questions. The first is how comprehensive and personal victims' statements should be considered from a normative point of view; the second is whether judges manage to decide about sentences without being subconsciously influenced by expressive narratives.

The first question is a matter for sentencing theory, but within the scope of this article I can only mention one point. It makes sense to distinguish between *remote harms* (negative consequences for victims later in their lives) and the *immediate harm in its individualised dimensions*. An example for the former would be unemployment causally linked to the crime but occurring a year later. Immediate harm can have an individualised dimension if, for instance, a person experiences physical pain more intensely than others, or a blow fractures particularly thin bones, or if a victim's old age or personal attitudes towards sex[69] deepen the impact of rape. A punishment theory that defines crimes as violations of victims' rights does not support sentencing based on *all kind of consequences* that are only remotely connected to the criminal act. But immediate harms must be taken into account to compare crimes' seriousness – the concept of rights does not allow ranking of crimes that have violated the same right to non-intervention. These immediate harms should be ranked in a standardised way;[70] however, a particular victim's enhanced sensitivity can be an aggravating factor.[71] Sentencing theorists often put strong emphasis on offenders' fault and argue that unexpected and unfortunate consequences should not be taken into account.[72] The underlying idea that an offender must have been able to control the event in all details is, however, too ambitious.[73] General foreseeability is enough, and it is in general foreseeable that some persons and thus some victims are more sensitive and vulnerable than the average person. For these reasons, victims' account of their personal vulnerability matters for sentencing if it is necessary to understand the immediate harm done to them.[74]

J Roberts and E Erez, 'Communication in Sentencing: The Expressive Function of Victim Impact Statements', in A Bottoms and J Roberts (eds), above n 16, 232.

[69] See A Bottoms, 'The "Duty to Understand": What Consequences for Victim Participation?' in A Bottoms and J Roberts (eds), above n 16, 17 at 20.

[70] See A von Hirsch and N Jareborg, 'Gauging Criminal Harm: A Living-Standard Analysis' (1991) 11 *Oxford Journal of Legal Studies* 1; A von Hirsch, *Deserved Criminal Sentences* (Oxford and Portland, Hart, 2017) 64–67.

[71] Bottoms, above n 69 at 30–37, speaks of 'appreciative descriptions'.

[72] See A von Hirsch, *Past Or Future Crimes: Deservedness and Dangerousness in the Sentencing of Criminals* (Manchester, Manchester University Press, 1986) 65; A Ashworth, *Sentencing and Criminal Justice*, 6th edn (Cambridge, Cambridge University Press, 2015) 133.

[73] Criminal law theorists who assign individuals' choices a central position (see for instance, L Alexander and K Ferzan, *Crime and Culpability: A Theory of Criminal Law* (Cambridge, Cambridge University Press, 2009) ch 5) put too much emphasis on control. Ambitious visions of choice and control are illusionary as the pathways to events of all sorts and the effects of human actions are shaped by bad luck at many junctures: see M Moore, *Placing Blame* (Oxford, Oxford University Press, 1997) ch 5.

[74] M Wasik, 'Crime Seriousness and the Offender-Victim-Relationship in Sentencing' in A Ashworth and M Wasik (eds), above n 6, 103 at 125.

Other content in expressive victim statements, for example relating to remote harm and/or other reflections about their coping with the crime should be met with empathy and respect, but it is ultimately the sentencing judge's task to filter out the relevant aspects.

The main worries about expressive victim statements are rooted in psychology. They might undermine normative standards by evoking inappropriate emotions[75] and by exerting subconscious influence on judges. Even professional judges who are determined to base their sentencing decisions only on normatively relevant facts might be unwittingly influenced by expressions of strong emotions or personal appearances.[76] Psychological influences might raise overall sentence severity, and/or clash with the principle of equal treatment of offenders. Within the limited scope of this chapter, it is not possible to resolve the question of psychological impact. This is a matter of empirical research. If there are well-founded and strong indicators that judges do not manage to maintain the necessary degree of inner neutrality when confronted with expressive victim statements, and if this problem cannot be solved by institutional arrangements such as written rather than oral statements, these would be strong countervailing reasons against expressive victim statements. The crucial point for my purpose again is: emphasising the role of victims in punishment theory *does not automatically deliver answers for all aspects of sentencing*. It does set the course for some issues, but does not allow final conclusions on most controversial points.

VI. CONCLUSION

Justifications of state punishment that rely on a single rationale are not convincing. Without denying the importance of preventive reasoning and other collective interests, a satisfying theory should include references to victims' interests if the crime in question victimised an individual. Two lines of argument support this conclusion. First, we would have to expect negative consequences if the state were not to react to intrusions into the personal sphere of citizens. Victims' emotions and retaliatory urges must be channelled to avoid retaliatory violence or disappointed retreat. Secondly, for normative reasons the state must respond to behaviour that violates rights to non-intervention. Granting citizens the right that other citizens must not interfere with their bodily integrity, property, etc entails a duty for the state not to ignore such violations. Victims have the right to have the case examined, the right to obtain confirmation that a legal right to non-intervention has been violated, the right to have the degree of wrongdoing

---

[75] S Bandes, 'Empathy, Narrative, and Victim Impact Statements' (1996) 63 *University of Chicago Law Review* 361.
[76] See for a more positive assessment Roberts and Erez, above n 68 at 247–48.

assessed, and the right that the offender is censured. In most cases, censure must be expressed through hard treatment in order to convey an accurate and serious message. From this account of state punishment, it does not follow that the state must necessarily give crime victims a stronger position in criminal proceedings and sentencing. Victims' rights are only prima facie rights that must be weighed against other considerations such as the principle of equality or the limitation of resources available for prosecutions. Whether it is a good idea that victims can, for instance, appeal against the dismissal of cases and give accounts of their suffering in trials, depends on complex considerations that transcend the area of punishment theory.

12

Penal Desert and the Passage of Time

ANTJE DU BOIS-PEDAIN

HAT AN UNUSUALLY long time has passed between the commission of a criminal offence and its subsequent prosecution is taken by all criminal justice systems to raise special issues concerning the legitimacy of prosecution and punishment. Some leave such issues to be considered in the exercise of prosecutorial discretion, with a residual authority for trial judges to stop late prosecutions under 'abuse of process' rules. Others impose statutory limitation periods on the prosecution of some or all offences; where this is done, prosecution and punishment are then time-barred irrespective of a perceived public interest in conducting a late prosecution in the instant case. This chapter does not seek to provide a comprehensive analysis of such issues. To do so, it would have to engage with the range and variety of reasons that (on most theories of state punishment) have a bearing on, and help underpin, a state's criminal justice system as well as individual instances of the infliction of punishment. Instead, it addresses a more circumscribed question – a question, however, which (on nearly all theories of punishment) identifies a necessary precondition for imposing punishment. This is the question whether, notwithstanding the amount of time that has passed between the offender's commission of the crime and his subsequent trial and punishment, the offender still *deserves* to be punished for his crime.

I. CHALLENGING THE DESERT RELATION

A desert statement has the following general form: 'D deserves p for X'. In the context of our discussion 'X' stands for the commission of a criminal offence, 'D' stands for the agent to whom the commission of this offence is imputed, and 'p' stands for a specific amount of punishment. If we factor in the dimension of time, the basic desert relation can be restated as follows: '$D_{(NOW)}$ deserves $p_{(NOW)}$ for $X_{(THEN)}$' – (NOW) indicating the speaker's present time, and (THEN) indicating the time at which D committed X.

Note that the basic desert statement is diachronic. This is in fact typical of desert statements: it is only for the briefest of moments that 'then' is 'now'.

For practical purposes, all desert claims exhibit a diachronic pattern, suggesting that the basic desert relation should itself be understood diachronically.

On a widely held view of penal desert, it may appear evident that 'with the commission of the criminal deed the two parameters, wrongdoing and culpability, are permanently fixed and cannot be changed subsequently'.[1] Taken together with what has been termed the 'ledger' or 'book-keeping view' of penal desert, which holds that 'any unfair advantage enjoyed at an earlier time should be balanced by a corresponding later burden',[2] this implies that the type and severity of a particular deserved punishment will also remain time-invariant. Penal ill-desert (once it has arisen) stays 'on the books'. No subsequent development can change or remove this entry from the ledger; all such developments can do is produce offsetting entries that balance out the crime.[3] But there are others who disagree, not just with the 'ledger view' of desert but also, and specifically, with the stability of desert claims over time.

The passage of time has been taken to undermine the desert relation in different ways. Some authors contend that it puts pressure on the imputability of X to D. When analysed carefully, these views however do not so much attack the connection between D and X, as they attack the culprit's identity. Accepting that $X_{(THEN)}$ is properly imputable to $D_{(THEN)}$, these authors drive a wedge between $D_{(NOW)}$ and $D_{(THEN)}$, and deny *on this basis* that $D_{(NOW)}$ can deserve $p_{(NOW)}$ for $X_{(THEN)}$. Only $D_{(THEN)}$ (or, at any rate, some $D_{(BEFORE\ NOW)}$) deserved p for $X_{(THEN)}$.

Second, the passage of time can put pressure on the connection between $X_{(THEN)}$ and $p_{(NOW)}$. Perhaps $p_{(NOW)}$ is not deserved because $X_{(THEN)}$ no longer constitutes a suitable desert basis[4] for p? Authors who take this view argue that the primary or socially significant meaning of X changes with time. At the time of its commission (and for some time thereafter), the socially significant meaning of X is that X constitutes a criminal offence. X matters *qua* crime. Now, by

---

[1] A Kaufmann, *Das Schuldprinzip: eine strafrechtlich-rechtsphilosophische Untersuchung*, 2nd edn (Heidelberg, Universitätsverlag Winter, 1976) 259 (my translation). Kaufmann makes this point when addressing the potential relevance of post-offence conduct for sentencing.

[2] G Sher, *Desert* (Princeton NJ, Princeton University Press, 1989) 83. See also ibid at 95: 'In general, what is significant about an improper burden or benefit will not be its temporal location, but only its occurrence within a life.' This is so, according to Sher, because the relevant unit is the temporally extended person. Sher explicitly states that his principle of diachronic fairness applies to the benefits-and-burdens account of punishment which he adopts (ibid at 97).

[3] See eg Sher, above n 2, ch 5 and J Finnis, 'Responses', in J Keown and RP George (eds), *Reason, Morality, and Law: The Philosophy of John Finnis* (Oxford, Oxford University Press, 2013) 459 at 508.

[4] The desert basis is the characteristic or prior activity in virtue of which a person deserves something (J Feinberg, 'Justice and Personal Desert', in his *Doing and Deserving. Essays in the Theory of Responsibility* (Princeton, Princeton University Press, 1970) 55 at 58). As Feinberg also states, any desert statement must necessarily identify the desert basis; a person cannot deserve something for no particular reason at all (ibid). Pointing out the desert basis, however, falls short of a full justification of a desert claim. For this, we need to refer to the specific values and principles that ground a particular desert basis. As Sher explains, 'most desert-claims ... are grounded in values rather than in obligations' (above n 2 at 21), and for much of his book Sher is concerned to identify 'the more local principles and values ... associated with specific desert-bases' (above n 2 at 52).

contrast, X no longer matters *qua* crime. Its socially significant meaning now lies elsewhere, and for this reason X no longer constitutes a desert basis for the imposition of punishment.

It is also possible to hold, third, that the passage of time affects the appropriateness of $p_{(NOW)}$ to be imposed on $D_{(NOW)}$ – even on the assumption that the acts of $D_{(THEN)}$ are properly imputed to $D_{(NOW)}$, and that $X_{(THEN)}$ continues to provide a desert basis for $p_{(NOW)}$. Most of these views draw on reasons other than a weakening of the desert relation over time, or a diminishing amount of desert. Rather, they point to factors *other than desert* that should matter in the apportionment of punishment.[5] To the extent that they do, they fall outside my topic. What is within the remit of my topic is, however, the question whether (assuming the crime-related parameters of desert have remained constant) the type and duration of the punishment deserved by D immediately after the commission of the offence is necessarily identical to the type and duration of the punishment he deserves now, or whether he may genuinely deserve greater or less severe punishment.

Glossing over some conceptual nuances, I take the statement that 'D still deserves to be punished for X with p' to be equivalent to the claim that 'it would not be unfair for $D_{(NOW)}$ to be punished for $X_{(THEN)}$ with $p_{(NOW)}$'. It is, however, a different question whether '$D_{(NOW)}$ ought to be punished for $X_{(THEN)}$ with $p_{(NOW)}$'. That $D_{(NOW)}$ 'ought to be punished with $p_{(NOW)}$' follows only from the consideration of all factors that a given criminal justice system, and the justification for state punishment that underpins it, hold relevant in the instant case. 'Ought' is used in this 'all relevant things considered' way.[6] To the extent that the full consideration takes into account factors beyond D's desert, we cannot conclude from the fact that $D_{(NOW)}$ deserves $p_{(NOW)}$ for $X_{(THEN)}$, that $D_{(NOW)}$ ought to be punished with $p_{(NOW)}$ for $X_{(THEN)}$.

Desert theory holds that an offender's punishment should be proportionate to the harm caused by his crime and his level of culpability. Within relatively narrow limits the determinants of desert have thus crystallised, and the amount of 'desert' for a criminal act is consequently fixed at the point of completion of the offence.[7] While there can be special reasons for extending this timeframe

---

[5] Both historically and in the contemporary literature, considerations of forward-looking aspects or aims of punishment, eg that D's punishment no longer serves an important social purpose because the old crime no longer constitutes a present threat to social peace, that D presents no future risk and/or that he is socially well integrated, such that punishment is unnecessary for his rehabilitation, have been prominent reasons in favour of criminal limitation periods. For an overview of such arguments, see M Asholt, *Verjährung im Strafrecht* (Tübingen, Mohr Siebeck, 2016) esp at 116–41.

[6] The same distinction between desert-claims and all-things-considered oughts is drawn by Feinberg, above n 4 at 60.

[7] For a full discussion of how to calibrate harm and culpability, and of special issues pertaining to particular categories of offenders, see A von Hirsch and A Ashworth, *Proportionate Sentencing: Exploring the Principles* (Oxford, Oxford University Press, 2005). Here, von Hirsch and Ashworth suggest in Appendix 1 that the fact that an unusually long time has elapsed between the commission of the offence and its prosecution, can permit equity-based mitigation of punishment (which also implies that they do not view this fact as affecting either harm or culpability levels).

in order to properly answer the question how much harm is attributable to the offence (say, latent harms have blossomed, initially unknown late-onset harms have materialised, reactive or secondary harms have occurred that are attributable to the original crime), and while (more controversially) there may be grounds for allowing certain post-offence conduct of the offender to influence, prior to sentence, the level of harm or the level of culpability that is attributed to the offender in respect of his crime,[8] the basic position remains that it is *the harm and culpability encapsulated in this crime* that determines how much punishment an offender deserves.[9]

This chapter addresses the ways in which the passage of time has been taken to destabilise the desert relation between D's commission of crime X, and his punishment. In section II, it investigates how the crime's dimension as a wrongful harm is affected by time. Against authors who assume the crime to be on a unidirectional slide towards 'historicisation', I maintain that the picture is more uneven, as even long-ago crimes can experience 'diachronic spikes' in their social significance. The effect of time on the actuality of the crime depends on context, and that context changes with time. Section III turns to the effects of time on an agent's culpability. Drawing on the tripartite model of moral responsibility put forward by David Shoemaker, it shows and explains culpability shifts over time – and particularly, how time affects what the crime tells us about D's self/character. I deny, however, that the attribution-relation can be entirely severed by profound personality changes over time. Against this, I argue that biographical-biological agential identity rather than psychological connectedness matters for continuing responsibility-ascription. Culpability levels can be modified over time but culpability continues to attach to the agent for as long as his biographical-biological identity persists. In section IV, I address the question how time affects penal desert. Beyond factoring in shifts in culpability and harm that have occurred since the commission of the offence, the calibration of the deserved punishment also needs to take into account the location of the punishment in the offender's life-course. Some adjustments to the form punishment takes may have to be made even when the aim is to achieve equivalent levels of penal severity. I also explore why, and how, the fact that late punishment no longer occupies its usual place in the sequence of events that shape an offender's life can undermine the conclusion that the offender still deserves to be punished.

---

[8] For such an argument, see JV Roberts and H Maslen, 'After the Crime: Post-offence Conduct and Penal Censure', in AP Simester, A du Bois-Pedain and U Neumann (eds), *Liberal Criminal Theory: Essays for Andreas von Hirsch* (Oxford, Hart, 2014) 87.

[9] But see Julian Roberts and Netanel Dagan (in this collection), who argue that offenders can bring down the culpability-based component of their deserved sentence by responding appropriately to their punishment – what they call the 'dynamic censure' perspective. When this occurs in the process of a punishment's continuing imposition the offender acquires a moral right to an appropriate modification of his sentence to reflect his subsequently reduced level of desert. For further discussion of Roberts' and Dagan's view, see section IV below.

II. THE TEMPORALITY OF THE WRONG

It is a familiar fact of life that harms brought about through wrongful actions may take time to emerge or develop fully, and judges and juries frequently have to decide whether late-maturing or reactive harms can still be laid at the wrongdoer's door. The issue in such cases is causation (or what in the continental tradition is referred to as imputation). Where the connection between D's action and a harmful outcome is mediated by an ever-growing range of additional influences and events, we encounter not only evidential uncertainties about the continuing effectiveness of D's contribution but also a normative concern: whether (given all else that has happened since) it is still fair to ascribe responsibility for the outcome to D.[10]

Some theorists connect this issue to the question which concerns us here – the effect that the mere passage of time may have on the quality of a wrong *qua* wrong.[11] This association is encouraged by the language used to formulate the relevant causation doctrines, such as whether the initial causal event has become merely part of the 'setting' in which other causes operate.[12] If a wrong can lose its salience *as a cause* on account of the many other things that happen as time moves on, can it not also lose its salience *as a wrong* or crime, and simply become history instead?

Focusing on when a penal response by the state is appropriate, in the German literature an argument has been developed that, with the passage of time, crimes lose their valence as crimes that call for a penal response. This argument's philosophical underpinnings rest on the corroding influence of time on the significance of an act as a criminal wrong. The idea is that crimes instantiate certain legal relations between perpetrators, victims and the state/polity, and time has a corrosive effect on the current significance of these relations. At the point of its commission, the crime gives rise to a web of legal claims that the legal system is there to enforce. But no legal claim lasts forever. An expectation of limited duration is built into the system.[13] If, somewhat differently,

---

[10] This issue has been extensively discussed in the German literature, also in relation to the application of limitation periods. See, eg, C Gomez-Rivero, 'Zeitliche Dimension und objektive Zurechnung' (2001) 148 *Goltdammer's Archiv für Strafrecht* 283 and S Gless, 'Zeitliche Differenz zwischen Handlung und Erfolg – insbesondere als Herausforderung an das Verjährungsrecht' (2006) 153 *Goltdammer's Archiv für Strafrecht* 689.

[11] See, eg, Asholt, above n 5 at 418–37. Compare also J Coleman and A Sarch, 'Blameworthiness and Time' (2012) *Legal Theory* 1. Their paper, which is centrally about the appropriateness of reactive emotions over time, includes an extensive discussion of the potential difference made by the much-later materialisation of what was initially only a fairly small risk of a late-onset harm (at 16 ff).

[12] This formulation occurs frequently in causation judgments, eg *R v Smith* [1959] 2 Q.B. 35 (at 43); *R v Hughes* [2013] UKSC 56 at [23].

[13] See esp. Asholt, above n 5 at 279–82, R Bloy, *Die dogmatische Bedeutung der Strafausschließungs- und Strafaufhebungsgründe* (Berlin, Duncker & Humblot, 1976). For a philosophical argument that builds explicitly on the temporal fragility of legal entitlements, see YG Hong, *Zeitablauf als Grenze des staatlichen Strafanspruchs. Eine Studie zu den rechtsphilosophischen Grundlagen der Verjährung unter besonderer Berücksichtigung der Problematik der Unverjährbarkeit* (Frankfurt, Peter Lang, 2005).

we think with Nils Christie of crimes as social 'conflicts',[14] the point is that these 'conflicts' eventually die down by themselves, leaving the criminal justice system with nothing to respond to. The polity must treat such evaporated conflicts as 'past', as ones that cannot now be legitimately processed through the criminal justice system. The suggestion is not that 'history heals all wounds' but that it turns everything into history – into a fact that is worth noting and remembering, but that is no longer a call to reactive action now. 'For the perpetrator [and, one should probably add, the victim], the crime becomes part of his life story; for the polity it becomes part of its social history of criminality.'[15] But how confident can we be that crimes are thus 'historicised'? To address the soundness of this assumption, we need to look more closely at the temporal dimension of crime and its meaning.

A. The Shifting Significance of Crimes over Time from the Victim's and the Polity's Points of View

Consider a case decided by the Court of Appeal for England and Wales in 2015.[16] GB was tried, convicted and sentenced at the age of 68 for indecent assaults and incest committed upon his sister in the 1960s, when GB was 15 and his sister 14. The family of six had lived in very cramped circumstances, the children sleeping in the same bed. GB had lived an exemplary life since reaching adulthood and had often helped out his sister. His sister had had a troubled existence and had increasingly come to blame GB's sexual abuse of her when they were children for the difficulties she experienced in her subsequent life. The prosecution was brought after GB's sister had confronted GB about what he had done to her when they were children, and she had taped that conversation, including his admissions and apology to her. GB was initially sentenced to 15 months' imprisonment, which was replaced by the Court of Appeal with a non-custodial sentence. In reducing the sentence, the Court did not raise the question whether the amount of time that had passed since the commission of the offence was, as such, a mitigating factor. In explaining why it was wrong *in this case* to impose a more severe sentence on the adult than would have faced the youth (something that can occur, within limits, in the move from sentencing a youth to sentencing an adult for what the adult did as a youth on account of a shift away from educational intervention as the main purpose of the sentence), the Court stressed that: '[A]s an adult, he has led an honest and industrious life for 50 years. He has been of considerable assistance to all his family, including the complainant and her immediate family. He is remorseful. He has acknowledged what he did and

---

[14] N Christie, 'Conflicts as Property' (1977) 17 *British Journal of Criminology* 1.
[15] Bloy, above n 13 at 189 (my translation).
[16] *R v GB* [2015] EWCA Crim 1501.

he has been punished'.[17] A mild, non-custodial sentence was thus considered appropriate even allowing for the fact that the offence had caused substantial harm to the complainant, who may well have expected a heavier sentence.[18]

A commentator on the case, concerned by the apparent pointlessness of 'prosecuting a man of 67 [of, in his adult life, exemplary character] for his improper behaviour with a sister of similar age when they were 13, 14 and 15', took the case to raise the question whether prescription periods should be introduced at least for offences committed by juveniles.[19] When prescription is thus thrown into the ring, the basic thought is that there is a temporality to demands of justice because there is a temporality to the wrong itself. This temporality is a complex matter. We can see this by following German criminal law scholar Martin Asholt's example of exploring the effects of time on the quality of a wrong through the prism of a late nineteenth-century German novel, *Effi Briest*.[20] The novel is set among the Prussian upper classes. Effi's husband, Baron von Innstetten, who is more than 20 years Effi's senior and married Effi when she was just a teenager, discovers nearly ten years after the fact that, early on in their marriage, his wife had an affair with another man. After much to-ing and fro-ing he calls the other man to a duel. But he does reflect, in conversation with a friend, that it was perhaps unfortunate that he found out about the affair before even more time had passed. Had he discovered it only when he was already in his seventies, and Effi well into middle-age, it would have been wrong to act on the fact of the affair to reassert his honour. As things are, he feels that he must still act on it to defend his family's honour, even though it is clear that the affair is over, and has long been so.

Time thus affects the wrong done by Effi and her lover to her husband's honour in multiple ways. First of all, Innstetten understands the honour norm itself, according to which he is now expected to reassert his family honour by calling the ex-lover to a duel, as one which has a temporal limitation built into it. At some (unspecified) point in time, the norm no longer demands – or even conceivably justifies – his shooting of his wife's former lover in a duel. Secondly, even though Innstetten still takes action against the adulterer, the passage of time has already affected his grounds for doing so. If he had discovered the affair when it was still 'hot' (or very recent), we can imagine – as Innstetten himself imagines – that he would have called the other man to a duel out of anger and jealousy, and the duel would have been a welcome outlet for both.

---

[17] Ibid at [21].

[18] Ibid at [22].

[19] See the editor John Spencer's brief comment following the case summary in *Archbold Review*, Issue 2, 25 March 2016, 5.

[20] For an English edition of the novel, see T Fontane, *Effi Briest* [1896] translated by H Rorrison and introduced by H Chambers (London, Penguin, 2000). For Asholt's discussion of the story (which differs from mine), see above n 5 at 224 and 263.

Now (he admits to his friend), he isn't angry or passionate about the affair. *Qua* cuckolded husband ('victim' of the wrong) he is tempted to let it go. What sways him in his decision to call the other man to a duel is his belief that he has no choice but to uphold the relevant social norm. As the affair has already become public knowledge, he would be perceived as unprincipled if he failed to act.

In Innstetten's case, the perspectives of the victim and of the normative community on the susceptibility of the wrong to fading over time are aligned. But a case like that of GB, with which I started this section, complicates the assumption of a fading of the wrong over time. Here, the wrong seems to have festered with the complainant. While it may have appeared at earlier phases in her life that – like the defendant – she had left these experiences behind her, as time went on she seems to have become more and more preoccupied with what he had done to her and how it had shaped her life. Some of that increase in significance may well have been due to her repeated experience of marriage breakdown and her search for the reasons. And it is quite possible that a third-party observer might reach the view that her own interpretation of the causes of her personal difficulties was mistaken; that much of it rebounded on her and had nothing to do with the defendant's crimes against her. But the point is that, from her perspective, his sexually abusing her *was* the explanation, and it led to her growing obsession with confronting him with his crimes and with seeing him punished.

B. Temporality, Diachronic Significance and Different Affected Entities' Time Frames

The case of GB thus reminds us that there is no linearity in how the passage of time affects the significance of the wrong. The basic assumption that, with time, wrongs stop being 'actual' (demanding to be addressed in the here and now), and become 'historical' or 'matters of mere historical interest', may not be accurate, both as regards their individual-psychological significance and as regards their collective-societal importance. Indeed, we find it perfectly possible to make sense of the suggestion that a certain wrong 'matters more today' than it did at the time of its commission. This is so because wrongs do not so much get historicised as that they are always already contextualised, and their context changes as time moves on.

If we accept that the significance of a wrong is not firmly linked to the linear flow of time but depends in part on its context, a context that can change significantly through future developments, we can see why wrongs have the potential for 'diachronic spikes' in their significance long after the fact. It is not unusual for people to come to wish, years after the event, that they 'hadn't let this or that go' – and that wish need not be based on having nothing better to do than dwelling on 'old stuff' but can well arise from some external factor that makes the long-ago wrong seem particularly important now.

A second point is also implicit in our discussion: the wrong matters differently to 'the public' and to the individuals affected by it. 'The public' may well consider that a particular wrong is no longer worth bringing up against D, or conversely may wish to bring it up even though the victim can hardly recall the experience. More problematically, the reasons why a crime is taken to have kept or increased its social significance may have nothing at all to do with the perpetrator and the victim in the particular case. It is not implausible to think that the decision to prosecute GB owed less to a desire to meet the expectations of the complainant than to a sense that the prosecution service could not afford to be seen to decline to prosecute sexual crimes committed in a domestic context against a young victim – given the police and prosecution authorities' frankly atrocious historical record of failing to take (the victims of) these offences seriously enough.[21] Minus the context of a still-festering public scandal about systemic failures spanning decades to protect the victims of child sex offences, it is quite possible that no prosecution would have been brought against GB. For the criminal law, the temporality question thus links up with the question of whose time frame ought to matter most for resort to criminal punishment. The examples we have considered destabilise the notion that we can predict with confidence when a criminal wrong is no longer part of our present-day concerns but merely a matter of historical interest.

Our discussion has therefore not clearly supported the assumption underlying the 'historicisation' model: that wrongful harms fairly regularly, consistently and, as it were, unidirectionally, lose their significance as wrongful harms over time. It has, however, also illustrated a particularly grave risk that improper considerations might influence and, indeed, become determinative of, prosecutorial choices. How would we, for example, react if Effi, aged 70, demanded the prosecution of her husband (by then in his nineties) for the murder of her lover, stating that the older she got, the more it rankled her that her husband had shot her lover, firmly believing that every unhappiness in her later life, of which there were many, could be traced back to this essential fact?[22] Given the time at which the novel is set, we have to imagine that Effi's demand would be made in the early 1930s, in a country that had, in the meantime, lost the First World War, experienced ravaging economic collapse and a revolution that ousted the Kaiser and created the Weimar Republic, a fragile political entity at best where

---

[21] England has for some years been undergoing a spate of late prosecutions for historic sex offences, and with depressing frequency it emerges from the facts that the victims did complain to police (or other authorities) at the time but were dismissed as unreliable, with no proper investigations into the allegations being conducted. These late prosecutions have thus both a morally compensatory and an institutional dimension to them, the latter consisting in police and prosecution authorities being keen to signal that they have broken with their old, improper, ways.

[22] The character in the novel dies young and broken. By contrast, the young aristocratic woman whose fate inspired Fontane's story (and who had been in love with, and planning to marry, her illicit lover when her husband killed him in a duel) lived to the venerable age of 99, dying only in 1952. See Helen Chambers' Introduction to *Effi Briest*, above n 20 at ix.

the remnants of Prussian officer culture were to some official eyes a threat to the stability of the government. So it is not hard to imagine that her call for prosecution would have fallen on receptive ears, the state having some considerable interest in driving home the message that duels and other honour killings are not honourable killings but ordinary murder. Should, therefore, 90-year-old Innstetten be brought to court? I confess I am just as conflicted about the right answer as I was at the start of this section, and clutch at the thought – rather than think it a full answer – that this was a very serious crime and that this *categorisation* surely still matters. The fairly impure and opportunistic motivations of complainant (revenge) and prosecutor (political message-sending) that I have sketched in this paragraph may simply clutter the picture. They may strike us as inappropriate but not make us doubt that punishment would be deserved.

III. THE TEMPORALITY OF GUILT

Under a narrow conception of culpability that reduces this concept to *mens rea*, it is difficult to see how an agent's level of culpability cannot be fixed at the commission of the crime. He will have acted intentionally, knowingly, recklessly, carelessly or negligently, and that's that. But hardly anyone thinks that this notion of culpability is exhaustive. Philosophical investigations into our blaming responses reveal that, emotionally and practically, we react to a much wider range of culpability determinants than simply the agent's *mens rea* at the time of the action. We care about the motives and motivations that stood behind his culpable choice, about the degree to which the agent identifies with these motives and motivations, about circumstantial and historical factors that influenced the agent in forming these attitudes, about how settled these attitudes are, etc. Sentencing decisions in particular engage with these additional factors and concerns.[23] Culpability in this wider sense is what German criminal law theorists mean with the expression 'criminal guilt'.

In this section, I draw on a tripartite model of responsibility developed by the philosopher David Shoemaker to explore how culpability assessments in respect of the same past act might change over time. Those familiar with Shoemaker's work may be surprised by this choice, given that Shoemaker himself has argued that his conception of moral responsibility is inapplicable to judgments of criminal responsibility.[24] Without being able to go into this discussion here,

---

[23] For a sustained analysis of sentencing practice, see CB Hessick, 'Motive's Role in Criminal Punishment' (2006) 80 *Southern Californian Law Review* 89.

[24] See D Shoemaker, 'Blame and Punishment' in DJ Coates and NA Tognazzini (eds), *Blame: Its Nature and Norms* (Oxford, Oxford University Press, 2012) 100 and D Shoemaker, 'On Criminal and Moral Responsibility' in M Timmons (ed), *Oxford Studies in Normative Ethics* vol 3 (Oxford, Oxford University Press, 2013) 154.

I believe (as do other critics of Shoemaker's work, who have argued the point at length) that Shoemaker is mistaken in this regard.[25] In any event, my use of Shoemaker's model in the context of the present discussion must stand or fall on its own terms.

In what follows, I will use the term responsibility interchangeably with culpability and guilt. The reason is that the different dimensions of responsibility Shoemaker gives such nuanced accounts of, in substance concern what criminal lawyers more standardly address under the heading of culpability, and what some moral philosophers, and German criminal-law scholars, incorporate into their conception of guilt.[26]

With these preliminary clarifications out of the way, we can turn to presentation and application of the model.

A. The Tripartite Model of Responsibility and Culpability Shifts over Time

Shoemaker holds that an agent can be a proper target of responsibility-assessments along three different axes: answerability, which tracks the agent's quality of judgment; accountability, which tracks the agent's quality of intersubjective regard; and attributability, which tracks the agent's quality of character.[27] (I will sometimes use the compound terms answerability-responsibility, accountability-responsibility and attributability-responsibility to underline the specific sense in which Shoemaker employs these concepts.[28])

Answerability-responsibility addresses the agent's conduct as an instance of his rational agency. To be answerable, D must be so constituted that we can engage with him in a dialogue about his reasons for what he did. On this axis of assessment, others respond to the agent's conduct with approval or disapproval,

---

[25] The most comprehensive discussion of objections and counter-arguments can be found in D Lefkowitz, 'Blame and the Criminal Law' (2015) 6 *Jurisprudence* 451. See also RA Duff, 'Moral and Criminal Responsibility: Answering and Refusing to Answer', available at https://papers.ssrn.com/sol3/papers.cfm?abstract_id=3055111 (version of 18 December 2017).

[26] For the philosophical literature, see eg G Taylor, *Pride, Shame, and Guilt. Emotions of Self-Assessment* (Oxford, Clarendon Press, 1985), ch 4 (with particular emphasis on the connection between guilt feelings and the self-conception of agents). For the German criminal-law literature, see Kaufmann, above n 1. The literature on blame and blameworthiness also has significant conceptual overlap.

[27] Most fully set out in D Shoemaker, *Responsibility from the Margins* (Oxford, Oxford University Press, 2015).

[28] The compound terms are helpful in avoiding confusion, since these terms otherwise tend to be associated with the steps of a criminal-law enquiry, with attribution referring to the agency-requirement-stage, answerability to what arises when all offence elements have been found against the agent, and accountability referring to the liability finding that follows when, in addition, the agent has no supervening defence. As Shoemaker uses these terms, they stand for different clusters of concerns that form part of a full culpability assessment. Other philosophers employ them as well with rather different meanings.

and the agent himself thinks of his action with satisfaction or regret. When holding D answerability-responsible, we thus focus on how D's action speaks to D's judgement. Holding D answerable means that we evaluate his action as an expression of D's rationality.[29]

That an agent is accountable means, for Shoemaker, that his act is one for which D can potentially be confronted with an angry response; this in turn depends on what the act tells us about the quality of D's regard for other people.[30] When we hold an agent accountability-responsible, we thus evaluate his action with regard to his interpersonal dispositions, and we condemn him to the extent that his reasons betray a culpable failure to treat other persons with due regard for their interests and rights. In an earlier article, Shoemaker connects accountability-responsibility to norm-violations, suggesting that someone is accountability-responsible when he 'flouts relationship-defining demands'.[31] This dimension of responsibility is often emphasised in criminal-law contexts. Shoemaker links it to (and, in fact, tracks it through) sanctioning behaviours, in the following way: 'What it must mean to hold someone to account is precisely to sanction that person, whether it be via the expression of a reactive attitude, public shaming, or something more psychologically or physically damaging.'[32]

Attributability is the notion Shoemaker reserves for the connection between an action and the agent's self or character.[33] When a deed X is attributable to D in Shoemaker's sense, it makes D subject to moral appraisal as a person; others evaluate D with admiration or disdain in respect of X. We hold an agent attributability-responsible when we take his act to reflect on his traits, values and commitments more generally, on what Shoemaker terms his 'deep self'. Attributability-responsibility is about what kind of person the agent is, and about how the action in question speaks to that.[34]

To get a sense of this conception of the self, think of agents as possessing 'volitional webs that are ... relevant to motivation and expressive of the agents' ... selves, regardless of those agents' subjective attitudes toward these features'.[35] According to a long philosophical tradition that starts with Locke, human beings are self-constituting agents: we construct ourselves in part through our thinking, self-reflection, and feelings, and in part through our actions. Our actions are thus not somehow external to us and separable from our 'inner being'; rather they emanate from and are emanations of our selves. Looking at

---

[29] For a fuller account of answerability, see Shoemaker, above n 27, ch 2.

[30] Addressed fully in Shoemaker ibid, ch 3.

[31] D Shoemaker, 'Attributability, Answerability, and Accountability: Toward a Wider Theory of Moral Responsibility' (2011) 121 *Ethics* 602, at 623.

[32] Ibid.

[33] See generally, Shoemaker, above n 27, ch 1.

[34] See Shoemaker, above n 31 at 611.

[35] D Shoemaker, 'Responsibility without Identity' (2012) 18 *Harvard Review of Philosophy* 109 at 126.

an action as self-constituting activity, we can ask questions such as: what sort of person does that action constitute me as; what sort of person is that action bringing into being?[36]

This is the proper context for considering whether the act was a lapse or the implementation of a prior plan, and (if the former) what sort of lapse it was. But it is important to be clear how the answers to such questions reflect on an agent's culpability. Philosophers sometimes talk as if an act that is not in accordance with my considered values, deep-seated preferences and commitments, second-order desires, and the like, forms no part of my character or true self.[37] That is, of course, nonsense. The important question is not whether it reflects on my character, but how.

Part of the confusion is owed to a tendency to essentialise the notion of character, and the role played by an agent's values in action. We are then tempted to ask whether the agent has good or bad values and traits, and identify his values and traits with his 'character'. Against this, George Sher maintains that the values and traits which such statements refer to are not the bedrock from which an action springs, but are 'merely an incidental consequence' of a 'vastly broader combination of desires, beliefs, and dispositions' that form an agent's internal makeup at a particular time, none of which need be bad in themselves.[38] Sher uses this argument to show how what we think of as a 'lapse' is connected to an agent's character. A lapse is produced by a confluence of traits and action tendencies that are not in themselves morally bad but coalesce on a particular occasion to produce a morally evil act – say, lead a generally decent agent to act cruelly on a particular occasion.[39] As Sher points out, that act of cruelty is then quite properly described as a lapse or an act that was 'out of character' for the agent – but in a sense that does not block attribution of responsibility, and blame, since it is true about the agent 'both that cruelty is no part *of* his character and that this particular cruel act is firmly rooted *in* his character.'[40]

Sher demonstrates thereby that a lapse is as much based in D's character as an act that stems from a consciously pursued personal campaign or commitment. But (as Sher's discussion also implies) if we attribute an act to D as a lapse, we are condemning D for something different (and usually less serious) than when we attribute an act to D as flowing from a commitment on his part.

---

[36] Compare on the self-generative aspects of agency (and their complicated relation to guilt) Taylor, above n 26 at 92–97 and 134–35. (For further discussion, see section III B below). Taylor also correctly locates second-order desires and weakness of will in the problem of agential integrity rather than responsibility (114 ff) and offers valuable insights on agents without integrity (at 114 and 129).

[37] I do not mean to suggest that the philosophers in question also want to defend this view. It may be more a case of using language and descriptions of agency that invite this (mis-)understanding.

[38] G Sher, *In Praise of Blame* (Oxford, Oxford University Press, 2005) 47.

[39] G Sher, 'Blameworthy Action and Character' (2002) 64 *Philosophy and Phenomenological Research* 381.

[40] Ibid at 389 (emphasis in original).

This is so even when the lapse is one that (as Nomy Arpaly nicely explains) reveals D's deep-seated preferences and desires, rather than a mere fleeting attitude or concern that is born of the occasion and the opportunity.[41] We are inclined to view as less reprehensible the paedophile who believes that what he dreams of doing to children would be wrong to do, and therefore makes considerable efforts to resist temptation, from which he has lapsed, than the paedophile who believes that what he is doing to children is (his) right, since it serves his pleasure.

We can now also put aside a potential worry of those who think character-assessments should have no place in assessments of criminal guilt. As Sher explains,

> By ... tracing the features of the act that make it bad to the interaction of a number of desires, beliefs, and dispositions, none of which need itself be bad, we may hope to avoid the objection that what justifies us in condemning the agent is something that would equally well justify us in condemning him if he did not act badly; while by demonstrating that the same desires, beliefs, and dispositions that collectively give rise to the act's badness are in addition collectively crucial to the agent's identity, we may also hope to establish the needed link between his act's badness and him.[42]

What this means is that every action that makes it past the fairly minimal agency-requirements of the criminal law opens the agent up to responsibility-appraisals along all three axes of Shoemaker's model.

How does Shoemaker's model help us make sense of culpability shifts over time? This we can see by looking at an example which I have adapted slightly from one introduced by Andrew Khoury:[43]

> Jane insults her brother at t_1. The insulting remark slipped out during an argument with her brother and surprised Jane. She realised immediately that her brother felt very hurt by it. At the time she felt, to some extent, bad about what she'd said but also a little pleased with herself for having spoken her mind. Time goes by and:
>
> *(Alternative A)* At t_2, Jane no longer feels bad about the insult at all. Quite the contrary: it fills her with satisfaction to recall her brother's shocked face and his inability to think of a good retort. If she had to do it all over again she would make an even more cutting remark. In fact, the first insult was something of a dam-breaker and she has insulted her brother on other occasions since.
>
> *(Alternative B)* At t_2, Jane feels ashamed of the spark of self-satisfaction she felt after insulting her brother. She doesn't want to be a nasty person. She has resolved to watch her tongue in the future. In fact, since the original insult she has not insulted her brother again, even though they have had plenty more disagreements. She wants to apologise to her brother but so far has not found the right moment to do so.

---

[41] N Arpaly, 'Moral Psychology's Drinking Problem' in I Fileva (ed), *Questions of Character* (Oxford, Oxford University Press, 2016) 121 at 129.

[42] Sher, above n 38 at 40.

[43] AC Khoury, 'Synchronic and Diachronic Responsibility' (2013) *Philosophical Studies* 735 (description of Jane's case adapted from the versions presented by Khoury on 737 and 742).

How would we analyse Jane's guilt in terms of Shoemaker's model? As regards answerability, when Jane made the insulting remark at t_1 she was carried away during an argument with her brother and the insulting remark 'just came out' before she had thought about it. Jane is clearly able to give an account of the reasons for her action, an account that (if she is honest) will include that the insult picked up on some things she really does think and feel about her brother, although she would not normally express them in this way. She can give an explanation for her action that we can engage with, and that explanation reveals the insult as an intentional but spontaneous utterance whose expression owes much to a failure of self-monitoring ('watching her mouth') in the heat of the argument. Turning to accountability, the making of the insult does show a failure of interpersonal regard. Clearly, at that moment part of what Jane meant to express was contempt for her brother in respect of the features of his personality the insult picked up on. She also wanted to hurt his feelings (although she was at best dimly aware of that). Finally, consider her attributability-responsibility. How deep-seated or ingrained that failure of regard is, we don't really know. It could be more akin to a moral lapse, or it could be a quite pervasive aspect of her character – though one that she has so far not revealed to others, and may not have become fully aware of herself. But the insult brings up the issue, even for her. It puts this potential aspect of her moral make-up on the table for her, awaiting self-reflection and self-inspection.

In *Alternative A*, such self-inspection leads her to endorse the unrestrained insulter that her first insult revealed to her as a possible self. True, she only by accident 'stumbled over' the insulter who had been lurking inside her; she had no awareness of that potential self before her verbal outburst. When it happened, though, she saw the kind of sister that the insult created, and that was the sort of sister she wanted to be from now on. In *Alternative B*, by contrast, self-inspection leads Jane to reject the kind of person that the insult makes her. It clashes with her previous self-image of herself as a polite and well-disciplined person who can occupy the moral high ground, and she cares very much about being that person. The kind of sister the insult creates – someone who feels self-satisfaction at having successfully hurt the feelings of her brother – is not compatible with that self-image. The insulter must be expelled from her self – and, ideally, she would even expel the insult itself from the relational record (hence her desire to apologise to her brother).

It is probably not pushing intuition too much to assume that most people will agree that Jane is less culpable for the insult in *Alternative B* than in *Alternative A*.[44] In *Alternative B*, the overall assessment of Jane's culpability leads us to address the insult as a mere lapse – a moment of weakness by which she let herself down. In *Alternative A*, by contrast, we look upon the insult as the first manifestation of the person Jane truly wants to be. She may have thought of

---

[44] Khoury, focusing on the related concept of blameworthiness, concludes that Jane is more blameworthy in (his version of) *Alternative A* than *Alternative B* (ibid at 742).

herself as a polite and well-disciplined person who can occupy the moral high ground, but when she discovered how good it feels not to be that person she never looked back. In *Alternative A*, she is the kind of person who enjoys insulting people (though she did feel a little bad about it that first time), as opposed to the Jane in *Alternative B* who feels bad about insulting people (though she did feel a spark of self-satisfaction about it that first time). So the insult reflects differently on Jane as a person in these scenarios, and more badly on her in *Alternative A* than in *Alternative B*.

My analysis here has treated Jane's reactions to her utterance of the insult as revealing something about what was going on at the time she made that insult. But it is, of course, just as plausible to analyse her reactions as something that comes only, and affects how things are, *after* the insult. This is a crucial difference for those who maintain that criminal desert must take D's culpability at t_1 as the desert basis and, at least in principle, treat diminished (or, for that matter, enhanced) culpability levels at t_2 as irrelevant. Everything then turns on whether we treat the further information that D's reactions and subsequent behaviour provide us with, as evidence about his precise culpability level at t_1, or as indicative of his 'developed' culpability level at t_2.[45] To my mind, it is simply impossible to know which of the two it is. Take GB, whose case we have already looked at in section II.[46] We simply do not know whether GB was always going to be a decent adult, even partly in reaction to feeling bad about what he had done to his sister, such that the abuse of his sister is by his subsequent life 'revealed' to us as a lapse from moral standards he has always endorsed, or whether he did not have those standards at the time but later came to see the wrongness of his (old) ways and changed accordingly – such that the question would be whether he should be given credit for a remorseful change of self, with no claim that this later change tells us anything about the level of guilt he had when he committed these crimes.

What follows from this for me is that, if we want to justify in the criminal-law context the sort of culpability assessment that Shoemaker's conception of attributability-responsibility invites us to make, we have to defend the view that an agent's reaction to the crime is properly part of gauging his culpability in respect of the crime – and that it simply doesn't matter in this context whether he 'changed' subsequently in reacting to the crime, or not. This is the position I will defend in the next sub-section with reference to Gabriele Taylor's work on guilt. Before we can turn to this issue, however, we have to address a different question. Since adopting this view means accepting that genuine changes in culpability levels may occur over time, we need to engage with the arguments of

---

[45] This appears to be Roberts' and Maslen's position in respect of how, and why, post-offence conduct may matter in an assessment of D's culpability for the crime. See Roberts and Maslen, above n 8 at 98–100 and 102 (suggesting that the decisive question is whether the offender's post-offence conduct provides evidence of his weak commitment to the offence at the time of its commission, and that we should look upon it as doing just that).

[46] *R v GB* [2015] EWCA Crim 1501, discussed in the text at nn 15–19 above.

those who think that a person's change over time has an even more radical effect on the agent's responsibility for her past actions.

B. Guilt, Identity and Integrity over Time

The thought that D has *after the crime* become the sort of person who would never do this sort of thing, can be taken not merely to show that D's culpability level is now lower than we would have assessed it contemporaneously, because we are confident that it is *now* true that the act was merely a lapse and not an expression of traits D cultivates and cherishes: it can be taken to show that $D_{(NOW)}$ is just so different from $D_{(THEN)}$ that the former cannot be held responsible for the actions of the latter. This conclusion seems particularly tempting when a lot of time has passed and D's personality change has been profound and all-encompassing, such that one has real difficulty seeing any trace of his former self in him now. Different philosophers have been drawn to this view.[47] I will respond here to a version of the argument advanced by Andrew Khoury, which I will refer to as the 'non-identity challenge'.

Khoury argues that what matters for our responsibility for our past acts is not our physical or biographical identity with the past agent, but instead depends on a sufficient degree of 'psychological connectedness' between our past and present self (or what I refer to as $D_{(THEN)}$ and $D_{(NOW)}$).[48] Relevant psychological connectedness depends on the persistence of those of 'the agent's psychological properties [beliefs, desires, values, and so on][49] ... that gave rise to the action; those that make up the motivational structure that brought about the act'.[50] $D_{(NOW)}$ is responsible at t_2 for what $D_{(THEN)}$ did at t_1 when we can establish a connection between 'those psychological elements that issued in the action and the agent's later psychology',[51] summing up the position thus: 'what matters

---

[47] The most well-known of these is D Parfit, *Reasons and Persons* (Oxford, Oxford University Press, 1984) 326.

[48] Khoury, above n 43. In a joint paper with Benjamin Matheson ('Is Blameworthiness Forever?', forthcoming in the *Journal of the American Philosophical Association*, available at https://phil-papers.org/rec/KHOIBF-2) Khoury and Matheson argue further that, since blameworthiness presupposes a flaw in the subject, a now-flawless subject (or one that no longer has the flaw in question) is no longer blameworthy for past acts that stemmed from that flaw. If one were to take this as an independent argument, it would have the counterintuitive implication that anyone who immediately 'learns their lesson' when they commit a particular wrong (say, someone's happy excitement when taking unreasonable risks in traffic is, after a 'near-miss' episode of overtaking dangerously, immediately replaced with an aversion to taking such risks), is instantaneously no longer blameworthy for the act that stemmed from the flaw. That can't be right. I therefore view the 'now-flawless subject' argument as a mere embellishment or illustration of when an agent at t_2 is relevantly 'psychologically disconnected' from that same agent at t_1, and do not address it separately in the text.

[49] The insertion takes up the phrase used by Khoury a few lines further down from the quoted sentence to clarify what he means by psychological elements. See Khoury, above n 43 at 741.

[50] Ibid at 741.

[51] Ibid at 741–42.

for [responsibility at t_1] is the [quality of will] with which one acted and what matters for [responsibility at t_2] is the persistence of those qualities of will'.[52]

It is important to note that Khoury and I are in agreement about a key issue: that, if t_1 stands for the moment when D commits the crime and t_2 for the moment when D is held liable for his crime by a criminal court, it is D's culpability at t_2 that constitutes the reference point for the punishment D deserves.[53] But I disagree with Khoury's view that in order to hold $D_{(NOW)}$, at t_2, responsible for what $D_{(THEN)}$ did at t_1, we have to *transfer* $D_{(THEN)}$'s responsibility across to $D_{(NOW)}$. No such transfer is necessary. $D_{(NOW)}$ is responsible for what $D_{(THEN)}$ did at t_1 because $D_{(NOW)}$ is *biographically and biologically* fully continuous with $D_{(THEN)}$. In other words: they are the same agent. Simple agential identity, not psychological connectedness, provides the foundation for holding D responsible at t_2 for acts carried out at t_1.

The misstep in Khoury's argument becomes clear when we focus on his reason for rejecting the simple 'identical agent' view. After discussing the example of Jane's insult, Khoury concludes (as I have done above) that in *Alternative B*, Jane is a lot less blameworthy for the insult at t_2 than she was at t_1. This he takes to show that 'the mere fact that one is the person who committed some past act does not guarantee that responsibility freely transfers', because 'If this were so then there would be no difference in Jane's blameworthiness for the insult at t_2 in the above example'.[54] As is clear from my discussion above, I agree with Khoury that our culpability assessments of Jane's culpability for the insult change between t_1 and t_2. But that doesn't mean we have a problem. We arrive at this conclusion after considering Jane's responsibility at t_2 with regard to what her act at t_1 signifies about her quality of judgement, quality of regard and quality of character. The mistake is to assume that a responsibility *transfer* from Jane at t_1 to Jane at t_2 is necessary in order to establish Jane's culpability at t_2 for an act she performed at t_1, and that we are in the business of 'transferring' responsibility from Jane at t_1 to Jane at t_2 when we perform this culpability assessment at t_2 on the lines I set out above. All we need to do is appreciate that Jane is an agent situated in time.

The logic of agency requires of us to think of ourselves as reason-responsive (including desire-responsive) choosers, and that means that we must be capable of (self-) reflection as well as of imaginative projection, and we must accept that the reasons that apply to us before we act continue to support (or fail to support) an act after we have performed it; they are in that sense time-invariant. The metaphysical preconditions of desert (personal continuity and 'survival' of reasons into the post-event time) are the metaphysical preconditions for 'living in time', for relating to each other as agents who persist over time and whose choices and lives can be made sense of in terms of a history of choices and their

---

[52] Ibid at 742.
[53] See ibid at 745.
[54] Ibid at 739.

consequences. The logic that desert-claims presuppose is no other than the logic of agency.[55]

This also explains why (contrary to what Asholt suggests in passing[56]) it is not possible to develop Hegel's argument for time limits on claims for the return of misappropriated property to its rightful owner into a defence of prescription of prosecution. Our will cannot retreat from our past acts after the fact, as it can retreat from objects that have been taken from us and are no longer in our possession (eventually we will let them go inwardly). Our past acts remain our past acts, and our very existence as agents is bound up with perception, and acceptance, of that truth. Consider also Jeffrie Murphy's explanation for why he thinks that the 'Give yourself a break; you were just a kid' reaction to feeling bad as an adult for the hurt he caused his father on a particular occasion when he was a young boy, is shallow:

> To disavow the self of one's past – even one's childhood self – blocks, among other things, one's ability to understand the sense in which one may see oneself as having experienced moral growth and the path by which further moral growth may be possible. And is not all bad conscience directed towards the past?[57]

It is true that we can subsequently influence the meaning of our actions, in the sense that it is up to us how these actions sit in the larger context of our life history. In fact, insofar as very serious wrongdoing is concerned, it is plausible to think that we have to engage in such an exercise. It is, as Gabriele Taylor explains, a psychological necessity as we have to find a way of integrating the wrong we have done with our agential self-image.[58] We have to develop a conception of ourselves that enables us to live with ourselves as the perpetrators of this serious wrong.[59] But what we cannot do is change the fact of having committed the wrong, and therefore our integrative efforts must (short of madness) continue to acknowledge our past agency. To that extent we all are – as a colleague of mine put it in discussion with me – 'hostages of our former selves'.

Through the focus on the agent's guilt-adaptive strategies, we can also see an important difference between serious and venial crimes. Someone who has committed murder cannot inwardly walk away from what he did. He must react through some big inner adjustment – either by embracing the initially alien

---

[55] Sher, above n 2, ch 9. It was, in fact, Sher's interest in agency and responsibility that led him to focus on desert: ibid at xii–xiii.

[56] Asholt, above n 5 at 273–74.

[57] JG Murphy, 'Shame Creeps Through Guilt and Feels like Retribution' (1999) 18 *Law and Philosophy* 327 at 341.

[58] Taylor, above n 26 at 93 ff.

[59] Compare Herbert Morris: 'I do not believe that one can begin to explain the suffering attached to one's disobeying conscience without emphasizing a person's deep attachment to being a person of the sort partly defined by one's conscience. ... We are attached to the source of the command and thus disobedience becomes like self-betrayal. ... [W]e experience a form of fragmentation; there is a breakdown in our sense of wholeness.' (H Morris, 'Reflections on Feeling Guilty' (1981) 40 *Philosophical Studies* 187 at 189).

murderous self that showed itself in that act, or by taking active steps to expel that self and its traces.[60] Either way, *who he is now is profoundly enmeshed with that deed; he wouldn't be the person he is now without it.* By contrast, where the wrongdoing is more venial, even if it was victimising, one can make sense of the thought that D never felt put on the spot for long enough that he couldn't have become the person he is now except in response to that crime. Again, this doesn't sever the link. But it does suggest that, as time moves on, the crime has less and less to do with who he is. Guilt thus matters differently in cases of serious crimes – particularly those that have done grave harm to their victims – than it does in other, less serious or victimless cases of wrongdoing.[61] The latter are cases where we might accept a weakening of the attribution relation over time, as D becomes less and less 'like' the person who committed the offence. We do not accept such a weakening effect, though, when we think the commission of the offence was such a heinous violation of core human norms that D will be the person he is now (partly but importantly) on account of how he has reacted to the offence in his efforts at self-restoration. This is so even if these efforts have also resulted in him being a morally much better person now compared to the person he was when he committed the offence. The serious crime's significance for the agent's narrative history is bound to increase with time in light of his unavoidable strategies of self-adaptation. We draw our conclusions about what the agent's crime says about him also from the meaning he has given that crime in his life.[62]

IV. THE TEMPORALITY OF DESERT

As pointed out in section I, responsibility judgments are necessarily diachronic – perhaps we should even say 'doubly diachronic': Firstly, any judgment that an agent is blameworthy for a past act builds on a finding that, given the reasons

---

[60] For a fascinating discussion drawing on Macbeth, see Taylor, above n 26 at 94–96.

[61] Murphy is right to stress the importance of harm in this context: 'what tends to cause the most painful pangs of guilty conscience in morally mature persons … is not just wrong[doing] but *wrongful injury to others*' (Murphy, above n 57 at 335, emphasis original).

[62] This also provides a response to Khoury, above n 43 at 743, who points to the character Red from the prison film *The Shawshank Redemption* as an example of someone who no longer bears responsibility for his past actions. Red, now an old man and a morally courageous and exemplary character, is serving a life sentence for a murder he committed as a teenager. In response to the question put to him at a parole hearing whether he 'is sorry for what he did', he responds gruffly: 'Not a day goes by I don't feel regret, and not because I'm in here … I look back on myself the way I was … stupid kid who did that terrible crime … wish I could talk sense into him. … But I can't. That kid's long gone, this old man is all that's left, and I have to live with that.' Khoury thinks that this remark illustrates 'the frustration that Red feels being psychologically continuous but not connected with "the stupid kid who did that terrible crime"'. I think that interpretation is mistaken. What the quote does illustrate, as powerfully as one could wish, is the profound connection between Red as he is now and the stupid kid he was then. 'Not a day goes by' that he doesn't think about that kid, because that kid's crime required a deep self-adjustment. While his adjustment shows that he has reduced his guilt levels in response to the crime, it does not – and cannot – show that he is disconnected from it.

that applied to the agent at that time, it was wrong then for him to act as he did. These reasons are diachronically valid, in that the very reasons that should have made him act differently prospectively are also reasons that support the retrospective judgment that he should have acted differently. Secondly, we judge the person in front of us as sufficiently connected to that past agent that our judgment of that past agent carries across to him.[63]

We can also see now that time affects desert judgments in another way, too. Sher's analysis of desert initially suggests that desert lasts for a person's lifetime – simply because according to his principle of diachronic fairness, the point in time at which the remedial correction is performed, is irrelevant.[64] An undeserved benefit or burden of a particular kind and size have occurred at t_1, and until such time when they are remedied define the kind and size of the inverse burden or benefit that would balance things out. But on closer inspection, this 'timing does not matter' view of desert cannot be right. As we have seen, desert-claims are not fully formed at the moment of the injurious event and uninfluenced by the timing of their performance. To the contrary: desert-claims are multi-dimensionally time-sensitive. This means that we should let drop the 'ledger image' when addressing questions of desert. The question is rather: what does a person deserve *now* in respect of a past event and subsequent developments? And – as Sher reminds us at other points in his book – the answers to such questions are 'area-specific', because they depend on the specific values that underlie desert claims in this area of moral practice.[65]

What shapes penal desert? In a nutshell: wrongful harm; culpability; and personal agency – the latter consisting in the fact that crime and punishment are events or processes located within the life course and biographical history of a natural person. We have explored the first two and said something about how they are influenced by time. We should now say something about the third.

Penal desert, because it is about holding agents responsible for certain of their past actions, presupposes the kinds of structures and values on which the very possibility of human agency depends. According to philosopher Marya Schechtman, in order for a person to be an agent, she needs to have 'a sense of [her]self as a persisting individual whose actions should cohere with [her] beliefs, values and desires … and whose current actions have implications for the future' such that she is able to 'see [her life] as unfolding in an intelligible manner' (what Schechtman calls a 'narrative self-conception').[66] Schechtman continues: 'It is this kind of temporally extended life which creates

---

[63] Sher, above n 2, ch 9.

[64] Sher, above n 2 at 95: 'if a moral rule demands that M refrain from harming N at t_1, this will reflect only the fact that t_1 is among the moments at which M might harm N. In general, what is significant about an improper burden or benefit is not its temporal location, but only its occurrence within a life.'

[65] Sher, above n 2 at xii: 'desert need not have any single normative basis. Indeed, different classes of desert-claims may owe their justification to irreducibly different principles and values'.

[66] M Schechtman, *The Constitution of Selves* (Ithaca, NY, Cornell University Press, 1996) 159.

persons, and which makes the four [basic] features [of personal existence] part of our lives'.[67]

These four basic features are given by Schechtman as: survival; moral responsibility; self-interested concern; and compensation.[68] Note that, by 'compensation', Schechtman effectively means positive desert. This is clear from her comment that: 'Punishment can in fact be seen as the flip side of compensation. Whereas it seems right to reward virtuous action with something that is pleasant to the virtuous subject, it also seems right to detract from the ill-gotten pleasures of the vicious subject.'[69] Since it seems rather implausible that negative desert would be any less basic than positive desert, it seems that the fourth feature would rather more accurately be stated as 'desert'.

What a person negatively deserves by way of punishment is some kind of sanction. In the most general form, an imposition of a sanction will involve making the person experience a setback to one or more of his/her interests or resources. Such setbacks affect individuals in different ways depending on when and under what circumstances they are imposed on them across their life course. Given this placement of a sanction in the unfolding trajectory of D's life, we have to be sensitive to the possibility that what is effected by nominally identical sanctions when imposed at different times in D's life, is different. Even if our aim is to punish $D_{(NOW)}$ exactly as severely as we would have punished $D_{(THEN)}$, the determination of the 'punitive match' is sensitive to timing: the *impact* of the punishment on D changes due to changes in D's circumstances that have occurred in the meantime. *What* sanction is commensurate to D's crime in terms of its penal severity must be calibrated afresh, even if he does *not* now deserve greater or lesser punishment than he deserved immediately after the offence. This is so because even if he still deserves the same punishment, to bring about the same effect in penal severity, the punishment's nominal shape must be adapted to present circumstances. As regards fines, it might be that the adaptation nominally needs to increase the sum of the fine, not just to take account of inflation but also to take account of what may be D's far increased means. In the case of a fine, what matters is how the sum that his punishment would have consisted of then would have impacted on his resources then. Assuming that D is now a much higher earner, either the sum has to increase to the point where it achieves a comparable penal impact, or (if the offence doesn't allow such increases) we may have to opt for some form of community service to make D feel his punishment at all.

A change in the severity of a punishment that results from such impact-conscious adjustments is merely an apparent one. Because $D_{(NOW)}$ is less sensitive to punishment's effects than $D_{(THEN)}$, a punishment of the same severity as was deserved at the time of the crime, would now under-punish D.

---

[67] Ibid at 160.
[68] Ibid at 2.
[69] Ibid at 158.

More troubling than the risk of under-punishing D by imposing a nominally unadjusted sanction is the risk of over-punishing D by doing so. This risk is particularly acute in respect of sentences of imprisonment. The impact of a period of imprisonment on a person's life course varies – again, not in a linear manner, but due to what imprisonment deprives a person of in respect of their overall life plan and life chances. When it comes to sentences of fairly short to moderate duration, we can use as a rough guide for changes in severity the proportion of an offender's remaining life span that imprisonment deprives him of. But we also have to appreciate that the biographical structure of human lives gives certain time periods particular significance. An offender who receives a 20-year-sentence at age 18, when this sentence will make him miss various biographical landmarks of an ordinarily progressing life, is arguably punished more severely than an offender who receives a 20-year-sentence while in the final stages of a life previously lived in freedom.

Sometimes this temporality leads us to a yet different perspective: the idea that 'D, due to the failure to apprehend him earlier, has already had a better life than he deserved' and that for this reason, even a rather ineffectual punishment – a punishment that 'comes too late' to achieve any of the primary penal objectives – should still be imposed, and served. This reaction to the passage of time as *having increased* the undeserved benefits of the offender and hence *strengthened* the case for his punishment follows neatly from 'the idea that one who has committed some serious wrong should not be able to live a life of "freedom and contentment" – should not be able to carry on as if she had done no wrong'.[70] Matravers has described this as the 'claim that a situation in which those who have done wrong nevertheless flourish is somehow "out of kilter"'.[71] It is most likely to carry significant weight with us when the wrongdoing was particularly heinous or when the offender continues to enjoy the fruits of his crime.

But there is another reason why we are sometimes troubled about imposing a deserved punishment very long after the fact, a reason that is connected more generally to *crime and punishment as events in the life-course of an offender*. We might be bothered by the thought that if D had been apprehended, tried and punished at the time, he would by now have put the punishment behind him. Punishment now will rupture his life course more severely than punishment then would have done. One might be tempted to dismiss the worry – holding on to the thought that 'Well, it's his own fault, he could have confessed then and been done with it'. But while this is a valid point, it doesn't change the fact that punishment now affects him differently from punishment then, and if we accept that this is the case then it must affect our reaction.

---

[70] RA Duff, 'Penal Communications: Recent Work in the Philosophy of Punishment' (1996) 20 *Crime and Justice* 1 at 31 (quoting JG Murphy, 'Hatred: A Qualified Defense' in JG Murphy and J Hampton, *Forgiveness and Mercy* (Cambridge, Cambridge University Press, 1988) 88 at 91).

[71] M Matravers, *Justice and Punishment: The Rationale of Coercion* (Oxford, Oxford University Press, 2000) 74.

We are troubled by this thought especially in cases where D has made significant positive changes to his self since he committed the crime. Because the agent's subsequent (and particularly his self-adaptive) history informs our culpability assessment, it may seem unfair to refuse to treat as significant subsequent profound self-reform – unfair in the sense that we now would appear to be 'reducing' the agent to being 'the perpetrator of crime X' when we react to him only qua 'perpetrator of crime X'. This is perhaps why one possible reaction to late apprehension for a crime is to think that 'we shouldn't punish now because, had the punishment been timely, both the crime and the punishment would now have receded in importance to the point where they hardly matter for anyone's present life'. By having escaped punishment thus far, the offender has also missed the natural progression by which he would have left the crime behind him. We can see now why even on a ledger view of desert, the contextual shifts to culpability levels mean that we cannot simply brush this consideration aside with the thought that 'the hypothetical world in which D would already have been punished' is in no way relevant to the world in which 'D has not yet been punished'. The German Constitutional Court, when it had to rule on the validity of a retrospective extension of the period of prescription for murder, argued (among other things) that 'at least where the crimes in question makes D liable to life imprisonment', such retrospective extension could give no cause for concern.[72] The thought appears to be that, where the crime is such that D is liable to *life imprisonment*, we are already of the view that we may treat D harshly on account of this crime *for the rest of his life*. By contrast, it is not so clear whether we may treat D harshly at any subsequent point in time during his life for just any other crime he committed at some point that he was not apprehended and punished for yet. As we have seen in section III, D's culpability levels, particularly for serious crimes, are affected by his subsequent self-adjustive efforts. To the extent that such efforts decrease his culpability, he deserves to be credited for them even if they have not been undertaken in response to punishment as part of a penal dialogue.[73]

V. CONCLUSION: THE INSTABILITY OF DESERT

This chapter has affirmed, on desert-based grounds, the practice of the courts to judge a defendant on the 'fully contextualised' basis of what we can say now about the harm his crime did, as well as what it really says about him to have

---

[72] BVerfGE 25, 269 (concerning the retrospective extension of prescription periods for certain serious crimes).

[73] I therefore go further than Roberts and Dagan in this collection for whom the reduction in culpability only results from how the offender reacts to his *punishment*. In section III B of this chapter, I hope to have shown that the reduction in culpability results from how the offender reacts to his *crime*. These reactions can include, but are not exhausted by, reactions to his punishment.

committed this crime. We can now see why considerations of temporality should lead us to assess the significance of the old crime 'in the here and now' (with the possible, but by no means certain, conclusion that 'nothing has changed since the time he did this'). Both the significance of the legal relations and claims instituted by the commission of a crime, and the perpetrator's culpability, are influenced by developments over time. Moreover, punishment is necessarily imposed on persons who are, in Schechtman's words, 'agent(s) situated in time' – confronting us with further considerations affecting the calibration of what punishment an agent now deserves for his past acts. Yet in most cases – particularly those of serious victimising crimes – we will reach the view that the defendant still deserves to be punished, and will be able to say how much punishment he deserves.

The broader question of whether, all things considered, such deserved punishment should be imposed remains open. Sher tells us that 'that the urge to blame is bound up with a commitment to morality itself', and explains that,

> anyone who combined a future-oriented commitment to morality with an indifference to past transgressions would have a perpetually unstable set of desires. If someone wanted people to do the right thing from now on but did not care whether they had done the right thing in the past, then what he cared about would be constantly changing. As each moment slipped from the future into the past, he would have to relinquish his desire that he and other people do the right thing at that moment.[74]

In other words, it is just incoherent to want people to act rightfully in the future but not to care about whether they have acted rightfully in the past. This point applies to any normative order, whether it is constituted as morality or as law. But it is just as obvious that the quest to respond always to what people have done in the past can become quixotic. As Melissa Lane has observed: 'If there were no intuitive or tacit statute of limitations on most wrong-doing, every decision about what to do, or ethical judgment about what should or shouldn't be done, would be hampered by the need to take account of an indefinite series of interaction in the remote past'.[75]

Criminal justice systems have to find a balance between these two poles. They must be guided in doing so by the thought that penal desert is a concept most deeply grounded in human agency, and that this commits them to acknowledging and responding to the temporal instability of desert.

---

[74] Sher, above n 38 at 135–36.
[75] M Lane, 'Time and Morality in Political Ethics' in G Pfleiderer and C Rehmann-Sutter (eds), *Zeithorizonte des Ethischen. Zur Bedeutung der Temporalität in der Fundamental- und Bioethik* (Stuttgart, Kohlhammer, 2006) 15 at 19.

13

Censure, Dialogue and Reconciliation

ROB CANTON

O NE ELEMENT OF most conventional definitions of punishment is that it must involve an imposition of some pain or deprivation, 'an evil, an unpleasantness'[1] – conventionally referred to as 'hard treatment'. Since it is not usually morally permissible so to afflict others, this imposition calls for justification; and retributive justifications of punishment have, until relatively recently, centred on attempts to show that hard treatment is required as a deserved and just response to a criminal wrong, or is at least permissible (in a way that punishment of the innocent is not). In drawing attention to the expressive and communicative aspects of punishment, however, Feinberg[2] pointed to a core element of punishment that was absent from (or at least under-emphasised in) the authoritative definitions put forward by Flew,[3] Benn[4] and Hart.[5] Punishment necessarily expresses *censure*: it communicates disapproval (whatever else it may convey and whatever form it may take) and this seems fundamental to the concept.

As Bennett insists, however, not just any response could count as an expression of disapproval. The relationship between the act of censure and the expression of denunciation is more than contingent: it is grounded in the emotional structure of censure. You cannot really be outraged unless you are disposed to act in certain ways. It is not just that these emotions tend to be expressed in this way, but that it is essential to them.[6] Hard treatment may be the best or perhaps even the only way to convey censure. Others have argued that hard treatment

---

[1] A Flew, 'The Justification of Punishment' (1954) 29 *Philosophy* 291 at 293.
[2] J Feinberg, 'The Expressive Function of Punishment' (1965) 49 *The Monist* 397.
[3] Flew, above n 1.
[4] S Benn, 'An Approach to the Problems of Punishment' (1958) 22 *Philosophy* 325.
[5] HLA Hart, *Punishment and Responsibility* (Oxford, Clarendon Press, 1968) 4.
[6] C Bennett, *The Apology Ritual: A Philosophical Theory of Punishment* (Cambridge, Cambridge University Press, 2008) 35ff.

is justified in itself because it adds a prudential (deterrent) incentive to refrain from offending, with consequent crime-reductive effects, in addition to the normative claims expressed in the censure.[7] In both types of account, however, the communication of censure is central.

I. CENSURE THEORY AND THE 'TREATMENT MODEL'

Censure theory originated in accounts of punishment that were wary of consequentialist justifications: the justification of punishment, it was argued, is not to be found solely or even mainly in its consequences, and the belief that punishment should be designed to reduce offending leads to flawed policy and to conspicuous injustices. *Doing Justice*[8] and other foundational texts in the emergence of a 'justice model' of punishment[9] aimed their most trenchant criticisms at a conception of rehabilitation which was then taken to be the dominant contemporary rationale for sentencing.[10] Roughly, this 'treatment model' supposed that offending was an expression or manifestation of some kind of pathological condition, perhaps a disease.[11] Punishment would then be futile (because offending would continue while this condition remained unremedied) and unjust, even in retributive terms (because the individual was not responsible for the condition which led to the offending and people ought not to be punished for that for which they are not responsible).

Critics argued that, understood in this way, rehabilitation seems fundamentally incompatible with most principles of justice. Prominent among these principles are desert and proportionality: to say that a punishment is undeserved or that it is disproportionate is to reject that punishment as unjust. However, the 'rehabilitative ideal',[12] as it was propagated at that time, dismissed the relevance

---

[7] A von Hirsch and A Ashworth, *Proportionate Sentencing: Exploring the Principles* (Oxford, Oxford University Press, 2005).

[8] A von Hirsch, *Doing Justice: The Choice of Punishments* (Report of the Committee for the Study of Incarceration) (New York, Hill and Wang, 1976).

[9] For example, American Friends Service Committee, *Struggle for Justice: A Report on Crime and Punishment in America* (New York, Hill and Wang, 1971).

[10] Whatever the position in the USA, its dominance in the UK is more disputable. It seems likely that the sentences of the court in England and Wales corresponded to a tariff that was mainly structured by the seriousness of the offence, understood as a function of harm and culpability, and by previous criminal record. 'Treatment' sanctions, notably probation, were outside of, and did not usually subvert, this tariff. (DA Thomas, *Principles of Sentencing: The Sentencing Policy of the Court of Appeal Criminal Division*, 2nd edn (London, Heinemann, 1979).

[11] It is sometimes not clear whether crime was regarded as an actual disease (a position mordantly rebutted by A Flew, *Crime or Disease?* (Basingstoke, Macmillan, 1973)) or whether it was *like* a disease – requiring assessment and treatment person-by-person. Arguably it is the latter position that was more common.

[12] F Allen, 'Criminal Justice, Legal Values and the Rehabilitative Ideal' (1959) 50 *Journal of Criminal Law, Criminology, and Police Science* 226.

of desert and readily countenanced disproportion. Desert, it was contended, was a concept made obsolete by the insights of the social sciences into the causes of human behaviour – or was at least on the road to obsolescence, as these sciences made their slow but sure progress towards these discoveries. Retributive proportionality, resting upon desert, therefore stood as a constraint on effective sentencing. It might be, for instance, that a less serious offence should appropriately attract a longer (than proportionate) sentence because of the treatment needs of the offender. Indeed, in many cases, sentences should be indeterminate since at the point of imposition it is plainly impossible to know how long a treatment process might take.[13]

To its critics, however, the 'treatment model' was said to meddle with people's souls, and was all the more insidious because it claimed to be doing so in their own interests. CS Lewis famously protested at the way in which 'the humanitarian theory of punishment' tramples over the constraints of justice:

> It will be in vain … to say, 'but this punishment is hideously unjust, hideously disproportionate to the criminal's deserts'. The experts, with perfect logic will reply, 'but nobody was talking about deserts. No one was talking about *punishment* in your archaic vindictive sense of the word. … Here are the statistics proving that this other treatment cures. What is your trouble?'[14]

Some retributivists, however, made concessions towards some of rehabilitation's ambitions. *Limiting retributivism*[15] proposes that rehabilitation (and other reductive aims) are legitimate penal objectives so long as the weight of the sentence is (relatively) proportionate and set within the parameters of what is deserved. In particular, a sentence may not be made longer than the offence merits in order to meet the individual's 'need for treatment'. If this can be ensured, rehabilitation may be properly pursued, although it must not involve coercion, manipulation or other forms of deception. Others have gone further in asserting a 'right to rehabilitation'.[16] Very many offenders have experienced

---

[13] It is to be remembered that England and Wales had, from 1908, a semi-indeterminate sentence known as 'borstal training'. The law set a minimum and maximum period of detention, but the term to be served was not set by the judge and would be determined by the trainee's perceived progress. Controversially, after the passing of the Criminal Justice Act 1961, borstal training became the sole way in which courts could pass a medium-term custodial sentence on an offender under 21. Borstal was abolished in 1982.

[14] CS Lewis, 'The Humanitarian Theory of Punishment' (1949) 6 *The Twentieth Century: An Australian Quarterly Review* 1; reprinted in (1953) 6 *Res Judicatae* 244, also in RJ Gerber and PD McAnany (eds), *Contemporary Punishment* (Notre Dame IN, University of Notre Dame Press, 1970) 194 (emphasis in original). For further exposition, see SB Babbage, 'CS Lewis and the Humanitarian Theory of Punishment' (1973) 4 *The Christian Lawyer* 36.

[15] See for example R Frase, 'Limiting Retributivism: The Consensus Model of Criminal Punishment' in M Tonry (ed), *The Future of Imprisonment in the 21st Century* (New York, Oxford University Press, 2003).

[16] E Rotman, 'Do Criminal Offenders have a Constitutional Right to Rehabilitation?' (1986) 77 *Journal of Criminal Law and Criminology* 102; S Lewis, 'Rehabilitation: Headline or Footnote in the New Penal Policy?' (2005) 52 *Probation Journal* 119.

considerable personal and/or social adversity, and it has been argued that the state accordingly has a duty to contribute to their becoming better fitted to avoid offending. The implications of this are that, in both its duration and form, the punishment should at the least try to avoid further prejudice to their circumstances. In particular, the state, at least arguably, has a compelling duty to try to redress any additional 'incidental'[17] disadvantages that may have resulted from the punishment itself (where, for example, imprisonment has left someone homeless). Appreciation of the political context in which the 'justice model' was first developed helps to explain why censure theory has mainly attended to the pronouncement of censure in the sentence of the court, and to the determination of a just punishment. The weight of the punishment has been the principal concern – which is to say (normally) its duration, since it is commonly imprisonment and the length of the term that people have in mind when they discuss these matters.[18] It should also be noted that most scholars have focused on relative, or ordinal, proportionality among sentences – for example, that more serious crimes should be assigned heavier punishments – rather than on cardinal proportionality, which aspires to impose the amount of hard treatment that an offence deserves (or at least, not to impose unjustly more or less than it deserves).[19]

Censure is much more than an expression of anger or reproach. Not to censure is to fail to acknowledge the wrongness of the deed and to dissociate oneself from conduct of this kind. Victims of abuse and atrocities often report how much this matters to them. Observers of such abuse cannot enjoy the indulgence of neutrality. To fail to express disapproval at the least – and sometimes indeed failing to act to demonstrate disapprobation – invites accusations of collusion or at least indifference to the victim's suffering. This was part of the critique of 'radical non-intervention', a policy advocated by Edwin Schur.[20] The insights of labelling theory had suggested that some reactions to wrongdoing were at least as likely to make things worse as they were to improve them, and the inference drawn was 'to leave the kids alone'.[21] But, as Braithwaite objected,[22] this sends quite the wrong message to everyone and dishonours victims in particular. In his influential exposition, Strawson[23] argued that our

---

[17] N Walker, *Why Punish?* (Oxford, Oxford University Press, 1991) 108.

[18] How the burdens of imprisonment can be equitably translated or converted into other forms of penalty, especially community penalties, without disturbing the proportions required by justice remains a notoriously vexed question.

[19] For the distinction, see M Matravers, 'Is Twenty-first Century Punishment Post-desert?' in M Tonry (ed), *Retributivism Has a Past, Has it a Future?* (New York, Oxford University Press, 2011) 30. Limiting retributivists remain concerned with cardinal 'outer limits' that act as a constraint on preventive aims.

[20] E Schur, *Radical Non-intervention: Rethinking the Delinquency Problem* (New Jersey, Prentice Hall, 1973).

[21] Ibid at 155.

[22] J Braithwaite, *Crime, Shame and Reintegration* (Cambridge, Cambridge University Press, 1979).

[23] PF Strawson, 'Freedom and Resentment' (1962) 48 *Proceedings of the British Academy* 187, reprinted in PF Strawson, *Freedom and Resentment and Other Essays* (London, Methuen, 1974).

'reactive attitudes' to the behaviour of others, which include resentment, blaming, gratitude, forgiveness and anger, are part of the very fabric of human exchange and reciprocity. Holding people accountable for what they do is integral to our associations with one another.[24]

II. THE INCOMPLETENESS OF CENSURE THEORY

This chapter considers some of the ways in which censure theory, for all its merits, is incomplete. Some of the challenges raised are familiar. For example, censure is a communication, typically if not perhaps necessarily,[25] and subject to all the hazards of misunderstanding that can affect any communication. If the communicative aspects of punishment are foregrounded, we cannot be indifferent to the effectiveness of the communication. Perhaps some censuring communications elicit defensiveness or defiance and a reciprocal 'resentment' (to use Strawson's term), rather than remorse. Certainly not all pronouncements of punishment will manage to convey what needs to be communicated to the several audiences concerned – the offender, the victim(s), the 'general public'. What is intended by the sentencer (a 'message' that is already likely to be complex) will be mediated by the expectations, preferences and prejudices of these audiences and cannot be assumed to be received as intended.[26] This is further complicated by the consideration that much of the language of punishment is allegorical and symbolic. As Duff puts it:

> The language of punishment is more than a purely verbal language. Punishment speaks to the offender, not just through the words that are said to her, but through the material forms that it takes. Imprisonment, fines, Community Service Orders, and other kinds of sentence have their own meanings … But this is a general point about the language of the law: it is a language rich in non-verbal symbols and meanings.[27]

The *form* of the punishment, then, as well as its weight, makes a difference to the potential and actual communication. Notably, imprisonment seems an inept means of communicating anything much more than rejection: prison is something that can be merely suffered or endured and in the nature of the case it need not ask much of the offender.[28] Again, as Duff implies, the way in which the sentence is put into effect can support or, as it may be, undermine or

---

[24] Ibid; see also Bennett, above n 6.

[25] T Metz, 'Censure Theory and Intuitions about Punishment' (2000) 19 *Law and Philosophy* 491.

[26] P Smith, *Punishment and Culture* (Chicago, University of Chicago Press, 2008).

[27] RA Duff, *Punishment, Communication and Community* (Oxford, Oxford University Press, 2001) 222.

[28] It is true that the best prison regimes do try to make constructive challenges and may elicit an active response, but a recalcitrant and unremorseful prisoner is still being punished.

subvert the original communication, at least so far as the offender is concerned. These are matters that need more attention than they have so far received. Those who are troubled by the hard treatment of punishing practices – 'the inflicting of pain, intended as pain', as Christie[29] challengingly characterises it – argue that we need to find other and better ways of expressing censure. Walgrave, for example, refers to the 'communicative aridity'[30] of retributive punishment and argues that restorative processes are much more fertile ground for effective communication.[31]

Yet while some proponents of restorative justice make a sharp distinction between what they regard as different and indeed incompatible conceptions of justice,[32] Duff argues that restorative and retributive justice are better understood as two sides of a coin.[33] The communication of censure is essential to both. The victim and the community have not only been harmed but also wronged and accordingly the response, whether described as retributive or restorative, has to make demands on the offender if it is to be recognised as a fitting expression of remorse and apology. Many censure theorists accordingly welcome restorative responses and are keen to develop a synergy between these approaches. Both approaches foreground the ideas of individual responsibility (which is sometimes taken to be precisely what some forms of rehabilitation deny) and of membership of a moral community.[34] However, while censure theory sometimes seems to rest satisfied once a just and proportionate sentence has been passed, it is at least arguable that this point is only the *beginning* of a punishment. We need to attend to what happens next before we can be confident that justice has been done. As Radzik says: 'We need some way of talking about the end state of cases of wrongdoing – some point at which we can describe the wrongful act as having been successfully resolved',[35] or, otherwise stated, we need some way to express the idea of the wrongdoer's return to full standing

---

[29] N Christie, *Limits to Pain* (Oxford, Martin Robertson, 1981) i.

[30] L Walgrave, 'Imposing Restoration instead of Inflicting Pain: Reflections on the Judicial Reaction to Crime', in A von Hirsch, J Roberts, A Bottoms, K Roach and M Schiff (eds), *Restorative Justice and Criminal Justice: Competing or Reconcilable Paradigms?* (Oxford, Hart, 2003) 61 at 65.

[31] A problem, however, is that censure should express disapproval in a manner that can be readily understood not only by offender and victim but by the community in general. While the public pronouncement of the crime and its punishment may be necessary for the reaffirmation and as necessary the clarification of norms, it risks evoking public vilification and stigma. A restorative justice encounter may not be able to respond to the wider social significance of the crime, cannot deal with crimes that have no specific victim and can communicate only to those present at the event. See: L Zedner, 'Reparation and Retribution: Are they Reconcilable?' (1994) 75 *Modern Law Review* 228.

[32] For references and discussion, see D Roche, 'Retribution and Restorative Justice' in G Johnstone and D Van Ness (eds), *Handbook of Restorative Justice* (London, Routledge, 2003) 75.

[33] RA Duff, 'Restoration and Retribution' in A von Hirsch et al, above n 30, 43 at 53.

[34] An expression introduced by Strawson, above n 23, and subsequently used by others, including Duff, above n 27.

[35] L Radzik, *Making Amends: Atonement in Morality, Law and Politics* (New York, Oxford University Press, 2009) 112.

within the moral community. In what follows, I will explore what that end state might look like, as well as how it might be accomplished, and in the process I will draw upon experiences of responding to wrong-doing in non-criminal justice contexts. It will be concluded that retributivism and rehabilitation have much more in common than their respective advocates usually recognise, even to the point of being inter-dependent in an adequate conception of justice.

III. RIGHTING WRONGS

To begin to explore the process from wrongdoing to resolution, it is instructive to look beyond the formal procedures of criminal justice. Proponents of restorative justice have often looked to pre-modern societies in this connection, where formal laws and criminal justice institutions may not exist and other ways of responding to wrongdoing are found. But another source of understanding could involve critical reflection on how (actual or perceived) wrongs are responded to in intimate groups like families or friendship groups. What follows is a sketch of a process that is not offered as a model or paradigm or archetype of responding to wrongs, but is, I want to claim, one that is entirely familiar. In a rather unscholarly way, I invite readers to draw upon their own experiences and reflections and to recognise the outlines of a process in which they themselves have (perhaps often) participated in all the roles – wrongdoers, wronged, allies, mediators, arbitrators.

> Some kind of (actual or supposed) wrong or transgression takes place. The wrongdoer is identified and rebuked or blamed. Blame here has two principal elements: (i) that a wrong has been done and (ii) that this person is responsible. The individual thus blamed can make their response by (varying degrees of) acceptance of fault,[36] or by denying (or softening) the allegation – that is, by challenging the claim that the act (or omission) was wrong and/or by disowning some or all responsibility for it.[37] In the ensuing exchanges, which may be (although are not always) acrimonious, appeal may be made to others – often other (perhaps senior) members of the family or friendship group, who may intervene (on or without the invitation of the parties) to take sides, or to mediate or arbitrate. Once the degree of fault has been more or less determined, remorse and apology may be expected and in some circumstances some kind of penalty and/or way of making amends agreed upon. This should be followed by forgiveness and reconciliation – the 'end state' to which Radzik refers.[38]

---

[36] Many transgressions may be rapidly and fully admitted – a reminder that these processes may not always be best characterised as 'conflicts' or 'disputes'.

[37] I have tried to argue elsewhere that children typically learn about right and wrong at the same time and through the same experiences as they learn about their personal responsibility for their conduct. See R Canton, *Why Punish? An Introduction to the Philosophy of Punishment* (London, Palgrave Macmillan, 2017) ch 2.

[38] Radzik, above n 35.

This account is, of course, far too simplistic. There are indefinitely many ways in which these transactions may evolve or be blocked. It is also too schematic – for instance, the question of blameworthiness may be re-opened when nego- tiation is taking place about the making of amends; forgiveness may come before apologies and may indeed enable its expression.[39] Even so, the contention here is that this is a process that is common, entirely familiar and one that is usually successful in re-establishing normal relations. It should also be said that (depending on the seriousness of the wrong) if the process is blocked or prema- turely terminated at any stage, a resolution is unlikely to be reached, resentment can linger and perhaps find later and damaging expression: there may be, as we say, *unfinished business*. But where this process is sufficiently completed – apolo- gies sought and given, forgiveness extended – it is an effective means of ensuring that normal relations are resumed.

Among the characteristics of this process are:

- It is (essentially) **dialogic** – blame invites a response (*What were you thinking? How could you?*). The nature of the response in turn prompts further exchanges. Where an acceptance of culpable wrongdoing is arrived at, remorse and apology are appropriate. Apology next expects an acceptance and moves towards forgiveness. It is to be noted that actions and symbols may be part of the dialogue, although it is very commonly a literal, verbal dialogue where the principals are the 'wrongdoer' and the wronged, with sometimes others contributing.

- It is charged with **emotions**, including (for example) anger, sadness, anxi- ety, resentment, defiance, guilt and shame. Just because these are intimate relationships, all concerned are typically anxious to achieve a restoration of peaceful relations. Any of the phases in this process may be blocked by a *feeling* (for instance, that blame has been unfairly ascribed, that apology has not been genuinely sought or granted, that forgiveness is withheld or grudg- ingly expressed).

- The process takes account of the **context** in which the act took place. While the act seems a natural starting point in this process, many wrongs have complex antecedents which, once understood, help in an understanding of how they came to be done. Often these antecedents must be taken into account in an adequate response. The significance of wrongdoing cannot be fully understood without attention to the context, especially that of prior and continuing relationships, in which all of this takes place. The dialogues (and certainly the quarrels) are unlikely to be confined to the immediately precipitating event. The parties deal with one another and are appraised in that context; they are not reduced to their roles in the 'index' incident.

---

[39] Although an expression of forgiveness when the wrong is denied is more likely to prompt resentment.

Relatedly, the **motives** and meanings with which the participants invest their actions are a common focus when talking about the act. *What were you thinking?* is not a question about intention, but about motive.

- **Search for reconciliation and a shared duty to achieve it.** Insisting that a good parent should respond to (and not ignore) a child's wrongdoing, John Braithwaite[40] urges that these responses take place within a shared understanding that the 'wrongdoer' is a valued member of the family and that everyone eagerly anticipates a time when the matter can be regarded as closed and normal relations re-established. In a healthy community, the wrongdoer may have particular obligations to acknowledge the wrong, express remorse and resolve to do better in future, but other members of that group are likely to be keen to accept their responsibilities to contribute for the benefit of the whole community and for the sake of the member who was responsible for the wrong. This often includes attempts to learn from the experience and reflections by all members of the community on what their contribution might be towards helping to avoid such incidents in future.

In the next section, comparisons will be made between these characteristics and those of formal professionalised criminal justice procedures.

IV. COMPARISON WITH CRIMINAL JUSTICE

At the outset, it is to be emphasised that there is no argument here that punishment within the context of the criminal justice system should seek to model its processes on the familiar practices of righting wrongs among intimates. Indeed, any idea that it should will rightly arouse suspicions about civil liberties and intrusiveness. Many scholars in the philosophy of punishment insist that their project is to explore justifications for punishment by the state; and they (often explicitly) claim that they will not be seeking a justification of other kinds of punishment. In particular, parental punishment is likely to need a very different kind of justification. For that matter, some people may feel uncomfortable about describing parental reproof as 'punishment' at all, regarding this as too crude a term to characterise the transactions that should take place in a loving relationship. Be that as it may, citizens are not the children of the state and the relationship is hardly a 'loving' one. The state's dealings ought not to be intimate and intrusive, but are properly constrained by the rights of citizens.

Nevertheless, the contention here is that there is much to be learnt from reflections on the processes of responding to 'wrongs' in families and among intimate groups. In particular, these ways of righting wrongs express and mould many of our intuitions about justice. It is in and through participation in these

---

[40] Braithwaite, above n 22 ch 4.

processes that people form their conceptions of what is fair. The extent to which intuitions are a reliable guide to moral behaviour is, of course, a deeply contested matter, but even so we are unlikely to be content with any theory that offends our intuitions radically – for example by countenancing punishment of innocent people or punishing anyone cruelly or excessively. Again, if part of the project of the philosophy of punishment is to enhance the quality of justice, attention must be paid to the intuitions and emotions of those we seek to persuade – feelings that may variously thwart or support initiatives for reform. The contention here is therefore that the practices of criminal punishment need to chime with our intuitions about justice, about wrongs and how to respond to them, what it is to express remorse and to apologise, and the point at which an end state has been achieved. The more criminal punishment jars with these sentiments, the more likely it will be that the normative legitimacy of criminal justice is called into question and offenders, victims or others may be left feeling that justice has not been fully served.

Comparisons and contrasts can illuminate both the process of informal responses to wrongdoing and criminal justice punishment. In what follows, points of comparison are therefore addressed as regards the four matters highlighted in the bullet points above (dialogue; emotions; context and motive; and search for reconciliation).

A. Dialogue

It has been argued that dialogue, interaction and exchange characterise responses to wrongdoing in non-criminal justice contexts, where there is commonly an exploration of motive and a subsequent negotiation about the meaning and significance of what has taken place. How might this apply to penal censure? Censure after all is not mere scolding or an expression of outrage, but a communication that invites a response and perhaps a subsequent dialogue. This view, associated especially with the work of Antony Duff,[41] has been criticised by Kimberley Brownlee, who argues that the concept of a dialogue does not offer a plausible way of understanding criminal punishment.[42] Setting out the criteria for reciprocal dialogue, she sees the act of punishment as having a performative function that alters (lowers) the legal status of the offender and so vitiates one of the necessary conditions for mutual, respectful dialogue. She also explores the so-called 'scripting problem'.[43] Certain responses are expected from the offender and indeed often (perhaps typically) *required*; and

---

[41] Duff, above n 27.

[42] K Brownlee, 'The Offender's Part in the Dialogue' in R Cruft, M Kramer and M Reiff (eds), *Crime, Punishment, and Responsibility: The Jurisprudence of Antony Duff* (Oxford, Oxford University Press, 2011) 54.

[43] Ibid at 55.

an exchange in which one party's script is predetermined falls short of respectful dialogue. A related issue is the conscientious offender (someone who does not accept the justice or legitimacy of a law that he has broken, or who wants to make political protest through their actions). Such a defendant may wish to engage in a very different kind of dialogue with the state, yet she must still do so within a 'blanket script of censure'.[44] In a response to Brownlee, Hannah Maslen defends the idea of dialogue.[45] Her particular concern is to make the case for the relevance to sentence of expressions of remorse by the defendant. This, she argues, is of relevance *pre-censure* – that is, before sentence, so that the censure can be 'responsive', responding appropriately to the offender's attitude.[46] This is a dialogue, then, that takes place before the legal status has been altered. As for the scripting problem, Maslen first notes that, for some versions of punishment-as-communication, such as that offered by von Hirsch and Ashworth,[47] the problem does not arise: the communication is an 'appeal',[48] which affords the offender the opportunity to respond, but allows her to respond as she wishes or not at all. Maslen goes on to argue that, even within Duff's account, the offender is not bound to rehearse a generic script. She may communicate a more nuanced message – for example, in the case of the conscientious offender the message might be that, for principled reasons, she broke the law of the land which she acknowledges a wider duty to respect.[49] Maslen insists that a lack of remorse should not increase the punishment: it is just a sign that the full penalty is merited. But in that case to depart from the expected script is to forgo the mitigation that would follow an expression of remorse. This complicates the idea of a dialogue: a communication of this kind is still constrained, for all its legitimacy, and scarcely 'reciprocal'.[50] Is it open to the offender (on pain of being disregarded or forfeiting mitigation) to articulate anything more than a 'remorseful' communication? Can the offender offer other interpretations of events?

Crucially, too, does the sentencing decision bring any dialogue to an end? Neither the judge nor the offender regards the pronouncement of sentence as part of a conversation. Indeed, the censured offender is (almost) never invited or given an opportunity to respond at court. Still, even if the judge cannot participate in the dialogue, perhaps 'the state' can? Several questions would then arise.

---

[44] Ibid at 61.

[45] H Maslen, *Remorse, Penal Theory and Sentencing* (Oxford, Hart, 2015) especially 108–16.

[46] Ibid at 113.

[47] Von Hirsch and Ashworth, above n 7, at 79–80; see also Maslen, above n 45 at 92, 115.

[48] Maslen, above n 45 at 115.

[49] Perhaps this is not entirely persuasive. Terrorists and anarchists may reject the legitimacy of the law and place themselves outside of the relevant 'moral community'. War criminals and deposed tyrants may 'refuse to recognise' the court. In such cases, the court cannot argue about its standing or about the justice of a law in the course of trial and punishment, though the position of the conscientious offender should sometimes prompt wider moral and political debate.

[50] Maslen, above n 45 at 101.

Who, precisely, would be the interlocutors in any continuing dialogue? May the offender make requests or even demands in response to the initial censure? How should the state respond to the wrongdoer's answers back? What is the objective of this exchange and at what point might the dialogue be felt to be suitably concluded? Later in this chapter, I shall try to argue that mutual and attentive communication, whether or not it amounts to a 'dialogue', should continue beyond the sentencing decision, be sustained during the period of punishment and continue until an end state has been achieved. It should be marked by careful and respectful attention to all participants. The state communicates censure to the offender and expects to be heard; the offender has a legitimate expectation that the state take notice of his perceptions and, above all, perhaps, his thoughts about what he may need if he is to avoid further offending – so that he might give behavioural expression to the commitment not to do it again, which is among the defining features of remorse.

B. Emotions

Emotions are not supposed to have a place in the court room, although it may well be thought that nothing about criminal justice can be properly comprehended without attention to emotions.[51] Counsel and judges are supposed to be professionally dispassionate. The offender's emotions rarely weigh with the court (with the conspicuous exception of remorse: see below); and while a victim's distress may be taken to aggravate the seriousness of the offence in some cases (although it is not agreed how much difference this ought to make), her feelings are not otherwise likely to be taken into account. It remains the case that the sense that justice has or hasn't been done can never be a dispassionate intellectual judgement, but always engages the emotions. In the case of punishment, it is among Durkheim's most important insights that it is precisely this emotionally evocative character that enables punishment to fulfil its 'function' of binding a community.[52] Stripped of these passions, this is not something that punishment is capable of doing.

C. Context and Motives

The focus of the criminal proceedings and of the sentencing decision is on the individual's act. The context in which this act took place is, at best, incidental and likely to enter into the case in mitigation (at best) or at worst be taken as a

---

[51] S Karstedt, I Loader and H Strang (eds), *Emotions, Crime and Justice* (Oxford, Hart, 2013).

[52] For an accessible summary and critique of Durkheim's position, see D Garland, *Punishment and Modern Society: A Study in Social Theory* (Oxford, Clarendon Press, 1990) especially chs 2 and 3.

story of excuses, seen to be self-serving when adduced on the defendant's behalf. Yet, as Christie comments: 'Many among us have, as laymen, experienced the sad moments of truth when our lawyers tell us that our best arguments in our fight against our neighbour are without any legal relevance whatsoever and that we for God's sake ought to keep quiet about them in court'.[53]

The relevant considerations of mental state in a British court of law are to do with intentions (and recklessness, knowledge of risks, negligence) and not motives. Attention will often be paid to motive in aggravation or mitigation. Yet in most other situations of responding to wrongs, an appreciation of motive is at the very heart of what the individual took herself to be doing and, for many philosophers, it is motive above all that determines the moral worth of an action. Motive is not just a further consideration, but makes it the act that it is, and is essential to its evaluation. Yet the context which is indispensable to understanding is something that the law cannot readily comprehend, and is therefore 'ruled out of court'. Developing Christie's metaphor of the state's 'theft' of conflicts,[54] Lucia Zedner has put it well: 'not only has the state 'stolen' the conflict, by the artifice of legal language it has transformed the drama and emotion of social interaction and strife into technical categories which can be subjected to the ordering practices of the criminal process'.[55]

In that process of transformation into manageable categories, criminal justice can lose everything about the crime that gives it meaning and significance – not only for the offender, but for the victim as well. The well-known criticism levelled against criminology by David Matza applies with as much force here. Preoccupations with correction and denunciation suppress a rounded and 'appreciative' understanding of offending which increases the possibility of 'losing the phenomenon – reducing it to that which it is not'.[56] Dismissing offender accounts as self-serving, the state loses opportunities to learn.

D. Search for Reconciliation and a Shared Duty to Support this

What a search for reconciliation might involve in the case of state punishment will be explored in more detail below, when we turn to the matter of rehabilitation. It is enough to note at this stage that if we are to take seriously the idea of a moral community, then the members of that community have a duty to concern themselves with the question of what is needed for reconciliation to be achieved and what active responsibilities they may have to bring this about. It is not easy to see what this might involve without careful attention to the perceptions and attitudes of the individual who offended, and this implies a dialogue with him.

---

[53] Christie, above n 29 at 4.
[54] N Christie, 'Conflicts as Property' (1977) 17 *British Journal of Criminology* 1.
[55] Zedner, above n 31 at 231.
[56] D Matza, *Becoming Deviant* (Englewood Cliffs, NJ, Prentice Hall, 1969) 17.

In summary, the argument in this section has been that in its focus on the pronouncement of sentence and the weight of the punishment, censure theory mainly disregards what should happen subsequently. It is therefore at risk of leaving any 'dialogue' confined to its use in mitigation. Censure theory may well accord with some intuitions about justice, but it is incomplete – especially in its relative disregard for what follows the expression of censure and its neglect of what might be involved in achieving a proper 'end state'. It has further been suggested that the more criminal justice procedures depart from some of the characteristics that mark informal processes, the more they risk jarring with intuitions about proper punishment and thus to feelings that justice has not been done. The argument now proceeds to look at the particular case of *remorse,* which is usually considered to be a wholly desirable response to justified censure, and which helps to make censure a communication and not simply an expression of outrage.

V. REMORSE AND APOLOGY, FORGIVENESS AND RECONCILIATION

One example of the fact that it is impossible (even if it were desirable) to eliminate 'the emotional' from the formal processes of punishment (despite all efforts to do so) is the phenomenon of remorse. This weighs especially with courts and indeed with those who appraise their sentencing decisions. In many jurisdictions, if a defendant shows remorse convincingly, it is likely to lead to a lighter punishment.[57] In 2013, remorse was found to have been taken into account in mitigation of sentence by higher criminal courts in England and Wales in 22 per cent of cases – more than twice as often as any other mitigating factor.[58] Conversely, a *lack of remorse*, often mentioned by judges to account for a heavier sentence,[59] is referred to specifically in sentencing guidelines.[60]

But why should remorse matter?[61] Remorse cannot change the past and I am not aware of any evidence that remorse can be shown to be associated with better behaviour in future – a consequentialist consideration in any case.

---

[57] N Smith, *Justice Through Apologies: Remorse, Reform, and Punishment* (New York, Cambridge University Press, 2014).

[58] Sentencing Council, *Crown Court Sentencing Survey January – December 2013* (2015) available online at www.sentencingcouncil.org.uk/wp-content/uploads/CCSS-Annual-2013.pdf (accessed December 2016).

[59] N Walker, *Aggravation, Mitigation and Mercy in English Criminal Justice* (Oxford, Blackstone, 1999).

[60] Sentencing Guidelines Council, *Overarching Principles: Seriousness* (2004) available online at www.sentencingcouncil.org.uk/wp-content/uploads/web_seriousness_guideline.pdf (accessed December 2016).

[61] It can be argued that it doesn't. See M Bagaric and K Amarasekara, 'Feeling Sorry? – Tell Someone who Cares: The Irrelevance of Remorse in Sentencing' (2001) 40 *Howard Journal of Criminal Justice* 364.

There are at least two ways of understanding this 'why?' question, however. One way is to take it as a normative question – about why remorse may properly or should be taken to make a difference to censure and punishment. Hannah Maslen has comprehensively addressed the question in this sense,[62] concluding that the 'responsive censure' argument is a persuasive explanation. Censure must address the offender with due regard to her present understanding; where her understanding includes her remorse, the appropriate message of censure changes. Since the censure *is* the punishment, moreover, a change in a message of censure entails a variation in the level of punishment. As we have seen, Maslen further argues that a lack of remorse should not aggravate – entailing only that the full censure must be conveyed – while remorse before sentence means that less censure and consequently a lower level of punishment is called for.[63]

Yet there is another way in which the question 'why does remorse matter?' can be understood, namely, as a question about human psychology, about the mainsprings of a widespread human sentiment that remorse makes a difference. McCullough[64] explains why reconciliation is so fundamental and argues that expressions of remorse through apology are a signal of a willingness to reconcile, in the absence of which the wrongdoer is implying a preparedness to persist in his misbehaviour. This might explain common reactions to a lack of remorse and why, however normatively unjustifiable this may be in the context of responsive censure, it is often regarded as aggravating and meriting an increase in sentence.[65] As we all learn from our earliest experiences of reactions to wrongdoing, an expression of remorse is fitting and engages us emotionally, inducing sentiments of forgiveness – whatever its place in an ethical sentencing policy.

Aptly describing remorse as 'a complex syndrome involving affect, beliefs, desires, intentions and, often, action', Maslen identifies its characteristics as follows:

- the agent must painfully perceive himself to have done something he considers to be morally wrong (typically harming someone else);
- the agent must see himself as blameworthy, leading to self-condemnation;
- the agent's primary focus must be on the person wronged, and only secondarily on the agent as wrongdoer;
- there must be a wish to atone, to apologise or make amends;
- there must be an intention not to do it again.[66]

---

[62] Maslen, above n 45.
[63] Ibid ch 5.
[64] M McCullough, *Beyond Revenge: The Evolution of the Forgiveness Instinct* (San Francisco, John Wiley, 2008).
[65] Walker, above n 59 at 55.
[66] Maslen above n 45 at 6.

If apology is taken to be the public expression of remorse (one may feel remorseful in private), another element could be added – that of *explanation*.[67] As we have seen, this seems fundamental to making progress towards an 'end state' after wrongdoing. It is, however, notoriously, a difficult business. A ready explanation can sound glib or facile and indeed altogether too much like an excuse. Yet a person who has been wronged commonly wants to know why (motive – not intent) and may well be unable to feel that a complete resolution has been reached without some such account.

Part of the critique levelled against formal criminal justice procedures by the proponents of restorative justice is precisely that it frustrates these expressions of remorse. Acceptance of wrongdoing will be compromised where legal advice about the prosecution's ability to prove their case leads to a plea of not guilty. The prospect of punishment often focuses a defendant's concern on himself (which is psychologically understandable, however morally regrettable) rather than the victim, whose pains he may seek to deny or to minimise in the course of a defence or a mitigation. Apology is typically expressed not by the wrongdoer, but by a professional advocate on his behalf in the familiar and easy formulas of mitigation. Similarly, the wish to atone can be difficult to articulate and even harder to accomplish, especially since most of the sentences of the court make few demands on the offender in relation to the offence and do not include any active making of amends.

Just as censure invites remorse, apology seeks, minimally, a recognition that apology has been offered; further, that it has been appreciated and accepted; and finally that some adequate end state has been achieved. It has been proposed that in many informal processes that end state is the granting of forgiveness. Like remorse, forgiveness involves affective, cognitive and behavioural elements. If forgiveness has truly been granted, the forgiver should act in a manner that expresses this. These reflections raise at least two matters of interest. First, punishment theory usually attends to the responsibilities of the offender, but achieving the end state calls for (at least) the forbearance of other people and often for their active participation. Second, can the state 'forgive'? If not, what is the appropriate criminal justice counterpart to forgiveness?

Further reflection on apology can be instructive here. Apology is due first of all to the victim(s), but as Tavuchis remarks:

> A consummate apology, no matter how personal or private an act, is rarely the sole concern of the principals. It is not easily contained because it inevitably touches upon the lives and convictions of interested others while raising both practical and moral questions that transcend the particular situation that prompted it.[68]

---

[67] A Lazare, *On Apology* (New York, Oxford University Press, 2004).
[68] N Tavuchis, *Mea Culpa: A Sociology of Apology and Reconciliation* (Stanford, Stanford University Press, 1991) 14.

In a similar way, just to the extent that the wrong has had its impact on 'interested others', they will be concerned to see that the apology has been tendered, and may themselves expect in some circumstances to be among the recipients of the apology. In intimate groups, all may have to be involved in forgiveness: where resentment lingers, an 'end state' has not been arrived at. Forgiveness, however, is sometimes said to be the prerogative of victims[69] and perhaps the most that can be expected in the context of criminal justice is *reconciliation*. Forgiveness seems too emotionally freighted a concept to be applicable to the form of resolution that can be expected of a state or of most of its citizens. Perhaps the resolution sought is that the state's dealings with the (ex-)offender (and of those others who were not directly affected by the original wrong) should come to be on the same basis as its dealings with other citizens. Foucault saw this as *the requalification of the juridical subject*.[70] Once the punishment has been served, the offender is restored to his/her civil rights. To see what this might involve we may need to turn (to the likely consternation of at least some censure theorists) to the idea of rehabilitation.

VI. REHABILITATION

A. Psychological or Correctional Rehabilitation

The rehabilitation that was the particular target of the retributive critique of the 1970s should be seen as psychological or correctional rehabilitation, which assumes that crime is the expression of some kind of flaw or sickness that requires 'treatment' if further offending is to be prevented. As we have seen, limiting retributivism can countenance psychological intervention so long as it is voluntary, which is to say not coercive, deceptive or otherwise manipulative. There are, however, other ways of understanding rehabilitation, associated with varying assumptions 'about the nature, characteristics and entitlements of people who commit offences',[71] as well as the reasons behind their offending and ideas about how it may be influenced in future. Fergus McNeill rightly insists that 'both the concept and the project of rehabilitation compel and require' other ways of regarding it and goes on to set out 'four forms' of rehabilitation.[72] As well as psychological rehabilitation, then, McNeill distinguishes legal, moral

---

[69] Radzik, above n 35 at 120.

[70] For exposition and discussion, see AE Bottoms, 'Neglected Features of Contemporary Penal Systems' in D Garland and P Young (eds), *The Power to Punish: Contemporary Penality and Social Analysis* (London, Gower, 1983) 166 at 177. See also the chapter by Bottoms in this volume.

[71] P Raynor and G Robinson, *Rehabilitation, Crime and Justice* (Basingstoke, Palgrave Macmillan, 2009) 16.

[72] F McNeill, 'Four Forms of "Offender" Rehabilitation: Towards an Interdisciplinary Perspective' (2012) 17 *Legal and Criminological Psychology* 18 at 19. My debt to this paper will be apparent.

and social rehabilitation. These are conceptually separate, although bound up with one another in interesting ways. My argument here is that these forms of rehabilitation are not only compatible with just punishment and appropriate censure, but are a requirement of it.

B. Legal Rehabilitation

Legal rehabilitation is the restoration of the individual to his/her full civil rights once a punishment has been duly served, and no fresh offences have been committed. It is well expressed in the French expression *rétablir dans ses droits*.[73] The title of the Rehabilitation of Offenders Act represents this sense of the word: the legislation relates not to psychological change, but to people's entitlements in relation to their past offending (especially with regard to disclosure of previous convictions when seeking employment). Rehabilitation in this sense does not depend upon personal reform, but is a right that follows from the due completion of the lawfully imposed sentence. It is in this sense that rehabilitation is closest to the Foucauldian idea of juridical requalification.[74] Understood in this way, legal rehabilitation is conceptually quite distinct from the personal reform which psychological rehabilitation tries to bring about. And just as legal rehabilitation does not depend on personal change, psychological change, no matter how convincingly demonstrated, does not ensure legal rehabilitation: some offences (or more exactly some sentences) are never 'spent', so that legal rehabilitation is never granted.[75]

C. Social Rehabilitation

Distinct again is the idea of social rehabilitation.[76] By this may be understood a full and effective opportunity to have access to the resources of civil society. Once again, this is conceptually distinct from (and not dependent upon) personal reform. Where legal rehabilitation has not taken place, however, full social rehabilitation is impossible: the law would be continuing to countenance different entitlements for ex-offenders. (They may, for example, be lawfully discriminated against in the employment market.) Nor does legal rehabilitation guarantee social rehabilitation; it may be, for example, that the law would not

---

[73] F McNeill, 'Probation, Credibility and Justice' (2011) 58 *Probation Journal* 9. This conception of rehabilitation is also discussed by W McWilliams and K Pease, 'Probation Practice and an End to Punishment' (1990) 29 *Howard Journal of Criminal Justice* 14.

[74] See above, n 70.

[75] For an excellent review, see S Maruna, 'Judicial Rehabilitation and the "Clean Bill of Health" in Criminal Justice' (2011) 3 *European Journal of Probation* 97.

[76] My account differs slightly from McNeill's here and later.

directly bar access to services and resources, but these would even so remain effectively unavailable because of the distinct needs and circumstances of (most obviously) former prisoners. It is in pursuit of social rehabilitation that the probation service advocates on behalf of offenders and liaises with responsible agencies, recognising that social inclusion and fair opportunities must accompany changes in ex-offenders' attitudes, motivations and abilities,[77]

D. Moral Rehabilitation

Moral rehabilitation is an exceptionally important idea that needs a much fuller development. McNeill sees this as a matter of earning redemption – perhaps through reparation – but however this is to be accomplished, it entails acceptance into the moral community whose values were flouted by the offence. In fact, McNeill's definition of social rehabilitation – 'something that is broader, deeper and more subjective; specifically, the informal social recognition and acceptance of the reformed ex-offender'[78] – expresses this well and this is, as it seems to me, better characterised as *moral* rehabilitation. The terminology, perhaps, is less important than the ideas behind it. This conception of rehabilitation is certainly distinct: someone might have committed himself to personal change, found acknowledgement of this by legal recognition and enjoy full and fair access to the resources of civil society, but still be viewed with suspicion or active mistrust. Indeed, however this is to be achieved, the gaining of *trust* seems to be central to moral rehabilitation. In a significant respect, this form of rehabilitation is the most difficult to achieve. Judgements about character can be exceptionally hard to change. In the context of intimate relationships, the position is very different. Christie explains:

> All other things being equal, though obviously they are not, it seems to be a plausible hypothesis that the greater the amount of information on the totality of the life of the relevant system members, the less useful (and needed) are generalized concepts such as 'sickness', 'madness' – and 'crime'. The system members come to know so much about each other, that the broad concepts in a way become too simple. They do not add information, they do not explain.[79]

A challenge for criminal justice is to avoid reducing any offender to the worst thing he ever did.[80]

A more complete understanding of rehabilitation, then, requires a commitment from the offender to try to change, but also a legal recognition of their

---

[77] R Canton, *Probation: Working with Offenders* (Abingdon, Routledge, 2011) ch 8 and *passim*.
[78] McNeill, above n 72 at 18.
[79] Christie, above n 29 at 10.1.
[80] B Stevenson, *We need to talk about an injustice* (2012) available online at www.ted.com/talks/bryan_stevenson_we_need_to_talk_about_an_injustice?language=en (accessed January 2017).

entitlement to be restored to civic status, social inclusion (by which may be under-stood fair and effective access to opportunities) and regaining membership of a moral community. Raynor and Robinson speak of 'relational reintegration'.[81] As in the case of intimate associations, this often calls for more than forbear-ance, but for active steps from others. McNeill puts the matter well:

> Rehabilitation, therefore, is not just about sorting out the individual's readiness for or fitness for reintegration; it is as much about rebuilding the social relationships without which reintegration is impossible. Any would-be supporter of rehabilitation has to do more than try to sort out 'offenders'; s/he needs to mediate relationships between people trying to change and the communities in which change is impeded or impelled; s/he also has to mediate the role and limits of the state itself in the process.[82]

What if this cannot be achieved? In other contexts, the failure to achieve a harmonious end state can lead to the severing of relationships (separations, family rifts, expulsion from friendship groups, resignation, dismissal from employment, striking off or defrocking, varying degrees of ostracism). In contrasting reintegrative with stigmatising and rejecting forms of shaming, Braithwaite[83] cogently argues that rejection is likely to lead to further offend-ing, as well as being psychologically damaging to the individuals concerned.[84] It can also impoverish the community by excluding members of worth and with contributions to make, as well as coarsening the sensibilities and blunting the compassion of the community. Yet this failure to support and recognise rehabili-tation is also unjust: it implies an extended and perhaps indefinite punishment that exceeds and is (*ex hypothesi*) out of proportion to the just punishment originally imposed. It is in this respect that, while rehabilitation must respect the parameters of a just punishment, desert-based accounts, including censure theory, should aspire to that just end state that we have been referring to as rehabilitation.

VII. SUMMARY AND CONCLUSIONS

It has been argued in this chapter that censure theory should seek to develop the implications of the idea of a dialogue. It must not rest content with attention to the pronouncement of sentence, its weight or even its form. Maslen's concept of responsive censure[85] should be built upon to explore a continuing process that moves through remorse and apology to reconciliation.

What might this look like? One important component of this dialogue concerns the manner in which the sentence is put into effect. This aspect has

---

[81] Raynor and Robinson, above n 71 at 160. Cf Maruna, above n 75.

[82] McNeill, above n 69 at 17.

[83] Braithwaite, above n 22.

[84] K Williams, 'Ostracism' (2007) 58 *Annual Review of Psychology* 425.

[85] Maslen, above n 45.

been relatively neglected in the literature, but any account of punishment that foregrounds communication must consider not only the pronouncement of the punishment, but also its implementation. In principle, the way in which the sentence is put into effect could support or, as it may be, undermine the message of the censure. Most offences – and all of the most serious ones – represent a disregard or disdain for the rights and interests of victims. The penal response should accordingly affirm the values of respect for others not only in words but in practice. Practitioners, notably prison and probation staff, should try to realise these values by demonstrating a consistent respect for the offender's worth, dignity and interests. For example, individuals should be involved to the fullest extent possible when decisions are made that directly affect them. The idea of pro-social modelling[86] captures one aspect of this. Pro-social model-ling matters not just for any contingent influence on individuals' subsequent behaviour, but is among the ways in which the value of respect for other people is communicated to them.

The dialogue will include verbal exchanges between offenders and staff. It is likely to involve attempts to elicit individuals' understanding of why they behaved as they did, taking their perspective with complete seriousness even when it is necessary to challenge some of their attitudes. This is, emphatically, not to be understood as some form of preaching or moralised scolding. Censur-ing should call for more than a passive acceptance and many people will need to struggle with the realities of what they have done before they can come to feel remorseful. While this may require new skills for some staff and sometimes a rather different conception of their role, some such dialogic practices are already quite common. For example, raising awareness of the victim is standard in many offending behaviour programmes and involves precisely this level of moral exploration and engagement.

A sketch has been offered here of the mechanisms for righting wrongs that are familiar to us all in other contexts. It was not argued that criminal punish-ment should emulate this process in all respects, but it has been suggested that reflection on these mechanisms may expose common intuitions about the significance of wrongdoing and advancement towards an end state. If these intuitions are frustrated, there will be doubts that justice has been done and the legitimacy of criminal justice called into question. Further, perhaps, the more that we push at the concept of a moral community, the closer its responses to wrongs are likely to come to the processes of righting wrongs within fami-lies and friendship groups. This is because a moral community cares about its members, treats them with concern and respect and will be anxious to bring about an end state in which the ex-offender can thrive in their associations with other members of the community.

---

[86] S Rex and A Matravers (eds), *Pro-social Modelling and Legitimacy* (Cambridge, Institute of Criminology 1998); S Cherry, *Transforming Behaviour: Pro-social Modelling in Action* (Cullompton, Willan, 2005).

The traditional disputes between proponents of rehabilitation and of 'doing justice' need to be reframed to take account of developments in rehabilitation theory. Rehabilitation is more than the correctional rehabilitation that attracted the criticism of an earlier generation and, in the more rounded conception advanced by McNeill,[87] it is not only compatible with censure theory but required by it. Following McNeill and Maruna,[88] it has been argued that the state and civil society have active duties if reconciliation is to be achieved and justice done and felt to be done. Censure theory and restorative justice theorists have recognised a synergy between their respective projects,[89] uniting around the notion of membership of a moral community. Rehabilitation can find this same common cause and need not be seen to be in opposition to restorative justice.[90] For all their different origins, approaches and emphases, these three paradigms share a conception of responding to wrongdoing by affirming the responsibility of wrongdoers, attempting to elicit their commitment to make amends and their subsequent acceptance in the moral community from which their offending estranged them. They also can (and variably do) insist on the reciprocal duties of the community. As Duff puts it: 'Reconciliation is what the repentant wrongdoer seeks with those she has wronged – *and what they must seek with her if they are still to see her as a fellow citizen.*'[91]

Censure makes a statement about the values of a community, but a moral community should enact (not just proclaim) its values. The way in which censure is communicated, the manner in which it meets a response, and the subsequent transactions that move towards an end state will also give expression to these values. Among the values that a community should affirm is a belief in the worth of all its members and a belief in the possibility of change. If we take seriously the idea of a moral community, that community has a duty not only to censure but also to support offenders in their aspiration to desist. This includes developing an understanding, in dialogue with the individual, about how they can best be supported in their endeavours to live a life in which offending has no place. This includes fair and effective access to the resources of civil society and, at the least, precludes the unfair discrimination that so often besets individuals, especially those leaving prison. It is among the insights of community justice[92] that a crime is an indication of a social problem and the community is negligent

---

[87] McNeill, above n 72.

[88] Maruna, above n 75.

[89] Explored by several of the contributors to von Hirsch et al, above n 30. See also J Shapland, G Robinson and A Sorsby, *Restorative Justice in Practice: Evaluating What Works for Victims and Offenders* (Cullompton, Willan, 2011).

[90] As argued by, for example, P Carlen, *Against Rehabilitation: For Reparative Justice* (22nd Eve Saville Memorial Lecture, 2012) available online at www.crimeandjustice.org.uk/resources/against-rehabilitation-reparative-justice (accessed January 2017).

[91] Duff, above n 27 at 109 (emphasis added).

[92] See for example T Clear and D Karp, *The Community Justice Ideal: Preventing Crime and Achieving Justice,* (Boulder CO, Westview, 1999).

if it fails to try to learn from the event. Offenders have distinctive contributions to make in enhancing this learning. This is among the ways that, as Christie insisted, 'conflicts' can be of value to a community.[93] In the dialogue to which censure theory has given so much attention, there has been consideration of the unwilling offender – that individual who is not prepared to participate in a dialogue. This chapter has tried to raise the further question of the unwilling state. When offenders seek to communicate something other than the remorse expected of them, or seek the active support of society in their endeavours not to offend again, in too many places and at too many times their representations are met by a deafening silence from the state.

---

[93] Christie, above n 54.

14

Fairness, Equality, Proportionality and Parsimony: Towards a Comprehensive Jurisprudence of Just Punishment

MICHAEL TONRY

C ONTEMPORARY RETRIBUTIVE THEORIES, and mixed theories incorporating retributive elements, do not provide adequate guidance for thinking about justice in the imposition of criminal punishments. If punishment were unidimensional, involved only first offenders convicted of a single offence, and based solely on censuring blameworthy behaviour, theorising would be easier: offenders should be censured, and punished, precisely as much as they deserve relative to the censure and punishment of others convicted of the same and different offences. In mixed theories, punishments of individuals should never exceed what is deserved relative to the punishments of others. All that would be needed is a sufficiently discriminant ordinal scale of offence seriousness tied to proportionate punishments. Theories of punitive justice, however, cannot be unidimensional.

Much writing on punishment mistakenly treats the subject in theoretical isolation. It ignores the reality, as Isaiah Berlin observed, that difficult problems almost always implicate competing normative principles: 'The world that we encounter in ordinary experience is one in which we are faced with choices between ends equally ultimate, and claims equally absolute, the realization of some of which must inevitably involve the sacrifice of others.'[1]

The way forward becomes clearer when we recognise that punishment implicates not only blameworthiness, crime prevention, and norm reinforcement but

---

[1] I Berlin, *Liberty* (H Hardy ed) (Oxford, Oxford University Press, 2002) 213–14.

also fairness, equality, and human dignity. A comprehensive jurisprudence of just punishment would incorporate four principles:

- *Justice as Fairness*: Processes for responding to crimes should be publicly known, implemented in good faith, and applied even-handedly.[2]

- *Justice as Equal Treatment*: Defendants and offenders should be treated as equals; their interests should be accorded respect and concern when decisions affecting them are made.[3]

- *Justice as Proportionality*: Offenders should never be punished more severely than can be justified by their blameworthiness in relation to the severity of punishments justly imposed on others for the same and different offences.[4]

- *Justice as Parsimony*: Offenders should never be punished more severely than can be justified by appropriate, valid, normative purposes.[5]

Those are not airy-fairy propositions. They describe what people accused or convicted of crimes would want for themselves or their loved ones. They are minimum, interacting requirements of a just system of punishment.

The proposition that values and principles other than those narrowly related to punishment are germane is not novel, even if uncommon in our time. Both Immanuel Kant and Jeremy Bentham described instances in which there are good reasons for not imposing otherwise deserved or appropriate punishments. Kant observed that the sovereign 'will want to avoid adversely affecting the feelings of the people' and can in some capital cases assume the role of the judge to impose some other penalty.[6] Bentham wrote that otherwise appropriate punishments should not be imposed when too many people would have to be punished, making the aggregate punishment too great; when punishment would cause the loss of the offender's 'extraordinary value' to the community; when community opinion is strongly that the offence or offender should not be punished, or punished so much; and when relations with foreign powers would be undermined.[7] The point in recalling those qualifications is not to endorse them, or to discuss their merits, but to point out that even such usually single-minded folk recognised that extrinsic considerations may sometimes limit actions that punishment theories might otherwise justify.

---

[2] Eg, J Rawls, 'Justice as Fairness' (1958) 67 *The Philosophical Review* 164; J Rawls, *A Theory of Justice* (Cambridge, MA, Harvard University Press, 1971).

[3] Eg, R Dworkin, *Taking Rights Seriously* (Cambridge, MA, Harvard University Press, 1978).

[4] Eg, I Kant, 'The Penal Law and the Law of Pardon' [1787] in I Kant, *The Metaphysical Elements of Justice* (J Ladd tr) (Indianapolis, Liberal Arts Press/Bobbs-Merrill, 1965) 99–108.

[5] J Bentham, *An Introduction to Principles of Morals and Legislation* [1789] (JH Burns and HLA Hart eds) (London, Athlone Press, 1970), 179 (the principle of 'frugality' of punishment); N Morris, *The Future of Imprisonment* (Chicago, University of Chicago Press, 1974).

[6] Kant, above n 4 at 104.

[7] Bentham, above n 5 at 103–04.

In this chapter, I explain why retributive theories, including censure theory, cannot by themselves adequately elucidate what a just punishment system would look like. My focus is primarily on the United States because that is the country I know best and because problems of unjust punishment are more extreme and systemic there than elsewhere in developed countries. In the first section, I canvass a series of dilemmas that expose the inability of retributive theories by themselves adequately to resolve fundamental problems. These include the multiple offence paradox, assessments of blameworthiness, and practical problems in the administration of the criminal law. The paradox – that punishments per offence are usually decreased when two or more offences are sentenced simultaneously, but increased when they are sentenced successively – receives greatest attention. It poses an insoluble problem for retributive theories and for mixed theories that incorporate retributive elements.

In the second section, I step back to describe the intellectual and policy contexts of the 1960s and 1970s when widespread support in our time for retributive theories emerged. Their flowering usefully addressed troubling problems of unjust punishment in that period, enriched understanding of sentencing as a process, and constructively influenced policy developments. The context of the 2010s, and the most pressing contemporary problems, however, are very different.

In the third section, I discuss the considerable merits, and limits, of retributive and mixed theories as guides to just punishment. As ideal theories, retributive accounts offer useful devices for consideration of what just punishment might look like in a fully just society. As the multiple offence paradox illustrates, however, retributive and mixed theories do not provide sufficiently rich frameworks for explanation and justification of sentencing and punishment in the real world.

In the final section, I elaborate on a normative framework for just punishment that incorporates retributive ideas within a wider set of values. Ordinal proportionality based on offence seriousness is a fundamental component.[8] It provides tools for inter-offence comparisons. It also sets intelligible limits on just punishments. So, however, independently, do fairness, equality and human dignity.

---

[8] Writers on punishment distinguish between cardinal and ordinal desert. Cardinal desert refers to punishments that are morally deserved in an absolute sense. God may know what those punishments are, but human beings do not; intuitions vary widely. Andreas von Hirsch in 1992 proposed a vocabulary for addressing this problem by distinguishing absolutely (cardinally) from relatively (ordinally) deserved punishments. Calculations based on ordinal desert provide a logic for deciding what people convicted of a particular offence deserve relative to what people convicted of the same and other offences deserve. Once offences are scaled according to seriousness, and ceilings and floors of punishment scales are set, particular offences can be linked to corresponding degrees of punishment severity. See: A von Hirsch, 'Proportionality in the Philosophy of Punishment' in M Tonry (ed), *Crime and Justice: A Review of Research* volume 16 (Chicago, University of Chicago Press, 1992) 15.

I. THE LIMITED REACH OF RETRIBUTIVISM

The value and limitations of censure or blameworthiness as foundational concepts becomes evident when emphasis shifts from courts to offenders. Few would disagree that a core function of criminal convictions and punishments imposed by judges is authoritative, normative expression of censure for wrongdoing. Big disagreements emerge, however, when the focus shifts from judges to offenders. To decide how much censure one offender deserves relative to deserved censures of others, a convincing measure of blameworthiness is needed. Developing one that is generalisable is not easy. Large conceptual disagreements and practical impediments stand in the way.

A. Conceptual Impediments

Retributive theories that link deserved punishments to the seriousness of the crimes of which people are convicted cannot by themselves resolve two inescapable problems: the multiple offence paradox; and assessment of blameworthiness. First, the emerging if exiguous literature on punishment for multiple crimes exposes a paradox that retributive theories, whether positive ones that specify punishments that must be imposed,[9] or negative ones that set upper limits,[10] cannot adequately address or explain.[11] Punishments of people convicted of multiple crimes are often discounted if sentences are imposed at one time (a 'bulk discount') but enhanced if imposed at different times (a 'recidivist premium').[12] This is perverse. Exactly the same sets of crimes can be handled either way – in one omnibus prosecution or in a series – depending on how prosecutors choose to proceed or on the happenstance of when offences come to light. This is a serious problem: most convicted offenders are concurrently convicted of multiple offences, have been previously convicted, or both.

Second, most retributive punishment theories assume that assessments of blameworthiness can be made more or less objectively, on the basis of the

---

[9] Eg, RA Duff, *Punishment, Communication, and Community* (New York, Oxford University Press, 2001).

[10] Eg, N Morris, above n 5; RS Frase, *Just Sentencing: Principles and Procedures for a Workable System* (New York, Oxford University Press, 2013).

[11] Negative retributivism is sometimes described as a prohibition against punishing innocent people (eg, JL Mackie, 'Morality and the Retributive Emotions' (1982) 1 *Criminal Justice Ethics* 3; MT Cahill, 'Punishment Pluralism' in MD White (ed), *Retributivism: Essays on Theory and Practice* (New York, Oxford University Press, 2011) 25). This is a non-sequitur. There is no coherent retributive sense in which innocent people deserve to be punished: 'Retributivists believe in punishment only when it is deserved and will always oppose it when it is not deserved' (J Murphy, 'Last Words on Retributivism' in J Jacobs and J Jackson (eds), *The Routledge Handbook of Criminal Justice Ethics* (Abingdon, Routledge, 2016) ch 2 at 30.

[12] K Reitz, 'The Illusion of Proportionality: Desert and Repeat Offenders', in JV Roberts and A von Hirsch (eds), *Previous Convictions at Sentencing: Theoretical and Applied Perspectives* (Oxford, Hart, 2010) 137.

offence of conviction perhaps modified by circumstances such as weapon use, gratuitous violence, or a victim's special vulnerability that seem inextricably related to the seriousness of the crime. Serious arguments have been made, however, that decisions about punishment should incorporate subjective assessments of the offender's blameworthiness and of the foreseeable effects of contemplated punishments on him/her as a unique individual.

i. The Multiple Offence Paradox

Only a few writers, including George Fletcher, Richard Singer and Mirko Bagaric, reject the recidivist premium in principle.[13] However, the few efforts that have been made to justify it are unpersuasive. I am not alone in my scepticism. Richard Lippke similarly concludes, 'Like others, I find the arguments given on behalf of recidivist premiums unconvincing'.[14]

One unconvincing argument is that repeat offenders are somehow more blameworthy than first-timers because earlier convictions impose special duties on them not to offend again.[15] Everyone, however, has a civic responsibility not to commit crimes. It is hard to imagine why the civic responsibility to obey the law is greater for the previously convicted. It cannot be because greater knowledge or self-control can reasonably be imputed to them. Most repeat offenders no doubt know that behaviour they contemplate is unlawful, but so do most first offenders. Members of both groups sometimes commit offences under extreme social, economic or circumstantial pressures, or influenced by deviant subcultural norms, that make law abidingness especially difficult. This might or might not make them less blameworthy, but it offers no basis for differentiating between them. An empirically grounded argument can be made that prior convictions should mitigate punishments for subsequent crimes. Collateral effects of prior convictions make it foreseeably more difficult for former offenders than for non-offenders to live law-abiding lives.[16]

Other unconvincing arguments supporting the recidivist premium assert that repeat offending is evidence of bad character[17] or constitutes disrespect or defiance of the court, the criminal law, or the state.[18] Defiance, disrespectfulness

---

[13] G Fletcher, *Rethinking Criminal Law* (Boston, Little Brown, 1978); RG Singer, *Just Deserts: Sentencing Based on Equality and Desert* (Lexington, MA, Ballinger 1979); M Bagaric, 'Double Punishment and Punishing Character: The Unfairness of Prior Convictions' (2010) 19 *Criminal Justice Ethics* 10.

[14] RL Lippke, 'The Ethics of Recidivist Premiums' in Jacobs and Jackson (eds), above n 11 ch 1.

[15] Y Lee, 'Repeat Offenders and the Question of Desert' in Roberts and von Hirsch (eds), above n 12, 49.

[16] A Ashworth and M Wasik, 'Sentencing the Multiple Offender: in Search of a "Just and Proportionate" Total Sentence' in J Ryberg, JV Roberts JW de Keijser (eds), *Sentencing Multiple Crimes* (New York, Oxford University Press, 2018) 211.

[17] Y Lee, 'Multiple Offenders and the Question of Desert' in Ryberg et al (eds), above n 16, 113.

[18] C Bennett, '"More to Apologise For": Can We Find a Basis for the Recidivist Premium in a Communicative Theory of Punishment?' in Roberts and von Hirsch (eds), above n 12, 73.

and bad character, however, are not criminal offences in a liberal democratic state.[19]

Almost no one rejects the bulk discount in principle, with the tentative exception of Jesper Ryberg who canvasses possible arguments for it and finds none he judges to be persuasive.[20] Richard Lippke offers the most extensive analysis to date of what a jurisprudence of bulk discounts might look like.[21] Policy justifications have been offered. One is that the discount is supported by broadly shared intuitions.[22] A second is that no punishment should be so 'crushing' that it deprives a person of a large fraction of his/her remaining life[23] or a high proportion of the prime years of life.[24] A third is that bulk discounts can be justified as extensions of mercy based on judges' holistic assessments of offenders.[25] These propositions, however, are ad hoc, unembedded in broader general theories, and ungeneralisable.

There is convincing empirical evidence that majorities of the public, judges, and offenders approve of both the bulk discount and the recidivist premium.[26] Some argue that those broadly shared intuitions justify the paradox either because democratic values require acknowledgment of widely shared beliefs or because failure to do so will undermine the legitimacy of law and the legal process in citizens' minds.[27] Common intuitions, however, by themselves cannot offer a principled justification for anything. Widely shared intuitions, for example, about racial, gender, ethnic and sexual preference differences, or in our time

---

[19] Von Hirsch's argument that punishments should be discounted for first offences, and possibly a few more, is somewhat different (A von Hirsch, 'Desert and Previous Convictions at Sentencing' (1981) 65 *Minnesota Law Review* 91; A von Hirsch, 'Proportionality and the Progressive Loss of Mitigation: Some Further Reflections' in Roberts and von Hirsch (eds), above n 11, 1). It expresses a policy preference based on the premise that first and early offences may have been 'out of character' and thus warrant less-than-deserved punishment. This is a characterological claim. Von Hirsch elsewhere argued to the contrary that sentencing should not be based on characterological 'whole life judgments': A von Hirsch, *Past and Future Crimes: Deservedness and Dangerousness in the Sentencing of Criminals* (Manchester, Manchester University Press, 1986).

[20] Ryberg was a decade ahead of the game, canvassing these issues in detail long before others began writing about them: see J Ryberg, 'Recidivism, Multiple Offending and Legal Justice' (2001) 36 *Danish Yearbook of Philosophy* 69.

[21] RL Lippke, 'Retributive Sentencing, Multiple Offenders, and Bulk Discounts' in White (ed), above n 11, 212.

[22] JV Roberts and JW de Keijser, 'Sentencing the Multiple Conviction Offender: Diminished Culpability for Related Criminal Conduct', in Ryberg et al (eds), above n 16, 137.

[23] For example N Jareborg, 'Why Bulk Discounts in Multiple Offence Sentencing?' in A Ashworth and M Wasik (eds), *Fundamentals of Sentencing Theory: Essays in Honour of Andrew von Hirsch* (Oxford, Oxford University Press 1998); Ashworth and Wasik, above n 16.

[24] AE Bottoms, 'Exploring an Institutionalist and Post-Desert Theoretical Approach to Multiple Offence Sentencing' in Ryberg et al (eds), above n 16, 31.

[25] AE Bottoms, 'Five Puzzles in von Hirsch's Theory of Punishment', in Ashworth and Wasik (eds), above n 23, 53.

[26] JV Roberts, *Punishing Persistent Offenders: Exploring Community and Offender Perspectives* (Oxford, Oxford University Press, 2008).

[27] For example JV Roberts, 'The Future of State Punishment: The Role of Public Opinion in Sentencing' in M Tonry (ed), *Retributivism Has a Past, Has It a Future?* (Oxford, Oxford University Press, 2011) 101.

about the moral worthiness of immigrants, are often empirically indefensible and normatively repellent.

No one has satisfactorily offered principled justification for why punitive punches should be pulled when people are sentenced for multiple offences but swung harder when they have previously been convicted. This is not a small failure. These issues arise in a large majority of criminal cases. The typical defendant is not a first-timer charged with a single offence but a recidivist offender charged with multiple offences.

Table 14.1 presents 2009 American data (taken from an official US Department of Justice publication) on multiple current charges of felony defendants in the state courts of the country's 75 most populous counties.[28] Fifty-five per cent of all felony defendants' cases involved multiple charges, including 61 to 68 per cent of violent crimes and 53 percent of property crimes.[29]

Table 14.1 Multiple charges, by most serious felony, 75 largest US counties (2009) (percentages)

Most serious charge	No other charge	Other charges
All felonies	45%	55%
Violence	37%	63%
Murder	39%	61%
Rape	32%	68%
Robbery	39%	61%
Property	47%	53%
MV Theft	48%	52%
Burglary	33%	67%
Drugs	46%	54%

Source: Reaves (n 28), table 2.

Table 14.2, taken from the same publication, presents data on prior convictions. Overall, 60 per cent of felony defendants had at least one prior conviction; 43 per cent had prior felony convictions. Thirty per cent had two or more prior felony convictions. Eleven per cent had more than four. For specific offences, 48 per cent of murder defendants had prior convictions as did 53 per cent of all violent crime defendants, 56 per cent of property crime defendants, and 66 per cent of drug defendants.

---

[28] BA Reaves, *Felony Defendants in Large Urban Counties, 2009 – Statistical Tables* (Washington, DC, US Department of Justice Bureau of Justice Statistics, 2013). These data are the most recent available at the time of writing.

[29] The American experience is paralleled elsewhere. Professor Anthony Doob in private communication reported that Statistics Canada data for 2014 show that nationally 60% of convictions involved more than one offence, ranging from 55% in Quebec to 72% in the Yukon.

Table 14.2 Prior convictions, by most serious felony, 75 largest US counties (2009) (percentages)

Most serious charge	No prior convictions	Misdemeanor convictions only	One felony only	Two to four felonies	Four-plus felonies
All felonies	40%	17%	13%	19%	11%
Violence	47%	16%	13%	16%	8%
Murder	52%	9%	13%	14%	13%
Rape	49%	15%	14%	12%	10%
Robbery	48%	13%	13%	17%	9%
Property	44%	16%	11%	16%	13%
Motor vehicle theft	38%	14%	11%	20%	17%
Burglary	39%	17%	13%	18%	13%
Drugs	34%	16%	13%	22%	15%

Source: Reaves (n 28), table 7.

Those data do not indicate cumulative percentages of all multiple-conviction defendants, that is, including both those subject to multiple current charges and those facing one or more current charges who had previous convictions. Some defendants charged only with one felony no doubt had prior convictions. Data on prior arrests of felony defendants show that three-quarters had previously been arrested, ranging from two-thirds for murder and rape to nearly 80 per cent for motor vehicle theft, burglary and drugs.[30] The first-time defendant with a clean record is not a mythological beast, but he/she is far from the norm.

ii. Blameworthiness

Assessments of blameworthiness are difficult and contested. Nothing inherent in any retributive theory entails a particular approach. Assessments and resulting punishments might be based, objectively, solely on the seriousness of the crimes of which individuals are convicted or, subjectively, on crimes' distinctive features and the social, psychological, economic and situational circumstances causally related to their commission.[31] Criminal law in English-speaking countries takes no account of motives, caring only about the classic *mens rea* categories of intention, knowledge, recklessness and negligence. It allows only limited space for defences of duress, necessity, immaturity, emotional distress

---

[30] Reaves, above n 28.

[31] For example, A von Hirsch, *Doing Justice: The Choice of Punishments* (Report of the Committee for the Study of Incarceration) (New York, Hill and Wang, 1976); M Tonry, 'Can Deserts Be Just in an Unjust World?' in AP Simester, U Neumann and A du Bois-Pedain (eds), *Liberal Criminal Theory: Essays for Andreas von Hirsch* (Oxford, Hart, 2014) 141.

and mental disability; and usually none at all for harms resulting from imperfect self-defence and other honest but unreasonable mistakes. If the law does not take account of these and other complexities of human lives, decisions about punishment can take account of what HLA Hart approvingly called informal mitigation.[32] Nigel Walker suggested that, if we take moral blameworthiness seriously, assessments should be subjective.[33] That, he observed, is how the Recording Angel would do it.

A similar question can be asked about the effects of punishments on individuals. Adam Kolber and others have proposed that punishment decisions should take account of their foreseeable subjective effects on individuals.[34] Otherwise, the suffering caused by seemingly generic punishments will be radically different. Claustrophobic and mentally ill people, for example, will be affected by close confinement substantially differently than are people who are not similarly afflicted. Confinement of people with dependent children will have substantially different direct and collateral effects than does confinement of the childless. Imprisonment may mean very different things to a young gang leader, an employed middle-aged parent, and someone who is seriously ill. To ignore such things in relation to comparably culpable people, however culpability is measured, is to accept huge differences in the pains imposed upon them.

B. Practical Impediments

The practical impediments are no less confounding. These problems are most acute in the United States where 95–98 per cent of convictions in almost all jurisdictions result from guilty pleas, most emerging from diverse forms of plea negotiation. Practices vary widely. In many charge bargains, some among multiple charges of similar offences are dismissed. Even in a world of bulk discounts, this reduces sentences. In other charge bargains, defendants are allowed to plead guilty to less serious crimes (eg, theft or sexual assault); more serious charges (eg, robbery or rape) are dismissed. Conviction numbers and labels thus become fundamentally misleading. In sentence bargaining, defendants plead guilty to the offences charged, but in exchange for an agreed sentence. In fact, in bargaining,

---

[32] HLA Hart, *Punishment and Responsibility: Essays in the Philosophy of Law* (Oxford, Oxford University Press, 1968).

[33] N Walker, *Why Punish?* (Oxford, Oxford University Press, 1991).

[34] Kolber's article revived ideas at least two centuries old (A Kolber, 'The Subjective Experience of Punishment' (2009) 109 *Columbia Law Review* 182). Jeremy Bentham was adamant that punishments must be adjusted to offenders' 'sensibilities' (Bentham, above n 5 at 169). Immanuel Kant called for attention 'to the special sensibilities of the upper classes' so that the privileged will be punished equivalently to the poor. His most vivid example is of a 'man of a higher class' who would be condemned to 'solitary and painful confinement' for an offence for which a 'social inferior' would be called upon to apologise 'because by this means, in addition to the discomfort suffered, the pride of the offender will be painfully affected, and thus his humiliation will compensate for the offense as like for like' (Kant, above n 4 at 101–02).

prosecutors agree not to allege facts that if proven would result in a mandatory minimum sentence, trigger policies that prescribe aggravated penalties, or offend idiosyncratic judicial sensibilities that lawyers believe make harsher penalties more likely. Patterns of plea negotiation often vary substantially between counties within a state – charge dismissals in some, charge reductions in some, and sentence agreements in others. People convicted of the same nominal crime will often have engaged in very different behaviours. Many different kinds of acts reflecting diverse degrees of objective blameworthiness are hidden behind the names of the offences of which people are convicted. Finally, a 'trial tax' almost always results in harsher sentences for defendants convicted at trial than they would otherwise have received.[35]

These problems are not uniquely American.[36] Plea bargaining in England and Wales is less ornate than in the United States, but results in as much as a one-third reduction in sentence for defendants who plead guilty early. From the defendant's perspective, the English trial tax is 50 per cent. This is considerably higher than is conventional in the United States. Although unconstrained US-style plea negotiation exists nowhere in continental Europe, defendants offered transactions in Belgium and the Netherlands or conditional dismissals in Germany and Austria receive punishments but avoid convictions, thereby being treated better than are others charged with comparable crimes who are not offered or who refuse the same accommodation. Scandinavian penal orders result in convictions but otherwise raise the same issue. Italian and French courts offer expedited procedures and reduced punishments to defendants deemed by prosecutors to be deserving.

Blameworthiness is thus difficult to define in theory and harder to characterise in practice. That does not, of course, make concepts of censure and blameworthiness unimportant, but it does show that they can provide at best partial accounts of how a principled system of punishment should operate. Like the shadows flickering on the walls of Plato's cave, they provide impressions of what punitive justice might look like in an ideal world, but that is not where we live.

II. THE FLOWERING OF RETRIBUTIVE THEORY

Retributive punishment theories have so completely displaced consequentialism in scholarly writing that only oldsters remember when they re-emerged in the English-speaking countries from a century or more's slumber. At least through

---

[35] AC Kim, 'Underestimating the Trial Penalty: An Empirical Analysis of the Federal Trial Penalty and Critique of the Abrams Study' (2015) 84 *Mississippi Law Journal* 1195.

[36] The assertions in the preceding paragraph about the United States are uncontroversial descriptions of well-documented practices. Sources for assertions about other countries' legal systems in this paragraph can be found in M Tonry (ed), *Sentencing Policies and Practices in Western Countries – Comparative and Cross-national Perspectives* (Chicago, University of Chicago Press, 2016).

the 1960s, consequentialism reigned supreme in the United States and was influential elsewhere. Herbert Wechsler, the *Model Penal Code's* chief architect, believed in the principles and values that underlay indeterminate sentencing.[37] He viewed the conviction as an expression of censure but saw punishment as an instrumental device: 'The rehabilitation of an individual who has incurred the moral condemnation of the law is in itself a social value of importance, a value, it is well to note, that is and ought to be the prime goal'.[38] Two decades earlier, Wechsler and Columbia law professor Jerome Michael expressed beliefs that were not then controversial. They observed that retribution may represent 'the unstudied belief of most men' but averred that 'no legal provision can be justified merely because it calls for the punishment of the morally guilty by penalties proportioned to their guilt, or criticized merely because it fails to do so'.[39] A decade before that, Harvard law professor Sheldon Glueck, a leading intellectual supporter of indeterminate sentencing, observed: 'The old argument was that punishment was necessary as a "just retribution" or requital of wickedness. No thoughtful person today seriously holds this theory of sublimated social vengeance.'[40]

Wechsler's, Michael's and Glueck's rejection of retributivism was the mainstream view from the 1920s onward. In the 1950s and 1960s, Barbara Wootton[41] in England and Karl Menninger[42] in the United States went a step further and proposed the elimination altogether of moral fault, what lawyers call *mens rea*, in the criminal law. Nigel Walker's 1969 *Sentencing in a Rational Society*, the first modern book in English on sentencing policy and theory, was wholly utilitarian.[43]

Mainstream theoretical writing on punishment theory containing retributivist ideas, however, began to revive in the 1950s in the work of Norval Morris,[44] John Rawls[45] and HLA Hart.[46] They, and Edmund Pincoffs,[47] Rawls's student, author of *The Rationale of Legal Punishment*, the first modern monograph in English on punishment philosophy, argued for mixed theories that in various ways combined utilitarian preventive goals with retributivist limits on

---

[37] American Law Institute, *Model Penal Code: Proposed Official Draft* (Philadelphia, American Law Institute, 1962).

[38] H Wechsler, 'Sentencing, Correction, and the Model Penal Code' (1961) 109 *University of Pennsylvania Law Review* 465 at 468.

[39] J Michael and H Wechsler, *Criminal Law and Its Administration* (Chicago, Foundation, 1940) 7, 11.

[40] S Glueck, 'Principles of a Rational Penal Code' (1928) 41 *Harvard Law Review* 453 at 456.

[41] B Wootton, *Crime and the Criminal Law* (London, Stevens, 1963).

[42] K Menninger, *The Crime of Punishment* (New York, Viking, 1966).

[43] N Walker, *Sentencing in a Rational Society* (London, Allen Lane, 1969).

[44] N Morris, 'Sentencing Convicted Criminals' (1953) 27 *Australian Law Review* 186.

[45] J Rawls, 'Two Concepts of Rules' (1955) 64 *Philosophical Review* 3.

[46] HLA Hart, 'Prolegomenon to the Principles of Punishment' (1959) 60 *Proceedings of the Aristotelian Society (New Series)* 1, reprinted in Hart, above n 32, 1.

[47] E Pincoffs, *The Rationale of Legal Punishment* (Atlantic Highlands, NJ, Humanities Press, 1966).

punishment. In the 1960s, philosophers on both sides of the Atlantic began to develop systematic retributive arguments. Americans including Herbert Morris, Joel Feinberg and Jeffrie Murphy offered retributive theories of different sorts.[48] HLA Hart in *Punishment and Responsibility* in 1968 cited a number of British philosophers who did likewise.[49] Harold Acton in 1969 presented writings by several.[50]

Retributivist writing by philosophers and penal theorists blossomed, and soon became predominant. Consequentialist theorising largely disappeared, except most prominently in the restorative justice writings of John Braithwaite and Philip Pettit.[51] The debates occurred primarily between positive retributivists who argued that judges must impose deserved punishments and negative retributivists who argued that judges may but need not impose maximally deserved punishments, but never more than that. 'Mixed' theories incorporate retributivist ideas to set maximum and sometime minimum limits, but within those limits, permit instrumental considerations such as deterrence, incapacitation, rehabilitation and moral education to be taken into account.

In retrospect, at least in the United States, the movement away from consequentialism and toward retributivism was a response to the perceived failings of indeterminate sentencing of the sort that the *Model Penal Code*, and Wechsler, celebrated. The broad discretions accorded judges and parole boards, and the absence of officials' accountability for decisions in individual cases, were said to produce unwarranted disparities, to foster capricious and idiosyncratic decisions, and to create unacceptable risks of racial and ethnic bias. The evidence in support of those claims was overwhelming.[52] These critiques are not surprising. The civil rights, prisoners' rights, and due process movements in the United States reached their peaks in the 1960s and early 1970s, and these were precisely the kinds of injustices those movements attacked. The 'rights revolution' represented by John Rawls's *A Theory of Justice*, Ronald Dworkin's *Taking Rights Seriously*, and Robert Nozick's *Anarchy, State, and Utopia* helped shape an intellectual climate that emphasised fairness and equal treatment.[53]

---

[48] H Morris, 'Persons and Punishment' (1966) 52 *Monist* 475; J Feinberg, *Doing and Deserving* (Princeton, Princeton University Press, 1970); J Murphy, 'Marxism and Retribution' (1973) 2 *Philosophy and Public Affairs* 217.

[49] HLA Hart, above n 32.

[50] HB Acton (ed), *The Philosophy of Punishment* (London, St Martin's Press, 1969).

[51] Braithwaite and Pettit accept that retributive considerations should set upper limits on punishment, but otherwise explicitly reject the salience of retributive ideas. See J Braithwaite and P Pettit, *Not Just Deserts: A Republican Theory of Criminal Justice* (Oxford, Oxford University Press, 1990); J Braithwaite and P Pettit, 'Republicanism and Restorative Justice: An Explanatory and Normative Connection' in J Braithwaite and H Strang (eds), *Restorative Justice: Philosophy to Practice* (Burlington, VT, Ashgate, 2001).

[52] N Morris and M Tonry, *Between Prison and Probation: Intermediate Sanctions in a Rational Sentencing System* (Chicago, University of Chicago Press, 1990).

[53] Rawls, above n 2; Dworkin, above n 3; R Nozick, *Anarchy, State, and Utopia* (Cambridge, MA, Harvard University Press, 1974).

In policy terms, the shift toward retributivist ideas proved immensely influential, and not only in the United States. Government reports in Australia, Canada and England and Wales followed suit.[54] Almost no scholarly writer after the mid-1970s defended indeterminate sentencing or full-blown consequentialist punishment theories. Sentencing reforms – detailed statutory standards, guidelines of various sorts, mandatory minimums – proliferated. In the US, a third of the states abandoned parole release. Sentencing commissions and legislatures declared 'punishment' to be the primary purpose of sentencing. The Minnesota Sentencing Commission debated a choice between 'Just Deserts' and 'Modified Just Deserts' sentencing models, opting for the latter.[55] In England, the Home Office in 1990 endorsed 'Just Desserts' in its explanation of proposed sentencing law changes.[56]

I rehearse all of this to emphasise and reiterate a point that Matt Matravers has made: the retributivist revival occurred neither in a vacuum nor from turbulence in university philosophy departments, but in response to what were widely believed to be stark injustices.[57] By emphasising blameworthiness as a limit on the discretions of officials, it aimed to right wrongs. This remedial emphasis is nothing new. The writings of Cesare Beccaria and Jeremy Bentham,[58] which laid the foundations of nineteenth- and twentieth-century consequentialism, and of Immanuel Kant and Georg Wilhelm Friedrich Hegel,[59] which played the same role for retributivism, were reactions to the excesses of the *ancient regime* that Michel Foucault[60] and many others described, and are better understood when that is recognised. One sign of this reactive reality in the 1970s is in the final chapter of von Hirsch's 1976 book *Doing Justice*.[61] After agonising about the criminogenic influence of the life circumstances of the socially disadvantaged, he nonetheless rejected the idea of a social adversity discount in sentencing in favour of uniform offence-based standards. He acknowledged the resulting social injustice. However, he found solace in the belief that a desert-based system would at least spare the disadvantaged the even harsher punishments their greater risks of reoffending, and racial and class bias, often produced under indeterminate

---

[54] Australian Law Reform Commission, *Sentencing of Federal Offenders* (Canberra, Australian Government Publishing Service, 1980); Canadian Sentencing Commission, *Sentencing Reform: A Canadian Approach* (Ottawa, Canadian Government Publishing Centre, 1987); Home Office, *Crime, Justice, and Protecting the Public* (London, Her Majesty's Stationery Office, 1990).

[55] A von Hirsch, KA Knapp and M Tonry, *The Sentencing Commission: Guidelines for Criminal Sanctions* (Boston, Northeastern University Press, 1987).

[56] The report's drafters referred to 'Just Deserts'. Her Majesty's Stationery Office in its wisdom changed what was presumably believed to be a misspelling (Home Office, above n 54).

[57] M Matravers, 'Is Twenty-First Century Punishment Post-Desert?' in Tonry (ed), above n 27.

[58] C Beccaria, *On Crimes and Punishment* [5th edn, 1766] R Bellamy (ed), R Davis (tr) (Cambridge, Cambridge University Press, 1995); Bentham, above n 5.

[59] Kant, above n 4; GWF Hegel, *Elements of the Philosophy of Right* [1821] AW Wood (ed), HB Nisbet (tr) (Cambridge, Cambridge University Press, 1991).

[60] M Foucault, *Discipline and Punish: The Birth of the Prison* translated by A Sheridan (New York, Vintage, 1977).

[61] Von Hirsch, above n 31.

sentencing. *Doing Justice* was not an exercise in decontextualised theory, but an effort to influence how Americans thought about sentencing in the real world.

III. TWO CHEERS FOR CENSURE AND OTHER RETRIBUTIVE THEORIES

There are many kinds of primarily retributive theories. Various kinds of benefits and burdens, social contract, and equilibrium theories were popular in the 1960s and 1970s. In slightly different ways, Herbert Morris, Jeffrie Murphy and Andrew von Hirsch argued that people in a democratic society benefit from public order and security, including others' law-abidingness, and are obligated in return to accept various burdens and responsibilities of citizenship.[62] Punishment was conceptualised as a device for depriving offenders of unfair benefits gained through offending. Within a decade, these theories fell from favour, in large part from recognition that the gravamen of serious crimes, rape or other serious violent acts, for example, is not simply that offenders receive unfair benefits, and that imposing offsetting burdens on them cannot rectify their wrongs.

Three new kinds of retributive theories emerged. Communicative theories offered by, for example, Joel Feinberg, Herbert Morris and Jean Hampton emphasised that what distinguishes criminal punishments from other official burdens such as administrative penalties and taxes is that they communicate judgments about moral wrongdoing.[63] Censure theories offered by Antony Duff and Andrew von Hirsch focused more narrowly on moral blameworthiness and authoritative denunciation of wrongdoing.[64] Penance theories most famously associated with Antony Duff sought through punishment to facilitate offenders' understanding of why what they did was wrong and to attach or reattach them to good values.[65]

The lines that separate different kinds of retributive theory blur. HLA Hart, JC Cottingham, John Mackie and Nigel Walker, among many others, offered lengthy, somewhat different, taxonomies.[66] Retributive theories have co-existed and competed since the early 1970s with mixed theories of the sorts that Norval Morris and HLA Hart offered.[67] Morris's 'limiting retributivism' has been the most influential. It recognises maximum and sometimes minimum retributive punishments for particular crimes and, when threshold evidentiary criteria are

---

[62] H Morris, above n 48; Murphy, above n 48; von Hirsch, above n 31.

[63] Feinberg, above n 48; H Morris, 'A Paternalist Theory of Punishment' (1981) 18 *American Philosophical Quarterly* 26; J Hampton, 'The Moral Education Theory of Punishment' (1984) 13 *Philosophy and Public Affairs* 208.

[64] RA Duff, *Trials and Punishments* (Cambridge, Cambridge University Press, 1986); A von Hirsch, *Censure and Sanctions* (Oxford, Oxford University Press, 1993).

[65] Duff, above n 9.

[66] HLA Hart, above n 32; Mackie, above n 11; Walker, above n 33; JG Cottingham, 'Varieties of Retributivism' (1979) 29 *Philosophical Quarterly* 238.

[67] N Morris, above n 5; HLA Hart, above n 32.

satisfied, permits punishments above the minimum on the basis of instrumental considerations. It is the governing normative framework of the recent *Model Penal Code – Sentencing*.[68]

To my mind, censure and similar theories that apportion punishment to blameworthiness are the most convincing retributive theories, including in their limiting roles in mixed theories. Censure theories take as their predicate the seriousness of blameworthy behaviour committed by morally autonomous human beings, and thereby limit the intrusions on liberty the state may justly impose as punishment. As Jeffrie Murphy has observed:

> To the degree that a retributive outlook on punishment involves a respect for the dignity of human beings as free and responsible agents … then retributivism surely makes an important point … Some concept of desert, if not what might be called 'desert all the way down', is vital to our conception of ourselves and others as responsible beings, having the value that Kant called 'dignity'.[69]

Communicative and penance theories seek to reattach offenders to good values, demonstrate to them and others the wrongfulness of their acts, and offer them opportunities to establish or re-establish their status as equal citizens. Sometimes they rest on implausible and sometimes uncomfortable analogies: parents attempting to socialize children, residential religious communities, academic departments, or relations between teachers and students.[70] They founder on at least three problems: why offenders who are genuinely remorseful need be punished at all; handling of offenders firmly attached to non-majority or subcultural values; and handling of offenders whose conditions of life make law-abidance especially difficult. They often stumble over the target audience. To the extent that a goal is norm reinforcement or victim vindication, it is hard to see why such theories are not essentially or largely consequentialist. Censure theories face none of these problems and need not offer tortured explanations of how they should be addressed.

Some communicative theories are facially implausible. One example is Jean Hampton's argument that punishment should be understood as an institution for communicating acknowledgment to victims and others of the wrongfulness of the harms victims have suffered.[71] Conviction and punishment of particular offenders may provide that acknowledgment. However, cases which are not tried because the defendant is incompetent or beneath the age of criminal responsibility, or in which the defendant was acquitted on grounds of insanity or because of a successful affirmative defence, evidentiary problems, or a fact-finders' judgment that probative standards have not been met, do not. It would

---

[68] American Law Institute, *Model Penal Code – Sentencing*, Tentative Draft No 1 (Philadelphia, American Law Institute, 2007).

[69] J Murphy, *Punishment and the Moral Emotions: Essays in Law, Morality, and Religion* (New York, Oxford University Press, 2012) 86.

[70] Morris, above n 63; Duff, above n 9; Bennett, above n 18.

[71] Hampton, above n 63.

be odd to criticise any of those entirely legitimate outcomes because they do not acknowledge victim suffering.

IV. A COMPREHENSIVE JURISPRUDENCE OF JUST PUNISHMENT

Questions of justice in punishment cannot be answered by invocation only of retributive and consequentialist theories. They are 'monist' which, asserted Isaiah Berlin, implies the false view that all moral questions have a single correct answer and that all these answers dovetail within a single, coherent moral system.[72] In the introduction to this chapter, I quoted Berlin's famous assertion about value pluralism and the inevitability of conflicts between implications of equally important first principles. Berlin characterised Kantian retributivist and Benthamite utilitarian theories as monist.

A just punishment system would be pluralist. It would in Ronald Dworkin's terms treat offenders with equal concern and respect, allowing each to be assessed according to appropriate criteria in his/her individual circumstances and situation. It would in John Rawls's terms be fair, using procedures and standards that are transparent, consistent and even-handed. It would in James Whitman's terms be respectful of human dignity, taking account of the likely effects of punishments on offenders and their prospects for later living satisfying lives.[73]

Determining just punishments in individual cases is intrinsically difficult and raises conflicts of the kind that Berlin described. Nuanced differences between defendants and suspects, and among offences, lead practitioners to handle seemingly similar offences in different ways. Issues of social and racial justice are salient in every courtroom and every country. Whether extreme social and economic disadvantage should provide a defence to criminal charges or an appropriate basis for systematic mitigation of punishment is one. Whether evidence of social, racial, ethnic or religious bias in the operation of criminal justice systems should be taken into account at sentencing is another. Whether all infliction of pain including state punishment is an evil, as Bentham believed,[74] and should always lead to imposition of the least restrictive possible punishment, or none at all, is a third.

Matt Matravers rightly observed that: 'The issue is not one of reconciling [punishment] practices to desert ... but rather it is one of thinking about the requirements of liberal justice as a whole'.[75] If the requirements of liberal justice

---

[72] Berlin, above n 1.

[73] Dworkin, above n 3; Rawls, above n 2; J Whitman, 'The Two Western Cultures of Privacy: Dignity versus Liberty' (2004) 113 *Yale Law Journal* 1151; J Whitman, 'Presumption of Innocence or Presumption of Mercy?: Weighing Two Western Modes of Justice' (2016) 94 *Texas Law Review* 933.

[74] Bentham, above n 5 at 158.

[75] Matravers, above n 57.

are considered as a whole, it is clear – as the multiple offence paradox and myriad subjective differences between seemingly comparable cases demonstrate – that values other than punishment-as-censure-or-desert need to be taken into account.

Incorporation of fairness, equal treatment and human dignity values into a comprehensive jurisprudence of punishment raises three major matters.[76] First, these additional values are independently important and not simply side constraints on the pursuit of retributive or consequentialist aims. Ronald Dworkin long ago wrote of 'rights as trumps'.[77] Fairness, equal treatment and human dignity need to be recognised as trumps on punishment. Retributive or consequentialist logic may sometimes appear to justify punishments that other values forbid. When that happens, the punitive logic must give way. For example, part of the explanation the German Constitutional Court gave for declaring unconstitutional full life sentences without possibility of release is that they are incompatible with human dignity: no human being should be denied the possibility of hope for a better life.[78] Similar ideas underlie the much shorter maximum prison sentences authorised in continental European than in Anglo-Saxon legal systems. They also underlie the ad hoc propositions – 'crushing sentences', taking too large a portion of an individual's remaining life, mercy – that are offered to explain the bulk discounts received by people convicted of multiple offences.

Second, the multiple values that punishment implicates are not simply alternatives; all set independent limits. American criminal codes usually provide that the purposes of the criminal law, punishment or sentencing include at least imposition of deserved punishment, deterrence, incapacitation and rehabilitation. Those lists serve as buffets from which judges may choose. Elsewhere in this volume, Matt Matravers proposes something like a buffet when he calls for a 'plural' rather than a 'mixed' account of punishment in which censure and deterrence are independent governing principles. 'The results may well be counter-intuitive (one might end up threatening more severe hard treatment for less serious, but harder to detect, crimes than for more serious, more easily detected, crimes),' he observes, but such an approach 'is not inconsistent so long as censure and deterrence are independent' guiding principles.[79] This is not very different from Henry M Hart's classic refutation of the *Model Penal Code*'s

---

[76]'Equal treatment' here and below is used not literally to mean identical or the same treatment but as shorthand for Dworkin's 'treatment as an equal' with respect and concern: Dworkin, above n 3.

[77]Ibid.

[78]BVerfG, judgment of 21 June 1977, BVerfGE 45, 187 (*lebenslange Freiheitsstrafe*). The court distinguished between a structured possibility of early release (which would make the sentence constitutional) and reliance simply on executive clemency, which it declared insufficient for constitutionality.

[79]M Matravers, 'Rootless Desert and Unanchored Censure', in this volume.

primarily rehabilitative purposes.[80] He observed that deterrence, rehabilitation, incapacitation, norm reinforcement, satisfaction of the 'community's sense of just retribution' and 'even socialized vengeance' all have roles to play and that judges and parole boards must take account of them case by case as they are pertinent.[81]

Matravers' example and Henry Hart's elaboration underlay the core problems of consequentialist theories and indeterminate sentencing that retributive theorists in the 1970s sought to address and remedy. Punishing lesser crimes more harshly than greater ones defies common morality and undermines basic social norms. Conferring authority on individual judges to choose among and apply irreconcilable purposes assures outcomes that are often based more on judicial idiosyncrasies, personalities and ideologies than on differences between offences and offenders. Such broad authority is especially vulnerable to influence by invidious considerations.

Third, a comprehensive jurisprudence of just punishment would require subjective assessments of blameworthiness. David Luban has observed that 'subjectivity' lies at the heart of human dignity and that 'having human dignity means having a story of one's own'. Subjectivity is essential: 'Human beings have ontological heft because each of us is an "I", and I have ontological heft. For others to treat me as though I have none fundamentally denigrates my status in the world. It amounts to a form of humiliation that violates my human dignity'.[82] Plutarch observed of boys playing by a stream on a summer day, 'Though boys throw stones at frogs in sport, yet the frogs do not die in sport but in earnest'.[83] The frog's perspective, Luban's 'I's' perspective, cannot justly be ignored. A just sentencing system must harness the tension between the requirement of fairness that there be general standards that apply to all and the requirement of justice that all ethically important grounds for distinguishing between individuals be taken into account.

In the introduction, I described a comprehensive jurisprudence of just punishment as consisting of Justice as Fairness, Justice as Equal Treatment, Justice as Proportionality, and Justice as Parsimony. Blameworthiness and censure play central roles. No sentencing system could be said to be just unless it sets rigid upper limits (keyed to blameworthiness) on the severity of punishment, and unless values of fairness, equal treatment and human dignity are respected.

---

[80] Both Matravers and Henry Hart explicitly refer to the purposes of the criminal law rather than of punishment or sentencing, but appear to subsume punishment's within the criminal law's purposes. HLA Hart, by contrast, distinguishes between the – for him, preventative – purposes of the criminal law and the purposes of punishment: above, n 46.

[81] HM Hart, 'The Aims of the Criminal Law' (1958) 23 *Law and Contemporary Problems* 401 at 401.

[82] D Luban, *Legal Ethics and Human Dignity* (Cambridge, Cambridge University Press, 2007) 70–72.

[83] Plutarch, 'Whether Land or Sea Animals Are Cleverer' in *Moralia* volume 12, H Cherniss (tr) (Cambridge, MA, Harvard University Press, 1957) 355.

Human dignity underlies the case for fairness, which largely concerns process, the case for treatment as an equal, which largely concerns substantive decision-making, and the case for parsimony, which concerns the avoidance of gratuitous harm. At least rhetorically, it seems to me useful to identify fairness, equal treatment and parsimony as separate requirements of justice rather than describe them as embedded within a single 'Justice as Human Dignity'.

This proposed jurisprudence of just punishment allows judges to make indi-vidualised assessments of blameworthiness, and insists that gratuitous harm not be done. It recognises the complexity and myriad differing circumstances of human lives. It cannot resolve fundamental issues of social and racial injustice but empowers judges to make individualised subjective assessments of offend-ers' circumstances and blameworthiness within the constraints set by the four principles of punitive justice.

It provides solutions to the multiple offence paradox. The bulk discount is morally necessary. Without it, punishments would be so severe that they would be incompatible with human dignity and so mechanical that they would fail to treat offenders and their interests with equal respect and concern. The recidivist premium to the contrary is morally unjustifiable; depriving individuals of the bulk of their remaining lives is as objectionable when it is done piecemeal as when it is done at one time. Some of the objections are familiar ones. Impo-sition of increments of additional punishment because of earlier convictions is double counting, effectively punishing offenders a second time for prior offences. Punishing a subsequent offence more severely than a first offender is punished for the same offence breaks the link between blameworthiness and deserved punishment. In addition, all of the concerns that animate the bulk discount arise. Aggregate punishments rapidly become crushing and deprive offenders of unjustly large shares of their lives. If the potential aggregate sever-ity of sentences for multiple current convictions call for mercy, the burdens of recidivist premiums call at least as loudly.

This proposed jurisprudence of just punishment provides a firm foundation for the parsimony principle. Richard Lippke has argued that 'parsimony' is an empty concept because both retributive and consequentialist theories explicitly reject punishments more severe than are theoretically justifiable.[84] Parsimony is better understood, however, as deriving not from punishment principles but from the equality and human dignity principles with which punishment prac-tices must be reconciled. Bentham was adamant: 'All punishment is mischief: all punishment in itself is evil … If it ought at all to be admitted, it ought only to be admitted in as far as it promises to exclude some greater evil'.[85] His view was bedded within utilitarianism. It is better viewed as coming from outside.

---

[84] R Lippke, 'Parsimony and the Sentencing of Multiple Offenders' in Ryberg et al (eds), above n 16, 95.

[85] Bentham, above n 5 at 158.

The requirement that all people be treated with equal respect and concern can help address the problem of 'just deserts in an unjust society'. Punishments of people living fundamentally disadvantaged lives, or who are powerfully affected by mental disabilities or acute problems of drug dependence, should be determined subjectively in terms of the choices and possibilities available to them and not on the false premise that the hard realities of their lives were different.

There is one important problem, however, that the proposed jurisprudence cannot meaningfully address: determination of cardinally deserved punishments and the anchoring points of penalty scales that are necessary for any system of proportionate punishments to work.[86] Those judgments depend on cultural attitudes toward crime, criminals and punishment severity that vary widely and that no mechanical or theoretical fix can resolve. Palpable differences exist between countries in such matters: think only of contrasts between the United States and Scandinavia or between England and Switzerland. Achieving acceptance of ideas about ordinal proportionality and the moral necessity of inter-offence comparisons in punishment is a more easily achievable goal, and constitutes steps in the right direction.

The issues discussed in the preceding paragraphs require much fuller exploration and elaboration than is possible here. The important thing to recognise, however, is that they raise problems that punishment theories now in use cannot adequately address but that a normative framework incorporating fundamental principles of fairness, equality, proportionality and parsimony could.

Moving toward a comprehensive jurisprudence of just punishment will require partial abandonment or substantial amplification of most retributive and mixed theories of punishment. This change may not be as unlikely as some may believe. It will require a paradigm shift, which Thomas Kuhn demonstrated seldom happens in the physical sciences until prevailing ways of thinking change sufficiently to absorb unfamiliar, seemingly heretical ideas.[87] However, that is what happened when retributive punishment theories replaced consequentialist ones in the minds of most philosophers and academic lawyers in the 1960s and 1970s. The American law professor Albert Alschuler in 1978 bewilderedly described the recent sea change in attitudes toward indeterminate sentencing: 'That I and many other academics adhered in large part to this reformative viewpoint only a decade or so ago seems almost incredible to most of us today'.[88] Robert Nozick in 1981 explained how such things happen:

> When a philosopher sees that premises he accepts logically imply a conclusion he has rejected until now, he faces a choice: he may accept this conclusion or reject

[86] N Lacey and H Pickard, 'The Chimera of Proportionality: Institutionalising Limits on Punishment in Contemporary Social and Political Systems' (2015) 78 *Modern Law Review* 216.

[87] T Kuhn, *The Structure of Scientific Revolutions* (Chicago, University of Chicago Press, 1962).

[88] A Alschuler, 'Sentencing Reform and Prosecutorial Power '(1978) 126 *University of Pennsylvania Law Review* 550 at 552.

one of the previously accepted premisses ... His choice will depend on which is greater, the degree of his commitment to the various premisses or the degree of his commitment to denying the conclusion. It is implausible that these are independent of how strongly he wants certain things to be true. The various means of control over conclusions explain why so few philosophers publish ones that (continue to) upset them.[89]

It is time for proponents of retributive and mixed theories to adopt and argue for new 'premisses'.

[89] R Nozick, *Philosophical Explanations* (Cambridge, MA, Harvard University Press, 1981) 2–3.

Index